Fifth Edition

Crossing Cultures

Readings for Composition

Henry Knepler
Emeritus, Illinois Institute of Technology

Myrna Knepler
Northeastern Illinois University

Annie Knepler
University of Illinois, Chicago

Ellie Knepler

Allyn and Bacon
Boston • London • Toronto • Sydney • Tokyo • Singapore

Series Editor: Joe Opiela
Marketing Manager: Lisa Kimball
Production Administrator: Rob Lawson
Composition and Prepress Buyer: Linda Cox
Editorial-Production Service: Omegatype Typography, Inc.
Manufacturing Buyer: Suzanne Lareau
Cover Administrator: Linda Knowles

Library of Congress Cataloging-in-Publication Data

Crossing cultures : readings for composition / [compiled by] Henry
    Knepler ... [et al.] — 5th ed.
        p.   cm.
    Includes bibliographical references (p. 399) and index.
    ISBN 0-205-26829-3
    1. College readers.   2. Pluralism (Social sciences)—Problems,
exercises, etc.   3. Report writing—Problems, exercises, etc.
4. Culture—Problems, exercises, etc.   5. English language—
Rhetoric.   6. Readers—Social sciences.   I. Knepler, Henry W.
PE1417.C75   1998
808'.0427—dc21   97-10121
                                                            CIP

Printed in the United States of America
10 9 8 7 6 5 4 3 2   02 01 00 99 98

Contents

Rhetorical Contents   xiii

Preface   xvii

Acknowledgments   xxi

PART ONE   Growing Up   1

Elizabeth Wong   **The Struggle to Be an All-American Girl   4**
"…my brother and I had to go to Chinese school. No amount of kicking, screaming, or pleading could dissuade my mother, who was solidly determined to have us learn the language of our heritage."

Gary Soto   **The Jacket   8**
"I threw my books on the bed and approached the jacket slowly, as if it were a stranger whose hand I had to shake."

Maya Angelou   **Graduation   13**
"Days before, we had made a sign for the Store, and as we turned out the lights Momma hung the cardboard over the doorknob. It read clearly: CLOSED. GRADUATION."

Lindsy Van Gelder   **The Importance of Being Eleven: Carol Gilligan Takes on Adolescence   25**
"Instead of living comfortably inside their own skin, they measure themselves against an idealized, perfect girl."

Maxine Hong Kingston   **Girlhood among Ghosts   31**
"When I went to kindergarten and had to speak English for the first time, I became silent."

Grace Paley   **The Loudest Voice**   36

"We learned 'Holy Night' without an error. 'How wonderful!' said Miss Glacé, the student teacher. 'To think that some of you don't even speak the language!'"

Mike Rose   **I Just Wanna Be Average**   43

"It's popular these days to claim you grew up on the streets."

Countee Cullen   **Incident**   57

"Now I was eight and very small."

PART TWO   Heritage   59

John Tarkov   **Fitting In**   62

"Every father has a vision of what he'd like his son to be. Every son has a vision in kind of his father."

Toni Morrison   **A Slow Walk of Trees**   67

"His name was John Solomon Willis, and when at age 5 he heard from the old folks that 'the Emancipation Proclamation was coming,' he crawled under the bed."

Harry Mark Petrakis   **Barba Nikos**   72

"One of our untamed games was to seek out the owner of a pushcart or a store, unmistakably an immigrant, and bedevil him with a chorus of insults and jeers. To prove allegiance to the gang it was necessary to reserve our fiercest malevolence for a storekeeper or peddler belonging to our own ethnic background."

Michael Novak   **In Ethnic America**   78

"We did not feel this country belonged to us. We felt fierce pride in it, more loyalty than anyone could know. But we felt blocked at every turn."

Anton Shammas **Amérka, Amérka: A Palestinian Abroad in the Land of the Free 85**

"We travel light, empty-pocketed, with the vanity of those who think home is a portable idea, something that dwells mainly in the mind or within a text."

Wendy Rose **Three Thousand Dollar Death Song 94**

"From this distant point we watch our bones/auctioned with our careful beadwork...."

PART THREE   Families   97

Sun Park **Don't Expect Me to Be Perfect 100**

"If I were a genius, I would not mind being treated like one. But since I am not, I do."

Jane Howard **Families 103**

"Good families are much to all their members, but everything to none."

Deb Price **Gay Partners Need to Make a Name for Themselves 109**

"Is she my 'girlfriend' or my 'significant other'? My 'longtime companion' or my 'lover'?"

Ruth Breen **Choosing a Mate 113**

"Choice is not one of the terms I would use to describe my marriage."

Alfred Kazin **The Kitchen 117**

"All my memories of that kitchen are dominated by the nearness of my mother sitting all day long at her sewing machine, by the clacking of the treadle against the linoleum floor, by the patient twist of her right shoulder as she automatically pushed at the wheel with one hand...."

Arlene Skolnick **The Paradox of Perfection 121**

"The image of the perfect, happy family makes ordinary families seem like failures."

Theodore Roethke   **My Papa's Waltz**   **129**

"You…waltzed me off to bed/Still clinging to your shirt."

PART FOUR   Identities   131

Marcus Mabry   **Living in Two Worlds**   **135**

"In mid-December I was at Stanford, among the palm trees and weighty chores of academe…. Once I got home to New Jersey, reality returned."

Maria L. Muñiz   **Back, but Not Home**   **139**

"I want to return because the journey back will also mean a journey within. Only then will I see the missing piece."

Gish Jen   **An Ethnic Trump**   **143**

"That my son, Luke, age 4, goes to Chinese-culture school seems inevitable to most people, even though his father is of Irish descent. For certain ethnicities trump others; Chinese, for example, trumps Irish."

Nicolette Toussaint   **Hearing the Sweetest Songs**   **146**

"We're all just temporarily abled, and every one of us, if we live long enough, will become disabled in some way."

Eva Hoffman   **Lost in Translation**   **150**

"…as I hear my choked-up voice straining to assert itself, as I hear myself missing every beat and rhythm that would say "funny" and "punch line," I feel a hot flush of embarrassment."

Judith Ortiz Cofer   **The Myth of the Latin Woman: I Just Met a Girl Named María**   **155**

"You can leave the island, master the English language, and travel as far as you can, but if you are a Latina…the island travels with you."

Malcolm X **Hair**   **162**

"I took the little list of ingredients…to a grocery store, where I got a can of Red Devil lye, two eggs, and two medium-sized white potatoes."

Nell Bernstein **Goin' Gangsta, Choosin' Cholita: Teens Today "Claim" a Racial Identity**   **165**

"For April and her friends, identity is not a matter of where you come from, what you were born into, what color your skin is. It's what you wear, the music you listen to, the words you use—everything to which you pledge allegiance, no matter how fleetingly."

Gwendolyn Brooks **The Pool Players: Seven at the Golden Shovel**   **172**

"We real cool. We/Left school"

PART FIVE   Encounters   175

Brent Staples **Night Walker**   **178**

"…I soon gathered that being perceived as dangerous is a hazard in itself."

Piri Thomas **Alien Turf**   **183**

"This crap kept up for a month. They tried to shake me up. Every time they threw something at me, it was just to see me jump."

Walter White **I Learn What I Am**   **195**

"In the flickering light the mob swayed, paused, and began to flow toward us. In that instant there opened up within me a great awareness; I knew then who I was. I was a Negro,…"

Michael Dorris **For the Indians, No Thanksgiving**   **201**

"Only good Indians are admitted into this tableau, of course: those who accept the manifest destiny of a European presence and are prepared to adopt English dining customs and, by inference, English everything else."

Jeanne Wakatsuki Houston and James D. Houston   **Arrival at Manzanar   205**

"Mama took out another dinner plate and hurled it at the floor, then another and another, never moving, never opening her mouth, just quivering and glaring at the retreating dealer, with tears streaming down her cheeks."

Dwight Okita   **In Response to Executive Order 9066: All Americans of Japanese Descent Must Report to Relocation Centers   212**

"My best friend is a white girl named Denise—/we look at boys together."

PART SIX   How We Live   215

Daniel Meier   **One Man's Kids   219**

"My work is not traditional male work.... My energy is not spent in pursuing, climbing, achieving, conquering, or cornering some goal or object."

Geraldine Brooks   **Unplugged   223**

"I'd rather go fishing than watch the fishing channel."

Pico Iyer   **Home Is Every Place   227**

"I am a multinational soul on a multicultural globe where more and more countries are as polyglot and restless as airports."

Lars Eighner   **On Dumpster Diving   234**

"Quite a number of people, not all of them of the bohemian type, are willing to brag that they found this or that piece in the trash. But eating from Dumpsters is what separates the dilettanti from the professionals."

Barbara Brandt   **Less Is More: A Call for Shorter Work Hours   246**

"Americans often assume that overwork is an inevitable fact of life—like death and taxes. Yet a closer look at other times and other nations offers some startling surprises."

Barbara Ehrenreich and Annette Fuentes **Life on the Global Assembly Line** 252

"Multinational corporations and Third World governments alike consider assembly-line work—whether the product is Barbie dolls or missile parts—to be 'women's work.'"

Aurora Levins Morales **Class Poem** 261

"…and I am through apologizing. I am going to strip apology from my voice…"

PART SEVEN New Worlds 265

Bette Bao Lord **Walking in Lucky Shoes** 268

"…shoes that took me up a road cleared by the footfalls of millions of immigrants before me—to a room of my own."

Michel Guillaume St. Jean de Crèvecoeur **What Is an American?** 272

"Here individuals of all nations are melted into a new race of men, whose labours and posterity will one day cause great change in the world."

Recapture the Flag: 34 Reasons to Love America 277

"The way immigration transforms the nation's eating habits: Wieners, potatoes, pizza, chow mein, spaghetti, tacos, egg rolls, curry, mock duck, pad thai."

Anzia Yezierska **Soap and Water** 280

"Every time I had to come to the dean's office for a private conference, I prepared for the ordeal of her cold scrutiny, as a patient prepares for a surgical operation."

Malcolm Gladwell **Black Like Them** 287

"Garden City was no place for a black person. But that is the point. Rosie and Noel are from Jamaica. They don't consider themselves black at all."

Joseph Bruchac **Ellis Island**   **299**

"Like millions of others,/I too come to this island,/nine decades the answerer/of dreams."

PART EIGHT   Other Worlds   301

Margaret Atwood   **Canadians: What Do They Want?**   **305**

"It's hard to explain to Americans what it feels like to be a Canadian."

Mark Salzman   **Teacher Mark**   **310**

"'Chinese parents love their children, but they also think that children are like furniture. They own you, and you must make them comfortable until they decide to let you go.'"

John David Morley   **Living in a Japanese Home**   **318**

"The most striking feature of the Japanese house was lack of privacy; the lack of individual, inviolable space."

Laura Bohannan   **Shakespeare in the Bush**   **324**

"They threatened to tell me no more stories until I told them one of mine....Realizing that here was my chance to prove *Hamlet* universally intelligible, I agreed."

Jonathan Swift   **A Modest Proposal**   **335**

"...a fair, cheap, and easy method of making these children sound, useful members of the commonwealth..."

George Orwell   **Shooting an Elephant**   **343**

"In Moulmein, in lower Burma, I was hated by large numbers of people—the only time in my life that I have been important enough for this to happen to me."

Jamaica Kincaid   **On Seeing England for the First Time**   **351**

"The space between the idea of something and its reality is always wide and deep and dark. The longer they are kept apart—idea of thing, reality of a thing—the wider the width, the deeper the depth, the thicker and darker the darkness."

Gloria Anzaldúa **To live in the Borderlands means you** **361**
"To survive the Borderlands/you must live *sin fronteras*/be a crossroads."

PART NINE **Communicating** **365**

Gloria Naylor **The Meaning of a Word** **369**
"I was later to go home and ask the inevitable question that every black parent must face—'Mommy, what does "nigger" mean?'"

Amy Tan **Mother Tongue** **373**
"I spend a great deal of my time thinking about the power of language—the way it can evoke an emotion, a visual image, a complex idea, or a simple truth."

Joshua Gamson **Do Ask, Do Tell** **380**
"For lesbians, gay men, bisexuals, drag queens, transsexuals—and combinations thereof—watching daytime television has got to be spooky. Suddenly, there are renditions of you, chattering away in a system that otherwise ignores or steals your voice at every turn."

Jack G. Shaheen **The Media's Image of Arabs** **390**
"With my children, I have watched animated heroes Heckle and Jeckle pull the rug from under 'Ali Boo-Boo, the Desert Rat,' and Laverne and Shirley stop 'Sheik Ha-Mean-ie' from conquering 'the U.S. and the world.'"

Lisel Mueller **Why We Tell Stories** **395**
"Because the story of your life becomes your life."

Credits **399**

Author/Title Index **403**

Rhetorical Contents

Description (Selections that contain substantial descriptive passages)
Gary Soto, *The Jacket*   8
Mike Rose, *I Just Wanna Be Average*   43
Alfred Kazin, *The Kitchen*   117
Walter White, *I Learn What I Am*   195
Geraldine Brooks, *Unplugged*   223
Lars Eighner, *On Dumpster Diving*   234
John David Morley, *Living in a Japanese Home*   318
George Orwell, *Shooting an Elephant*   343

Narration (Personal)
Elizabeth Wong, *The Struggle To Be an All-American Girl*   4
Gary Soto, *The Jacket*   8
Maya Angelou, *Graduation*   13
Maxine Hong Kingston, *Girlhood among Ghosts*   31
Mike Rose, *I Just Wanna Be Average*   43
John Tarkov, *Fitting In*   62
Toni Morrison, *A Slow Walk of Trees*   67
Sun Park, *Don't Expect Me to Be Perfect*   100
Ruth Breen, *Choosing a Mate*   113
Marcus Mabry, *Living in Two Worlds*   135
Maria L. Muñiz, *Back, but Not Home*   139
Gish Jen, *An Ethnic Trump*   143
Nicolette Toussaint, *Hearing the Sweetest Songs*   146
Eva Hoffman, *Lost in Translation*   150
Judith Ortiz Cofer, *The Myth of the Latin Woman: I Just Met a Girl Named María*   155
Malcolm X, *Hair*   162
Brent Staples, *Night Walker*   178
Piri Thomas, *Alien Turf*   183
Walter White, *I Learn What I Am*   195
Jeanne Wakatsuki Houston and James D. Houston, *Arrival at Manzanar*   205
Daniel Meier, *One Man's Kids*   219
Pico Iyer, *Home Is Every Place*   227

Lars Eighner, *On Dumpster Diving*   234
Bette Bao Lord, *Walking in Lucky Shoes*   268
Malcolm Gladwell, *Black Like Them*   287
Mark Salzman, *Teacher Mark*   310
George Orwell, *Shooting an Elephant*   343
Jamaica Kincaid, *On Seeing England for the First Time*   351
Amy Tan, *Mother Tongue*   373

Narration (Observation and reporting)
Anton Shammas, *Amérka, Amérka: A Palestinian Abroad in the Land of the Free*   85
Nell Bernstein, *Goin' Gangsta, Choosin' Cholita*   165
Geraldine Brooks *Unplugged*   223
Barbara Ehrenreich and Annette Fuentes, *Life on the Global Assembly Line*   252
Malcolm Gladwell, *Black Like Them*   287
Laura Bohannan, *Shakespeare in the Bush*   324
Joshua Gamson, *Do Ask, Do Tell*   380

Definition
Jane Howard, *Families*   103
Deb Price, *Gay Partners Need to Make a Name for Themselves*   109
Ruth Breen, *Choosing a Mate*   113
Gish Jen, *An Ethnic Trump*   143
Judith Ortiz Cofer, *The Myth of the Latin Woman: I Just Met a Girl Named María*   155
Nicolette Toussaint, *Hearing the Sweetest Songs*   146
Nell Bernstein, *Goin' Gangsta, Choosin' Cholita*   165
Daniel Meier, *One Man's Kids*   219
Lars Eighner, *On Dumpster Diving*   234
Michel Guillaume St. Jean de Crèvecoeur, *What Is an American?*   272
Malcolm Gladwell, *Black Like Them*   287
Gloria Naylor, *The Meaning of a Word*   369

Classification and Division
Jane Howard, *Families*   103
Nell Bernstein, *Goin' Gangsta, Choosin' Cholita*   165
Barbara Ehrenreich and Annette Fuentes, *Life on the Global Assembly Line*   252
Recapture the Flag: 34 Reasons to Love America   277

Comparison and Contrast
Toni Morrison, *A Slow Walk of Trees*   67

Ruth Breen, *Choosing a Mate*   113
Marcus Mabry, *Living in Two Worlds*   135
Gish Jen, *An Ethnic Trump*   143
Judith Ortiz Cofer, *The Myth of the Latin Woman: I Just Met a Girl Named María*   155
Nell Bernstein, *Goin' Gangsta, Choosin' Cholita*   165
Michael Dorris, *For the Indians, No Thanksgiving*   201
Daniel Meier, *One Man's Kids*   219
Pico Iyer, *Home is Every Place*   227
Michel Guillaume Jean de Crèvecoeur, *What Is an American?*   272
Malcolm Gladwell, *Black Like Them*   287
Margaret Atwood, *Canadians: What Do They Want?*   305
Mark Salzman, *Teacher Mark*   310
John David Morley, *Living in a Japanese Home*   318
Laura Bohannan, *Shakespeare in the Bush*   324
Jamaica Kincaid, *On Seeing England for the First Time*   351
Amy Tan, *Mother Tongue*   373

Cause and Effect

Gary Soto, *The Jacket*   8
Lindsy Van Gelder, *The Importance of Being Eleven: Carol Gilligan Takes on Adolescence*   25
Arlene Skolnick, *The Paradox of Perfection*   121
Nell Bernstein, *Goin' Gangsta, Choosin' Cholita*   165
Walter White, *I Learn What I Am*   195
Geraldine Brooks, *Unplugged*   223
Barbara Brandt, *Less is More: A Call for Shorter Work Hours*   246
Jonathan Swift, *A Modest Proposal*   335
George Orwell, *Shooting an Elephant*   343
Jamaica Kincaid, *On Seeing England for the First Time*   351
Amy Tan, *Mother Tongue*   373
Jack G. Shaheen, *The Media's Image of Arabs*   390

Argument and Persuasion

Maya Angelou, *Graduation*   13
Mike Rose, *I Just Wanna Be Average*   43
Ruth Breen, *Choosing a Mate*   113
Judith Ortiz Cofer, *The Myth of the Latin Woman: I Just Met a Girl Named María*   155
Malcolm X, *Hair*   162
Pico Iyer, *Home Is Every Place*   227
Lars Eighner, *On Dumpster Diving*   234
Barbara Brandt, *Less Is More: A Call for Shorter Work Hours*   246

Barbara Ehrenreich and Annette Fuentes, *Life on the Global Assembly Line*   252

Malcolm Gladwell, *Black Like Them*   287

Margaret Atwood, *Canadians: What Do They Want?*   305

Jonathan Swift, *A Modest Proposal*   335

George Orwell, *Shooting an Elephant*   343

Jamaica Kincaid, *On Seeing England for the First Time*   351

Amy Tan, *Mother Tongue*   373

Joshua Gamson, *Do Ask, Do Tell*   380

Jack G. Shaheen, *The Media's Image of Arabs*   390

Irony, Humor, and Satire

Grace Paley, *The Loudest Voice*   36

Michael Dorris, *For the Indians, No Thanksgiving*   201

Geraldine Brooks, *Unplugged*   223

Margaret Atwood, *Canadians: What Do They Want?*   305

Jonathan Swift, *A Modest Proposal*   335

Poetry

Countee Cullen, *Incident*   57

Wendy Rose, *Three Thousand Dollar Death Song*   94

Theodore Roethke, *My Papa's Waltz*   129

Gwendolyn Brooks, *The Pool Players: Seven at the Golden Shovel*   172

Dwight Okita, *In Response to Executive Order 9066: All Americans of Japanese Descent Must Report to Relocation Centers*   212

Aurora Levins Morales, *Class Poem*   261

Joseph Bruchac, *Ellis Island*   299

Gloria Anzaldúa, *To live in the Borderlands means you*   361

Lisel Mueller, *Why We Tell Stories*   395

Preface

When we created the first edition of *Crossing Cultures* in 1983, we imagined a book that would encompass the "diverse ways in which men and women live in different societies and social circumstances." Our hope was to challenge and engage students by presenting them with readings that would expand and reinforce their understanding of people both similar to and different from themselves. This idea still holds true.

As multiculturalism has increasingly become a part of our vocabulary, its meaning has both broadened and deepened in scope. As writers have looked further into how we, as individuals and cultures, shape our identity, the questions have become more complex. We may question how we define our identity and to what extent it is something we are born with or raised into. How is it signified by behavior, dress, and talk? Also, we increasingly feel allegiance to more than one identity, given or chosen. How do we express our individuality, while integrating our loyalties? How do changes in technology and communication affect how we think about culture and identity?

NEW SELECTIONS IN THE FIFTH EDITION

We have tried to make the fifth edition of *Crossing Cultures* broader in scope and more current. Nineteen new selections have been added, all written recently. Often they expand on and complicate the idea of cultural identity. Several new authors—including Gish Jen, Judith Ortiz Cofer, Aurora Levins Morales, and Gloria Anzaldúa—write about the choices and conflicts they face because of their allegiance to more than one culture. Malcolm Gladwell, Nell Bernstein, and Jamaica Kincaid each explore the extent to which identity is created, chosen, or imposed.

Other authors define themselves as belonging to a culture based on something other than race, religion, or ethnicity. Deb Price and Joshua Gamson, for example, question how gays and lesbians define identity in a society that is often hostile, or misinformed. Nicolette Toussaint writes of living in two worlds, the deaf and the hearing.

A new section, "How We Live," deals with the meaning we give to work, leisure, and home. Daniel Meier reflects on his choice of a job that brings him personal satisfaction, if not societal approbation. Barbara Brandt questions our devotion to the work ethic. Lars Eighner describes a life without a home, and Pico Iyer a life with multiple and transient homes. When television brings the world in full color into our homes, Geraldine Brooks questions whether too often we watch life instead of live it.

We have kept classic selections by Michel Guillaume St. Jean de Crève-coeur, Jonathan Swift, and George Orwell because the issues they highlight—American identity, dehumanization of the "other," and personal responsibility within a political structure—are as relevant today as ever. For the same reason, we have also kept a few older journalistic selections, such as Barbara Ehrenreich and Annette Fuentes's description of work in developing countries, and Michael Novak's recently reissued explanation of the attitudes of white ethnics.

NEW FEATURES IN THE FIFTH EDITION

Since many students respond well to visual prompts, we have selected a relevant photo for the beginning of each chapter. Each photo is accompanied by a set of questions that relate both to the photograph and to the theme of the chapter. Realizing that poetry also can serve as a stimulus for writing, we have added questions for the poems that end each chapter.

USING CROSS-CULTURAL THEMES

The success of this book and our experiences teaching have convinced us that cross-cultural subjects work well in a composition course. They provide strong and meaningful topics for discussion and writing, both by broadening students' perspectives and allowing them to draw on stories and themes from their own lives. Multicultural selections challenge accepted beliefs by asking students to consider the lives, ideas, aspirations—and prejudices—of people who are very different from them. At the same time, reading, and having one's classmates read, selections related to one's own culture is likely to heighten students' self-assurance and prompt them to reflect on the meaning of their own experience. This reflection and reaction to reading and class discussion can often be the starting point for writing that "belongs" to the student, yet extends beyond his or her own (perhaps limited) experience of the world.

The readings in *Crossing Cultures* have been collected from a variety of sources and are meant to reflect a broad range of perspectives, ideas, and rhetorical styles. Each selection has also been chosen because it is "a good read" whose subject and style will engage college students and provide material for thoughtful reflection both within and beyond their composition classes.

CROSSING CULTURES AS A COMPOSITION TEXT

Clearly, students produce stronger writing when they are motivated to write—engaged by content that is thematically interesting and challenging. However, more is needed to turn that interest into good writing. *Crossing Cultures* provides many tools to help students develop stronger reading and composition skills. Each selection in the book is followed by a set of exercises that can be used for class discussions or as writing prompts. "Some of the Issues" aids students in careful reading by providing questions that help them clarify and analyze the meaning of the essay. "The Way We Are Told" asks students to examine the author's rhetorical strategies and points out the significance and effect of stylistic choices we make when we compose. Each exercise section concludes with "Some Subjects for Writing," which can be used as prompts for essays and/or journal entries. Asterisks indicate questions or writing topics that refer to more than one selection, often giving students the chance to compare and contrast two different views of the same subject.

The arrangement of the book allows the instructor flexibility and structure. *Crossing Cultures* contains selections of varying length, difficulty, and style. Selections are arranged thematically; each section begins with an accessible essay, moving on to more challenging and difficult readings. There is also a supplementary Rhetorical Table of Contents that organizes the readings based on the writers' stylistic patterns.

Acknowledgments

It was Henry Knepler's idea to create this anthology fifteen years ago. Although he wasn't able to actively participate in this revision, his vision and ideas are present throughout.

We wish to thank the editorial and production staff at Allyn and Bacon. Joe Opiela devoted his considerable enthusiasm and expertise to initiating the project, and to seeing it through from beginning to end. Kate Tolini provided prompt, thoughtful, and thorough answers to numerous questions big and small, always with cheerful encouragement. Rob Lawson skillfully coordinated the many details involved in the production of this book. Susan Duane and Sarah Evertson carefully selected the photos that begin each chapter. Kathy Robinson and Mary Young at Omegatype did a superlative job of managing the book's copyediting and pre-print production.

Several readers and reviewers gave us expert advice and suggestions for improving the text. We thank the reviewers arranged by the publisher: Susan Naomi Bernstein, Shippensburg University; Susan Chin, DeVry Institute of Technology, Decatur; Trudy Katzer, Brooklyn College; and Brian K. Reed, Bethune Cookman College.

We are grateful to Kathleen Kane for her work on the fourth edition; she provided new ideas and valuable contributions, many of which remain in this edition.

Many thanks to Ann Christophersen, Linda Bubon and all the staff at Women & Children First bookstore (especially Ellen Larrimore, Liz Wermcrantz, Caryn Aviv, and Jennifer Carns) for flexibility, patience, and generous sharing of resources. A big belated thank you to Mary Bowers for computer time and help, both licit and illicit. To Ann Generali, Susan Borrelli, and Cyndi Jaffe Schacher, thank you for your grounded wisdom and encouragement. And to Felice Newman, a special thank you for inspiration, helpful advice, and welcome distraction.

Many of the ideas for this edition were sparked by conversations with friends and colleagues. Rory Donnelly, Don Sorsa, Hal Adams, Mary Zajak, Jennifer Cohen, and Ann Feldman gave us input which, either directly or indirectly, led to insights and epiphanies. Veronda Pitchford at University of Illinois Chicago and the library staff at Northeastern Illinois University provided invaluable help in locating hard-to-find materials.

Irek Lapinski understood the importance of this project and provided us with the quiet time to be able to complete it.

Crossing Cultures

1
Growing Up

As we grow up, our awareness of the world around us gradually expands. The learning process begins at birth and never stops. We get to know our physical surroundings—a crib, perhaps, then a room, a house. We become aware of a parent and learn that if we cry, that parent will do something for us. We also learn that others want things from us; much of the time these demands are designed to stop us from doing what we want at that moment. Communication, we find, works in both directions.

What we learn depends of course on our environment, although we do not know that in our early lives. Then we believe that our way of talking—our language—is the only one, and that the way things happen is the only way they can be done. For many Americans, the earliest experiences are confined to one culture. Sooner or later we learn, however, that we coexist with people whose experience or upbringing differs from ours. The discovery of that fact may come as a shock, particularly when we find at the same time that our culture is in some way not welcomed or accepted, that there is a barrier between ours and "theirs," a barrier that we cannot readily cross.

Each author in Part One confronts that barrier while growing up. Elizabeth Wong wants to be an "all-American girl" and fights her mother's attempt to have her keep her Chinese background. Gary Soto's despised jacket, ugly, torn, and several sizes too large, becomes inflated in importance in the author's mind into a symbol of what keeps him from fitting in. Maya Angelou, an African-American student in a segregated elementary school in Arkansas in the 1940s, recoils from the condescending attitude of the white speaker at her graduation from the eighth grade. Lindsey Van Gelder, by looking at both her own life and at important sociological studies, analyzes the changes girls go through when they reach age eleven, and lose their boldness and spontaneity in an effort to conform to

┌───┐

⌐ THINKING ABOUT THE THEME *"Growing Up"*─────────

1. How do you respond to the photograph on the facing page? Without writing a complete essay, jot down some answers to the following questions and discuss your answers with the rest of the class.

   How old do you think the girl in the photo is?

   What does her expression tell you about how she's feeling?

   Consider her clothing. What does it tell you about this moment in her life?

   Why might the photographer have chosen to photograph her in this particular setting?

2. We all have rituals or events in our early lives that mark turning points—confirmation, communion, bar mitvahs or bat mitvahs, quincenera, to name a few. Describe one of these moments in your life. Try to recapture your feelings at the time. Were you proud, frightened, ambivalent? Were your feelings different than those of the adults around you?

3. The sign on the door could imply that the young girl is being welcomed into her future. Think back to a time when you were about the age of the girl in the picture. How did you think about your future then? How do you think about it now?

4. Select a photo of yourself when you were younger. Create a story that begins with the image in your photograph.

└───┘

society's notion of how women should behave. Maxine Hong Kingston, brought up in a Chinese environment, turns silent when she enters public school.

Grace Paley's short story tells about school administrators who, with great unconcern, impose a Christmas pageant on children whose culture is non-Christian. Mike Rose, with the help of a dedicated teacher, overcomes the limiting boundaries of working-class life and undereducation. Finally, Countee Cullen speaks simply but tellingly of his first confrontation, at age eight, with prejudice.

The Struggle to Be an All-American Girl

ELIZABETH WONG

Elizabeth Wong's mother insisted that she learn Chinese and be aware of her cultural background. In her essay, which first appeared in the Los Angeles Times, *Wong vividly portrays her childhood resistance to her mother's wishes and the anger and embarrassment she felt. Chinese school interfered with her being, as she puts it, "an all-American girl." Here, writing as a young adult, she recognizes in herself a sense of loss.*

Elizabeth Wong is a playwright and television writer who grew up in Los Angeles's Chinatown and worked as a news reporter for ten years before quitting in 1988 to write plays. Her first play premiered off Broadway in 1991. She received a B.A. from the University of Southern California in 1980 and an M.F.A. from New York University in 1991. She currently teaches in the theater department at Bowdoin College in Maine.

It's still there, the Chinese school on Yale Street where my brother and I used 1
to go. Despite the new coat of paint and the high wire fence, the school I knew 10 years ago remains remarkably, stoically the same.

Every day at 5 P.M., instead of playing with our fourth- and fifth-grade 2
friends or sneaking out to the empty lot to hunt ghosts and animal bones, my brother and I had to go to Chinese school. No amount of kicking, screaming, or pleading could dissuade my mother, who was solidly determined to have us learn the language of our heritage.

Forcibly, she walked us the seven long, hilly blocks from our home to 3
school, depositing our defiant tearful faces before the stern principal. My only memory of him is that he swayed on his heels like a palm tree, and he always clasped his impatient twitching hands behind his back. I recognized him as a repressed maniacal child killer, and knew that if we ever saw his hands we'd be in big trouble.

We all sat in little chairs in an empty auditorium. The room smelled like 4
Chinese medicine, an imported faraway mustiness. Like ancient mothballs or dirty closets. I hated that smell. I favored crisp new scents. Like the soft French perfume that my American teacher wore in public school.

4

5   There was a stage far to the right, flanked by an American flag and the flag of the Nationalist Republic of China, which was also red, white and blue but not as pretty.

6   Although the emphasis at the school was mainly language—speaking, reading, writing—the lessons always began with an exercise in politeness. With the entrance of the teacher, the best student would tap a bell and everyone would get up, kowtow, and chant, "Sing san ho," the phonetic for "How are you, teacher?"

7   Being ten years old, I had better things to learn than ideographs copied painstakingly in lines that ran right to left from the tip of a *moc but*, a real ink pen that had to be held in an awkward way if blotches were to be avoided. After all, I could do the multiplication tables, name the satellites of Mars, and write reports on *Little Women* and *Black Beauty*. Nancy Drew, my favorite book heroine, never spoke Chinese.

8   The language was a source of embarrassment. More times than not, I had tried to disassociate myself from the nagging loud voice that followed me wherever I wandered in the nearby American supermarket outside Chinatown. The voice belonged to my grandmother, a fragile woman in her seventies who could outshout the best of the street vendors. Her humor was raunchy, her Chinese rhythmless, patternless. It was quick, it was loud, it was unbeautiful. It was not like the quiet, lilting romance of French or the gentle refinement of the American South. Chinese sounded pedestrian. Public.

9   In Chinatown, the comings and goings of hundreds of Chinese on their daily tasks sounded chaotic and frenzied. I did not want to be thought of as mad, as talking gibberish. When I spoke English, people nodded at me, smiled sweetly, said encouraging words. Even the people in my culture would cluck and say that I'd do well in life. "My, doesn't she move her lips fast," they would say, meaning that I'd be able to keep up with the world outside Chinatown.

10   My brother was even more fanatical than I about speaking English. He was especially hard on my mother, criticizing her, often cruelly, for her pidgin speech—smatterings of Chinese scattered like chop suey in her conversation. "It's not 'What it is,' Mom," he'd say in exasperation. "It's 'What *is* it, what *is* it, what *is* it!'" Sometimes Mom might leave out an occasional "the" or "a," or perhaps a verb of being. He would stop her in mid-sentence: "Say it again, Mom. Say it right." When he tripped over his own tongue, he'd blame it on her: "See, Mom, it's all your fault. You set a bad example."

11   What infuriated my mother most was when my brother cornered her on her consonants, especially "r." My father had played a cruel joke on Mom by assigning her an American name that her tongue wouldn't allow her to say. No matter how hard she tried, "Ruth" always ended up "Luth" or "Roof."

12   After two years of writing with a *moc but* and reciting words with multiples of meanings, I finally was granted a cultural divorce. I was permitted to stop Chinese school.

I thought of myself as multicultural. I preferred tacos to egg rolls; I enjoyed   13
Cinco de Mayo[1] more than Chinese New Year.

At last, I was one of you; I wasn't one of them.   14

Sadly, I still am.   15

EXERCISES

Some of the Issues

1. Cite some of the characteristics of the Chinese school as Wong describes it; how does it differ from her American school?
2. Why was the Chinese language "a source of embarrassment" to Wong? What are her feelings about speaking English?
3. Consider the last sentence: "Sadly, I still am." Why "sadly"?
*4. Read Maxine Hong Kingston's "Girlhood among Ghosts." Compare Kingston's attitude toward Chinese school with Wong's.
*5. Read Maria Muñiz's "Back, but Not Home." What similarities do you notice in her experiences and Wong's? What differences?

The Way We Are Told

6. Consider the title. To what extent does Wong succeed in becoming the "all-American girl" she wanted to be? Explain why the title could be considered ironic.
7. What details does Wong give about her experience in Chinese school to make her feelings explicit? What senses does she appeal to?
8. How does the description of the principal in paragraph 3 reflect the fact that Wong sees him through the eyes of a child?
9. In paragraph 14, whom do "you" and "them" refer to?
10. Wong does not state a thesis directly. Nevertheless, a thesis statement that sums up the essay could be constructed. What might the thesis be? What do you think the author would gain or lose by stating it directly?

Some Subjects for Writing

11. Describe an experience you disliked. Try, like Wong, to build your case by the way you describe the details.

---

[1]Fifth of May. Mexican national holiday marking Mexico's victory over France at Puebla in 1862.
*Asterisks used in this context denote questions and essay topics that draw on more than one selection.

12. What does one gain or lose by assimilating into the mainstream culture? How might it affect one's family ties and self-awareness? Base your conclusions on both observation of others and personal knowledge.

*13. Read Maria Muñiz's "Back, but Not Home." Compare Wong's and Muñiz's attitudes toward their respective cultures. How does each woman's experience explain her attitude?

The Jacket

GARY SOTO

Gary Soto is a poet and prose writer influenced by his working-class Mexican-American roots. His writing style is simple and direct; it describes the particulars of everyday life while at the same time offering a glimpse of larger, more universal themes.

This selection takes a specific object, a jacket, and uses it to describe a feeling and mood at a particular time in the author's life. Most of us have shared the experience of having a piece of clothing take on a significance beyond its practical purpose.

Soto, born in 1952, has published numerous works of fiction and poetry for young adults and children, as well as several volumes of poetry for adults. He has chronicled his childhood in three volumes of memoirs: Living Up the Street *(1985),* Lesser Evils *(1988), and* Small Faces *(1986), from which this essay is taken.*

My clothes have failed me. I remember the green coat that I wore in fifth and sixth grade when you either danced like a champ or pressed yourself against a greasy wall, bitter as a penny toward the happy couples.

When I needed a new jacket and my mother asked what kind I wanted, I described something like bikers wear: black leather and silver studs, with enough belts to hold down a small town. We were in the kitchen, steam on the windows from her cooking. She listened so long while stirring dinner that I thought she understood for sure the kind I wanted. The next day when I got home from school, I discovered draped on my bedpost a jacket the color of day-old guacamole. I threw my books on the bed and approached the jacket slowly, as if it were a stranger whose hand I had to shake. I touched the vinyl sleeve, the collar, and peeked at the mustard-colored lining.

From the kitchen mother yelled that my jacket was in the closet. I closed the door to her voice and pulled at the rack of clothes in the closet, hoping the jacket on the bedpost wasn't for me but my mean brother. No luck. I gave up. From my bed, I stared at the jacket. I wanted to cry because it was so ugly and so big that I knew I'd have to wear it a long time. I was a small kid, thin as a young tree, and it would be years before I'd have a new one. I stared at the jacket, like an enemy, thinking bad things before I took off my old jacket, whose sleeves climbed halfway to my elbow.

4   I put the big jacket on. I zipped it up and down several times and rolled the cuffs up so they didn't cover my hands. I put my hands in the pockets and flapped the jacket like a bird's wings. I stood in front of the mirror, full face, then profile, and then looked over my shoulder as if someone had called me. I sat on the bed, stood against the bed, and combed my hair to see what I would look like doing something natural. I looked ugly. I threw it on my brother's bed and looked at it for a long time before I slipped it on and went out to the backyard, smiling a "thank you" to my mom as I passed her in the kitchen. With my hands in my pockets I kicked a ball against the fence, and then climbed it to sit looking into the alley. I hurled orange peels at the mouth of an open garbage can, and when the peels were gone I watched the white puffs of my breath thin to nothing.

5   I jumped down, hands in my pockets, and in the backyard, on my knees, I teased my dog, Brownie, by swooping my arms while making bird calls. He jumped at me and missed. He jumped again and again, until a tooth sunk deep, ripping an L-shaped tear on my left sleeve. I pushed Brownie away to study the tear as I would a cut on my arm. There was no blood, only a few loose pieces of fuzz. Damn dog, I thought, and pushed him away hard when he tried to bite again. I got up from my knees and went to my bedroom to sit with my jacket on my lap, with the lights out.

6   That was the first afternoon with my new jacket. The next day I wore it to sixth grade and got a D on a math quiz. During the morning recess Frankie T., the playground terrorist, pushed me to the ground and told me to stay there until recess was over. My best friend, Steve Negrete, ate an apple while looking at me, and the girls turned away to whisper on the monkey bars. The teachers were no help: they looked my way and talked about how foolish I looked in my new jacket. I saw their heads bob with laughter, their hands half covering their mouths.

7   Even though it was cold, I took off the jacket during lunch and played kick-ball in a thin shirt, my arms feeling like braille from goose bumps. But when I returned to class I slipped the jacket on and shivered until I was warm. I sat on my hands, heating them up, while my teeth chattered like a cup of crooked dice. Finally warm, I slid out of the jacket but put it back on a few minutes later when the fire bell rang. We paraded out into the yard where we, the sixth graders, walked past all the other grades to stand against the back fence. Everybody saw me. Although they didn't say out loud, "Man, that's ugly," I heard the buzz-buzz of gossip and even laughter that I knew was meant for me.

8   And so I went, in my guacamole-colored jacket. So embarrassed, so hurt, I couldn't even do my homework. I received C's on quizzes and forgot the state capitals and the rivers of South America, our friendly neighbor. Even the girls who had been friendly blew away like loose flowers to follow the boys in neat jackets.

9   I wore that thing for three years until the sleeves grew short and my fore-arms stuck out like the necks of turtles. All during that time no love came to

me—no little dark girl in a Sunday dress she wore on Monday. At lunchtime I stayed with the ugly boys who leaned against the chainlink fence and looked around with propellers of grass spinning in our mouths. We saw girls walk by alone, saw couples, hand in hand, their heads like bookends pressing air together. We saw them and spun our propellers so fast our faces were blurs.

I blame that jacket for those bad years. I blame my mother for her bad taste   10
and her cheap ways. It was a sad time for the heart. With a friend I spent my sixth-grade year in a tree in the alley, waiting for something good to happen to me in that jacket, which had become the ugly brother who tagged along wherever I went. And it was about that time that I began to grow. My chest puffed up with muscle and, strangely, a few more ribs. Even my hands, those fleshy hammers, showed bravely through the cuffs, the fingers already hardening for the coming fights. But that L-shaped rip on the left sleeve got bigger; bits of stuffing coughed out from its wound after a hard day of play. I finally Scotch-taped it closed, but in rain or cold weather the tape peeled off like a scab and more stuffing fell out until that sleeve shriveled into a palsied arm. That winter the elbows began to crack and whole chunks of green began to fall off. I showed the cracks to my mother, who always seemed to be at the stove with steamed-up glasses, and she said that there were children in Mexico who would love that jacket. I told her that this was America and yelled that Debbie, my sister, didn't have a jacket like mine. I ran outside, ready to cry, and climbed the tree by the alley to think bad thoughts and watch my breath puff white and disappear.

But whole pieces still casually flew off my jacket when I played hard, read   11
quietly, or took vicious spelling tests at school. When it became so spotted that my brother began to call me "camouflage," I flung it over the fence into the alley. Later, however, I swiped the jacket off the ground and went inside to drape it across my lap and mope.

I was called to dinner: steam silvered my mother's glasses as she said grace;   12
my brother and sister with their heads bowed made ugly faces at their glasses of powdered milk. I gagged too, but eagerly ate big rips of buttered tortilla that held scooped-up beans. Finished, I went outside with my jacket across my arm. It was a cold sky. The faces of clouds were piled up, hurting. I climbed the fence, jumping down with a grunt. I started up the alley and soon slipped into my jacket, that green ugly brother who breathed over my shoulder that day and ever since.

EXERCISES

Some of the Issues

1. How does the narrator describe the jacket he wants? How does he describe the jacket his mother buys for him? What do these descriptions say about the narrator's self-image as an adolescent?

2. Why does the narrator call the jacket a "stranger whose hand I had to shake" in paragraph 2?
3. Why do you think the narrator's mother buys him such a large jacket?
4. How does the incident in paragraph 5 foreshadow events later in the story?
5. What problems or misfortunes does the narrator attribute to the jacket? To what extent do you think his perceptions differ from reality?
6. Although there is little or no direct discussion of class and ethnicity in the story, there is a sense that both are important. How is this apparent?
7. Throughout the essay, Soto refers to the jacket in many different ways: "a stranger" (paragraph 2), "an enemy" (paragraph 3). Make a list of the various words and phrases he uses to describe the jacket. How do his perceptions of the jacket change? What does the jacket come to symbolize by the last line of the story?
*8. Read Malcolm X's "Hair." Compare Malcolm's attitude toward his hair with Soto's view of the jacket. How do their approaches differ? How are they similar?

How We Are Told

9. Throughout the essay, Soto uses short, simple sentences in combination with longer, more complex ones. How or why are these short sentences effective?
10. Soto uses many similes and metaphors in the story. Find as many of them as you can and discuss which ones you feel are most effective. How do they work as a stylistic tool?
*11. Read Piri Thomas's "Alien Turf." Whereas Soto uses vivid images throughout the story, allowing the reader to visualize certain scenes or moments, Thomas uses dialogue that lets the reader "hear" the action. Discuss the difference between these two methods of description. Why might one author choose to emphasize one over the other?

Some Subjects for Writing

12. Soto uses the jacket to provide focus and continuity in his story. Write an essay in which, like Soto, you focus on one object and its significance in your life. What did this object mean to you? What metaphors and similes would you use to describe this object?
13. Some people feel that clothes make the person. How true is the statement, "You are what you wear"? What kinds of judgments do we make about individuals based on the way they dress? Write an essay in which you analyze the importance placed on clothing in our society. Depending on the focus of your essay, you may want to take into consideration some of the following issues: school uniforms; gang-related clothing and insignias; fashion

magazines and the fashion industry; or the relationship between clothing and musical/artistic taste.

14. Keeping in mind Soto's use of visual imagery, create a comic book based on the story of the jacket. Which scenes would you illustrate? In what places would you use captions or bubbles for dialogue?

Graduation

MAYA ANGELOU

Maya Angelou was born Marguerite Johnson in St. Louis in 1928, and was raised by her grandmother in Stamps, Arkansas. She grew up in a rigidly segregated society. The Civil War had ended slavery but had not eliminated segregation. In fact, several decisions of the Supreme Court reaffirmed its legality. In the case of Plessy v. Ferguson *(1896) in particular, the Court gave its approval to segregation, declaring it to be constitutional as long as the affected facilities, such as public schools, were "separate but equal." Schools were separate after that in large parts of the country, but not equal, as Angelou's memory of the early 1940s demonstrates. In 1954 the Supreme Court reversed itself in* Brown v. Board of Education, *declaring that segregation was "inherently unequal" and, therefore, unconstitutional.*

Angelou—writer, actor, and civil rights activist—is the author of numerous books of poetry, which have been collected in The Complete Collected Poems *(1994).* I Know Why the Caged Bird Sings *(1970), from which this selection is taken, is the first in a series of auto-biographical prose works that includes* Gather Together in My Name *(1975),* Singin' and Swingin' and Merry Like Christmas *(1976) and* The Heart of a Woman *(1981).*

On January 20, 1993, at the invitation of President Clinton, before a crowd of 200,000, Angelou delivered the first original poem written especially for a presidential inauguration, entitled "On the Pulse of Morning."

1   The children in Stamps trembled visibly with anticipation. Some adults were excited too, but to be certain the whole young population had come down with graduation epidemic. Large classes were graduating from both the grammar school and the high school. Even those who were years removed from their own day of glorious release were anxious to help with preparations as a kind of dry run. The junior students who were moving into the vacating classes' chairs were tradition-bound to show their talents for leadership and management. They strutted through the school and around the campus exerting pressure on the lower grades. Their authority was so new that occasionally if they pressed a little too hard it had to be overlooked. After all, next term was coming, and it never hurt a sixth grader to have a play sister in the eighth grade, or a tenth-year stu-

dent to be able to call a twelfth grader Bubba. So all was endured in a spirit of shared understanding. But the graduating classes themselves were the nobility. Like travelers with exotic destinations on their minds, the graduates were remarkably forgetful. They came to school without their books, or tablets or even pencils. Volunteers fell over themselves to secure replacements for the missing equipment. When accepted, the willing workers might or might not be thanked, and it was of no importance to the pregraduation rites. Even teachers were respectful of the now quiet and aging seniors, and tended to speak to them, if not as equals, as beings only slightly lower than themselves. After tests were returned and grades given, the student body, which acted like an extended family, knew who did well, who excelled, and what piteous ones had failed.

Unlike the white high school, Lafayette County Training School distinguished itself by having neither lawn, nor hedges, nor tennis court, nor climbing ivy. Its two buildings (main classrooms, the grade school and home economics) were set on a dirt hill with no fence to limit either its boundaries or those of bordering farms. There was a large expanse to the left of the school which was used alternately as a baseball diamond or a basketball court. Rusty hoops on the swaying poles represented the permanent recreational equipment, although bats and balls could be borrowed from the P.E. teacher if the borrower was qualified and if the diamond wasn't occupied.   2

Over this rocky area relieved by a few shady tall persimmon trees the graduating class walked. The girls often held hands and no longer bothered to speak to the lower students. There was a sadness about them, as if this old world was not their home and they were bound for higher ground. The boys, on the other hand, had become more friendly, more outgoing. A decided change from the closed attitude they projected while studying for finals. Now they seemed not ready to give up the old school, the familiar paths and classrooms. Only a small percentage would be continuing on to college—one of the South's A & M (agricultural and mechanical) schools, which trained Negro youths to be carpenters, farmers, handymen, masons, maids, cooks and baby nurses. Their future rode heavily on their shoulders, and blinded them to the collective joy that had pervaded the lives of the boys and girls in the grammar school graduating class.   3

Parents who could afford it had ordered new shoes and ready-made clothes for themselves from Sears and Roebuck or Montgomery Ward. They also engaged the best seamstresses to make the floating graduating dresses and to cut down secondhand pants which would be pressed to a military slickness for the important event.   4

Oh, it was important, all right. Whitefolks would attend the ceremony, and two or three would speak of God and home, and the Southern way of life, and Mrs. Parsons, the principal's wife, would play the graduation march while the lower-grade graduates paraded down the aisles and took their seats below the platform. The high school seniors would wait in empty classrooms to make their dramatic entrance.   5

6   In the Store I was the person of the moment. The birthday girl. The center. Bailey had graduated the year before, although to do so he had to forfeit all pleasures to make up for his time lost in Baton Rouge.

7   My class was wearing butter-yellow piqué dresses, and Momma launched out on mine. She smocked the yoke into tiny crisscrossing puckers, then shirred the rest of the bodice. Her dark fingers ducked in and out of the lemony cloth as she embroidered raised daisies around the hem. Before she considered herself finished she had added a crocheted cuff on the puff sleeves, and a pointy crocheted collar.

8   I was going to be lovely. A walking model of all the various styles of fine hand sewing and it didn't worry me that I was only twelve years old and merely graduating from the eighth grade. Besides, many teachers in Arkansas Negro schools had only that diploma and were licensed to impart wisdom.

9   The days had become longer and more noticeable. The faded beige of former times had been replaced with strong and sure colors. I began to see my classmates' clothes, their skin tones, and the dust that waved off pussy willows. Clouds that lazed across the sky were objects of great concern to me. Their shiftier shapes might have held a message that in my new happiness and with a little bit of time I'd soon decipher. During that period I looked at the arch of heaven so religiously my neck kept a steady ache. I had taken to smiling more often, and my jaws hurt from the unaccustomed activity. Between the two physical sore spots, I suppose I could have been uncomfortable, but that was not the case. As a member of the winning team (the graduating class of 1940) I had outdistanced unpleasant sensations by miles. I was headed for the freedom of open fields.

10   Youth and social approval allied themselves with me and we trammeled memories of slights and insults. The wind of our swift passage remodeled my features. Lost tears were pounded to mud and then to dust. Years of withdrawal were brushed aside and left behind, as hanging ropes of parasitic moss.

11   My work alone had awarded me a top place and I was going to be one of the first called in the graduating ceremonies. On the classroom blackboard, as well as on the bulletin board in the auditorium, there were blue stars and white stars and red stars. No absences, no tardinesses, and my academic work was among the best of the year. I could say the preamble to the Constitution even faster than Bailey. We timed ourselves often: "WethepeopleoftheUnitedStates inordertoformamoreperfectunion…" I had memorized the Presidents of the United States from Washington to Roosevelt in chronological as well as alphabetical order.

12   My hair pleased me too. Gradually the black mass had lengthened and thickened, so that it kept at last to its braided pattern, and I didn't have to yank my scalp off when I tried to comb it.

13   Louise and I had rehearsed the exercises until we tired out ourselves. Henry Reed was class valedictorian. He was a small, very black boy with hooded eyes, a long, broad nose and an oddly shaped head. I had admired him for years

because each term he and I vied for the best grades in our class. Most often he bested me, but instead of being disappointed I was pleased that we shared top places between us. Like many Southern Black children, he lived with his grandmother, who was as strict as Momma and as kind as she knew how to be. He was courteous, respectful and soft-spoken to elders, but on the playground he chose to play the roughest games. I admired him. Anyone, I reckoned, sufficiently afraid or sufficiently dull could be polite. But to be able to operate at a top level with both adults and children was admirable.

His valedictory speech was entitled "To Be or Not to Be." The rigid tenth-grade teacher had helped him write it. He'd been working on the dramatic stresses for months.   14

The weeks until graduation were filled with heady activities. A group of small children were to be presented in a play about buttercups and daisies and bunny rabbits. They could be heard throughout the building practicing their hops and their little songs that sounded like silver bells. The older girls (non-graduates, of course) were assigned the task of making refreshments for the night's festivities. A tangy scent of ginger, cinnamon, nutmeg and chocolate wafted around the home economics building as the budding cooks made samples for themselves and their teachers.   15

In every corner of the workshop, axes and saws split fresh timber as the woodshop boys made sets and stage scenery. Only the graduates were left out of the general bustle. We were free to sit in the library at the back of the building or look in quite detachedly, naturally, on the measures being taken for our event.   16

Even the minister preached on graduation the Sunday before. His subject was, "Let your light so shine that men will see your good works and praise your Father, Who is in Heaven." Although the sermon was purported to be addressed to us, he used the occasion to speak to backsliders, gamblers and general ne'er-do-wells. But since he had called our names at the beginning of the service we were mollified.   17

Among Negroes the tradition was to give presents to children going only from one grade to another. How much more important this was when the person was graduating at the top of the class. Uncle Willie and Momma had sent away for a Mickey Mouse watch like Bailey's. Louise gave me four embroidered handkerchiefs. (I gave her three crocheted doilies.) Mrs. Sneed, the minister's wife, made me an underskirt to wear for graduation, and nearly every customer gave me a nickel or maybe even a dime with the instruction "Keep on moving to higher ground," or some such encouragement.   18

Amazingly the great day finally dawned and I was out of bed before I knew it. I threw open the back door to see it more clearly, but Momma said, "Sister, come away from that door and put your robe on."   19

I hoped the memory of that morning would never leave me. Sunlight was itself still young, and the day had none of the insistence maturity would bring it in a few hours. In my robe and barefoot in the backyard, under cover of going to   20 see about my new beans, I gave myself up to the gentle warmth and thanked God that no matter what evil I had done in my life He had allowed me to live to see this day. Somewhere in my fatalism I had expected to die, accidentally, and never have the chance to walk up the stairs in the auditorium and gracefully receive my hard-earned diploma. Out of God's merciful bosom I had won reprieve.

21   Bailey came out in his robe and gave me a box wrapped in Christmas paper. He said he had saved his money for months to pay for it. It felt like a box of chocolates, but I knew Bailey wouldn't save money to buy candy when we had all we could want under our noses.

22   He was as proud of the gift as I. It was a soft-leather-bound copy of a collection of poems by Edgar Allan Poe, or, as Bailey and I called him, "Eap." I turned to "Annabel Lee" and we walked up and down the garden rows, the cool dirt between our toes, reciting the beautifully sad lines.

23   Momma made a Sunday breakfast although it was only Friday. After we finished the blessing, I opened my eyes to find the watch on my plate. It was a dream of a day. Everything went smoothly and to my credit. I didn't have to be reminded or scolded for anything. Near evening I was too jittery to attend to chores, so Bailey volunteered to do all before his bath.

24   Days before, we had made a sign for the Store, and as we turned out the lights Momma hung the cardboard over the doorknob. It read clearly: CLOSED, GRADUATION.

25   My dress fitted perfectly and everyone said that I looked like a sunbeam in it. On the hill, going toward the school, Bailey walked behind with Uncle Willie, who muttered, "Go on, Ju." We wanted him to walk ahead with us because it embarrassed him to have to walk so slowly. Bailey said he'd let the ladies walk together, and the men would bring up the rear. We all laughed, nicely.

26   Little children dashed by out of the dark like fireflies. Their crepe-paper dresses and butterfly wings were not made for running and we heard more than one rip, dryly, and the regretful "uh uh" that followed.

27   The school blazed without gaiety. The windows seemed cold and unfriendly from the lower hill. A sense of ill-fated timing crept over me, and if Momma hadn't reached for my hand I would have drifted back to Bailey and Uncle Willie, and possibly beyond. She made a few slow jokes about my feet getting cold, and tugged me along to the now-strange building.

28   Around the front steps, assurance came back. There were my fellow "greats," the graduating class. Hair brushed back, legs oiled, new dresses and pressed pleats, fresh pocket handkerchiefs and little handbags, all homesewn. Oh, we were up to snuff, all right. I joined my comrades and didn't even see my family go in to find seats in the crowded auditorium.

29   The school band struck up a march and all classes filed in as had been rehearsed. We stood in front of our seats, as assigned, and on a signal from the choir director, we sat. No sooner had this been accomplished than the band started to play the national anthem. We rose again and sang the song, after

which we recited the pledge of allegiance. We remained standing for a brief minute before the choir director and the principal signaled to us, rather desperately I thought, to take our seats. The command was so unusual that our carefully rehearsed and smooth-running machine was thrown off. For a full minute we fumbled for our chairs and bumped into each other awkwardly. Habits change or solidify under pressure, so in our state of nervous tension we had been ready to follow our usual assembly pattern: the American national anthem, then the pledge of allegiance, then the song every Black person I knew called the Negro National Anthem. All done in the same key, with the same passion and most often standing on the same foot.

Finding my seat at last, I was overcome with a presentiment of worse things   30
to come. Something unrehearsed, unplanned, was going to happen, and we were going to be made to look bad. I distinctly remember being explicit in the choice of pronoun. It was "we," the graduating class, the unit, that concerned me then.

The principal welcomed "parents and friends" and asked the Baptist minis-   31
ter to lead us in prayer. His invocation was brief and punchy, and for a second I thought we were getting back on the high road to right action. When the principal came back to the dais, however, his voice had changed. Sounds always affected me profoundly and the principal's voice was one of my favorites. During assembly it melted and lowed weakly into the audience. It had not been in my plan to listen to him, but my curiosity was piqued and I straightened up to give him my attention.

He was talking about Booker T. Washington,[1] our "late great leader," who   32
said we can be as close as the fingers on the hand, etc.... Then he said a few vague things about friendship and the friendship of kindly people to those less fortunate than themselves. With that his voice nearly faded, thin, away. Like a river diminishing to a stream and then to a trickle. But he cleared his throat and said, "Our speaker tonight, who is also our friend, came from Texarkana to deliver the commencement address, but due to the irregularity of the train schedule, he's going to, as they say, 'speak and run.'" He said that we understood and wanted the man to know that we were most grateful for the time he was able to give us and then something about how we were willing always to adjust to another's program, and without more ado—"I give you Mr. Edward Donleavy."

Not one but two white men came through the door offstage. The shorter   33
one walked to the speaker's platform, and the tall one moved over to the center seat and sat down. But that was our principal's seat, and already occupied. The dislodged gentleman bounced around for a long breath or two before the Baptist minister gave him his chair, then with more dignity than the situation deserved, the minister walked off the stage.

---

[1]African-American leader (1856–1915) and founder of Tuskegee Institute who advocated economic self-reliance for American Blacks.

34   Donleavy looked at the audience once (on reflection, I'm sure that he wanted only to reassure himself that we were really there), adjusted his glasses and began to read from a sheaf of papers.

35   He was glad "to be here and to see the work going on just as it was in the other schools."

36   At the first "Amen" from the audience I willed the offender to immediate death by choking on the word. But Amens and Yes, sir's began to fall around the room like rain through a ragged umbrella.

37   He told us of the wonderful changes we children in Stamps had in store. The Central School (naturally the white school was Central) had already been granted improvements that would be in use in the fall. A well-known artist was coming from Little Rock to teach art to them. They were going to have the newest microscopes and chemistry equipment for their laboratory. Mr. Donleavy didn't leave us long in the dark over who made these improvements available to Central High. Nor were we to be ignored in the general betterment scheme he had in mind.

38   He said that he had pointed out to people at a very high level that one of the first-line football tacklers at Arkansas Agricultural and Mechanical College had graduated from good old Lafayette County Training School. Here fewer Amens were heard. Those few that did break through lay dully in the air with the heaviness of habit.

39   He went on to praise us. He went on to say how he had bragged that "one of the best basketball players at Fisk sank his first ball right here at Lafayette County Training School."

40   The white kids were going to have a chance to become Galileos and Madame Curies and Edisons and Gauguins, and our boys (the girls weren't even in on it) would try to be Jesse Owenses[2] and Joe Louises.[3]

41   Owens and the Brown Bomber were great heroes in our world, but what school official in the white-goddom of Little Rock had the right to decide that those two men must be our only heroes? Who decided that for Henry Reed to become a scientist he had to work like George Washington Carver, as a bootblack, to buy a lousy microscope? Bailey was obviously always going to be too small to be an athlete, so which concrete angel glued to what county seat had decided that if my brother wanted to become a lawyer he had to first pay penance for his skin by picking cotton and hoeing corn and studying correspondence books at night for twenty years?

42   The man's dead words fell like bricks around the auditorium and too many settled in my belly. Constrained by hard-learned manners I couldn't look behind me, but to my left and right the proud graduating class of 1940 had dropped

[2](1913–1980) African-American winner of four Olympic gold medals in track and field.
[3]African-American boxer (1914–1981) and heavyweight champion of the world from 1937–1949. Also known as the Brown Bomber.

their heads. Every girl in my row had found something new to do with her hand-kerchief. Some folded the tiny squares into love knots, some into triangles, but most were wadding them, then pressing them flat on their yellow laps.

On the dais, the ancient tragedy was being replayed. Professor Parsons sat,   43
a sculptor's reject, rigid. His large, heavy body seemed devoid of will or willing-ness, and his eyes said he was no longer with us. The other teachers examined the flag (which was draped stage right) or their notes, or the windows which opened on our now-famous playing diamond.

Graduation, the hush-hush magic time of frills and gifts and congratulations   44
and diplomas, was finished for me before my name was called. The accomplish-ment was nothing. The meticulous maps, drawn in three colors of ink, learning and spelling decasyllabic words, memorizing the whole of *The Rape of Lucrece*[4]—it was for nothing. Donleavy had exposed us.

We were maids and farmers, handymen and washerwomen, and anything   45
higher that we aspired to was farcical and presumptuous.

Then I wished that Gabriel Prosser and Nat Turner had killed all whitefolks   46
in their beds and that Abraham Lincoln had been assassinated before the signing of the Emancipation Proclamation, and that Harriet Tubman had been killed by that blow on her head and Christopher Columbus had drowned in the *Santa María*.

It was awful to be Negro and have no control over my life. It was brutal to   47
be young and already trained to sit quietly and listen to charges brought against my color with no chance of defense. We should all be dead. I thought I should like to see us all dead, one on top of the other. A pyramid of flesh with the white-folks on the bottom, as the broad base, then the Indians with their silly toma-hawks and teepees and wigwams and treaties, the Negroes with their mops and recipes and cotton sacks and spirituals sticking out of their mouths. The Dutch children should all stumble in their wooden shoes and break their necks. The French should choke to death on the Louisiana Purchase (1803) while silkworms ate all the Chinese with their stupid pigtails. As a species, we were an abomina-tion. All of us.

Donleavy was running for election, and assured our parents that if he won   48
we could count on having the only colored paved playing field in that part of Arkansas. Also—he never looked up to acknowledge the grunts of acceptance—also, we were bound to get some new equipment for the home economics build-ing and the workshop.

He finished, and since there was no need to give any more than the most   49
perfunctory thank-you's, he nodded to the men on the stage, and the tall white man who was never introduced joined him at the door. They left with the atti-tude that now they were off to something really important. (The graduation cer-emonies at Lafayette County Training School had been a mere preliminary.)

[4]Shakespeare's poem (1594) based on a Roman legend.

50   The ugliness they left was palpable. An uninvited guest who wouldn't leave. The choir was summoned and sang a modern arrangement of "Onward, Christian Soldiers," with new words pertaining to graduates seeking their place in the world. But it didn't work. Elouise, the daughter of the Baptist minister, recited "Invictus," and I could have cried at the impertinence of "I am the master of my fate, I am the captain of my soul."

51   My name had lost its ring of familiarity and I had to be nudged to go and receive my diploma. All my preparations had fled. I neither marched up to the stage like a conquering Amazon, nor did I look in the audience for Bailey's nod of approval. Marguerite Johnson, I heard the name again, my honors were read, there were noises in the audience of appreciation, and I took my place on the stage as rehearsed.

52   I thought about colors I hated: ecru, puce, lavender, beige and black.

53   There was shuffling and rustling around me, then Henry Reed was giving his valedictory address, "To Be or Not to Be." Hadn't he heard the whitefolks? We couldn't *be*, so the question was a waste of time. Henry's voice came out clear and strong. I feared to look at him. Hadn't he got the message? There was no "nobler in the mind" for Negroes because the world didn't think we had minds, and they let us know it. "Outrageous fortune"? Now, that was a joke. When the ceremony was over I had to tell Henry Reed some things. That is, if I still cared. Not "rub," Henry, "erase." "Ah, there's the erase." Us.

54   Henry had been a good student in elocution. His voice rose on tides of promise and fell on waves of warnings. The English teacher had helped him to create a sermon winging through Hamlet's soliloquy. To be a man, a doer, a builder, a leader, or to be a tool, an unfunny joke, a crusher of funky toadstools. I marveled that Henry could go through with the speech as if we had a choice.

55   I had been listening and silently rebutting each sentence with my eyes closed; then there was a hush, which in an audience warns that something unplanned is happening. I looked up and saw Henry Reed, the conservative, the proper, the A student, turn his back to the audience and turn to us (the proud graduating class of 1940) and sing, nearly speaking,

> "Lift ev'ry voice and sing
> Till earth and heaven ring
> Ring with the harmonies of Liberty…"*

It was the poem written by James Weldon Johnson. It was the music composed by J. Rosamond Johnson. It was the Negro national anthem. Out of habit we were singing it.

---

*"Lift Ev'ry Voice and Sing"—words by James Weldon Johnson and music by J. Rosamond Johnson. Copyright by Edward B. Marks Music Corporation. Used by permission.

Our mothers and fathers stood in the dark hall and joined the hymn of   56
encouragement. A kindergarten teacher led the small children onto the stage and
the buttercups and daisies and bunny rabbits marked time and tried to follow:

"Stony the road we trod
Bitter the chastening rod
Felt in the days when hope, unborn, had died.
Yet with a steady beat
Have not our weary feet
Come to the place for which our fathers sighed?"

Every child I knew had learned that song with his ABC's and along with   57
"Jesus Loves Me This I Know." But I personally had never heard it before.
Never heard the words, despite the thousands of times I had sung them. Never
thought they had anything to do with me.

On the other hand, the words of Patrick Henry had made such an impres-   58
sion on me that I had been able to stretch myself tall and trembling and say, "I
know not what course others may take, but as for me, give me liberty or give me
death."

And now I heard, really for the first time: 59

"We have come over a way that with tears
has been watered,
We have come, treading our path through
the blood of the slaughtered."

While echoes of the song shivered in the air, Henry Reed bowed his head,   60
said "Thank you," and returned to his place in the line. The tears that slipped
down many faces were not wiped away in shame.

We were on top again. As always, again. We survived. The depths had been   61
icy and dark, but now a bright sun spoke to our souls. I was no longer simply a
member of the proud graduating glass of 1940; I was a proud member of the
wonderful, beautiful Negro race.

EXERCISES

Some of the Issues

1. How does Angelou establish the importance of the graduation? How does
   she build it stage by stage?

2. Why does Angelou distinguish between the high school graduates (paragraph 3, end) and the eighth-graders like herself? How do their attitudes differ? Why is she happier?

3. How does Angelou describe her rising expectations for "the great day" in paragraphs 15 through 23?

4. At what point in the narrative do we first get the idea that things may be going wrong with the "dream of a day"? What are later indications that something is wrong?

5. In paragraph 29 the children are confronted with a change in the usual order of things. Why does Angelou make this seem important? Why does the principal "rather desperately" signal for the children to sit down?

6. How do the first words Mr. Donleavy says indicate what his attitude is?

7. In paragraphs 50 through 60 Angelou describes her shifting thoughts and emotions. Explain them in your own words and relate them to the conclusion reached in paragraph 61.

*8. Read Jamaica Kincaid's "On Seeing England for the First Time." How does Angelou's anger after hearing Mr. Donleavy's speech resemble Kincaid's anger at the end of her article? What is the source of anger in each case?

The Way We Are Told

9. Paragraph 1 talks about the graduates and their schoolmates. Paragraphs 2 and 3 describe the school. Why does Angelou write in that order? What distinguishes paragraph 1 from 2 and 3 in addition to the content?

10. Explain the irony Angelou sees in Henry Reed's "To Be or Not to Be" speech.

Some Subjects for Writing

11. Have you ever experienced an event—a dance, a party, a trip—that you looked forward to and that turned out to be a disaster? Or have you ever dreaded an event, such as an interview or a blind date, that turned out better than you had expected? Tell it, trying to make the reader feel the anticipation and the change through the specific, descriptive details you cite, rather than by direct statements. (You will find that the indirect way—making the reader feel or see the event—is more effective than simply saying, "I was bored" or "I found out it was a great evening after all.")

12. In his speech, Mr. Donleavy offers only sports figures like Jesse Owens and Joe Louis as cultural heroes for African-American students. Reflect on famous persons whom you have admired as role models. Write an essay in which you examine the importance of role models and cultural heroes in determining how we see ourselves.

13. Describe a ceremony you have witnessed or participated in. Do it in two separate essays. In the first, describe the event simply in a neutral way. In the second, tell it from the point of view of a witness or participant.

*14. Read Grace Paley's "The Loudest Voice." Compare Mr. Donleavy's insensitivity to that shown by Shirley's teachers in the story. Cite specific instances to explain similarities and differences.

The Importance of Being Eleven: Carol Gilligan Takes on Adolescence

LINDSY VAN GELDER

In this 1990 Ms. *article, Lindsy Van Gelder reviews the results of a study on adolescent girls undertaken by a group of educational psychologists at Harvard University (known as the Harvard Project) and published in* Making Connections: The Relational Worlds of Adolescent Girls at Emma Willard School *(1989). Their findings indicate that as girls approach adolescence, they undergo a crisis in response to what they perceive as the demands placed on girls and women in mainstream American culture. As a consequence, girls learn to "think in ways that differ from what they really think," and turn from outspoken to self-doubting.*

Van Gelder notes in this essay that as recently as a decade ago, there was not enough research on adolescent girls to "fill even a chapter in a psychology textbook." Recently there has been a small explosion of books published about the issues facing adolescent girls. Several of these books, including another book written by members of the Harvard Project, Meeting at the Crossroads: Women's Psychology and Girls' Development *(1992), have become national bestsellers.*

Van Gelder is chief writer for Allure *magazine and coauthor with Pamela Robin Brandt of* Are You Two...Together?: A Gay and Lesbian Travel Guide to Europe *(1991) and* The Girls Next Door: Into the Heart of Lesbian America *(1996). She was born in 1944 and has two daughters.*

1 The summer before sixth grade, I grew six inches. So, probably, did my breasts. In June, my nickname was "Ace," and my favorite possession was a pair of boys' black hightoppers with a decal of the Lone Ranger on the ankle; by September, I had given up sports (this being the pre-aerobics 1950s), changed my name to "Lyn," learned to sleep in iron maiden hair rollers, and begun getting crushes on boys instead of on their haberdashery. The adults in my life were visibly relieved at my "decision," and I remember being happy that I apparently seemed

to be the one in control. On the inside it felt more like putting a gun to my own head just before the enemy army burst through the ramparts. Around the same time as my fall from tomboy grace, but seemingly unrelated to it, I also stopped doing something else I loved: writing poetry. There was no reason to leave it behind; the poetry was the one part of my smart-ass fifth-grade self that teachers and parents wholeheartedly approved of. Nonetheless, it simply disappeared.

According to the ongoing research of Harvard University's Project on the Psychology of Women and the Development of Girls, I was hardly the only girl in our culture who, in one way or another, choked off her own voice at adolescence. The project—whose best known member is Carol Gilligan, author of *In a Different Voice*—has uncovered strong evidence that girls at puberty get the message that the culture doesn't value their experience; it literally doesn't want to listen to what they have to say. They "adjust" by stifling themselves. Indeed, in self-defense most of them stop even consciously knowing the things that the choked-off voice would want to say. 2

At 10 or 11, girls have clear-eyed views of the world and their own right to be heard, says Gilligan. "At this age, they're often called 'bossy'—a word that virtually disappears later on. They're not afraid of conflict. They care deeply about relationships, but they understand that there's often jealousy and anger in relationships as well as joy and comfort." Above all, they aren't worried about being "nice." 3

Consider the girl who is asked to complete the sentence "What gets me into trouble is" and adds: "Chewing gum and not tucking my shirt in (but it's usually worth it)." Or the girl who's mad at her friend for ignoring her when a third friend is around and who plans to "get even" by doing the same thing—at which point her friend will empathize with how *she* felt, and they can be friends again. Or the girl who gets annoyed when she thinks her family isn't paying enough attention to what she has to say at the dinner table—and whips out a whistle and blows it. In the stunned silence that follows, she cheerfully notes in a normal voice: "That's much nicer." 4

But by seventh grade, the girls have started to use the phrase "I don't know" as a sort of conversational mantra ("I thought it was, like—I don't know—a little unfair") or later, even to preface their opinions with remarks like "This may sound mediocre, but..." Instead of living comfortably inside their own skin, they measure themselves against an idealized, perfect girl. And they start to frame dilemmas in relationships not in terms of conflicts between two people but in terms of how "nice" and "good" and self-sacrificing they can be. One legacy of all this shoehorning into an impossible ideal is that girls' relationships (precisely the thing they really *were* "good" at) may become inauthentic—since one's "real" self needs constantly to be tamed, denigrated, glossed over, or buried. It's an endless loop—or it will be if we don't find our way back to what we all knew, effortlessly, in fifth grade. 5

As recently as a decade ago, according to Gilligan, there wasn't enough adolescent girl-specific research to fill even a chapter in a psychology textbook. 6

"The study of adolescence had been the study of males," Gilligan notes. "You'd have titles like 'The Psychological World of the Teenager: A Study of 175 Boys.' These studies were passing government review boards and peer review boards, and they were being published in journals, and they weren't studying girls. I think it's one of the most interesting pieces of intellectual history of this century that nobody saw this, neither women nor men."

7   Then in 1980 Robert Parker moved from a New England boys' prep school to become headmaster of Emma Willard, a girls' private high school near Albany, New York. Parker did notice that the trajectory into adulthood for his new female students seemed to be very different from that of boys. He invited Gilligan (whose *In a Different Voice* had focused on variations in the way men and women approach moral choices) to study his students. The book based on that research (*Making Connections: The Relational Worlds of Adolescent Girls at Emma Willard School*, edited by Gilligan, Nona P. Lyons, and Trudy J. Hanmer) has just been published by Harvard University Press.

8   "What could you possibly learn," one of the Emma Willard girls asked the researchers early on, "by studying *us*?" The girl may have been asking the question out of a typical conviction that girls don't really count, but the researchers themselves didn't have an agenda. The most basic question at the time was simply: "What will we hear about adolescence if we start listening to girls?" As the project grew, the group listened to girls beyond the Emma Willard sample: black, Irish, and Hispanic girls at after-school clubs in three inner-city Boston neighborhoods, as well as girls in public, private, coed, and all-girls school settings.

9   In hindsight, the breakthrough probably came when project member Lyn Mikel Brown began studying girls at a private school in the Midwest. Because it was an elementary as well as a secondary school, Brown had the opportunity to mount a five-year longitudinal comparative study of girls in four different age groups: second, fifth, seventh, and tenth grades. Brown saw changes among the age groups, and over time, saw individual girls change. As Gilligan notes, "It was as if we had been filling in a mosaic piece by piece. With Lyn's pieces, a real picture emerged: and the picture was of an 11-year-old."

10   That the 11-year-old's sea change might be a pivotal life event was also radical news. "As psychologists we're used to thinking of early childhood as the most crucial time," Gilligan explains. The project's research certainly suggests, however, that psychologists should look at adolescence when they look at girls. Gilligan also finds cultural clues pointing in the same direction: "Look at all the coming-of-age stories written by men, from *David Copperfield* to *Tom Jones* to *Portrait of the Artist*. They almost always begin in infancy or childhood. Then look at what women write. Jane Eyre was ten at the beginning of the novel. Claudia in Toni Morrison's *The Bluest Eye* is nine. Or look at Margaret Atwood's *Cat's Eye* or Jamaica Kincaid's *Annie John* or Carson McCullers's *Member of the Wedding*. It's much more likely that *our* stories start at nine or ten." The new work is likely to invite controversy precisely because the team members at this stage

analyze only girls' responses. Ironically, Gilligan's *In a Different Voice*, which did compare men and women, was attacked for providing ammunition to those who would use differences between men and women as a basis for discrimination.

I deliberately began this article with my own personal experience because, ultimately, research on girls doubles back to our own ten-year-old selves. I learned to write, and you learned to read, and the Harvard researchers learned to collect and interpret data precisely in the language of the culture that didn't hear what we had to say. The Journalism Voice I learned was one that insisted on pretending that the writer was "objective" and not part of the story. The Researcher Voice assumes no personal connection between interviewer and subject (in this case a girl who may in fact be looking for clues about life from a former girl—or vice versa). 11

Traditional research also assumes that interviews proceed in a linear way and can be codified according to long-standing traditions of social science. Project members felt in their guts that this approach wasn't fine-tuned to the way girls really talk about themselves—but what was the alternative? For several years, literally, the group wrestled with this basic dilemma of language. Ultimately, they came up with a method of interpreting interviews that proceeds from a metaphor not of language at all, but of music. Each interview is gone over four times, like a song played in four different keys, with researchers listening for different elements: the "plot" of whatever story is being told, the teller's sense of self, her concern for justice, and her sensitivity to caring. Researchers also listen for what *isn't* said. 12

"We now see what's said as polyphonic, and we listen for the counterpoint and the orchestration of voices," Gilligan explains. The metaphor seemed even more apt when project member Annie Rogers researched the etymology of the word "counterpoint" and found that it came from *contre-point*—or quilt-making. 13

Another image that project members are using a lot these days is that of "resistance." Not all girls stop knowing what they knew in fifth grade; some girls simply take that knowledge "underground" without losing it. "It's a brilliant but risky strategy," says Gilligan, "because when you're thirteen years old, it really *is* hard to confront the authority of the culture. So you keep your mouth shut, and you take a deep dive. Friendships become treacherous, because who do you trust? Will they turn out to be double agents?" 14

Current project work includes research into the role of friendships in adolescence and workshops on how to build resistance in girls. (Writing helps, since it keeps girls in touch with their own voice, as do activities that emphasize group efforts rather than competition.) The group is also studying girls whom society has labeled "at risk." Much preliminary research indicates that it may be precisely those "trouble-making" girls who are among the strongest resisters—and who may even drop out of school as a way to protect their sense of self. 15

Adds Gilligan: "It's often the ones who seem to be doing *well* who may, from our perspective, be the ones who are in trouble." 16

EXERCISES

Some of the Issues

1. What analogy does Van Gelder use to describe her internal response to the "decision" she made in the sixth grade (paragraph 1)? What does this image say about her feelings?
2. What can you infer about Van Gelder's parents' attitude toward her behavior at that time?
3. According to the research findings, why do girls change their personalities at adolescence (paragraph 2)?
4. How would you characterize the behavior of the girls cited in paragraph 4?
5. What are the noticeable features of the speech of seventh-grade girls quoted in paragraph 5? How do you interpret these patterns of speech?
6. Why do you suppose research on adolescence before 1980 focused only on male behavior?
7. Describe the procedure used to interpret the girls' responses to the interviewers. How does it differ from traditional research methods in the social sciences?
8. What strong claims about at-risk girls does the preliminary research purport?
9. Explain the significance of Gilligan's comment in the last lines of the article.

The Way We Are Told

10. What strategies does Van Gelder use in the first paragraph to capture the reader's attention?
11. What further motivation does she give (paragraph 11) for beginning in this way?
12. In paragraph 10, what other kinds of evidence does Gilligan examine to support the claim that age eleven is a critical psychological period for girls?
13. In paragraph 11, Van Gelder characterizes the "language" of our culture, i.e., the "Journalism Voice" and the "Researcher Voice." How is her "voice" different?

Some Subjects for Writing

14. Journal writing, poetry writing, and free writing are ways to stay in touch with our own voices. For one week, write for at least 10 minutes a day to see what you can discover about yourself. You might wish to begin by reflecting on some of the questions asked in the Harvard University Project:
    a. How would you describe yourself to yourself?
    b. A woman should always...
    c. What gets me into trouble is...

15. Examine several current magazines aimed at teenagers or young men or women. Looking at both the text and the photos, what images are presented of young men and young women? Write an essay in which you examine how these images might shape our views of gender roles.
16. In your opinion, is the development of boys radically different from that of girls? Use your own family history or that of friends and relatives to support your idea.

Girlhood among Ghosts

MAXINE HONG KINGSTON

Maxine Hong Kingston's parents came to America from China in the 1930s. She was born in Stockton, California, in 1940 and graduated from the University of California at Berkeley.

The following selection comes from The Woman Warrior: Memories of a Girlhood among Ghosts *(1976), for which Kingston received the National Book Critics Circle Award. The ghosts she refers to are of several kinds: the spirits and demons that Chinese peasants believed in, the ghosts of the dead, and, more significantly, the whole of non-Chinese America, peopled with strange creatures who seem very powerful but not quite human, and whose behavior is often inexplicable.*

Kingston continued her autobiography with China Men *(1981). Since then she has also written* Hawaii One Summer *(1981) and a novel,* Tripmaster Monkey *(1988). She teaches at the University of Hawaii.*

1   Long ago in China, knot-makers tied string into buttons and frogs, and rope into bell pulls. There was one knot so complicated that it blinded the knot-maker. Finally an emperor outlawed this cruel knot, and the nobles could not order it anymore. If I had lived in China, I would have been an outlaw knot-maker.

2   Maybe that's why my mother cut my tongue. She pushed my tongue up and sliced the frenum. Or maybe she snipped it with a pair of nail scissors, I don't remember her doing it, only her telling me about it, but all during childhood I felt sorry for the baby whose mother waited with scissors or knife in hand for it to cry—and then, when its mouth was wide open like a baby bird's, cut. The Chinese say "a ready tongue is an evil."

3   I used to curl up my tongue in front of the mirror and tauten my frenum into a white line, itself as thin as a razor blade. I saw no scars in my mouth. I thought perhaps I had had two frena, and she had cut one. I made other children open their mouths so I could compare theirs to mine. I saw perfect pink membranes stretching into precise edges that looked easy enough to cut. Sometimes I felt very proud that my mother committed such a powerful act upon me. At other times I was terrified—the first thing my mother did when she saw me was to cut my tongue.

4   "Why did you do that to me, Mother?"

5   "I told you."

"Tell me again."   6

"I cut it so that you would not be tongue-tied. Your tongue would be able   7
to move in any language. You'll be able to speak languages that are completely
different from one another. You'll be able to pronounce anything. Your frenum
looked too tight to do those things, so I cut it."

"But isn't 'a ready tongue an evil'?"   8

"Things are different in this ghost country."   9

"Did it hurt me? Did I cry and bleed?"   10

"I don't remember. Probably."   11

She didn't cut the other children's. When I asked cousins and other Chinese   12
children whether their mothers had cut their tongues loose, they said, "What?"

"Why didn't you cut my brothers' and sisters' tongues?"   13

"They didn't need it."   14

"Why not? Were theirs longer than mine?"   15

"Why don't you quit blabbering and get to work?"   16

If my mother was not lying she should have cut more, scraped away the rest   17
of the frenum skin, because I have a terrible time talking. Or she should not have
cut at all, tampering with my speech. When I went to kindergarten and had to
speak English for the first time, I became silent. A dumbness—a shame—still
cracks my voice in two, even when I want to say "hello" casually, or ask an easy
question in front of the check-out counter, or ask directions of a bus driver. I
stand frozen, or I hold up the line with the complete, grammatical sentence that
comes squeaking out at impossible length. "What did you say?" says the cab
driver, or "Speak up," so I have to perform again, only weaker the second time.
A telephone call makes my throat bleed and takes up that day's courage. It spoils
my day with self-disgust when I hear my broken voice come skittering out into
the open. It makes people wince to hear it. I'm getting better, though, Recently
I asked the postman for special-issue stamps; I've waited since childhood for
postmen to give me some of their own accord. I am making progress, a little
every day.

My silence was thickest—total—during the three years that I covered my   18
school paintings with black paint. I painted layers of black over houses and flowers and suns, and when I drew on the blackboard, I put a layer of chalk on top.
I was making a stage curtain, and it was the moment before the curtain parted
or rose. The teachers called my parents to school, and I saw they had been saving my pictures, curling and cracking, all alike and black. The teachers pointed
to the pictures and looked serious, talked seriously too, but my parents did not
understand English. ("The parents and teachers of criminals were executed,"
said my father.) My parents took the pictures home. I spread them out (so black
and full of possibilities) and pretended the curtains were swinging open, flying
up, one after another, sunlight underneath, mighty operas.

During the first silent year I spoke to no one at school, did not ask before   19
going to the lavatory, and flunked kindergarten. My sister also said nothing for
three years, silent in the playground and silent at lunch. There were other quiet

Chinese girls not of our family, but most of them got over it sooner than we did. I enjoyed the silence. At first it did not occur to me I was supposed to talk or to pass kindergarten. I talked at home and to one or two of the Chinese kids in class. I made motions and even made some jokes. I drank out of a toy saucer when the water spilled out of the cup, and everybody laughed, pointing at me, so I did it some more. I didn't know that Americans don't drink out of saucers.

20   I liked the Negro students (Black Ghosts) best because they laughed the loudest and talked to me as if I were a daring talker too. One of the Negro girls had her mother coil braids over her ears Shanghai-style like mine; we were Shanghai twins except that she was covered with black like my paintings. Two Negro kids enrolled in Chinese school, and the teachers gave them Chinese names. Some Negro kids walked me to school and home, protecting me from the Japanese kids, who hit me and chased me and stuck gum in my ears. The Japanese kids were noisy and tough. They appeared one day in kindergarten, released from concentration camp, which was a tic-tac-toe mark, like barbed wire, on the map.

21   It was when I found out I had to talk that school became a misery, that the silence became a misery. I did not speak and felt bad each time that I did not speak. I read aloud in first grade, though, and heard the barest whisper with little squeaks come out of my throat. "Louder," said the teacher, who scared the voice away again. The other Chinese girls did not talk either, so I knew the silence had to do with being a Chinese girl.

22   Reading out loud was easier than speaking because we did not have to make up what to say, but I stopped often, and the teacher would think I'd gone quiet again. I could not understand "I." The Chinese "I" has seven strokes, intricacies. How could the American "I," assuredly wearing a hat like the Chinese, have only three strokes, the middle so straight? Was it out of politeness that this writer left off strokes the way a Chinese has to write her own name small and crooked? No, it was not politeness; "I" is a capital and "you" is lowercase. I stared at the middle line and waited so long for its black center to resolve into tight strokes and dots that I forgot to pronounce it. The other troublesome word was "here," no strong consonant to hang on to, and so flat, when "here" is two mountainous ideographs. The teacher, who had already told me every day how to read "I" and "here" put me in the low corner under the stairs again, where the noisy boys usually sat.

23   When my second grade class did a play, the whole class went to the auditorium except the Chinese girls. The teacher, lovely and Hawaiian, should have understood about us, but instead left us behind in the classroom. Our voices were too soft or nonexistent, and our parents never signed the permission slips anyway. They never signed anything unnecessary. We opened the door a crack and peeked out, but closed it again quickly. One of us (not me) won every spelling bee, though.

24   I remember telling the Hawaiian teacher, "We Chinese can't sing 'land where our fathers died.'" She argued with me about politics, while I meant

because of curses. But how can I have that memory when I couldn't talk? My mother says that we, like the ghosts, have no memories.

After American school, we picked up our cigar boxes, in which we had   25
arranged books, brushes, and an inkbox neatly, and went to Chinese school, from 5:00 to 7:30 P.M. There we chanted together, voices rising and falling, loud and soft, some boys shouting, everybody reading together, reciting together and not alone with one voice. When we had a memorization test, the teacher let each of us come to his desk and say the lesson to him privately, while the rest of the class practiced copying or tracing. Most of the teachers were men. The boys who were so well behaved in the American school played tricks on them and talked back to them. The girls were not mute. They screamed and yelled during recess, when there were no rules; they had fistfights. Nobody was afraid of children hurting themselves or of children hurting school property. The glass doors to the red and green balconies with the gold joy symbols were left wide open so that we could run out and climb the fire escapes. We played capture-the-flag in the auditorium, where Sun Yat-sen[1] and Chiang Kai-shek's[2] pictures hung at the back of the stage, the Chinese flag on their left and the American flag on their right. We climbed the teak ceremonial chairs and made flying leaps off the stage. One flag headquarters was behind the glass door and the other on stage right. Our feet drummed on the hollow stage. During recess the teachers locked themselves up in their office with the shelves of books, copybooks, inks from China. They drank tea and warmed their hands at a stove. There was no play supervision. At recess we had the school to ourselves, and also we could roam as far as we could go—downtown, Chinatown stores, home—as long as we returned before the bell rang.

At exactly 7:30 the teacher again picked up the brass bell that sat on his desk   26
and swung it over our heads, while we charged down the stairs, our cheering magnified in the stairwell. Nobody had to line up.

Not all of the children who were silent at American school found voice at   27
Chinese school. One new teacher said each of us had to get up and recite in front of the class, who was to listen. My sister and I had memorized the lesson perfectly. We said it to each other at home, one chanting, one listening. The teacher called on my sister to recite first. It was the first time a teacher had called on the second-born to go first. My sister was scared. She glanced at me and looked away; I looked down at my desk. I hoped that she could do it because if she could, then I would have to. She opened her mouth and a voice came out that wasn't a whisper, but it wasn't a proper voice either. I hoped that she would not cry, fear breaking up her voice like twigs underfoot. She sounded as if she were trying to sing though weeping and strangling. She did not pause or stop to end the embarrassment. She kept going until she said the last word, and then she sat

---

[1](1866–1925) Chinese statesman and revolutionary leader.
[2](1887–1975) Chinese politician and general.

down. When it was my turn, the same voice came out, a crippled animal running on broken legs. You could hear splinters in my voice, bones rubbing jagged against one another. I was loud, though. I was glad I didn't whisper. There was one little girl who whispered.

EXERCISES

Some of the Issues

1. After reading the selection explain why Kingston says in the first paragraph, "In China, I would have been an outlaw knot-maker." Why does she call herself an outlaw? And, considering the legend she tells, why would she have been a knot-maker?
2. "Maybe that's why my mother cut my tongue." That startling sentence introduces a remembered conversation with her mother. Is it possible that the tongue-cutting never took place? What evidence do you find either way?
3. Kingston is silent in some situations but not in others. When is she silent and when not?
4. How did the American and the Chinese schools differ in the way they were run? In the way they affected the children?

The Way We Are Told

5. Kingston uses several symbols: the knot, the tongue, the Chinese word for *I*. Explain their meaning and use.
6. What is the effect of the first sentence of paragraph 2?
7. Kingston departs from strict chronological order in telling her story. What is the effect?

Some Subjects for Writing

8. Kingston describes times when she was embarrassed or "tongue-tied." Describe a time when you were afraid to speak. Include descriptions of your feelings before, during, and after the incident.
9. Kingston suggests that, in Chinese-American culture, girls are brought up very differently from boys. In your own experience of the culture in which you were raised does gender make an important difference in upbringing? Give examples in your answer.
*10. In Maxine Hong Kingston's story and in Grace Paley's "The Loudest Voice," the question of voice plays a major role. In an essay, compare and contrast the two central characters' experience of losing and finding a voice.

The Loudest Voice

GRACE PALEY

Grace Paley grew up in the Bronx, New York, where she was born in 1922. Her first published collection of short stories, The Little Disturbances of Man, *which appeared in 1959, contained the story included here. Since then she has published* Enormous Changes at the Last Minute *(1974),* Later the Same Day *(1985),* Leaning Forward *(1985), and* Long Walks and Intimate Talks *(1991). A complete volume of her fiction,* The Collected Stories, *was published in 1994.*

Most of Paley's stories are set in New York and treat the lives of a great range of people of different backgrounds, Jews, African-Americans, Italians, Puerto Ricans, and Irish. She is noted particularly for her ability to capture the flavor of American speech, and for using dialog as a way to establish character.

In her short story "The Loudest Voice" Grace Paley tells how an unthinking school administration dealt with the children under its authority. There are almost no Christian children in Shirley Abramowitz's grade school, but the teachers find it natural to foist a Christmas pageant on them. The results are hilarious as well as thought provoking.

There is a certain place where dumb-waiters boom, doors slam, dishes crash; every window is a mother's mouth bidding the street shut up, go skate somewhere else, come home. My voice is the loudest. 1

There, my own mother is still as full of breathing as me and the grocer stands up to speak to her. "Mrs. Abramowitz," he says, "people should not be afraid of their children." 2

"Ah, Mr. Bialik," my mother replies, "if you say to her or her father 'Ssh,' they say, 'In the grave it will be quiet.'" 3

"From Coney Island[1] to the cemetery," says my papa. "It's the same subway; it's the same fare." 4

I am right next to the pickle barrel. My pinky is making tiny whirlpools in the brine. I stop a moment to announce: "Campbell's Tomato Soup. Campbell's Vegetable Beef Soup. Campbell's S-c-otch Broth…" 5

[1]Brooklyn amusement park on the Atlantic Ocean.

6   "Be quiet," the grocer says, "the labels are coming off."

7   "Please, Shirley, be a little quiet," my mother begs me.

8   In that place the whole street groans: Be quiet! Be quiet! but steals from the happy chorus of my inside self not a tittle or a jot.

9   There, too, but just around the corner, is a red brick building that has been old for many years. Every morning the children stand before it in double lines which must be straight. They are not insulted. They are waiting anyway.

10   I am usually among them. I am, in fact, the first, since I begin with "A."

11   One cold morning the monitor tapped me on the shoulder. "Go to Room 409, Shirley Abramowitz," he said. I did as I was told. I went in a hurry up a down staircase to Room 409, which contained sixth-graders. I had to wait at the desk without wiggling until Mr. Hilton, their teacher, had time to speak.

12   After five minutes he said, "Shirley?"

13   "What?" I whispered.

14   He said, "My! My! Shirley Abramowitz! They told me you had a particularly loud, clear voice and read with lots of expression. Could that be true?"

15   "Oh yes," I whispered.

16   "In that case, don't be silly; I might very well be your teacher someday. Speak up, speak up."

17   "Yes," I shouted.

18   "More like it," he said. "Now, Shirley, can you put a ribbon in your hair or a bobby pin? It's too messy."

19   "Yes!" I bawled.

20   "Now, now, calm down." He turned to the class. "Children, not a sound. Open at page 39. Read till 52. When you finish, start again." He looked me over once more. "Now, Shirley, you know, I suppose, that Christmas is coming. We are preparing a beautiful play. Most of the parts have been given out. But I still need a child with a strong voice, lots of stamina. Do you know what stamina is? You do? Smart kid. You know, I heard you read 'The Lord is my shepherd' in Assembly yesterday. I was very impressed. Wonderful delivery. Mrs. Jordan, your teacher, speaks highly of you. Now listen to me, Shirley Abramowitz, if you want to take the part and be in the play, repeat after me, 'I swear to work harder than I ever did before.'"

21   I looked to heaven and said at once, "Oh, I swear." I kissed my pinky and looked at God.

22   "That is an actor's life, my dear," he explained. "Like a soldier's, never tardy or disobedient to his general, the director. Everything," he said, "absolutely everything will depend on you."

23   That afternoon, all over the building, children scraped and scrubbed the turkeys and the sheaves of corn off the schoolroom windows. Goodbye Thanksgiving. The next morning a monitor brought red paper and green paper from the office. We made new shapes and hung them on the walls and glued them to the doors.

The teachers became happier and happier. Their heads were ringing like   24
the bells of childhood. My best friend Evie was prone to evil, but she did not
get a single demerit for whispering. We learned "Holy Night" without an error.
"How wonderful!" said Miss Glacé, the student teacher "To think that some of
you don't even speak the language!" We learned "Deck the Halls" and "Hark!
The Herald Angels."... They weren't ashamed and we weren't embarrassed.

Oh, but when my mother heard about it all, she said to my father: "Misha,   25
you don't know what's going on there. Cramer is the head of the Tickets Committee."

"Who?" asked my father. "Cramer! Oh yes, an active woman."   26

"Active? Active has to have a reason. Listen," she said sadly, "I'm surprised   27
to see my neighbors making tra-la-la for Christmas."

My father couldn't think of what to say to that. Then he decided: "You're   28
in America! Clara, you wanted to come here. In Palestine the Arabs would be
eating you alive. Europe you had pogroms.[2] Argentina is full of Indians. Here
you got Christmas.... Some joke, ha?"

"Very funny, Misha. What is becoming of you? If we came to a new country   29
a long time ago to run away from tyrants, and instead we fall into a creeping
pogrom, that our children learn a lot of lies, so what's the joke? Ach, Misha, your
idealism is going away."

"So is your sense of humor."   30

"That I never had, but idealism you had a lot of."   31

"I'm the same Misha Abramovitch, I didn't change an iota. Ask anyone."   32

"Only ask me," says my mama, may she rest in peace. "I got the answer."   33

Meanwhile the neighbors had to think of what to say too.   34

Marty's father said: "You know, he has a very important part, my boy."   35

"Mine also," said Mr. Sauerfeld.   36

"Not my boy!" said Mrs. Klieg. "I said to him no. The answer is no. When   37
I say no! I mean no!"

The rabbi's wife said, "It's disgusting!" But no one listened to her. Under   38
the narrow sky of God's great wisdom she wore a strawberry-blond wig.

Every day was noisy and full of experience. I was Right-hand Man. Mr. Hil-   39
ton said: "How could I get along without you, Shirley?"

He said: "Your mother and father ought to get down on their knees every   40
night and thank God for giving them a child like you."

He also said: "You're absolutely a pleasure to work with, my dear, dear   41
child."

Sometimes he said: "For God's sakes, what did I do with the script? Shirley!   42
Shirley! Find it."

Then I answered quietly: "Here it is, Mr. Hilton."   43

---

[2]Organized massacres of Jews in turn-of-the-century Russia and in Nazi Germany.

44   Once in a while, when he was very tired, he would cry out: "Shirley, I'm just tired of screaming at those kids. Will you tell Ira Pushkov not to come in till Lester points to that star the second time?"

45   Then I roared: "Ira Pushkov, what's the matter with you? Dope! Mr. Hilton told you five times already, don't come in till Lester points to that star the second time."

46   "Ach, Clara," my father asked, "what does she do there till six o'clock she can't even put the plates on the table?"

47   "Christmas," said my mother coldly.

48   "Ho! Ho!" my father said. "Christmas. What's the harm? After all, history teaches everyone. We learn from reading this is a holiday from pagan times also, candles, lights, even Chanukah. So we learn it's not altogether Christian. So if they think it's a private holiday, they're only ignorant, not patriotic. What belongs to history, belongs to all men. You want to go back to the Middle Ages? Is it better to shave your head with a secondhand razor? Does it hurt Shirley to learn to speak up? It does not. So maybe someday she won't live between the kitchen and the shop. She's not a fool."

49   I thank you, Papa, for your kindness. It is true about me to this day. I am foolish but I am not a fool.

50   That night my father kissed me and said with great interest in my career, "Shirley, tomorrow's your big day. Congrats."

51   "Save it," my mother said. Then she shut all the windows in order to prevent tonsillitis.

52   In the morning it snowed. On the street corner a tree had been decorated for us by a kind city administration. In order to miss its chilly shadow our neighbors walked three blocks east to buy a loaf of bread. The butcher pulled down black window shades to keep the colored lights from shining on his chickens. Oh, not me. On the way to school, with both my hands I tossed it a kiss of tolerance. Poor thing, it was a stranger in Egypt.

53   I walked straight into the auditorium past the staring children. "Go ahead, Shirley!" said the monitors. Four boys, big for their age, had already started work as propmen and stagehands.

54   Mr. Hilton was very nervous. He was not even happy. Whatever he started to say ended in a sideward look of sadness. He sat slumped in the middle of the first row and asked me to help Miss Glacé. I did this, although she thought my voice too resonant and said, "Show-off!"

55   Parents began to arrive long before we were ready. They wanted to make a good impression. From among the yards of drapes I peeked out at the audience. I saw my embarrassed mother.

56   Ira, Lester, and Meyer were pasted to their beards by Miss Glacé. She almost forgot to thread the star on its wire, but I reminded her. I coughed a few times to clear my throat. Miss Glacé looked around and saw that everyone was in costume and on line waiting to play his part. She whispered, "All right..." Then:

Jackie Sauerfeld, the prettiest boy in first grade, parted the curtains with his   57
skinny elbow and in a high voice sang out:

"Parents dear
We are here
To make a Christmas play in time.
It we give
In narrative
And illustrate with pantomime."

He disappeared.   58
My voice burst immediately from the wings to the great shock of Ira, Lester,   59
and Meyer, who were waiting for it but were surprised all the same.
"I remember, I remember, the house where I was born…"   60
Miss Glacé yanked the curtain open and there it was, the house—an old   61
hayloft, where Celia Kornbluh lay in the straw with Cindy Lou, her favorite
doll. Ira, Lester, and Meyer moved slowly from the wings toward her, sometimes
pointing to a moving star and sometimes ahead to Cindy Lou.
It was a long story and it was a sad story. I carefully pronounced all the   62
words about my lonesome childhood, while little Eddie Braunstein wandered
upstage and down with his shepherd's stick, looking for sheep. I brought up
lonesomeness again, and not being understood at all except by some women
everybody hated. Eddie was too small for that and Marty Groff took his place,
wearing his father's prayer shawl. I announced twelve friends, and half the boys
in the fourth grade gathered round Marty, who stood on an orange crate while
my voice harangued. Sorrowful and loud, I declaimed about love and God and
Man, but because of the terrible deceit of Abie Stock we came suddenly to a
famous moment. Marty, whose remembering tongue I was, waited at the foot of
the cross. He stared desperately at the audience. I groaned, "My God, my God,
why hast thou forsaken me?" The soldiers who were sheiks grabbed poor Marty
to pin him up to die, but he wrenched free, turned again to the audience, and
spread his arms aloft to show despair and the end. I murmured at the top of my
voice, "The rest is silence, but as everyone in this room, in this city—in this
world—now knows, I shall have life eternal."
That night Mrs. Kornbluh visited our kitchen for a glass of tea.   63
"How's the virgin!" asked my father with a look of concern.   64
"For a man with a daughter, you got a fresh mouth, Abramovitch."   65
"Here," said my father kindly, "have some lemon, it'll sweeten your dispo-   66
sition."
They debated a little in Yiddish, then fell in a puddle of Russian and Polish.   67
What I understood next was my father, who said, "Still and all, it was certainly
a beautiful affair, you have to admit, introducing us to the beliefs of a different
culture."

68   "Well, yes," said Mrs. Kornbluh. "The only thing…you know Charlie Turner—that cute boy in Celia's class—a couple others? They got very small parts or no part at all. In very bad taste, it seemed to me. After all, it's their religion."

69   "Ach," explained my mother, "what could Mr. Hilton do? They got very small voices; after all, why should they holler? The English language they know from the beginning by heart. They're blond like angels. You think it's so important they should get in the play? Christmas…the whole piece of goods…they own it."

70   I listened and listened until I couldn't listen any more. Too sleepy, I climbed out of bed and kneeled. I made a little church of my hands and said, "Hear, O Israel…" Then I called out in Yiddish, "Please, good night, good night. Ssh." My father said, "Ssh yourself," and slammed the kitchen door.

71   I was happy. I fell asleep at once. I had prayed for everybody: my talking family, cousins far away, passersby, and all the lonesome Christians. I expected to be heard. My voice was certainly the loudest.

EXERCISES

Some of the Issues

1. In paragraphs 1 through 8 Paley tells about "a certain place." How does she describe it? Do we know what it looked like? What it sounded like? How do we know that it is a place in Shirley's memory?

2. In paragraph 9 we move to another place, just around the corner. How are we told about that place?

3. Shirley has the loudest voice in the school, but at some points she whispers or talks softly. When and why?

4. Mr. Hilton has a number of ways of getting Shirley and the other children to do what he wants them to do. What techniques does he use? How sincere do you think he is? How much do he and the other teachers seem to understand or care about the children in the school?

5. Shirley's mother and father disagree with one another at several points in the story. Find the points where they disagree. What position does the father take consistently? The mother?

6. In paragraph 24 Miss Glacé, the student teacher, makes a comment. Does she believe it is a compliment? Is it really? Does her remark, and others made by teachers in the school, give any indication of their attitudes toward the children and their families?

7. Read the last sentences of paragraph 24; who is referred to as "we"? As "they"?

8. Paragraphs 34 through 38 tell how the neighbors react to the upcoming school play. What is their reaction? Why does no one pay attention to the rabbi's wife?

9. Read paragraph 52. Explain the people's reaction to "the tree." Why is it a stranger in Egypt?
10. Paragraphs 57 through 62 tell about the actual performance of the Christmas play. What is the story being told in the play? What parts are each of the children playing? How well do the children seem to understand the story and their parts?
11. Examine the last paragraph. Whom does Shirley pray for and why? In what way can Shirley be said to have triumphed?

The Way We Are Told

12. Grace Paley is known for her good ear for dialog. She is said to create dialog that sounds natural and conveys a sense of her characters' personalities. A large part of this story is told through dialog. Examine it, and show how it conveys the sense of each character who speaks and how it carries the story along.
13. Did you find the story funny? If so, why? Does the humorous tone help or hinder its serious purpose?

Some Subjects for Writing

14. We know Shirley, and indeed all of the characters in the story, through their voices. Unlike many authors, Paley gives few visual descriptions. We are not told the color of Shirley's hair, or how tall she is, or even exactly how old she is. We may, however, be able to form images in our minds about what she and others are like, from our knowledge of what they say and how they say it. Imagine that "The Loudest Voice" is to be filmed. You are the casting director. Tell how you would visualize Paley's characters: Shirley, her parents, and the various teachers.
15. In this story Paley describes people and places by means of sound, not appearance. Write a paragraph giving a vivid description of a place you know well, using primarily sounds to describe it, and avoiding visual details as much as possible.
16. Have you ever, as a child or as an adult, participated in a cultural or religious ceremony that was unfamiliar to you, in which you perhaps felt out of place? Describe it in an essay.
*17. Like Paley, Maya Angelou in "Graduation" describes a school ceremony in which officials are insensitive to the lives of the children and their parents. How do the two situations differ? In what way are they the same? Explain in an essay.

I Just Wanna Be Average

MIKE ROSE

Mike Rose was born in Chicago in 1938 and, when he was seven, moved with his parents to the south side of Los Angeles. His parents, who had immigrated from Italy and arrived at Ellis Island in the 1910s and 1920s, never escaped poverty; however, they managed to save enough money to send Rose to a parochial school. He was an average student but, after junior high, was misplaced in the vocational education track in high school, where he "drifted to the level of a really mediocre and unprepared student." His experience in "Voc. Ed." illustrates how students placed in the lower tracks live down to the expectations of their classrooms. Fortunately, Rose's biology teacher noticed his ability, looked at his academic record, and discovered that his grades had been switched with those of another student named Rose. Subsequently, he was reassigned to the college track. In his senior year, he encountered a nontraditional teacher who opened up the world of poetry, ideas, language, and life and who helped Rose to get a scholarship to Loyola University in Los Angeles.

Rose became a teacher and worked with others on the margins of society: inner-city kids, Vietnam veterans, and underprepared adults. He is now the associate director of the writing program at UCLA, where he continues to teach underprepared students to enter and succeed in the academic world.

In the following excerpts from his book Lives on the Boundary *(1989), he relates how poverty contributes to deep, lasting feelings of self-doubt, and how one caring person can make a fundamental difference in the lives of others. Rose is also the author of* Possible Lives: The Promise of Public Education in America *(1995).*

1   The house was on a piece of land that rose about four feet up from heavily trafficked Vermont Avenue. The yard sloped down to the street, and three steps and a short walkway led up the middle of the grass to our front door. There was a similar house immediately to the south of us. Next to it was Carmen's Barber Shop. Carmen was a short, quiet Italian who, rumor had it, had committed his first wife to the crazy house to get her money. In the afternoons, Carmen could be found in the lot behind his shop playing solitary catch, flinging a tennis ball high into the air and running under it. One day the police arrested Carmen on

charges of child molesting. He was released but became furtive and suspicious. I never saw him in the lot again. Next to Carmen's was a junk store where, one summer, I made a little money polishing brass and rewiring old lamps. Then came a dilapidated real estate office, a Mexican restaurant, an empty lot, and an appliance store owned by the father of Keith Grateful, the streetwise, chubby boy who would become my best friend.

Right to the north of us was a record shop, a barber shop presided over by   2
old Mr. Graff, Walt's Malts, a shoe repair shop with a big Cat's Paw decal in the window, a third barber shop, and a brake shop. It's as I write this that I realize for the first time that three gray men could have had a go at your hair before you left our street.

Behind our house was an unpaved alley that passed, just to the north, a   3
power plant the length of a city block. Massive coils atop the building hissed and cracked through the day, but the doors never opened. I used to think it was abandoned—feeding itself on its own wild arcs—until one sweltering afternoon a man was electrocuted on the roof. The air was thick and still as two firemen—the only men present—brought down a charred and limp body without saying a word.

The north and south traffic on Vermont was separated by tracks for the old   4
yellow trolley cars, long since defunct. Across the street was a huge garage, a tiny hot dog stand run by a myopic and reclusive man named Freddie, and my dreamland, the Vermont Bowl. Distant and distorted behind thick lenses, Freddie's eyes never met yours; he would look down when he took your order and give you your change with a mumble. Freddie slept on a cot in the back of his grill and died there one night, leaving tens of thousands of dollars stuffed in the mattress.

My father would buy me a chili dog at Freddie's, and then we would walk   5
over to the bowling alley where Dad would sit at the lunch counter and drink coffee while I had a great time with pinball machines, electric shooting galleries, and an ill-kept dispenser of cheese corn. There was a small, dark bar abutting the lanes, and it called to me. I would devise reasons to walk through it: "'Scuse me, is the bathroom in here?" or "Anyone see my dad?" though I can never remember my father having a drink. It was dark and people were drinking and I figured all sorts of mysterious things were being whispered. Next to the Vermont Bowl was a large vacant lot overgrown with foxtails and dotted with car parts, bottles, and rotting cardboard. One day Keith heard that the police had found a human head in the brush. After that we explored the lot periodically, coming home with stickers all the way up to our waists. But we didn't find a thing. Not even a kneecap.

When I wasn't with Keith or in school, I would spend most of my day with   6
my father or with the men who were renting the one-room apartments behind our house. Dad and I whiled away the hours in the bowling alley, watching TV, or planting a vegetable garden that never seemed to take. When he was still

mobile, he would walk the four blocks down to St. Regina's Grammar School to take me home to my favorite lunch of boiled wieners and chocolate milk. There I'd sit, dunking my hot dog in a jar of mayonnaise and drinking my milk while Sheriff John tuned up the calliope music on his "Lunch Brigade." Though he never complained to me, I could sense that my father's health was failing, and I began devising child's ways to make him better. We had a box of rolled cotton in the bathroom, and I would go in and peel off a long strip and tape it around my jaw. Then I'd rummage through the closet, find a sweater of my father's, put on one of his hats—and sneak around to the back door. I'd knock loudly and wait. It would take him a while to get there. Finally, he'd open the door, look down, and quietly say, "Yes, Michael?" I was disappointed. Every time. Somehow I thought I could fool him. And, I guess, if he had been fooled, I would have succeeded in redefining things: I would have been the old one, he much younger, more agile, with strength in his legs.

7   The men who lived in the back were either retired or didn't work that much, so one of them was usually around. They proved to be, over the years, an unusual set of companions for a young boy. Ed Gionotti was the youngest of the lot, a handsome man whose wife had run off and who spoke softly and never smiled. Bud Hall and Lee McGuire were two out-of-work plumbers who lived in adjacent units and who weekly drank themselves silly, proclaiming in front of God and everyone their undying friendship or their unequivocal hatred. Old Cheech was a lame Italian who used to hobble along grabbing his testicles and rolling his eyes while he talked about the women he claimed to have on a string. There was Lester, the toothless cabbie, who several times made overtures to me and who, when he moved, left behind a drawer full of syringes and burnt spoons. Mr. Smith was a rambunctious retiree who lost his nose to an untended skin cancer. And there was Mr. Berryman, a sweet and gentle man who eventually left for a retirement hotel only to be burned alive in an electrical fire.

8   Except for Keith, there were no children on my block and only one or two on the immediate side streets. Most of the people I saw day to day were over fifty. People in their twenties and thirties working in the shoe shop or tile garages didn't say a lot; their work and much of what they were working for drained their spirits. There were gang members who sauntered up from Hoover Avenue, three blocks to the east, and occasionally I would get shoved around, but they had little interest in me either as member or victim. I was a skinny, bespectacled kid and had neither the coloring nor the style of dress or carriage that marked me as a rival. On the whole, the days were quiet, lazy, lonely. The heat shimmering over the asphalt had no snap to it; time drifted by. I would lie on the couch at night and listen to the music from the record store or from Walt's Malts. It was new and quick paced, exciting, a little dangerous (the church had condemned Buddy Knox's "Party Doll"), and I heard in it a deep rhythmic need to be made whole with love, or marked as special, or released in some

rebellious way. Even the songs about lost love—and there were plenty of them—
lifted me right out of my socks with their melodious longing:

> Came the dawn,
> and my heart and her love and the night
> were gone.
> But I know I'll never forget
> her kiss in the moonlight Oooo…
> such a kiss Oooo Oooo such a night…

In the midst of the heat and slow time the music brought the promise of its origins, a promise of deliverance, a promise that, if only for a moment, life could
be stirring and dreamy.

But the anger and frustration of South Vermont could prove too strong for   9
music's illusion; then it was violence that provided deliverance of a different
order. One night I watched as a guy sprinted from Walt's to toss something on
our lawn. The police were right behind, and a cop tackled him, smashing his
face into the sidewalk. I ducked out to find the packet: a dozen glassine bags of
heroin. Another night, one August midnight, an argument outside the record
store ended with a man being shot to death. And the occasional gang forays
brought with them some fated kid who would fumble his moves and catch a
knife.

It's popular these days to claim you grew up on the streets. Men tell violent   10
tales and romanticize the lessons violence brings. But, though it was occasionally
violent, it wasn't the violence in South L.A. that marked me, for sometimes you
can shake that ugliness off. What finally affected me was subtler, but more pervasive: I cannot recall a young person who was crazy in love or lost in work or
one old person who was passionate about a cause or an idea. I'm not talking
about an absence of energy—the street toughs and, for that fact, old Cheech had
energy. And I'm not talking about an absence of decency, for my father was a
thoughtful man. The people I grew up with were retired from jobs that rub away
the heart or were working hard at jobs to keep their lives from caving in or were
anchorless and in between jobs and spouses or were diving headlong into a barren tomorrow: junkies, alcoholics, and mean kids walking along Vermont looking to throw a punch. I developed a picture of human existence that tendered it
short and brutish or sad and aimless or long and quiet with rewards like afternoon naps, the evening newspaper, walks around the block, occasional letters
from children in other states. When, years later, I was introduced to humanistic
psychologists like Abraham Maslow and Carl Rogers, with their visions of self-
actualization, or even Freud with his sober dictum about love and work, it all
sounded like a glorious fairy tale, a magical account of a world full of possibility,
full of hope and empowerment. Sindbad and Cinderella couldn't have been
more fanciful.

11   Some people who manage to write their way out of the working class describe the classroom as an oasis of possibility. It became their intellectual playground, their competitive arena. Given the richness of my memories of this time, it's funny how scant are my recollections of school. I remember the red brick building of St. Regina's itself, and the topography of the playground: the swings and basketball courts and peeling benches. There are images of a few students: Erwin Petschaur, a muscular German boy with a strong accent; Dave Sanchez, who was good in math; and Sheila Wilkes, everyone's curly-haired heartthrob. And there are two nuns: Sister Monica, the third-grade teacher with beautiful hands for whom I carried a candle and who, to my dismay, had wedded herself to Christ; and Sister Beatrice, a woman truly crazed, who would sweep into class, eyes wide, to tell us about the Apocalypse.

12   All the hours in class tend to blend into one long, vague stretch of time. What I remember best, strangely enough, are the two things I couldn't understand and over the years grew to hate: grammar lessons and mathematics. I would sit there watching a teacher draw her long horizontal line and her short, oblique lines and break up sentences and put adjectives here and adverbs there and just not get it, couldn't see the reason for it, turned off to it. I would hide by slumping down in my seat and page through my reader, carried along by the flow of sentences in a story. She would test us, and I would dread that, for I always got Cs and Ds. Mathematics was a bit different. For whatever reasons, I didn't learn early math very well, so when it came time for more complicated operations, I couldn't keep up and started day-dreaming to avoid my inadequacy. This was a strategy I would rely on as I grew older. I fell further and further behind. A memory: The teacher is faceless and seems very far away. The voice is faint and is discussing an equation written on the board. It is raining, and I am watching the streams of water form patterns on the windows.

13   I realize now how consistently I defended myself against the lessons I couldn't understand and the people and events of South L.A. that were too strange to view head-on. I got very good at watching a blackboard with minimum awareness. And I drifted more and more into a variety of protective fantasies. I was lucky in that although my parents didn't read or write very much and had no more than a few books around the house, they never debunked my pursuits. And when they could, they bought me what I needed to spin my web.

14   One early Christmas they got me a small chemistry set. My father brought home an old card table from the secondhand store, and on that table I spread out my test tubes, my beaker, my Erlenmeyer flask, and my gas-generating apparatus. The set came equipped with chemicals, minerals, and various treated papers—all in little square bottles. You could send away to someplace in Maryland for more, and I did, saving pennies and nickels to get the substances that were too exotic for my set, the Junior Chemcraft: Congo red paper, azurite, glycerine, chrome alum, cochineal—this from female insects!—tartaric acid, chameleon paper, logwood. I would sit before my laboratory and play for hours. My

father rested on the purple couch in front of me watching wrestling or *Gunsmoke* while I measured powders or heated crystals or blew into solutions that my breath would turn red or pink. I was taken by the blends of names and by the colors that swirled through the beaker. My equations were visual and phonetic. I would hold a flask up to the hall light, imagining the veils of a million atoms dancing. Sulfur and alcohol hung in the air. I wanted to shake down the house.

One day my mother came home from Coffee Dan's with an awful story. The   15
teenage brother of one of her waitress friends was in the hospital. He had been fooling around with explosives in his garage "where his mother couldn't see him," and something happened, and "he blew away part of his throat. For God's sake, be careful," my mother said. "Remember poor Ada's brother." Wow! I thought. How neat! Why couldn't my experiments be that dangerous? I really lost heart when I realized that you could probably eat the chemicals spread across my table.

I knew what I had to do. I saved my money for a week and then walked with   16
firm resolve past Walt's Malts, past the brake shop, across Ninetieth Street, and into Palazolla's market. I bought a little bottle of Alka-Seltzer and ran home. I chipped up the wafers and mixed them into a jar of white crystals. When my mother came home, dog tired, and sat down on the edge of the couch to tell me and Dad about her day, I gravely poured my concoction into a beaker of water, cried something about the unexpected, and ran out from behind my table. The beaker foamed ominously. My father swore in Italian. The second time I tried it, I got something milder—in English. And by my third near-miss with death, my parents were calling my behavior cute. Cute! Who wanted cute? I wanted to toy with the disaster that befell Ada Pendleton's brother. I wanted all those wonderful colors to collide in ways that could blow your voice box right off.

But I was limited by the real. The best I could do was create a toxic antacid.   17
I loved my chemistry set—its glassware and its intriguing labels—but it wouldn't allow me to do the things I wanted to do. St. Regina's had an all-purpose room, one wall of which was lined with old books—and one of those shelves held a row of plastic-covered space novels. The sheen of their covers was gone, and their futuristic portraits were dotted with erasures and grease spots like a meteor shower of the everyday. I remember the rockets best. Long cylinders outfitted at the base with three slick fins, tapering at the other end to a perfect conical point, ready to pierce out of the stratosphere and into my imagination: X-fifteens and Mach 1, the dark side of the moon, the Red Planet, Jupiter's Great Red Spot, Saturn's rings—and beyond the solar system to swirling wisps of galaxies, to stardust.

Students will float to the mark you set. I and the others in the vocational classes   18
were bobbing in pretty shallow water. Vocational education has aimed at increasing the economic opportunities of students who do not do well in our schools. Some serious programs succeed in doing that, and through exceptional

teachers—like Mr. Gross in *Horace's Compromise*—students learn to develop hypotheses and troubleshoot, reason through a problem, and communicate effectively—the true job skills. The vocational track, however, is most often a place for those who are just not making it, a dumping ground for the disaffected. There were a few teachers who worked hard at education; young Brother Slattery, for example, combined a stern voice with weekly quizzes to try to pass along to us a skeletal outline of world history. But mostly the teachers had no idea of how to engage the imaginations of us kids who were scuttling along at the bottom of the pond.

19   And the teachers would have needed some inventiveness, for none of us was groomed for the classroom. It wasn't just that I didn't know things—didn't know how to simplify algebraic fractions, couldn't identify different kinds of clauses, bungled Spanish translations—but that I had developed various faulty and inadequate ways of doing algebra and making sense of Spanish. Worse yet, the years of defensive tuning out in elementary school had given me a way to escape quickly while seeming at least half alert. During my time in Voc. Ed., I developed further into a mediocre student and a somnambulant problem solver, and that affected the subjects I did have the wherewithal to handle: I detested Shakespeare; I got bored with history. My attention flitted here and there. I fooled around in class and read my books indifferently—the intellectual equivalent of playing with your food. I did what I had to do to get by, and I did it with half a mind.

20   But I did learn things about people and eventually came into my own socially. I liked the guys in Voc. Ed. Growing up where I did, I understood and admired physical prowess, and there was an abundance of muscle here. There was Dave Snyder, a sprinter and halfback of true quality. Dave's ability and quick wit gave him a natural appeal, and he was welcome in any clique, though he always kept a little independent. He enjoyed acting the fool and could care less about studies, but he possessed a certain maturity and never caused the faculty much trouble. It was a testament to his independence that he included me among his friends—I eventually went out for track, but I was no jock. Owing to the Latin alphabet and a dearth of *R*s and *S*s, Snyder sat behind Rose, and we started exchanging one-liners and became friends.

21   There was Ted Richard, a much-touted Little League pitcher. He was chunky and had a baby face and came to Our Lady of Mercy as a seasoned street fighter. Ted was quick to laugh and he had a loud, jolly laugh, but when he got angry he'd smile a little smile, the kind that simply raises the corner of the mouth a quarter of an inch. For those who knew, it was an eerie signal. Those who didn't found themselves in big trouble, for Ted was very quick. He loved to carry on what we would come to call philosophical discussions: What is courage? Does God exist? He also loved words, enjoyed picking up big ones like *salubrious* and *equivocal* and using them in our conversation—laughing at himself as the word hit a chuckhole rolling off his tongue. Ted didn't do all that well in

school—baseball and parties and testing the courage he'd speculated about took up his time. His textbooks were *Argosy* and *Field and Stream*, whatever newspapers he'd find on the bus stop—from the *Daily Worker* to pornography—conversations with uncles or hobos or businessmen he'd meet in a coffee shop, *The Old Man and the Sea*. With hindsight, I can see that Ted was developing into one of those rough-hewn intellectuals whose sources are a mix of the learned and the apocryphal, whose discussions are both assured and sad.

And then there was Ken Harvey. Ken was good-looking in a puffy way and   22
had a full and oily ducktail and was a car enthusiast…a hodad. One day in religion class, he said the sentence that turned out to be one of the most memorable of the hundreds of thousands I heard in those Voc. Ed. years. We were talking about the parable of the talents, about achievement, working hard, doing the best you can do, blah-blah-blah, when the teacher called on the restive Ken Harvey for an opinion. Ken thought about it, but just for a second, and said (with studied, minimal affect), "I just wanna be average." That woke me up. Average?! Who wants to be average? Then the athletes chimed in with the clichés that make you want to laryngectomize them, and the exchange became a platitudinous melee. At the time, I thought Ken's assertion was stupid, and I wrote him off. But his sentence has stayed with me all these years, and I think I am finally coming to understand it.

Ken Harvey was gasping for air. School can be a tremendously disorienting   23
place. No matter how bad the school, you're going to encounter notions that don't fit with the assumptions and beliefs that you grew up with—maybe you'll hear these dissonant notions from teachers, maybe from the other students, and maybe you'll read them. You'll also be thrown in with all kinds of kids from all kinds of backgrounds, and that can be unsettling—this is especially true in places of rich ethnic and linguistic mix, like the L.A. basin. You'll see a handful of students far excel you in courses that sound exotic and that are only in the curriculum of the elite: French, physics, trigonometry. And all this is happening while you're trying to shape an identity, your body is changing, and your emotions are running wild. If you're a working-class kid in the vocational track, the options you'll have to deal with this will be constrained in certain ways: You're defined by your school as "slow"; you're placed in a curriculum that isn't designed to liberate you but to occupy you, or, if you're lucky, train you, though the training is for work the society does not esteem; other students are picking up the cues from your school and your curriculum and interacting with you in particular ways. If you're a kid like Ted Richard, you turn your back on all this and let your mind roam where it may. But youngsters like Ted are rare. What Ken and so many others do is protect themselves from such suffocating madness by taking on with a vengeance the identity implied in the vocational track. Reject the confusion and frustration by openly defining yourself as the Common Joe. Champion the average. Rely on your own good sense. Fuck this bullshit. Bullshit, of course, is everything you—and the others—fear is beyond you: books, essays,

tests, academic scrambling, complexity, scientific reasoning, philosophical inquiry.

24 The tragedy is that you have to twist the knife in your own gray matter to make this defense work. You'll have to shut down, have to reject intellectual stimuli or diffuse them with sarcasm, have to cultivate stupidity, have to convert boredom from a malady into a way of confronting the world. Keep your vocabulary simple, act stoned when you're not or act more stoned than you are, flaunt ignorance, materialize your dreams. It is a powerful and effective defense—it neutralizes the insult and the frustration of being a vocational kid and, when perfected, it drives teachers up the wall, a delightful secondary effect. But like all strong magic, it exacts a price.

25 Jack MacFarland couldn't have come into my life at a better time. My father was dead, and I had logged up too many years of scholastic indifference. Mr. MacFarland had a master's degree from Columbia and decided, at twenty-six, to find a little school and teach his heart out. He never took any credentialing courses, couldn't bear to, he said, so he had to find employment in a private system. He ended up at Our Lady of Mercy teaching five sections of senior English. He was a beatnik who was born too late. His teeth were stained, he tucked his sorry tie in between the third and fourth buttons of his shirt, and his pants were chronically wrinkled. At first, we couldn't believe this guy, thought he slept in his car. But within no time, he had us so startled with work that we didn't much worry about where he slept or if he slept at all. We wrote three or four essays a month. We read a book every two to three weeks, starting with the *Iliad* and ending up with Hemingway. He gave us a quiz on the reading every other day. He brought a prep school curriculum to Mercy High.

26 MacFarland's lectures were crafted, and as he delivered them he would pace the room jiggling a piece of chalk in his cupped hand, using it to scribble on the board the names of all the writers and philosophers and plays and novels he was weaving into his discussion. He asked questions often, raised everything from Zeno's[1] paradox to the repeated last line of Frost's "Stopping by Woods on a Snowy Evening." He slowly and carefully built up our knowledge of Western intellectual history—with facts, with connections, with speculations. We learned about Greek philosophy, about Dante, the Elizabethan world view, the Age of Reason, existentialism. He analyzed poems with us, had us reading sections from John Ciardi's *How Does a Poem Mean?*, making a potentially difficult book accessible with his own explanations. We gave oral reports on poems Ciardi didn't cover. We imitated the styles of Conrad, Hemingway, and *Time* magazine. We wrote and talked, wrote and talked. The man immersed us in language.

---

[1]Zeno, a Greek philosopher, developed paradoxes to demonstrate that our common-sense notions of time and space are deceptive.

Even MacFarland's barbs were literary. If Jim Fitzsimmons, hung over and   27
irritable, tried to smart-ass him, he'd rejoin with a flourish that would spark the
indomitable Skip Madison—who'd lost his front teeth in a hapless tackle—to
flick his tongue through the gap and opine, "good chop," drawing out the single
"o" in stinging indictment. Jack MacFarland, this tobacco-stained intellectual,
brandished linguistic weapons of a kind I hadn't encountered before. Here was
this *egghead*, for God's sake, keeping some pretty difficult people in line. And
from what I heard, Mike Dweetz and Steve Fusco and all the notorious Voc. Ed.
crowd settled down as well when MacFarland took the podium. Though a lot
of guys groused in the schoolyard, it just seemed that giving trouble to this particular teacher was a silly thing to do. Tomfoolery, not to mention assault, had
no place in the world he was trying to create for us, and instinctively everyone
knew that. If nothing else, we all recognized MacFarland's considerable intelligence and respected the hours he put into his work. It came to this: The trou-
blemaker would look foolish rather than daring. Even Jim Fitzsimmons was
reading *On the Road*[2] and turning his incipient alcoholism to literary ends.

There were some lives that were already beyond Jack MacFarland's minis-   28
trations, but mine was not. I started reading again as I hadn't since elementary
school. I would go into our gloomy little bedroom or sit at the dinner table
while, on the television, Danny McShane was paralyzing Mr. Moto with the
atomic drop, and work slowly back through *Heart of Darkness*, trying to catch
the words in Conrad's sentences. I certainly was not MacFarland's best student;
most of the other guys in College Prep, even my fellow slackers, had better
backgrounds than I did. But I worked very hard, for MacFarland had hooked
me. He tapped my old interest in reading and creating stories. He gave me a
way to feel special by using my mind. And he provided a role model that wasn't
shaped on physical prowess alone, and something inside me that I wasn't quite
aware of responded to that. Jack MacFarland established a literacy club, to borrow a phrase of Frank Smith's, and invited me—invited all of us—to join.

There's been a good deal of research and speculation suggesting that the   29
acknowledgment of school performance with extrinsic rewards—smiling faces,
stars, numbers, grades—diminishes the intrinsic satisfaction children experience
by engaging in reading or writing or problem solving. While it's certainly true
that we've created an educational system that encourages our best and brightest
to become cynical grade collectors and, in general, have developed an obsession
with evaluation and assessment, I must tell you that venal though it may have
been, I loved getting good grades from MacFarland. I now know how subjective
grades can be, but then they came tucked in the back of essays like bits of scientific data, some sort of spectroscopic readout that said, objectively and publicly, that I had made something of value. I suppose I'd been mediocre for too

---

[2]Semiautobiographical novel by American Beat writer Jack Kerouac (1922–1969) about his
travels through the United States and Mexico.

long and enjoyed a public redefinition. And I suppose the workings of my mind, such as they were, had been private for too long. My linguistic play moved into the world; like the intergalactic stories I told years before on Frank's berry-splattered truck bed, these papers with their circled, red B-pluses and A-minuses linked my mind to something outside it. I carried them around like a club emblem.

30   One day in the December of my senior year, Mr. MacFarland asked me where I was going to go to college. I hadn't thought much about it. Many of the students I teach today spent their last year in high school with a physics text in one hand and the Stanford catalog in the other, but I wasn't even aware of what "entrance requirements" were. My folks would say that they wanted me to go to college and be a doctor, but I don't know how seriously I ever took that; it seemed a sweet thing to say, a bit of supportive family chatter, like telling a gangly daughter she's graceful. The reality of higher education wasn't in my scheme of things: No one in the family had gone to college; only two of my uncles had completed high school. I figured I'd get a night job and go to the local junior college because I knew that Snyder and Company were going there to play ball. But I hadn't even prepared for that. When I finally said, "I don't know," Mac-Farland looked down at me—I was seated in his office—and said, "Listen, you can write."

31   My grades stank. I had As in biology and a handful of Bs in a few English and social science classes. All the rest were Cs—or worse. MacFarland said I would do well in his class and laid down the law about doing well in the others. Still, the record for my first three years wouldn't have been acceptable to any four-year school. To nobody's surprise, I was turned down flat by USC and UCLA. But Jack MacFarland was on the case. He had received his bachelor's degree from Loyola University, so he made calls to old professors and talked to somebody in admissions and wrote me a strong letter. Loyola finally accepted me as a probationary student. I would be on trial for the first year, and if I did okay, I would be granted regular status. MacFarland also intervened to get me a loan, for I could never have afforded a private college without it. Four more years of religion classes and four more years of boys at one school, girls at another. But at least I was going to college. Amazing.

32   In my last semester of high school, I elected a special English course fashioned by Mr. MacFarland, and it was through this elective that there arose at Mercy a fledgling literati. Art Mitz, the editor of the school newspaper and a very smart guy, was the kingpin. He was joined by me and by Mark Dever, a quiet boy who wrote beautifully and who would die before he was forty. Mac-Farland occasionally invited us to his apartment, and those visits became the high point of our apprenticeship: We'd clamp on our training wheels and drive to his salon.

33   He lived in a cramped and cluttered place near the airport, tucked away in the kind of building that architectural critic Reyner Banham calls a *dingbat.*

Books were all over: stacked, piled, tossed, and crated, underlined and dog eared, well worn and new. Cigarette ashes crusted with coffee in saucers or spilled over the sides of motel ashtrays. The little bedroom had, along two of its walls, bricks and boards loaded with notes, magazines, and oversized books. The kitchen joined the living room, and there was a stack of German newspapers under the sink. I had never seen anything like it: a great flophouse of language furnished by City Lights and Café le Metro. I read every title. I flipped through paperbacks and scanned jackets and memorized names: Gogol, *Finnegan's Wake*, Djuna Barnes, Jackson Pollock, *A Coney Island of the Mind*, F. O. Matthiessen's *American Renaissance*, all sorts of Freud, *Troubled Sleep*, Man Ray, *The Education of Henry Adams*, Richard Wright, *Film as Art*, William Butler Yeats, Marguerite Duras, *Redburn*, *A Season in Hell*, *Kapital*. On the cover of Alain-Fournier's *The Wanderer* was an Edward Gorey drawing of a young man on a road winding into dark trees. By the hotplate sat a strange Kafka novel called *Amerika*, in which an adolescent hero crosses the Atlantic to find the Nature Theater of Oklahoma. Art and Mark would be talking about a movie or the school newspaper, and I would be consuming my English teacher's library. It was heady stuff. I felt like a Pop Warner athlete on steroids.

Art, Mark, and I would buy stogies and triangulate from MacFarland's   34 apartment to the Cinema, which now shows X-rated films but was then L.A.'s premiere art theater, and then to the musty Cherokee Bookstore in Hollywood to hobnob with beatnik homosexuals—smoking, drinking bourbon and coffee, and trying out awkward phrases we'd gleaned from our mentor's bookshelves. I was happy and precocious and a little scared as well, for Hollywood Boulevard was thick with a kind of decadence that was foreign to the South Side. After the Cherokee, we would head back to the security of MacFarland's apartment, slaphappy with hipness.

Let me be the first to admit that there was a good deal of adolescent passion   35 in this embrace of the avant-garde: self-absorption, sexually charged pedantry, an elevation of the odd and abandoned. Still it was a time during which I absorbed an awful lot of information: long lists of titles, images from expression-ist paintings, new wave shibboleths, snippets of philosophy, and names that read like Steve Fusco's misspellings—Goethe, Nietzsche, Kierkegaard. Now this is hardly the stuff of deep understanding. But it was an introduction, a phrase book, a Baedeker[3] to a vocabulary of ideas, and it felt good at the time to know all these words. With hindsight I realize how layered and important that knowl-edge was.

It enabled me to do things in the world. I could browse bohemian book-   36 stores in far-off, mysterious Hollywood; I could go to the Cinema and see events through the lenses of European directors; and, most of all, I could share an evening, talk that talk, with Jack MacFarland, the man I most admired at the

[3]Classic guidebook for travelers.

time. Knowledge was becoming a bonding agent. Within a year or two, the persona of the disaffected hipster would prove too cynical, too alienated to last. But for a time it was new and exciting: It provided a critical perspective on society, and it allowed me to act as though I were living beyond the limiting boundaries of South Vermont.

EXERCISES

Some of the Issues

1. Give a physical description of the neighborhood where Rose grew up.
2. How would you characterize the men who lived in the area (paragraph 7)?
3. Considering the view of life on Vermont Avenue, can you infer why Rose doesn't mention any women?
4. How do you think he felt about growing up in his neighborhood? What lines from the text support your idea?
5. The author says that his childhood days were quiet, lazy, and lonely. What kinds of neighborhood activities did attract his attention?
6. What defense mechanism did Rose develop to cope with school and the hopelessness of the neighborhood (paragraph 12)?
7. Rose spent hours with his chemistry set, yet he was disappointed that it didn't allow him "to do the things I wanted to do." Based on what you know about his life, what "things" do you suppose he had in mind?
8. According to Rose, what are the job skills that vocational education programs should teach (paragraphs 18 and 19)?
9. In paragraphs 22–24, how does Rose interpret Ken Harvey's sentence, "I just wanna be average"?
10. What kind of a person is Jack MacFarland? If you were a film director, which actor would you cast to play him?
11. What do you think was the key to MacFarland's success as a teacher?
12. The knowledge that Rose gained during his senior year enabled him "to do things in the world" and "to act as though I were living beyond the limiting boundaries of South Vermont." How does all this relate to his childhood dreams? Find lines from earlier portions of the text that support your idea.

The Way We Are Told

13. Reread Rose's description of his neighborhood (paragraphs 1–8). Which images best capture the feeling of place for you?
14. How would you characterize Rose's use of language in paragraph 18, "Students will float to the mark you set. I and the others in the vocational classes were bobbing in pretty shallow water." Can you find similar phrases in paragraphs 18–24 that continue the comparison?

Some Subjects for Writing

15. Rose describes several of his classmates in Voc. Ed. who attempted to cope with the "disorienting" atmosphere of their high school (paragraphs 20–24). Did you or any of your high school classmates develop special ways of coping with the system or with the teachers? Recount this experience.

16. In paragraphs 18–24, Rose sharply criticizes traditional vocational education programs. What kinds of programs do you think are appropriate for students who do not plan to go to college or who want to enter the job market immediately after high school?

17. Write a letter to your high school principal (you do not need to send it) explaining the ways in which the school was successful or unsuccessful in meeting your needs and those of students like you. If it seems relevant, make realistic suggestions for change.

18. Many high schools, perhaps including the one you attended, use "tracking" to place students in separate classes according to their presumed ability for academic success. Rose, as well as other educators, questions this system. Write an essay detailing the advantages or disadvantages of such a system for schools and their students. Consider the question of how and whether one can determine ahead of time if a student has the ability to succeed academically.

*19. Rose says that a mystique surrounds those who grow up in urban environments: "It's popular these days to claim you grew up on the streets" (paragraph 10). Do you agree? What cultural factors might influence this attitude? You might also want to read Nell Bernstein's "Goin' Gangsta, Choosin' Cholita."

Incident

COUNTEE CULLEN

Countee Cullen (1903–46) gained recognition for his poetry while still in high school and published his first volume of poetry at the age of 22. He attended New York University and Harvard and continued to publish poetry and fiction. "Incident" first appeared in Color *(1925).*

Once riding in old Baltimore
   Heart-filled head-filled with glee,
I saw a Baltimorean
   Keep looking straight at me.

Now I was eight and very small,
   And he was no whit bigger,
And so I smiled, but he poked out
   His tongue, and called me, "Nigger."

I saw the whole of Baltimore
   From May until December;
Of all the things that happened there
   That's all that I remember.

EXERCISES

Some of the Issues

1. What are the author's feelings toward the Baltimorean at the beginning of the poem? Why are these feelings significant?
2. How old is the Baltimorean? How is age significant in the poem?
3. Why is the incident the only thing the author remembers?
4. Read the poem aloud several times. Does his insistent meter and rhyme remind you of poems that children may recite? How does the music of the poem contrast with its subject?

Some Subjects for Writing

5. Write about an incident in which someone called you a name. Describe the incident and your reaction.

6. There is a saying: "Sticks and stones will break my bones, but names will never hurt me." Is this statement true? Write an essay in which you examine whether or not words and names can be harmful.

2
Heritage

Each of us inherits something: in some cases, it is money, property or some object—a family heirloom such as a grandmother's wedding dress or a father's set of tools. But beyond that, each of us inherits something else, something much less concrete and tangible, something we may not even be fully aware of. It may be a way of doing a daily task, or the way we solve a particular problem or decide a moral issue for ourselves. It may be a special way of keeping a holiday, or a tradition to have a picnic on a certain date. It may be something important or central to our thinking, or something minor that we have long accepted quite casually.

For many Americans who are descended from immigrants, refugees, former slaves, and native peoples, the notion of heritage often includes more than one culture. Often, such cross-cultural heritage gives rise to mixed feelings, especially in the children of immigrants. A sense of pride in the distant land a father or mother came from may be mingled with a sense of embarrassment when that parent tries—and does not quite succeed at—being part of the son's or daughter's new lifestyle. In the first selection, "Fitting In," John Tarkov, son of a Russian father, reveals such mingled sentiments. In the story "Barba Nikos" by Harry Mark Petrakis, the narrator illustrates the conflict that often arises between first- and second-generation immigrants when the ways of the Old Country—and their parents' accented English—become a source of embarrassment. Toni Morrison, granddaughter of a slave, describes in "A Slow Walk of Trees" how her parents and grandparents strove to overcome a set of obstacles, very different from those facing immigrants like John Tarkov's father or the old Greek grocer in "Barba Nikos."

Michael Novak's essay "In Ethnic America" is a defense of the people from eastern and southern Europe, millions of whom immigrated to the United States in the early twentieth century. Mostly of peasant origin, they have a

┌───┐

THINKING ABOUT THE THEME *"Heritage"*

1. The photos in the album tell part of the story of what seems to be a traditional wedding ceremony. Work with your classmates to describe some of the traditions common in North American weddings and what they symbolize.

2. Wedding traditions vary from culture to culture and within cultures in North America. With your classmates, discuss the various customs you are aware of and consider their meanings and roles in the culture. You might also examine whether or not these traditions have changed over time.

3. Observing tradition seems to be important for most people, not only in childhood but throughout adult life. We mark significant events in our lives, such as graduations, birthdays, anniversaries of various kinds, and national and/or religious holidays, with traditional activities, clothing, and foods. Some families or groups of friends even create rituals of their own. Examine a set of traditions you observe and its importance to you.

4. Photo albums, along with stories, common sayings, important objects, and family rituals often serve to help create a heritage, and to carry traditions and values forward to a new generation. Examine the role of one or more of these elements in your own upbringing.

5. In what ways did the traditions you grew up with help shape your character? Are there some that you feel you had to resist or modify? Why? Which have you embraced and why? Were there consequences either way?

└───┘

strong heritage of hard work—and silence, including a silent acceptance of the disregard for them, as Novak asserts, by mainstream America.

One general trait that is part of the American heritage is a belief in the importance of individual rights. In "Amérka, Amérka" Anton Shammas illustrates how immigrants can live in this country and keep their native traditions if they so choose. "This country is big," he says, "it has room not only for the newcomers, but for their portable homelands."

In the poem that ends the chapter, Wendy Rose, of Hopi-Miwok ancestry, uses a news story of the sale of her people's bones to a museum as a symbol of the stealing of Native American lands and culture.

Fitting In

JOHN TARKOV

John Tarkov is a writer and editor who lives in Queens, New York. "This newspaper" (paragraph 12) refers to the New York Times, *in whose* Sunday Magazine *the following selection was published on July 7, 1985. In this autobiographical essay, Tarkov speaks about the question of identity from the point of view of a second-generation American. He loves his Russian immigrant father and yet is exasperated by him—as much by his attempts to be American as by his foreignness.*

Russian Americans of John Tarkov's father's generation often encountered an added difficulty in integrating themselves into mainstream America. Deeply attached to their homeland, they were out of sympathy with the Communist government under Josef Stalin—a government, moreover, disliked and often feared by a majority of Americans.

Not quite two miles and 30 years from the church where these thoughts came to me, is a small, graveled parking lot cut out of the New Jersey pines, behind a restaurant and a dance hall. On road signs, the town is called Cassville. But to the several generations of Russian-Americans whose center of gravity tipped to the Old World, it was known as Roova Farms. I think the acronym stands for Russian Orthodox Outing and Vacation Association. In the summers, the place might as well have been on the Black Sea. 1

One day during one of those summers, my old man showed up from a job, just off a cargo ship. He made his living that way, in the merchant marine. With him, he had a brittle new baseball glove and a baseball as yet unmarked by human error. We went out to that parking lot and started tossing the ball back and forth; me even at the age of 8 at ease with the motions of this American game, him grabbing at the ball with his bare hands then sending it back with an unpolished stiff-armed heave. It was a very hot day. I remember that clearly. What I can't remember is who put the first scuff mark on the ball. Either I missed it, or he tossed it out of my reach. 2

I chased it down, I'm sure with American-kid peevishness. I wonder if I said anything. Probably I mouthed off about it. 3

Last winter, the phone call comes on a Saturday morning. The old man's heart had stopped. They had started it beating again. When I get to the hospital, 4 he's not conscious. They let me in to see him briefly. Then comes an afternoon of drinking coffee and leaning on walls. Around 4 o'clock, two doctors come out of coronary care. One of them puts his hand on my arm and tells me. A nurse takes me behind the closed door.

5   Two fragments of thought surface. One is primitive and it resonates from somewhere deep: *This all began in Russia long ago.* The other is sentimental: *He died near the sea.*

6   I joined the tips of the first three fingers of my right hand and touch them to his forehead, then his stomach, then one side of his chest, then the other. It's what I believe. I pause just briefly, then give him a couple of quick cuffs on the side of his face, the way men do when they want to express affection but something stops them from embracing. The nurse takes me downstairs to sign some forms.

7   He never did quite get the hang of this country. He never went to the movies. Didn't watch television on his own. Didn't listen to the radio. Ate a lot of kielbasa.[1] Read a lot. Read the paper almost cover to cover every day. He read English well, but when he talked about what he'd read, he'd mispronounce some words and put a heavy accent on them all. The paper was the window through which he examined a landscape and a people that were nearly as impenetrable to him as they were known and manageable to me. For a touch of home, he'd pick up *Soviet Life.* "I'm not a Communist," he used to tell me. "I'm a Russian." Then he'd catch me up about some new hydroelectric project on the Dnieper.

8   And so he vaguely embarrassed me. Who knows how many times, over the years, this story has repeated itself: the immigrant father and the uneasy son. This Melting Pot of ours absorbs the second generation over a flame so high that the first is left encrusted on the rim. In college, I read the literature—Lenski on the three-generation hypothesis, stuff like that—but I read it to make my grades, not particularly to understand that I was living it.

9   When he finally retired from the ocean, he took his first real apartment, on the Lower East Side, and we saw each other more regularly. We'd sit there on Saturday or Sunday afternoons, drinking beer and eating Chinese food. He bought a television set for our diversion, and, depending on the season, the voices of Keith Jackson and Ara Parseghian or Ralph Kiner and Lindsey Nelson would overlap with, and sometimes submerge, our own.

10   After the game, he'd get us a couple more beers, and we would become emissaries: from land and sea, America and ports of destination. We were never strangers—never that—but we dealt, for the most part, in small talk. It was a son trying—or maybe trying to try—to share what little he knew with his father, and flinching privately at his father's foreignness. And it was a father outspokenly proud of his son, beyond basis in reason, yet at times openly frustrated that the kid had grown up unlike himself.

---

[1]A type of sausage.

Every father has a vision of what he'd like his son to be. Every son has a   11
vision in kind of his father. Eventually, one of them goes, and the one remaining
has little choice but to extinguish the ideal and confront the man of flesh and
blood who was. Time and again it happens: The vision shed, the son, once
vaguely embarrassed by the father, begins to wear the old man's name and story
with pride.

Though he read it daily, the old man hated this newspaper. Sometimes I   12
think he bought it just to make himself angry. He felt the sports editor was trying to suppress the growth of soccer in America. So naturally, I would egg him
on. I'd say things like: "Yeah, you're right. It's a conspiracy. The sports editor
plus 200 million other Americans." Then we'd start yelling.

But when it came time to put the obituary announcements in the press, after   13
I phoned one in to the Russian-language paper, I started to dial *The Times*. And
I remembered. And I put the phone down. And started laughing. "O.K.," I said.
"O.K. They won't get any of our business."

So he went out Russian, like he came in. Up on the hill, the church is topped   14
by weathered gold onion domes—sort of like back in the Old Country, but in
fact just down the road from his attempt to sneak us both into America through
a side door in New Jersey, by tossing a baseball back and forth on a hot, still,
bake-in-the-bleachers kind of summer day.

I believe he threw the thing over my head, actually. It *was* a throwing error,   15
the more I think about it. No way I could have caught it. But it was only a baseball, and he was my father, so it's no big deal. I bounced a few off his shins that
day myself. Next time, the baseball doesn't touch the ground.

EXERCISES

Some of the issues

1. Tarkov begins his reminiscence with a description of a summer day.
   Describe the location and the event.
2. Paragraphs 4 through 6 abruptly change the time and location. What are
   Tarkov's thoughts and actions on that day?
3. Tarkov says of his father: "He never did quite get the hang of this country."
   What examples does he give?
4. What does the father say after reading *Soviet Life*, and what does he mean
   by it?
5. Explain the sentence in paragraph 8: "This Melting Pot of ours absorbs the
   second generation over a flame so high that the first is left encrusted on the
   rim."
6. Tarkov cites several incidents when his father's behavior embarrassed him.
   What are they? In your opinion, is Tarkov embarrassed because his father

was an immigrant, or does Tarkov feel what many children feel about their parents from time to time?

7. In several instances the roles of father and son seem to be reversed: the son is more knowledgeable than the father and at one point speaks in the father's voice. Cite come examples of this reversal of roles.

8. In paragraph 8 Tarkov mentions reading a book as a student, without realizing that it might have personal relevance to him. Why did he not understand it at that time?

9. What does paragraph 10 tell you about the relationship between father and son? Why are they "emissaries from land and sea"?

10. In paragraph 12 Tarkov describes an argument with his father. What is its significance?

11. Why did Tarkov decide not to put an obituary in the *New York Times?*

12. Examine the final paragraph. Why is it important to Tarkov to determine who was responsible for an error in a baseball game long ago?

The Way We Are Told

13. The essay begins with the description of a place—Roova Farms—and an activity—baseball. Why would Tarkov choose to describe this particular place and activity?

14. Tarkov looks at the relationship between himself and his father at several different points in their lives. How would the character of the essay be changed if he had put his account in chronological order?

15. Tarkov uses colloquial language or slang several times, such as "my old man" (paragraphs 2 and 4) and "mouthed off " (paragraph 3). Find some additional examples. Are such expressions appropriate in an otherwise serious essay?

16. Paragraph 7 contains several intentional sentence fragments. Identify them. What effect do they have?

17. Cite other examples of the use of informal and formal language. Is the combination effective for Tarkov's purposes?

Some Subjects for Writing

18. What person in your family are you most like or most often compared to? Write a careful description of that person's appearance and personality, emphasizing your similarities or differences.

19. In his essay Tarkov explains the ways in which he is both a part of and separate from his heritage. Write an essay in which you describe some specific aspect of your own heritage. Examine the ways in which you have departed from it, or have accepted it.

20. Tarkov writes about a relationship with one person that changes, yet in some ways stays the same over a long period of time. In an essay, describe your own relationship with someone whom you have known over a long time, perhaps your own parents, perhaps another relative or a friend of long standing. Give "snapshots" of at least three different periods in the relationship and explain how it has changed over time.

*21. Read Harry Mark Petrakis's "Barba Nikos." Tarkov and the character created by Petrakis both are children of immigrants to America, and both reflect on what their heritage meant to them in their youth, and later on. In your essay first describe and then compare their experiences and attitudes.

A Slow Walk of Trees

TONI MORRISON

Toni Morrison was born in 1931 in Lorrain, Ohio, a small town near Cleveland. She received a B.A. degree from Howard University and an M.A. from Cornell. Morrison is the author of six novels: The Bluest Eye *(1969),* Sula *(1973),* Song of Solomon *(1977),* Tar Baby *(1981); the 1987 Pulitzer Prize winner,* Beloved; *and* Jazz *(1992). She is also the author of a work of literary criticism,* Playing in the Dark: Whiteness and the Literary Imagination *(1993) and the editor of* Race-ing Justice, En-gendering Power: Essays on Anita Hill, Clarence Thomas, and the Construction of Social Reality *(1992). Morrison won the Nobel Prize for Literature in 1993.*

The article included here was first published in the New York Times Magazine *on July 4, 1976, the date of the American bicentennial. Morrison describes as well as contrasts the attitudes of her grandparents and parents toward the discrimination that was a central factor in their lives. In each of the two generations, she explains, the male had an essentially pessimistic outlook that nothing could be done; the female, on the other hand, set out to cope with whatever particular adversity was likely to befall her family. At the same time, Morrison sees a generational difference between the views of her grandparents and her parents that indicates some progress: an increased belief in the possibility of assuming control of their lives.*

1   His name was John Solomon Willis, and when at age 5 he heard from the old folks that "the Emancipation Proclamation was coming," he crawled under the bed. It was his earliest recollection of what was to be his habitual response to the promise of white people: horror and an instinctive yearning for safety. He was my grandfather, a musician who managed to hold on to his violin but not his land. He lost all 88 acres of his Indian mother's inheritance to legal predators who built their fortunes on the likes of him. He was an unreconstructed black pessimist who, in spite of or because of emancipation, was convinced for 85 years that there was no hope whatever for black people in this country. His rancor was legitimate, for he, John Solomon, was not only an artist but a first-rate carpenter and farmer, reduced to sending home to his family money he had made playing the violin because he was not able to find work. And this during

the years when almost half the black male population were skilled craftsmen who lost their jobs to white ex-convicts and immigrant farmers.

His wife, however, was of a quite different frame of mind and believed that all things could be improved by faith in Jesus and an effort of the will. So it was she, Ardelia Willis, who sneaked her seven children out of the back window into the darkness, rather than permit the patron of their sharecropper's existence to become their executioner as well, and headed north in 1912, when 99.2 percent of all black people in the U.S. were native-born and only 60 percent of white Americans were. And it was Ardelia who told her husband that they could not stay in the Kentucky town they ended up in because the teacher didn't know long division.

They have been dead now for 30 years and more and I still don't know which of them came closer to the truth about the possibilities of life for black people in this country. One of their grandchildren is a tenured professor at Princeton. Another, who suffered from what the Peruvian poet called "anger that breaks a man into children," was picked up just as he entered his teens and emotionally lobotomized by the reformatories and mental institutions specifically designed to serve him. Neither John Solomon nor Ardelia lived long enough to despair over one or swell with pride over the other. But if they were alive today each would have selected and collected enough evidence to support the accuracy of the other's original point of view. And it would be difficult to convince either one that the other was right.

Some of the monstrous events that took place in John Solomon's America have been duplicated in alarming detail in my own America. There was the public murder of a President in a theater in 1865 and the public murder of another President on television in 1963. The Civil War of 1861 had its encore as the civil rights movement of 1960. The torture and mutilation of a black West Point Cadet (Cadet Johnson Whittaker) in 1880 had its rerun with the 1970's murders of students at Jackson State College, Texas Southern and Southern University in Baton Rouge. And in 1976 we watch for what must be the thousandth time a pitched battle between the children of slaves and the children of immigrants—only this time, it is not the New York draft riots of 1863, but the busing turmoil in Paul Revere's home town, Boston.

Hopeless, he'd said. Hopeless. For he was certain that white people of every political, religious, geographical and economic background would band together against black people everywhere when they felt the threat of our progress. And a hundred years after he sought safety from the white man's "promise," somebody put a bullet in Martin Luther King's brain. And not long before that some excellent samples of the master race demonstrated their courage and virility by dynamiting some little black girls to death. If he were here now, my grandfather, he would shake his head, close his eyes and pull out his violin—too polite to say, "I told you so." And his wife would pay attention to the music but not to the sadness in her husband's eyes, for she would see what she expected to see—not the occasional historical repetition, but, *like the slow walk of certain species of trees from the flatlands up into the mountains,* she would see the signs of irrevocable and permanent change. She, who pulled her girls out of an inadequate school in the Cumberland Mountains, knew all along that the gentlemen from Alabama who had killed the little girls would be rounded up. And it wouldn't surprise her in the least to know that the number of black college graduates jumped 12 percent in the last three years: 47 percent in 20 years. That there are 140 black mayors in this country; 14 black judges in the District Circuit, 4 in the Courts of Appeals and one on the Supreme Court. That there are 17 blacks in Congress, one in the Senate; 276 in state legislatures—223 in state houses, 53 in state senates. That there are 112 elected black police chiefs and sheriffs, 1 Pulitzer Prize winner; 1 winner of the Prix de Rome; a dozen or so winners of the Guggenheim; 4 deans of predominantly white colleges.... Oh, her list would go on and on. But so would John Solomon's sweet sad music.

6   While my grandparents held opposite views on whether the fortunes of black people were improving, my own parents struck similarly opposed postures, but from another slant. They differed about whether the moral fiber of white people would ever improve. Quite a different argument. The old folks argued about how and if black people could improve themselves, who could be counted on to help us, who would hinder us and so on. My parents took issue over the question of whether it was possible for white people to improve. They assumed that black people were the humans of the globe, but had serious doubts about the quality and existence of white humanity. Thus my father, distrusting every word and every gesture of every white man on earth, assumed that the white man who crept up the stairs one afternoon had come to molest his daughters and threw him down the stairs and then our tricycle after him. (I think my father was wrong, but considering what I have seen since, it may have been very healthy for me to have witnessed that as my first black-white encounter.) My mother, however, *believed* in them—their possibilities. So when the meal we got on relief was bug-ridden, she wrote a long letter to Franklin Delano Roosevelt. And when white bill collectors came to our door, it was she who received them civilly and explained in a sweet voice that we were people of honor and that the debt would be taken care of. Her message to Roosevelt got through—our meal improved. Her message to the bill collectors did not always get through and there was occasional violence when my father (self-exiled to the bedroom for fear he could not hold his temper) would hear that her reasonableness had failed. My mother was always wounded by these scenes, for she thought the bill collector knew that she loved good credit more than life and that being in arrears on a payment horrified her probably more than it did him. So she thought he was rude because he was white. For years she walked to utility companies and department stores to pay bills in person and even now she does not seem convinced that checks are legal tender. My father loved excellence, worked hard (he held three jobs at once for 17 years) and was so outraged by the suggestion of

personal slackness that he could explain it to himself only in terms of racism. He was a fastidious worker who was frightened of one thing: unemployment. I can remember now the doomsday-cum-graveyard sound of "laid off" and how the minute school was out he asked us, "Where you workin'?" Both my parents believed that all succor and aid came from themselves and their neighborhood, since "they"—white people in charge and those not in charge but in obstructionist positions—were in some way fundamentally, genetically corrupt.

So I grew up in a basically racist household with more than a child's share   7
of contempt for white people. And for each white friend I acquired who made a small crack in that contempt, there was another who repaired it. For each one who related to me as a person, there was one who in my presence at least, became actively "white." And like most black people of my generation, I suffer from racial vertigo that can be cured only by taking what one needs from one's ancestors. John Solomon's cynicism and his deployment of his art as both weapon and solace, Ardelia's faith in the magic that can be wrought by sheer effort of the will; my mother's open-mindedness in each new encounter and her habit of trying reasonableness first; my father's temper, his impatience and his efforts to keep "them" (throw them) out of his life. And it is out of these learned and selected attitudes that I look at the quality of life for my people in this country now. These widely disparate and sometimes conflicting views, I suspect, were held not only by me, but by most black people. Some I know are clearer in their positions, have not sullied their anger with optimism or dirtied their hope with despair. But most of us are plagued by a sense of being worn shell-thin by constant repression and hostility as well as the impression of being buoyed by visible testimony of tremendous strides. There *is* repetition of the grotesque in our history. And there *is* the miraculous walk of trees. The question is whether our walk is progress or merely movement. O.J. Simpson leaning on a Hertz car *is* better than the Gold Dust Twins on the back of a soap box. But is "Good Times" better than Stepin Fetchit? Has the first order of business been taken care of? Does the law of the land work for us?

EXERCISES

Some of the Issues

1. Toni Morrison describes her grandfather as a pessimist and says that "his rancor was legitimate." Why does she call it legitimate? Toward whom was it directed?
2. What was the difference in basic outlook between Morrison's grandfather and grandmother? What did her grandmother believe? How does the author show that she lived up to her beliefs?

3. Why does Morrison cite the lives of John Solomon and Ardelia's two grandchildren in paragraph 3? How do these lives relate to her grandparents' beliefs? In what way does Morrison think these lives would have affected her grandparents' beliefs?
4. Reread paragraph 4. What bearing does what Morrison tells here have on the grandparents' views?
5. After rereading paragraph 5, explain the title of the essay. Whose beliefs does Morrison reflect in this paragraph?
6. Explain the distinction Morrison makes between the views of her grandparents and her parents. What is the difference between the views of her father and mother?
7. Morrison says: "So I grew up in a basically racist household." How does Morrison trace her views back to the influence of her parents and grandparents?

The Way We Are Told

8. Morrison uses a mix of personal anecdotes and more general observations, including statistics, to support her thesis. How are these used to support the idea of black progress or the lack of it?
9. As Morrison tells it, one each of her parents and grandparents was an optimist, the other a pessimist. Try to determine Morrison's own stand. Whose side is she on?

Some Subjects for Writing

10. How would you characterize your own family's outlook on life? Is it more on the optimistic or pessimistic side? How have your family's attitudes influenced you?
11. Which point of view, the optimistic one of Morrison's grandmother or the pessimistic one of her grandfather, best accounts for the trend in race relations in the United States in the past ten years? Cite specific events in the news or changes in media representation, or draw from personal experience and family history.

Barba Nikos

HARRY MARK PETRAKIS

Harry Mark Petrakis was born in St. Louis in 1923 but has spent most of his life in and around Chicago. A novelist and short story writer, his books include Pericles on 31st Street *(1965),* A Dream of Kings *(1966), and* Stelmark: A Family Recollection *(1970), from which the following selection is an excerpt.*

In more recent years he has written Reflections on a Writer's Life and Work *(1983) and published his* Collected Stories *(1983). Petrakis, himself of Greek descent, often sets the scene of his writing among Greek Americans and immigrants.*

The story Petrakis tells describes the strains that can come between first- and second-generation immigrants, when the ways of the Old Country—and their parents' accented English—become a source of embarrassment. Young people, trying to conform with their peers, may find this situation particularly trying.

Located in the eastern Mediterranean, Greece has some 10 million inhabitants. It gained its independence in the nineteenth century after centuries of rule by the Turkish empire. It is a relatively poor country, many of whose people have sought their fortunes elsewhere, often in the United States, which has a large population of Greek descent.

Ancient Greece, the Greece Barba Nikos talks about so proudly, has often been called "the cradle of Western civilization." Among its many small city states, Athens stands out as the first representative democracy. Of the earliest philosophers, poets, historians, and scientists whose works have been preserved, most are Athenians. Achilles, whom Barba Nikos mentions, is a mythical warrior who plays a central role in Homer's Iliad, *the epic poem about the war between the Greek city states and Troy. Alexander the Great, King of Macedonia, conquered the Middle East as far as India some 2,300 years ago. Marathon was not a race but a city in Greece where, in 490 B.C., the Athenians won a major battle against the invading Persians. According to legend, a Greek soldier ran from Marathon to Athens to carry the news of victory—before collapsing dead from the strain. He ran the same distance as the thousands who now run in marathons all over the world, except he ran it in full armor.*

1   There was one storekeeper I remember above all others in my youth. It was shortly before I became ill, spending a good portion of my time with a motley group of varied ethnic ancestry. We contended with one another to deride the customs of the old country. On our Saturday forays into neighborhoods beyond our own, to prove we were really Americans, we ate hot dogs and drank Cokes. If a boy didn't have ten cents for this repast he went hungry, for he dared not bring a sandwich from home made of the spiced meats our families ate.

2   One of our untamed games was to seek out the owner of a pushcart or a store, unmistakably an immigrant, and bedevil him with a chorus of insults and jeers. To prove allegiance to the gang it was necessary to reserve our fiercest malevolence for a storekeeper or peddler belonging to our own ethnic background.

3   For that reason I led a raid on the small, shabby grocery of old Barba Nikos, a short, sinewy Greek who walked with a slight limp and sported a flaring, handlebar mustache.

4   We stood outside his store and dared him to come out. When he emerged to do battle, we plucked a few plums and peaches from the baskets on the sidewalk and retreated across the street to eat them while he watched. He waved a fist and hurled epithets at us in ornamental Greek.

5   Aware that my mettle was being tested, I raised my arm and threw my half-eaten plum at the old man. My aim was accurate and the plum struck him on the cheek. He shuddered and put his hand to the stain. He stared at me across the street, and although I could not see his eyes, I felt them sear my flesh. He turned and walked silently back into the store. The boys slapped my shoulders in admiration, but it was a hollow victory that rested like a stone in the pit of my stomach.

6   At twilight when we disbanded, I passed the grocery alone on my way home. There was a small light burning in the store and the shadow of the old man's body outlined against the glass. Goaded by remorse, I walked to the door and entered.

7   The old man moved from behind the narrow wooden counter and stared at me. I wanted to turn and flee, but by then it was too late. As he motioned for me to come closer, I braced myself for a curse or a blow.

8   "You were the one," he said, finally, in a harsh voice.

9   I nodded mutely.

10   "Why did you come back?"

11   I stood there unable to answer.

12   "What's your name?"

13   "Haralambos," I said, speaking to him in Greek.

14   He looked at me in shock. "You are Greek!" he cried. "A Greek boy attacking a Greek grocer!" He stood appalled at the immensity of my crime. "All right," he said coldly. "You are here because you wish to make amends." His great mustache bristled in concentration. "Four plums, two peaches," he said. "That makes a total of 78 cents. Call it 75. Do you have 75 cents, boy?"

I shook my head.

"Then you will work it off," he said. "Fifteen cents an hour into 75 cents makes"—he paused—"five hours of work. Can you come here Saturday morning?"

"Yes," I said.

"Yes, Barba Nikos," he said sternly. "Show respect."

"Yes, Barba Nikos," I said.

"Saturday morning at eight o'clock," he said. "Now go home and say thanks in your prayers that I did not loosen your impudent head with a solid smack on the ear." I needed no further urging and fled.

Saturday morning, still apprehensive, I returned to the store. I began by sweeping, raising clouds of dust in dark and hidden corners. I washed the windows, whipping the squeegee swiftly up and down the glass in a fever of fear that some member of the gang would see me. When I finished I hurried back inside.

For the balance of the morning I stacked cans, washed the counter, and dusted bottles of yellow wine. A few customers entered, and Barba Nikos served them. A little after twelve o'clock he locked the door so he could eat lunch. He cut himself a few slices of sausage, tore a large chunk from a loaf of crisp-crusted bread, and filled a small cup with a dozen black shiny olives floating in brine. He offered me the cup. I could not help myself and grimaced.

"You are a stupid boy," the old man said. "You are not really Greek, are you?"

"Yes, I am."

"You might be," he admitted grudgingly. "But you do not act Greek. Wrinkling your nose at these fine olives. Look around this store for a minute. What do you see?"

"Fruits and vegetables," I said. "Cheese and olives and things like that."

He stared at me with a massive scorn. "That's what I mean," he said. "You are a bonehead. You don't understand that a whole nation and a people are in this store."

I looked uneasily toward the storeroom in the rear, almost expecting someone to emerge.

"What about olives?" he cut the air with a sweep of his arm. "There are olives of many shapes and colors. Pointed black ones from Kalamata, oval ones from Amphissa, pickled green olives and sharp tangy yellow ones. Achilles carried black olives to Troy and after a day of savage battle leading his Myrmidons, he'd rest and eat cheese and ripe black olives such as these right here. You have heard of Achilles, boy, haven't you?"

"Yes," I said.

"Yes, Barba Nikos."

"Yes, Barba Nikos," I said.

He motioned at the row of jars filled with varied spices. "There is origanon there and basilikon and daphne and sesame and miantanos, all the marvelous flavorings that we have used in our food for thousands of years. The men of

Marathon carried small packets of these spices into battle, and the scents reminded them of their homes, their families, and their children."

34   He rose and tugged his napkin free from around his throat. "Cheese, you said. Cheese! Come closer, boy, and I educate your abysmal ignorance." He motioned toward a wooden container on the counter. "That glistening white delight is feta, made from goat's milk, packed in wooden buckets to retain the flavor. Alexander the Great demanded it on his table with his casks of wine when he planned his campaigns."

35   He walked limping from the counter to the window where the piles of tomatoes, celery, and green peppers clustered. "I suppose all you see here are some random vegetables?" He did not wait for me to answer. "You are dumb again. These are some of the ingredients that go to make up a Greek salad. Do you know what a Greek salad really is? A meal in itself, an experience, an emotional involvement. It is created deftly and with grace. First, you place large lettuce leaves in a big, deep bowl." He spread his fingers and moved them slowly, carefully, as if he were arranging the leaves. "The remainder of the lettuce is shredded and piled in a small mound," he said. "Then comes celery, cucumbers, tomatoes sliced lengthwise, green peppers, origanon, green olives, feta, avocado and anchovies. At the end you dress it with lemon, vinegar, and pure olive oil, glinting golden in the light."

36   He finished with a heartfelt sigh and for a moment closed his eyes. Then he opened one eye to mark me with a baleful intensity. "The story goes that Zeus himself created the recipe and assembled and mixed the ingredients on Mount Olympus[1] one night when he had invited some of the other gods to dinner."

37   He turned his back on me and walked slowly again across the store, dragging one foot slightly behind him. I looked uneasily at the clock, which showed that it was a few minutes past one. He turned quickly and startled me. "And everything else in here," he said loudly. "White beans, lentils, garlic, crisp bread, kokoretsi, meat balls, mussels and clams." He paused and drew a deep, long breath. "And the wine," he went on, "wine from Samos, Santorini, and Crete, retsina and mavrodaphne, a taste almost as old as water…and then the fragrant melons, the pastries, yellow diples and golden loukoumades, the honey custard galatobouriko. Everything a part of our history, as much a part as the exquisite sculpture in marble, the bearded warriors, Pan[2] and the oracles at Delphi,[3] and the nymphs dancing in the shadowed groves under Homer's glittering moon." He paused, out of breath again, and coughed harshly. "Do you understand now, boy?"

---

[1] Highest point in Greece. Believed to be the home of the gods in early Greek mythology.
[2] Greek god of woods, fields, and fertility, Pan was part human and part goat.
[3] The ancient Greeks believed Delphi to be the site of the oracle who spoke the words of the god Apollo.

He watched my face for some response and then grunted. We stood silent   38
for a moment until he cocked his head and stared at the clock. "It is time for
you to leave," he motioned brusquely toward the door. "We are square now.
Keep it that way."

I decided the old man was crazy and reached behind the counter for my   39
jacket and cap and started for the door. He called me back. From a box he drew
out several soft, yellow figs that he placed in a piece of paper. "A bonus because
you worked well," he said. "Take them. When you taste them, maybe you will
understand what I have been talking about."

I took the figs and he unlocked the door and I hurried from the store. I   40
looked back once and saw him standing in the doorway, watching me, the swirling tendrils of food curling like mist about his head.

I ate the figs late that night. I forgot about them until I was in bed, and then   41
I rose and took the package from my jacket. I nibbled at one, then ate them all.
They broke apart between my teeth with a tangy nectar, a thick sweetness running like honey across my tongue and into the pockets of my cheeks. In the
morning when I woke, I could still taste and inhale their fragrance.

I never again entered Barba Nikos's store. My spell of illness, which began   42
some months later, lasted two years. When I returned to the streets I had forgotten the old man and the grocery. Shortly afterwards my family moved from
the neighborhood.

Some twelve years later, after the war, I drove through the old neighbor-   43
hood and passed the grocery. I stopped the car and for a moment stood before
the store. The windows were stained with dust and grime, the interior bare and
desolate, a store in a decrepit group of stores marked for razing so new structures could be built.

I have been in many Greek groceries since then and have often bought the   44
feta and Kalamata olives. I have eaten countless Greek salads and have indeed
found them a meal for the gods. On the holidays in our house, my wife and sons
and I sit down to a dinner of steaming, buttered pilaf like my mother used to
make and lemon-egg avgolemono and roast lamb richly seasoned with cloves of
garlic. I drink the red and yellow wines, and for dessert I have come to relish
the delicate pastries coated with honey and powdered sugar. Old Barba Nikos
would have been pleased.

But I have never been able to recapture the halcyon flavor of those figs he   45
gave me on that day so long ago, although I have bought figs many times. I have
found them pleasant to my tongue, but there is something missing. And to this
day I am not sure whether it was the figs or the vision and passion of the old
grocer that coated the fruit so sweetly I can still recall their savor and fragrance
after almost thirty years.

EXERCISES

Some of the Issues

1. Why do the gang members attack immigrants of their own ethnic group?
2. What is the first sign that the narrator will change his mind about his deed?
3. What is the boy's first reaction to the olives? How does it set the scene for later reactions?
4. What does Barba Nikos mean when he says, "a whole nation and a people are in this store"?
5. In what way do the last two paragraphs sum up the theme of the essay?

The Way We Are Told

6. In the first four paragraphs the author uses a number of rather unusual words and phrases for simple events: *motley, repast, untamed, bedevil, malevolence, to do battle*. What effect is achieved by this choice?
7. Contrast the tone of the narrative frame at the beginning and end of the selection with the telling of the story through dialog in the middle. What is the effect?
8. Examine the various references to Barba Nikos throughout the selection. What impression do we have of him in the beginning? How does it change?
9. List the various references linking food and drink to mythology. What is their purpose?

Some Subjects for Writing

10. Write an essay about a traditional family celebration that was important to you as a child. Describe in detail the rituals, ceremonies, and foods associated with it. Was symbolism involved? What meaning did the ceremony have for you in early life? Has that meaning changed as you have grown older?

In Ethnic America

MICHAEL NOVAK

Michael Novak, an American of Slovak descent, was born in Johnstown, Pennsylvania, in 1933 and has been a resident scholar at the American Enterprise Institute, a conservative think tank, since 1978. He holds honorary degrees from several universities. A prolific author, Novak's books include The American Vision *(1978),* The Spirit of Democratic Capitalism *(1982),* Moral Clarity in the Nuclear Age *(1983),* Freedom and Justice *(1984),* Character and Crime *(1986),* The Consensus on Family and Welfare *(1987), and* This Hemisphere of Liberty: A Philosophy of the Americas *(1992). Novak's writings examine the relationship between religion, politics, and economics.*

The selection included here is an excerpt from The Rise of the Unmeltable Ethnics *(1972), which was revised and reissued in 1996 as* Unmeltable Ethnics: Politics and Culture in American Life. *It is a spirited defense of the cultural roles of southern and eastern European immigrants to America. These immigrants, often referred to collectively as "ethnics," arrived in large numbers in the late nineteenth and early twentieth centuries. Mostly of peasant origin, they have been, Novak asserts, discriminated against in many ways. Yet, Novak claims, whereas other minorities who suffer from discrimination have aroused the sympathy and concern of many mainstream Americans, ethnics have been treated with neglect and often with scorn.*

Growing up in America has been an assault upon my sense of worthiness. It has also been a kind of liberation and delight. 1

There must be countless women in America who have known for years that something is peculiarly unfair, yet who only recently have found it possible, because of Women's Liberation, to give tongue to their pain. In recent months I have experienced a similar inner thaw, a gradual relaxation, a willingness to think about feelings heretofore shepherded out of sight. 2

I am born of PIGS—those Poles, Italians, Greeks, and Slavs, those non-English-speaking immigrants numbered so heavily among the workingmen of this nation. Not particularly liberal or radical; born into a history not white Anglo-Saxon and not Jewish; born outside what, in America, is considered the intellectual mainstream—and thus privy to neither power nor status nor intellectual voice. 3

4   Those Poles of Buffalo and Milwaukee—so notoriously taciturn, sullen, nearly speechless. Who has ever understood them? It is not that Poles do not feel emotion—what is their history if not dark passion, romanticism, betrayal, courage, blood? But where in America is there anywhere a language for voicing what a Christian Pole in this nation feels? He has no Polish culture left him, no Polish tongue. Yet Polish feelings do not go easily into the idiom of happy America, the America of the Anglo-Saxons and yes, in the arts, the Jews. (The Jews have long been a culture of the word, accustomed to exile, skilled in scholarship and in reflection. The Christian Poles are largely of peasant origin, free men for hardly more than a hundred years.) Of what shall the young man of Lackawanna think on his way to work in the mills, departing his relatively dreary home and street? What roots does he have? What language of the heart is available to him?

5   The PIGS are not silent willingly. The silence burns like hidden coals in the chest.

6   All four of my grandparents, unknown to one another, arrived in America from the same country in Slovakia. My grandfather had a small farm in Pennsylvania; his wife died in a wagon accident. Meanwhile, Johanna, fifteen, arrived on Ellis Island, dizzy from witnessing births and deaths and illnesses aboard the crowded ship. She had a sign around her neck lettered PASSAIC. There an aunt told her of a man who had lost his wife in Pennsylvania. She went. They were married. She inherited his three children.

7   Each year for five years Grandma had a child of her own. She was among the lucky; only one died. When she was twenty-two and the mother of seven (my father was the last), her husband died. "Grandma Novak," as I came to know her many years later, resumed the work she had begun in Slovakia at the town home of a man known to my father only as "the Professor"; she housecleaned and she laundered.

8   I heard this story only weeks ago. Strange that I had not asked insistently before. Odd that I should have such shallow knowledge of my roots. Amazing to me that I do not know what my family suffered, endured, learned, and hoped these last six or seven generations. It is as if there were no project in which we all have been involved, as if history in some way began with my father and with me.

9   The estrangement I have come to feel derives not only from lack of family history. Early in life, I was made to feel a slight uneasiness when I said my name. When I was very young, the "American" kids still made something out of names unlike their own, and their earnest, ambitious mothers thought long thoughts when I introduced myself.

10   Under challenge in grammar school concerning my nationality, I had been instructed by my father to announce proudly: "American." When my family moved from the Slovak ghetto of Johnstown to the WASP[1] suburb on the hill, my mother impressed upon us how well we must be dressed, and show good

[1]White Anglo-Saxon Protestant.

manners, and behave—people think of us as "different" and we mustn't give them any cause. "Whatever you do, marry a Slovak girl," was other advice to a similar end: "They cook. They clean. They take good care of you. For your own good." I was taught to be proud of being Slovak, but to recognize that others wouldn't know what it meant, or care.

Nowhere in my schooling do I recall any attempt to put me in touch with my   11
own history. The strategy was clearly to make an American of me. English literature, American literature, and even the history books, as I recall them, were peopled mainly by Anglo-Saxons from Boston (where most historians seemed to live). Not even my native Pennsylvania, let alone my Slovak forebears, counted for very many paragraphs. (We did have something called "Pennsylvania History" somewhere; I seem to remember its puffs for industry. It could have been written by a Mellon.[2]) I don't remember feeling envy or regret: a feeling, perhaps, of unimportance, of remoteness, of not having heft enough to count.

   The fact that I was born a Catholic also complicated life. What is a Catholic   12
but what everybody else is in reaction against? Protestants reformed "the whore of Babylon." Others were "enlightened" from it, and Jews had reason to help Catholicism and the social structure it was rooted in fall apart. The history books and the whole of education hummed in upon that point (for during crucial years I attended a public school): to be modern is decidedly not to be medieval; to be reasonable is not to be dogmatic; to be free is clearly not to live under ecclesiastical authority; to be scientific is not to attend ancient rituals, cherish irrational symbols, indulge in mythic practices. It is hard to grow up Catholic in America without becoming defensive, perhaps a little paranoid, feeling forced to divide the world between "us" and "them."

   We had a special language all our own, our own pronunciation for words   13
we shared in common with others (Augústine, contémplative), sights and sounds and smells in which few others participated (incense at Benediction of the Most Blessed Sacrament, Forty Hours, wakes, and altar bells at the silent consecration of the Host); and we had our own politics and slant on world affairs. Since earliest childhood, I have known about a "power elite" that runs America: the boys from the Ivy League in the State Department as opposed to the Catholic boys in Hoover's FBI who (as Daniel Moynihan once put it), keep watch on them. And on a whole host of issues, my people have been, though largely Democratic, conservative: on censorship, on communism, on abortion, on religious schools, etc. "Harvard" and "Yale" long meant "them" to us.

   We did not feel this country belonged to us. We felt fierce pride in it, more   14
loyalty than anyone could know. But we felt blocked at every turn. There were not many intellectuals among us, not even very many professional men. Laborers mostly. Small businessmen, agents for corporations perhaps. Content with a

[2]Famous Pittsburgh family of industrialists and financiers.

little, yes, modest in expectation, and content. But somehow feeling cheated. For a thousand years the Slovaks survived Hungarian hegemony and our strategy here remained the same: endurance and steady work. Slowly, one day, we would overcome.

15   A special word is required about a complicated symbol: sex. To this day my mother finds it hard to spell the word intact, preferring to write "s--." Not that much was made of sex in our environment. And that's the point: silence. Demonstrative affection, emotive dances, an exuberance Anglo-Saxons seldom seem to share; but on the realities of sex, discretion. Reverence, perhaps; seriousness, surely. On intimacies, it was as though our tongues had been stolen, as though in peasant life for a thousand years—as in the novels of Tolstoi, Sholokhov, and even Kosinski—the context had been otherwise. Passion, certainly; romance, yes; family and children, certainly; but sex rather a minor if explosive part of life.

16   Imagine, then, the conflict in the generation of my brothers, sister, and myself. Suddenly, what for a thousand years was minor becomes an all-absorbing investigation. Some view it as a drama of "liberation" when the ruling classes (subscribers to the *New Yorker,* I suppose) move progressively, generation by generation since Sigmund Freud, toward concentration upon genital stimulation, and latterly toward consciousness-raising sessions in Clit. Lib. But it is rather a different drama when we stumble suddenly upon mores staggering any expectation our grandparents ever cherished.

17   Yet more significant in the ethnic experience in America is the intellectual world one meets: the definition of values, ideas, and purposes emanating from universities, books, magazines, radio, and television. One hears one's own voice echoed back neither by spokesmen of "middle America" (so complacent, smug, nativist, and Protestant), nor by the "intellectuals." Almost unavoidably, perhaps, education in America leads the student who entrusts his soul to it in a direction which, lacking a better word, we might call liberal: respect for individual conscience, a sense of social responsibility, trust in the free exchange of ideas and procedures of dissent, a certain confidence in the ability of men to "reason together" and adjudicate their differences, a frank recognition of the vitality of the unconscious, a willingness to protect workers and the poor against the vast economic power of industrial corporations, and the like.

18   On the other hand, the liberal imagination has appeared to be astonishingly universalist and relentlessly missionary. Perhaps the metaphor "enlightenment" offers a key. One is *initiated into light.* Liberal education tends to separate children from their parents, from their roots, from their history, in the cause of a universal and superior religion.

19   In particular, I have regretted and keenly felt the absence of that sympathy for PIGS which simple human feeling might have prodded intelligence to muster, that same sympathy which the educated find so easy to conjure up for black culture, Chicano culture, Indian culture, and other cultures of the poor. In such

cases one finds the universalist pretensions of liberal culture suspended; some groups, at least, are entitled to be both different and respected. Why do the educated classes find it so difficult to want to understand the man who drives a beer truck, or the fellow with a helmet working on a site across the street with plumbers and electricians, while their sensitivities race easily to Mississippi or even Bedford-Stuyvesant?[3]

There are deep secrets here, no doubt, unvoiced fantasies and scarcely admitted historical resentments. Few persons in describing "middle Americans," "the silent majority," or Scammon and Wattenberg's "typical American voter" distinguish clearly enough between the nativist American and the ethnic American. The first is likely to be Protestant, the second Catholic. Both may be, in various ways, conservative, loyalist, and unenlightened. Each has his own agonies, fears, betrayed expectations. Neither is ready, quite, to become an ally of the other. Neither has the same history behind him here. Neither has the same hopes. Neither lives out the same psychic voyage, shares the same symbols, has the same sense of reality. The rhetoric and metaphors proper to each differ from those of the other.   20

There is overlap, of course. But country music is not a polka; a successful politician in a Chicago ward needs a very different "common touch" from the one needed by the county clerk in Normal.[4] The urban experience of immigration lacks that mellifluous, optimistic, biblical vision of the good America which springs naturally to the lips of politicians from the Bible Belt. The nativist tends to believe with Richard Nixon that he "knows America, and the American heart is good." The ethnic tends to believe that every American who preceded him has an angle, and that he, by God, will some day find one, too. (Often, ethnics complain that by working hard, obeying the law, trusting their political leaders, and relying upon the American dream, they now have only their own naiveté to blame for rising no higher than they have.)   21

Unfortunately, it seems, the ethnics erred in attempting to Americanize themselves before clearing the project with the educated classes. They learned to wave the flag and to send their sons to war. They learned to support their President—an easy task, after all, for those accustomed to obeying authority. And where would they have been if Franklin Roosevelt had not sided with them against established interests? They knew a little about communism—the radicals among them in one way, and by far the larger number of conservatives in another. To this day not a few exchange letters with cousins and uncles who did not leave for America when they might have, whose lot is demonstrably harder than their own and less than free.   22

Finally, the ethnics do not like, or trust, or even understand the intellectuals. It is not easy to feel uncomplicated affection for those who call you "pig," "fas-   23

[3]Low-income, predominantly African-American neighborhood in Brooklyn, NY.
[4]A small town in central Illinois.

cist," "racist." One had not yet grown accustomed to not hearing "hunkie," "Polack," "spic," "mick," "dago," and the rest.

24   At no little sacrifice, one had apologized for foods that smelled too strong for Anglo-Saxon noses; moderated the wide swings of Slavic and Italian emotion; learned decorum; given oneself to education, American style; tried to learn tolerance and assimilation. Each generation criticized the earlier for its authoritarian and European and old-fashioned ways. "Up-to-date" was a moral lever. And now when the process nears completion, when a generation appears that speaks without accent and goes to college, still you are considered "pigs," "fascists," and "racists." Racists? Our ancestors owned no slaves. Most of us ceased being serfs only in the last two hundred years—the Russians in 1861....

25   Whereas the Anglo-Saxon model appears to be a system of atomic individuals and high mobility, our model has tended to stress communities of our own, attachment to family and relatives, stability, and roots. Ethnics tend to have a fierce sense of attachment to their homes, having been homeowners for less than three generations: a home is almost fulfillment enough for one man's life. Some groups save arduously in a passion to *own*; others rent. We have most ambivalent feelings about suburban assimilation and mobility. The melting pot is a kind of homogenized soup, and its mores only partly appeal to ethnics: to some, yes, and to others, no.

26   It must be said that ethnics think they are better people than the blacks. Smarter, tougher, harder working, stronger in their families. But maybe many are not sure. Maybe many are uneasy. Emotions here are delicate; one can understand the immensely more difficult circumstances under which the blacks have suffered; and one is not unaware of peculiar forms of fear, envy, and suspicion across color lines. How much of this we learned in America by being made conscious of our olive skin, brawny backs, accents, names, and cultural quirks is not plain to us. Racism is not our invention; we did not bring it with us; we had prejudices enough and would gladly have been spared new ones. Especially regarding people who suffer more than we.

EXERCISES

Some of the Issues

1. What aspects of his own background does Novak single out? How do they relate to his opening statement?
2. Novak refers to his background in paragraph 3 and returns to his family history in paragraphs 6 through 8. What is his reason for inserting paragraphs 4 and 5 in between?
3. How does Novak's family history reflect the silence of the ethnics to which he refers?

4. In paragraph 14 Novak says, "We did not feel this country belonged to us." What has he said in the preceding part of the essay to substantiate that assertion?

5. Show the points Novak makes to contrast the ethnic and liberal outlooks on life in America.

6. What reasons does Novak give for the liberal, intellectual sympathy for African Americans, Chicanos, or Native Americans, but not for ethnics?

The Way We Are Told

7. Why does Novak make the analogy between the women's movement and his own "inner thaw" (paragraph 2)?

8. In paragraphs 4 and 5 Novak uses emotional terms to characterize ethnics. Find some of them, and then contrast them to the language of paragraphs 6 and 7. Can you explain the reasons for the difference between the two sets of paragraphs?

9. In paragraph 10 Novak refers to his people as "different." Different from whom? How does he show that difference? What do his comments imply about Americans?

10. On a few occasions Novak uses sarcasm, or satirizes the people he considers anti-ethnic, the "them" at the end of paragraph 12. Find some examples of satiric statements.

11. Look at the last sentence of paragraph 14. Do you hear any echoes?

Some Subjects for Writing

12. This essay was first published in 1972, but was republished, with only minor changes, in a second edition in 1996. Do you believe that Novak has taken into account changes in American life since 1972? Why or why not? Explain.

13. Novak considers himself to be a member of a forgotten minority, without the self-recognition or recognition by others that more established minority groups have. Consider his claim. Do you believe it is justified? Why or why not?

14. Novak's essay emphasizes social class as an important factor in the power that different groups have to influence American life. If all racial and ethnic discrimination and discrimination against women were to disappear, how important would discrimination based on social class still be? Write an essay explaining your views.

Amérka, Amérka:
A Palestinian Abroad
in the Land of the Free

ANTON SHAMMAS

Anton Shammas is a Palestinian born in Israel in 1950. He attended Hebrew University and came to the United States in 1987 as a Rockefeller Fellow at the University of Michigan. He is the author of the novel Arabesques *(1989) and has published numerous essays. Shammas teaches in the Department of Near Eastern Studies at the University of Michigan.*

Historic Palestine, on the eastern coast of the Mediterranean, is sacred land to three major religions—Judaism, Christianity, and Islam—and, throughout history, ownership of this land has been often and bitterly contested. After the Second World War, the part of Palestine known as the West Bank was administered by Jordan and known as West Jordan. Since the Israeli victory in the war of 1967, it has been occupied by Israel. The majority of inhabitants of the West Bank are Palestinian Arabs, though there are Israeli settlements in several communities.

In 1988, Jordan, under King Hussein, relinquished all of its claims to the Palestine Liberation Organization (PLO), which proclaimed a Palestinian state. In 1993, Israel and the PLO signed a peace agreement calling for the withdrawal of Israeli troops from areas of the West Bank.

In this essay published in Harper's *magazine in 1991, Shammas speaks of Arab immigrants who, although physically separated from their home in the Middle East, carry with them the spiritual and cultural heritage of their "lost Palestine."*

1   Some years ago, in San Francisco, I heard the following tale from a young, American-educated Palestinian engineer. We had found a rustic, trendy place and managed to find a quiet table. Over lukewarm beers, rather than small cups of lukewarm cardamomed coffee, we talked about his family, which had wandered adrift in the Arab world for some time before finding its moorings on the

West Coast, and in particular of a relative of his living to the south of San Francisco whom we were planning to visit the following day. We never did make that visit—that is a story, too—but the story about this man has fluttered inside my head ever since.

We will call him Abu-Khalil. Imagine him as a fortysomething Palestinian (he is now past sixty) whose West Bank homeland was, once again in his lifetime, caving in on him in June 1967 after what the Arabs call the Defeat of Hazieran 5 and the Israelis and Americans call the Six-Day War.[1] Where was he to spend the occupation years of his life? Where could he get as far away from the Israeli "benign" presence as his captive mind could go? The choices were essentially two: He could cross the Allenby Bridge to His Majesty's Jordan,[2] or he could take an unhijackable flight west, from Ben-Gurion Airport. He chose the latter, a plane that would carry him to the faraway U.S.A.—to those members of his large family (Arabs always seem to have *large* families) who had discovered the New World centuries after Columbus. (They had discovered the New World, as they would tell him later, in a sort of belated westbound revenge for the eastbound expulsion of their great ancestors from Andalusia/Spain the same year that Columbus's Spanish ships arrived on the shores of his imaginary India.)

To continue our tale: Abu-Khalil lands in San Francisco one warm September afternoon, clad in a heavy black coat that does not astonish his waiting relatives a bit, since they are familiar with the man's eccentricities. But what about the security guys at Ben-Gurion Airport? Didn't the out-of-season coat merit suspicion and a frisking? Apparently not. Abu-Khalil is, as far as I can tell, the only Palestinian to have seeped out through the thick security screenings at Ben-Gurion Airport—née Lydda—unsearched. How else to account for the fact that he had managed to carry on board with him a veritable Little Palestine—flora, fauna, and all?

His bags were heavy with small plants and seeds that went undetected by Israeli security. (It should be said, of course, that flora poised to explode is not what they look for in a Palestinian's luggage at Ben-Gurion Airport.) As for U.S. Customs Form 6059B, which inbound foreigners are graciously asked to fill out before they land—it prohibits passengers from importing "fruits, vegetables, plants, plant products, soil, meats, meat products, birds, snails, and other live animals and animal products"—our passenger, to the best of the storyteller's authorial knowledge (and mine), could not read English, and no American officer, lawful or otherwise, bothered to verify his declarations—albeit not made—through questioning, much less through physical search, these being two procedures that Palestinians are much accustomed to in their comings and goings in the Middle East.

---

[1]Two names (Arab and Israeli, respectively) for the armed conflict between Israel, Jordan, Syria, and Egypt in June of 1967.
[2]The West Bank had been administered by the neighboring country of Jordan under its king, Hussein, from 1949 until Israeli victory in 1967.

5   So that's how Abu-Khalil managed to bring to California some representative plants of Palestine, many still rooted in their original, fecund soil. It seems, however, that he took pride mainly—think of it as a feather in his kaffiyeh[3]—in his having managed to smuggle out of the West Bank, through Israel, and into the United States seven representative birds of his homeland. The duri, the hassoun, the sununu, the shahrur, the bulbul, the summan, and the hudhud, small-talk companion to King Solomon himself—they all surrounded him now in California, re-chirping Palestine away in his ears from inside their unlocked American cages. "They will not leave their open cages," Abu-Khalil would say, or so the story went, "till I leave mine."

6   Abu-Khalil's was a cage of his own making; he has not left it to this very day. But I was mainly interested in the birds, in their mute, wondrous migration. In the years that followed, I asked the storyteller, did they forget their mother chirp? Did they eventually adopt the mellow sounds of California? And how, I asked, did he manage to smuggle in these birds in the first place? "Well," said my friend, "he had a coat of many pockets, you see."

7   I found the story hard to believe at the time; but one has to trust the storyteller, even a Palestinian. After all, where else could the birds of Palestine go "after the last sky," in the words of the poet Mahmoud Darwish, but to the Land of the Free.

8   My storyteller and I belong to a different generation from Abu-Khalil's. We, and others like us, are too young to think of smuggling roots and soil, though not young enough to forget all about the birds we left behind. We travel light, empty-pocketed, with the vanity of those who think home is a portable idea, something that dwells mainly in the mind or within a text. Celebrating the modern powers of imagination and of fiction, we have lost faith in our old idols—memory, storytelling. We are not even sure anymore whether there ever was a home out there, a territory, a homeland. We owe allegiance to no memory; and we have adopted as our anthem Derek Walcott's perhaps too-often-quoted line: "I had no nation now but the imagination." Our language, Arabic, was de-territorialized by another, and only later did we realize that Arabic does not even have a word for "territory." The act of de-territorialization, then, took place outside our language, so we could not talk, much less write, about our plight in our mother tongue. Now we need the language of the Other for that, the language that can categorize the new reality and sort it out for us in upper and lower cases; the language that can re-territorialize us, as imaginary as that might be, giving us some allegedly solid ground. It is English for my San Francisco storyteller-friend, French for others, Hebrew for me: the unlocked cages of our own choices. In short, we are Palestine's post-Abu-Khalilians, if you like.

[3]Arab headdress.

Many Middle Eastern Abu-Khalils have immigrated to the U.S.A. over the   9
years, driven out of their respective homelands by wars, greedy foreigners, and
pangs of poverty. At the turn of the century, when the Ottomans—who had been
ruling the Middle East since 1517—were practicing some refined forms of their
famine policy, Arabs left their homes and families and sailed to the Americas.
Brazil and Argentina had their charm; Michigan, too. Today, Michigan is home
to the largest Arab-American community in North America. If you were to take
a stroll through the streets of Dearborn, a south-by-southwest suburb of
Detroit, the signs and names might remind you of some ancient legend.

Bereft of names and deeds, these Arabs came to Michigan to make names   10
for themselves as a twentieth-century self-mocking variation on the old Mesopotamian tradition of the *shuma shakanu*, the preservation of one's name and
deeds. That also was the original aim of those who followed Nimrod the Hunter
in his biblical endeavor to reach heaven and said, "Let us make us a name for
ourselves" (Gen. 11:4). An American heaven of sorts and, in this case, an American name; no concealed Nimrods.

Hoping for a happier ending than the biblical one, they have come from   11
places whose names Mark Twain, the great American nomenclator, traveling
with "the innocents abroad" some 123 years ago, found impossible to pronounce. "One of the great drawbacks to this country," he wrote in September
1867, from Palestine, "is its distressing names that nobody can get the hang
of.... You may make a stagger of pronouncing these names, but they will bring
any Christian to grief that tries to spell them. I have an idea that if I can only
simplify the nomenclature of this country, it will be of the greatest service to
Americans who may travel here in the future."

This may account for the notorious Hollywood tradition, many years after   12
tongue-in-cheek Twain, of assuming that all men Middle Eastern—if fortunate
enough to actually have names of their own in the films—should be called
Abdul. (In fact, Abdul is but the first half of a common Middle Eastern compound.) So all these anonymous Abduls are here now, trying, so far away from
home, to complete their names, in a new world that has been practicing the
renaming of things now for five centuries and counting.

* * * * *

From Fassuta, my small village in the Galilee,[4] émigrés went mainly to Brazil   13
and Argentina. My grandfather and his brothers and brother-in-law left for
Argentina in 1896, only to return home, empty-handed, a year later. Then, on
the eve of the First World War, my grandfather tried his luck again, this time
on his own, heading once more to Argentina (at least that's what he told my
grandmother the night before he took off), where he vanished for about ten
years, leaving behind three daughters and three sons, all of them hungry. His

[4]Region in what is now Northern Israel, on the border of Syria.

youngest son, my uncle Jiryes, followed in his footsteps in 1928, leaving his wife and child behind, never to come back.

14   One of my childhood heroes, an old villager whom we, the children of Fassuta, always blamed for having invented school, had actually been to Salt Lake City. I don't have the foggiest idea what he did there for three years before the Depression; his deeds remain a sealed and, I suspect, quite salty book, but he certainly did not betray the Catholic faith, no sir. I still remember him in the late 1950s, breathing down my neck during Mass at the village's church. He used to wear impeccable white American shirts under his Arab *abaya*,[5] even some thirty years after he had returned to the village. But that was the only American fingerprint on him; the rest was Middle Eastern.

15   The most famous American immigrant from my village, though, was M., my aunt Najeebeh's brother-in-law, Najeebeh being my father's sister. I hate to be finicky about the exact relationship, but that is simply the way it is in Arabic: There are different words to refer to the father's and the mother's side of the family. At any rate, M. left the village in the early 1920s and came back to visit his brothers some forty years later, with his non-Arabic-speaking sons. As a matter of fact, he was the only one of a long, winding line of immigrants who had really made it, or "had it fixed," as the Galileans would say. He came to own a chain of fast-food restaurants, quite famous in the Midwest. Before I myself left the Mideast for these parts, I went to see his nephews—my cousins—in the village and promised them, under oath, that I would certainly look M. up one day and introduce myself, or at least pop into one of his restaurants and, naturally, ask for a free meal. I have not yet done the former and am still keeping the latter for a rainy Michigan day. However, whenever I come across his chain's emblem, a plump plastic boy holding a plate high above his plumply combed head, I remember my late aunt Najeebeh and think how disconcerted she would be had she known what kind of a mnemonic-device-in-the-form-of-a-cultural-shock she had become for her nephew, in faraway Amérka, as it is called in my part of the world.

16   Upon first arriving in Amérka, one of my first cultural shocks was the otherwise trivial American fact that shirts had not only a neck size but also a sleeve size. Fassuta's Salt Lake City visitor and I, we both come from a culture where, insofar as shirts are concerned, one's arm length doesn't matter much. People in the Middle East are still immersed in figuring out the length of their postcolonial borders, personal and otherwise, and all indications show that a long time will elapse before they start paying attention to the lonely business of their sleeve size.

17   Which may or may not have something to do with the fact that in a culture with an oral background of storytelling, where choices continue, even in postcolonial times, to be made for you (be they by God, fate, nature, or the ruler),

[5]A cloak.

you don't enjoy the luxuries of the novel's world, where characters make their own choices and have to live, subsequently, with the consequences, sleeve size and all. The storyteller's world revolves around memory; the novelist's, around imagination. And what people in places like the Middle East are struggling to do, I think, is to shrug off the bondage of their memory and decolonize their imagination. So, in this regard, for a Middle Easterner to have a sleeve size would be a sign of such a decolonization.

My first stroll ever on American soil took place in a park along the Iowa River, in Iowa City. I was thirty years old, and there were so many things I had not seen before. On that day I saw my first squirrel. There are many jittery, frail creatures in the Middle East, but, to the best of my zoological knowledge, there are no squirrels. However, people do talk of the *sinjabi,* the squirrelish color. I remember thinking, during my walk, that if there were no squirrels in the Middle East, how come the Arabs use the word *sinjabi?* 18

Not long after the day I took my walk, I found out, as I had expected, that there were *sinjabs* in Iran and that the word *sinjabi* was derived from the Persian, a language that had given Arabic, long before the Koran, so many beautiful words. Some 1,300 years later, at the very time of my stay in Iowa, the Ayatollah Khomeini[6] was busy squirreling away some ideas about a new order, about the Mesopotamian tradition of the *shuma shakanu.* A half-world away, Salman Rushdie[7] was, apparently, squirreling away some counter-ideas of his own. It was not hard to imagine, later, who would play the Crackers, and who—or on whose—Nuts. 19

My Galilean friend J., not to be confused with the biblical author, came to America some sixteen years ago. We'd met at the Hebrew University in Jerusalem, in the early Seventies. He was my instructor in the Introduction to Arabic literature course, and I'm still indebted to him for teaching me the first steps of academic research and, most importantly, for being so decent a friend as to have unabashedly explained to me how I would never have the proper discipline. 20

At that time he was mulling over the idea that he should perhaps come to this country to work on a Ph.D. in modern Arabic literature. Once he had made up his mind, he started frantically looking for a wife with whom to share the burden of American self-exile. I asked him once whether it wouldn't be wiser to find himself an already naturalized American lady, to which he replied: "I'm looking for a woman that when I put my weary head against her arm, I want to hear her blood murmuring in Arabic." He did eventually find one, and they both immigrated to Amérka and have been happily listening to each other's blood ever since. 21

[6](1900–1989) Shiite muslim religious leader who had a powerful influence in Iran, especially after it became an Islamic republic in 1979.
[7](1947–) Indian-born British novelist whose book *The Satanic Verses* (1988) enraged many Muslims, including the Ayatollah Khomeini, who called for his death.

22   J. was looking for the blood tongue, for the primordial language, wherein the names of things, long before the confusion of tongues, were so deeply lodged in the things they designated that no human eye could decipher the sign. Had he been a Cabalist, he would have believed that what God introduced into the world was written words, not murmurings of blood. But J. came from the oral Middle East to the literate West, and he knew upon arriving in Amérka that he would be expected to trade in his mother tongue and keep the secret language circulating only in his veins.

23   I saw the already "naturalized" J. again, in Jerusalem, some ten years after he'd left. At the end of a very long night of catching up, he picked up a Hebrew literary magazine from my desk and browsed through it. Something caught his eye; he paused for a moment. "What is *this* doing here?" "This" turned out to be an ad for a famous Israeli brand of women's underwear. I wasn't sure what he meant. It was a full-page ad, an exact replica of the famous photograph of Marilyn Monroe standing on a grate in the street, her dress blowing above her waist. "You know what the reference is to, right?" I asked. No, he did not. And I thought, How could a bright guy like J. live for so long in the U.S.A., be an *American citizen*, and not be familiar with what I thought were the basics of American iconography?

24   I had been settled for a year in Ann Arbor when I went to visit J. and his wife in Ohio. Having just returned from a short visit to our Galilee home, I brought J., who has a green thumb, what he had asked me to: some local lubia peas for his thriving backyard garden. We were reminiscing late at night, with Fayruz, the famous Lebanese singer, on the stereo in the background and some Middle Eastern munchies on the coffee table, when I suddenly remembered that night in Jerusalem years before and the ad with the Marilyn knockoff. It would be nice if you did recognize the American icon, I thought to myself, but it is nice too that you can live in this country for decades without being forced to go native. You can always pick up your own fold of the huge map and chart yourself into it.

25   Now it is my fourth year in Ann Arbor. I moved in early in September of 1987, and for three months my relationship with the squirrels outside my window was quite good. "Quite good," as my English professor at the Hebrew University in Jerusalem used to say, means "yes, good, but there's no need to be so excited about it." So I was developing an unexciting relationship with these creatures, especially with one of them, whom I told myself I was able to tell from the others, although they all did look alike, if I may say so without prejudice. Anyway, I would open the door early in the morning to pick up the *New York Times* from the doorstep, and he would be goofing around its blue, transparent wrap (that's how the paper is home-delivered in Michigan), unalarmed by my invasion of *his* kingdom.

26   But one morning, as I reached down for the paper, he froze, all of a sudden, in the middle of one of his silly gesticulations, gaping at me in utter terror, and

then fled away as if I were about to—well, throw a stone at him. Maybe it was a morning in December 1987, and he had peeked at the *Times.* Maybe I will never cease to look east for my images and metaphors.

For J., for my friend in San Francisco, for me, the Old World will never   27
cease to hold us hostage in this way. Sometimes I think that no matter how deep I have traveled *into* the American life, I still carry my own miniature Abu-Khalils in my pockets and a miniature Middle East in my mind. There is little space for Amérka in the most private of my maps.

And speaking of maps, how many adult Americans know where the "heart-   28
broken piece of territory" Mark Twain was talking about actually is?

Still, would it matter if they did?   29

I don't think it would. After all, modern colonialism (sometimes euphemis-   30
tically referred to as "our American interests"), unlike its old-fashioned, European counterpart, is not geographically oriented. Geographical literacy is defunct; its demise was caused by the invention of the remote control. And if you happen to live in this vast country, your sense of geography is necessarily numbed by what Aldous Huxley would have called one's "local validity." Paradoxically, the vastness of the land provides Americans with a continental alibi. A look at the map of the U.S.A. from, say, a Palestinian point of view would psychologically suffice to make a clear-cut distinction between the American people and their government's policy. Unlike England, for instance, where every Brit seems to be living in London and has something or another to do with the business of running the rather rusty machinery of a worn-out colonialism, there is an utter distinction when it comes to the United States between the Americans on Capitol Hill and the *real* Americans who, on a good day, want absolutely nothing to do with Washington's follies.

Maybe that's why Abu-Khalil can feel at home in California, surrounded by   31
the artifacts of his lost Palestine. This country is *big;* it has enough room not only for the newcomers but also for their portable homelands. Among other achievements, Amérka has made homesickness obsolete.

EXERCISES

Some of the Issues

1. What is the significance of Abu-Khalil's smuggling seven birds out of Palestine to the United States? What do these birds represent?
2. How is Shammas's concept of home different from Abu-Khalil's? What historical events have shaped younger Arabs' views?
3. Explain what Shammas means by "unlocked cages of our own choices" in paragraph 8.

4. How does Shammas distinguish the storyteller from the novelist in paragraphs 8 and 17?
5. In paragraph 17, Shammas asserts that many Middle Easterners are struggling to cast off "the bondage of their memory and decolonize their imagination." What are the political implications of this statement?
6. Shammas's friend J. married an Arab woman before coming to America. Why is it important for him to keep "the secret language circulating only in his veins" (paragraph 22)?
7. In paragraph 23, what is the source of his friend J.'s confusion over the underwear ad in the Hebrew literary magazine? How does his friend's ignorance strike Shammas?
8. How do you understand the last line, "Amérka has made homesickness obsolete?"

The Way We Are Told

9. How does the squirrel metaphor in paragraphs 18 and 19 and 25–27 relate to the Middle Eastern experience?
10. Shammas uses part of Mark Twain's description of Palestine as that "most hopeless, dreary, heartbroken piece of territory out of Arizona" to underscore the fact that many Americans are geographically illiterate. He cites this American characteristic as a possible advantage. Why?
11. Find several examples of the author's humorous or sarcastic tone.
12. In paragraph 23, why is the word *naturalized* in quotation marks?

Some Subjects for Writing

13. If you were forced to leave home, what objects would you take with you? Write an essay in which you describe the objects and explain your choices.
14. "…Home is a portable idea, something that dwells mainly in the mind or within a text" (paragraph 8). In an essay, consider what home means to you and develop a personal definition of "home." Illustrate your idea with your experience and, if appropriate, the experiences of various authors in the text.

Three Thousand Dollar Death Song

WENDY ROSE

Wendy Rose, of Hopi and Miwok ancestry, was born in Oakland, California, in 1948. She received B.A. and M.A. degrees from the University of California at Berkeley. A visual artist, poet, and anthropologist, she is a frequent contributor of articles to anthologies and journals. She has published several volumes of poetry, including Going to War with All My Relations *(1993),* Bone Dance *(1994), and* Now Poof She Is Gone *(1994). Rose writes of herself, "I have often been identified as a 'protest poet' and although something in me frowns a little at being so neatly categorized, that is largely the truth."*

In the following poem, taken from Lost Copper *(1980), Rose examines the cost incurred, both material and spiritual, when museums collect and display Native American mummies, skeletons, artifacts, and sacred objects. For many of Native American ancestry, the exhibiting of these remains is a continued source of pain and disrespect. In recent years, Native activists and other groups have demanded that museums return bones for reburial; in 1990 a federal law took effect requiring the return of these items to the tribe or association.*

> *"Nineteen American Indian Skeletons from Nevada…valued at $3,000…"*
> —Museum invoice, 1975

Is it in cold hard cash? the kind
that dusts the insides of mens' pockets
lying silver-polished surface along the cloth.
Or in bills? papering the wallets of they
who thread the night with dark words. Or   5
checks? paper promises weighing the same
as words spoken once on the other side
of the grown grass and dammed rivers
of history. However it goes, it goes.
Through my body it goes   10
assessing each nerve, running its edges
along my arteries, planning ahead

for whose hands will rip me
into pieces of dusty red paper,
15 whose hands will smooth or smatter me
into traces of rubble. Invoiced now,
it's official how our bones are valued
that stretch out pointing to sunrise
or are flexed into one last foetal bend,
20 that are removed and tossed about,
catalogued, numbered with black ink
on newly-white foreheads.
As we were formed to the white soldier's voice,
so we explode under white students' hands.
25 Death is a long trail of days
in our fleshless prison.

From this distant point we watch our bones
auctioned with our careful beadwork,
our quilled medicine bundles, even the bridles
30 of our shot-down horses. You: who have
priced us, you who have removed us: at what cost?
What price the pits where our bones share
a single bit of memory, how one century
turns our dead into specimens, our history
35 into dust, our survivors into clowns.
Our memory might be catching, you know;
picture the mortars, the arrowheads, the labrets[1]
shaking off their labels like bears
suddenly awake to find the seasons have ended
40 while they slept. Watch them touch each other,
measure reality, march out the museum door!
Watch as they lift their faces
and smell about for us; watch our bones rise
to meet them and mount the horses once again!
45 The cost, then, will be paid
for our sweetgrass-smelling having-been
in clam shell beads and steatite,
dentalia[2] and woodpecker scalp, turquoise
and copper, blood and oil, coal
50 and uranium, children, a universe
of stolen things.

[1]*Labrets* are ornaments of wood or bone worn in a hole pierced through the lip.
[2]*Dentalia* refers to any marine mollusk resembling a tooth.

EXERCISES

Some of the Issues

1. How does Rose contrast the value of the skeletons to Native Americans with their value to others?
2. How does Rose describe the museum's physical treatment of Native American skeletons and cultural artifacts? How is that treatment symbolic of the treatment of Native American people?
3. Beginning in line 36, Rose describes a fantasy in which the bones will rise. What does she imagine them doing?
4. The word "cost" occurs several times in the poem. How does its meaning change throughout the poem?
5. Look at the list of "stolen things" at the end of the poem. In what order are items placed? Why?
6. How might museum officials justify a display of Native American skeletons and traditional art on the basis of its educational value?

Some Subjects for Writing

7. Write about an object that has meaning to you aside from its monetary value. What is its history and what makes it valuable to you?
*8. In "On Seeing England for the First Time," Jamaica Kincaid writes of being immersed in the culture of a colonial power while her own culture was ignored. Consider the case of a Native American child growing up in America. Would that child's experience be similar or dissimilar to Kincaid's? In what ways?

3

Families

The American family we used to consider the norm in the postwar generation of the 1940s and 1950s is now the minority. The traditional family in which children grow up in the same household with two biological parents who are married to each other is being replaced by an array of differently formed families. The selections in Part Three examine the lives of children in traditional families, the changing definition of family structures, and the notion of the "perfect" family.

What holds a family together? Child-parent relationships, particularly the expectations parents have for children, are explored in "Don't Expect Me to Be Perfect" by Sun Park, a 16-year-old Korean-American. Jane Howard in "Families," gives 10 characteristics she believes all "good" families must have. Her definition of family includes nontraditional families such as families based on friendship. Deb Price, in "Gay Partners Need to Make a Name for Themselves," explores the question of what name to call Joyce, the woman she shares her life with.

In "Choosing a Mate," Ruth Breen tells the story of her own marriage, arranged by her parents. She compares arranged marriages to "love" marriages and concludes that they are equally likely to succeed. Alfred Kazin recounts the story of his eastern European immigrant family living in the tenements of New York City early in the twentieth century. His family is held together by the ceaseless work and worry of his mother.

Arlene Skolnick's essay "The Paradox of Perfection" helps us to consider the family in the light of its historical development. As Skolnick reveals, the "traditional" family has actually not been the norm for society except in fairly recent times, and then only in some cultures. Finally, in a short poem by Theodore Roethke, we get a brief glimpse of a child's memory of his father, a memory filled with mixed emotions.

THINKING ABOUT THE THEME *"Families"*

1. If you saw the three people in the photograph on the street, what would you assume their relationship was? What specific aspects of the photo (gesture, physical appearance, facial expression) influenced your response?

2. Our culture presents us with many images of the "perfect" family. How are these images powerful? Are they dangerous, or do they present us with necessary models?

3. What roles does society assign to fathers and mothers in raising children? Do you agree with these roles? Why or why not?

4. What are some ways in which governments define family; for example, by laws about marriage, divorce, adoption or custody of children, or laws that affect financial decisions such as the sharing of benefits and pensions. Consider the definitions of family—governmental, religious, social—in the society that you know best. To what extent does your own definition of family correspond or differ?

Don't Expect Me to Be Perfect

SUN PARK

This essay first appeared in a 1990 special edition of Newsweek *for teenagers. Sun Park writes about some of the problems she and others face in trying to meet parental expectations.*

I am a 16-year-old Korean-American. My family has been in the United States for six years now. I'll be a junior next fall.

When I first came to the States, it took two years before I could speak English fluently. By the time I started middle school, I realized that most of my fellow students had never met many kids like me before. They had this idea, probably from TV and movies, that all Asians are nerds and all Asians are smart. It's true that some are. I know many smart people. But what about those Asians who aren't so smart? Having a reputation for brains is nice, I guess, but it can also be a pain. For instance, sometimes when my classmates do not know something, they come to me for the answer. Often I can help them. But when I can't, they get these weird expressions on their faces. If I were a genius, I would not mind being treated like one. But since I am not, I do.

The problem isn't just limited to the classroom. My mother and father expect an awful lot from me, too. Like so many Korean parents, and many ambitious American parents, they're very competitive and can't help comparing me with other kids. Mine always say to me, "So and so is smart, works so hard and is so good to his or her parents. Why can't you be more like him or her?" Because I am the oldest kid in my family, they expect me to set a good example for my younger sisters and relatives. They'd rather I concentrate on schoolwork than dating. They want me to be No. 1.

Most of the time I want to do well, too. I'm glad I take all honors classes. But now that I am at those levels, I have to be on my toes to keep doing well. The better I do, the more pressure I seem to place on myself. Because my parents want me to be perfect—or close to perfect—I find myself turning into a perfectionist. When I do a project and make one little error, I can't stand it. Sometimes I stay up as late as 2 A.M. doing homework.

I don't think I would be like this if my parents weren't motivating me. But I don't think they know what pressure can do to a teenager. It's not that they put me down or anything. They have plenty of faith in me. But to tell the truth, sometimes I really like to be lazy, and it would be nice just to take it easy and not worry so much about my grades all the time. Maybe my parents know this. Maybe that's why they encourage me to be better. Well, it still drives me crazy when they compare me with others. I wonder if those smart kids have parents like mine.

6   Sure, I'm proud of who I am, and I love my parents very much. But then there are times I just feel like taking a break and going far away from parents and teachers. Of course that's impossible, but it's always nice to dream about it.

Some of the Issues

1. What image of Asians do most of Park's classmates have? How does this image affect her relationships with other students?
2. How does she react to her parents' wishes that she achieve high marks?
3. What are some of the manifestations of her "perfectionism"? Do you think there is anything wrong with this behavior?
4. What is the author's attitude toward her parents? How do you know?

The Way We Are Told

5. Sun Park opens her essay with a short description of herself. Why might this be an effective way to begin?
6. How would you describe the tone of this essay? How does the author's audience affect her tone? Find specific phrases and words from the text to illustrate your answer.
7. What do you think is the author's purpose in writing this essay? What lines best express it?

Some Subjects for Writing

8. Do you know any perfectionists? Describe their behavior and characteristics. What is your own attitude toward perfectionism?
9. Sun Park wonders if other "smart kids have parents like mine." Have you ever felt this way? From your own school experiences, have you noticed any connection between academic achievement and parental involvement?
10. What were the attitudes in your household toward personal achievement? Were they stated explicitly or were they implicit? What was the attitude toward failure and how was failure defined?
11. Park dreams of "going far away from parents and teachers" as a solution to her problem. Have you ever had these feelings? Can you think of better options?

12. Read "The Media's Image of Arabs," in which Jack G. Shaheen enumerates the negative images of Arabs in the American media. Park believes that Asians are also depicted as stereotypes, yet with images that many would view as positive—intelligent and hard-working. Is one stereotype less damaging than another?

Families

JANE HOWARD

Jane Howard, born in Springfield, Illinois in 1935, is a reporter, editor, and writer. Among her books are Please Touch: A Guided Tour of the Human Potential Movement *(1970), the autobiographical* A Different Woman *(1973), and* Families *(1978). Her latest book is* Margaret Mead: A Life *(1984). She has taught at several universities.*

Howard explains 10 characteristics good families should have. Her definition of a family includes not only the one you are born into but also those you may develop through close friendships.

1   Each of us is born into one family not of our choosing. If we're going to go around devising new ones, we might as well have the luxury of picking their members ourselves. Clever picking might result in new families whose benefits would surpass or at least equal those of the old. The new ones by definition cannot spawn us—as soon as they do that, they stop being new—but there is plenty they can do. I have seen them work wonders. As a member in reasonable standing of six or seven tribes in addition to the one I was born to, I have been trying to figure which earmarks are common to both kinds of families.

2   (1) Good families have a chief, or a heroine, or a founder—someone around whom others cluster, whose achievements as the Yiddish word has it, let them *kvell,*[1] and whose example spurs them on to like feats. Some blood dynasties produce such figures regularly; others languish for as many as five generations between demigods, wondering with each new pregnancy whether this, at last, might be the messianic baby who will redeem us. Look, is there not something gubernatorial about her footstep, or musical about the way he bangs with his spoon on his cup? All clans, of all kinds, need such a figure now and then. Sometimes clans based on water rather than blood harbor several such personages at one time. The Bloomsbury Group[2] in London six decades ago was not much hampered by its lack of a temporal history.

3   (2) Good families have a switchboard operator—someone like my mother who cannot help but keep track of what all the others are up to, who plays Houston Mission Control to everyone else's Apollo. This role, like the foregoing one,

---

[1]To boast or gloat over accomplishments.
[2]Group of prominent London intellectuals, writers, and artists of the first quarter of the twentieth century.

is assumed rather than assigned. Someone always volunteers for it. That person often also has the instincts of an archivist, and feels driven to keep scrapbooks and photograph albums up to date, so that the clan can see proof of its own continuity.

(3) Good families are much to all their members, but everything to none. Good families are fortresses with many windows and doors to the outer world. The blood clans I feel most drawn to were founded by parents who are nearly as devoted to whatever it is they do outside as they are to each other and their children. Their curiosity and passion are contagious. Everybody, where they live, is busy. Paint is spattered on eyeglasses. Mud lurks under fingernails. Person-to-person calls come in the middle of the night from Tokyo and Brussels. Catchers' mitts, ballet slippers, overdue library books and other signs of extrafamilial concerns are everywhere.

(4) Good families are hospitable. Knowing that hosts need guests as much as guests need hosts, they are generous with honorary memberships for friends, whom they urge to come early and often and to stay late. Such clans exude a vivid sense of surrounding rings of relatives, neighbors, teachers, students and godparents, any of whom at any time might break or slide into the inner circle. Inside that circle a wholesome, tacit emotional feudalism develops: you give me protection, I'll give you fealty. Such treaties begin with, but soon go far beyond, the jolly exchange of pie at Thanksgiving for cake on birthdays. It means you can ask me to supervise your children for the fortnight you will be in the hospital, and that however inconvenient this might be for me, I shall manage to. It means I can phone you on what for me is a dreary, wretched Sunday afternoon and for you is the eve of a deadline, knowing you will tell me to come right over, if only to watch you type. It means we need not dissemble. ("To yield to seeming," as Buber[3] wrote, "is man's essential cowardice, to resist it is his essential courage…one must at times pay dearly for life lived from the being, but it is never too dear.")

(5) Good families deal squarely with direness. Pity the tribe that doesn't have, and cherish, at least one flamboyant eccentric. Pity too the one that supposes it can avoid for long the woes to which all flesh is heir. Lunacy, bankruptcy, suicide and other unthinkable fates sooner or later afflict the noblest of clans with an undertow of gloom. Family life is a set of givens, someone once told me, and it takes courage to see certain givens as blessings rather than as curses. Contradictions and inconsistencies are givens, too. So is the war against what the Oregon patriarch Kenneth Babbs calls malarkey. "There's always malarkey lurking, bubbles in the cesspool, fetid bubbles that pop and smell. But I don't put up with malarkey, between my stepkids and my natural ones or anywhere else in the family."

---

[3]Martin Buber (1878–1965) religious philosopher, influenced by the Hasidic Jewish tradition, whose views proclaimed the importance of a close personal relationship between God and man.

7   (6) Good families prize their rituals. Nothing welds a family more than these. Rituals are vital especially for clans without histories, because they evoke a past, imply a future, and hint at continuity. No line in the Seder service at Passover[4] reassures more than the last: "Next year in Jerusalem!" A clan becomes more of a clan each time it gathers to observe a fixed ritual (Christmas, birthdays, Thanksgiving, and so on), grieve at a funeral (anyone may come to most funerals; those who do declare their tribalness), and devises a new rite of its own. Equinox breakfasts and all-white dinners can be at least as welding as Memorial Day parades. Several of us in the old *Life* magazine years used to meet for lunch every Pearl Harbor[5] Day, preferably to eat some politically neutral fare like smorgasbord, to "forgive" our only ancestrally Japanese colleague Irene Kubota Neves. For that and other reasons we became, and remain, a sort of family.

8   "Rituals," a California friend of mine said, "aren't just externals and holidays. They are the performances of our lives. They are a kind of shorthand. They can't be decreed. My mother used to try to decree them. She'd make such a goddamn fuss over what we talked about at dinner, aiming at Topics of Common Interest, topics that celebrated our cohesion as a family. These performances were always hollow, because the phenomenology of the moment got sacrificed for the *idea* of the moment. Real rituals are discovered in retrospect. They emerge around constitutive moments, moments that only happen once, around whose memory meanings cluster. You don't choose those moments. They choose themselves." A lucky clan includes a born mythologizer, like my blood sister, who has the gift of apprehending such a moment when she sees it, and who cannot help but invent new rituals everywhere she goes.

9   (7) Good families are affectionate. This is of course a matter of style. I know clans whose members greet each other with gingerly handshakes or, in what pass for kisses, with hurried brushes of side jawbones, as if the object were to touch not the lips but the ears. I don't see how such people manage. "The tribe that does not hug," as someone who has been part of many *ad hoc* families recently wrote to me, "is no tribe at all. More and more I realize that everybody, regardless of age, needs to be hugged and comforted in a brotherly or sisterly way now and then. Preferably now."

10   (8) Good families have a sense of place, which these days is not achieved easily. As Susanne Langer wrote in 1957, "Most people have no home that is a symbol of their childhood, not even a definite memory of one place to serve that purpose…all the old symbols are gone." Once I asked a roomful of supper guests who, if anyone, felt any strong pull to any certain spot on the face of the earth. Everyone was silent, except for a visitor from Bavaria. The rest of us seemed to know all too well what Walker Percy means in *The Moviegoer* when

[4]Jewish festival that commemorates the Israelites' exodus from Egypt.
[5]Site of American naval base in the Hawaiian Islands. The surprise attack on December 7, 1941, by Japanese aircraft brought the United States into World War II.

he tells of the "genie-soul of the place which every place has or else is not a place [and which] wherever you go, you must meet and master or else be met and mastered." All that meeting and mastering saps plenty of strength. It also underscores our need for tribal bases of the sort which soaring real estate taxes and splintering families have made all but obsolete.

So what are we to do, those of us whose habit and pleasure and doom is our   11
tendency, as a Georgia lady put it, to "fly off at every other whipstitch?" Think in terms of movable feasts, for a start. Live here, wherever here may be, as if we were going to belong here for the rest of our lives. Learn to hallow whatever ground we happen to stand on or land on. Like medieval knights who took their tapestries along on Crusades, like modern Afghanis with their yurts, we must pack such totems and icons as we can to make short-term quarters feel like home. Pillows, small rugs, watercolors can dispel much of the chilling anonymity of a sublet apartment or motel room. When we can, we should live in rooms with stoves or fireplaces or anyway candlelight. The ancient saying still is true: Extinguished hearth, extinguished family. Round tables help, too, and as a friend of mine once put it, so do "too many comfortable chairs, with surfaces to put feet on, arranged so as to encourage a maximum of eye contact." Such rooms inspire good talk, of which good clans can never have enough.

(9) Good families, not just the blood kind, find some way to connect with   12
posterity. "To forge a link in the humble chain of being, encircling heirs to ancestors," as Michael Novak has written, "is to walk within a circle of magic as primitive as humans knew in caves." He is talking of course about babies, feeling them leap in wombs, giving them suck. Parenthood, however, is a state which some miss by chance and others by design, and a vocation to which not all are called. Some of us, like the novelist Richard P. Brickner, "look on as others name their children who in turn name their own lives, devising their own flags from their parents' cloth." What are we who lack children to do? Build houses? Plant trees? Write books or symphonies or laws? Perhaps, but even if we do these things, there still should be children on the sidelines, if not at the center, of our lives. It is a sadly impoverished tribe that does not allow access to, and make much of, some children. Not too much, of course: it has truly been said that never in history have so many educated people devoted so much attention to so few children. Attention, in excess, can turn to fawning, which isn't much better than neglect. Still, if we don't regularly see and talk to and laugh with people who can expect to outlive us by twenty years or so, we had better get busy and find some.

(10) Good families also honor their elders. The wider the age range, the   13
stronger the tribe. Jean-Paul Sartre[6] and Margaret Mead,[7] to name two spectac-

[6](1905–1980) French existential philosopher and author.
[7](1901–1978) Popular American anthropologist known for her work in comparing habits and beliefs of varied cultures.

ularly confident former children, have both remarked on the central importance of grandparents in their own early lives. Grandparents now are in much more abundant supply than they were a generation or two ago when old age was more rare. If actual grandparents are not at hand, no family should have too hard a time finding substitute ones to whom to give unfeigned homage. The Soviet Union's enchantment with day care centers, I have heard, stems at least in part from the state's eagerness to keep children away from their presumably subversive grandparents. Let that be a lesson to clans based on interest as well as to those based on genes.

EXERCISES

Some of the Issues

1. In paragraph 1, and elsewhere in her book *Families*, Howard suggests that people should build their own families, "devising new ones" with friends, supplementing (or replacing) natural families. What do you think of her idea?
2. In offering her 10 "earmarks...common to both kinds of families" does she distinguish at any time between "natural" and "new" families? If so, in what way?
3. Look at each of the 10 points, and consider if each one is convincing. If you agree with Howard, try to add evidence from your own experience. If you disagree, try to develop counterarguments. Are there any points you would add? Why?
*4. Read Alfred Kazin's "The Kitchen." Which of the 10 points fit that family and why?
5. Howard's definitions are implicitly based on mainstream American culture. On the basis of your experience or reading, would you say that her definitions hold for families in another culture?

The Way We Are Told

6. Each of the 10 points begins in exactly the same way. What is the effect of this repetition?
7. Describe how each of the points is constructed. How is the content arranged? How consistent is the arrangement?
8. Howard frequently uses a specific example to talk about a general idea, for example the last two sentences of point 3; or, in point 4, "you can ask me to supervise your children for the fortnight you will be in the hospital." Find other examples. What is their effect?

Some Subjects for Writing

9. Select a topic similar to Howard's, for example, "The good citizen," or "An educated person," or "An effective teacher." Then treat it as Howard might, developing the points one by one that together constitute a definition of the subject.

10. Some writers and sociologists have compared gangs to families. In your opinion, are gangs families? Argue for or against that proposition.

11. Howard's definition of families includes families of friends, as well as the family that she was born into. She also talks about the virtues of choosing "new families whose benefits would surpass or at least equal those of one's birth family." What role do close friendships play in life? Is that role similar to or different from roles played by one's blood relationships? You may want to consider whether or not friendships play the same role in the lives of men and women.

Gay Partners Need to Make a Name for Themselves

DEB PRICE

On May 8, 1992, Deb Price began the first nationally syndicated column on gay issues to appear in mainstream newspapers. While news organizations have increased coverage of gay and lesbian issues in recent years, Price offered readers something unique: life from a gay perspective. The essay reprinted here is the column that introduced Price and her lover Joyce Murdoch, also a writer, to newspaper readers, and asked the question, "So tell me America, how do I introduce Joyce?"

Deb Price's columns have been collected in And Say Hi to Joyce *(1995), co-authored with Murdoch. Price's column, written for both gay and straight audiences, covers a wide range of topics including gay and lesbian parenting, gay marriage, and problems facing gay teenagers. The book also chronicles the responses, both positive and negative, that Price received when she began to write about her life for mainstream America.*

The question of whether gays and lesbians should have the legal right to marry is a hotly contested one in both the gay and straight communities. Legally sanctioned marriage affords tangible benefits such as shared health insurance and specific legal rights and privileges—for example adoption, inheritance, and immigration—that are denied to gay and lesbian couples. Marriage also affords intangible social benefits and recognition in the eyes of society. Although gay marriage is not currently legal in the United States, many major corporations and universities have recently begun extending benefits to same-sex partners. Though Price is not specifically arguing in this essay for the right to marry, she does demand that Joyce be recognized as the woman she shares her life with, whatever name she chooses to call her by.

Deb Price is formerly the news editor of the Washington Bureau of The Detroit News *and holds a B.A. and M.A. in literature from Stanford University. She and Joyce live in the Washington, D.C. area.*

There's no confusion when a woman says: "This is my husband." But how do I introduce the woman I've lived with for six years to my boss?   1

Is she my "girlfriend" or my "significant other"? My "long-time companion" or my "lover"?   2

Who says the gay rights movement hasn't made a lot of progress? In just one hundred years, we've gone from the love that dare not speak its name to the love that doesn't know its name.   3

It sometimes seems as if we speak most clearly about our relationships once they are over: 4

"My ex."   5

The term is blunt with a lingering air of possessiveness.   6

No one thinks you mean ex-roommate or ex-business partner. They know ex-actly what your relationship used to be.   7

Documentary maker Debra Chasnoff brought this little dilemma of mine to world attention at the Academy Awards this year when she thanked her "life partner."   8

No sooner had she uttered these words than gay couples turned to each other on couches all across America and said, "Honey, did you hear that? That means she's a lesbian, right?"   9

Those of us who live in the land of the gay euphemism were pretty sure and won the bet. But to me, "life partner" sounds like what you become when you buy a health club membership.   10

Beyond that, if I break up with my life partner, do I have to refer to the next woman I live with as my "after life partner"?   11

But what are the alternatives?   12

"Significant other" sounds as though it should only be used by straight liberals who don't care who's doing what with whom—they just want to know how many people are coming to the barbecue.   13

"Longtime companion" sounds like the obituary-page creation that it is.   14

"Girlfriend" can be fun in the right crowd, but I feel pretty silly using it in mixed company to describe a thirty-eight-year-old professional.   15

"Domestic partner" always has a certain sarcastic ring to it for those of us whose dust bunnies breed like rabbits.   16

And then there's "spouse," "the woman I live with," and the psycho-babble guaranteed to land me on the couch for the night, "my relationship."   17

This vocabulary vacuum is a perennial problem for gay couples.   18

In *Borrowed Time: An AIDS Memoir*, Paul Monette said he and Roger Horwitz settled on "friend." They decided the most likely alternative, "lover," had a "beaded, sixties topspin."   19

But "lover" is the term Craig Dean uses to describe the man whose name he wants joined with his on a marriage license. Dean says "lover" underscores a vexing reality that "we're not legally married."   20

21   If he wins his lawsuit against the District of Columbia to marry, he says he'll call Patrick Gill his "husband."

22   The tabloids, on the other hand, have come up with "date-mates" and "gal pals" to describe lesbian couples. And, for the first time ever in 1990, the Census Bureau counted us as "unmarried partners."

23   Yet most of the time, straight people and straight forms have no category to describe us.

24   "Check one. Are you married, single, widowed or divorced?"

25   Help me out on this one. Maybe I should cross out "single" and print in "double." Or, when things are really going great at home, "a party of two."

26   Let's face it, none of the terminology out there fits me—or us. Whatever phrase I use, I end up sounding like a foreigner who hasn't quite gotten the hang of American colloquialisms.

27   Do we need a unique word to describe gay coupledom? Maybe we should seize a word, as we did with "gay," and make it ours. Or is it simply part of gay culture to have a love that answers to many names?

28   Surely a little ingenuity will solve this problem. So tell me, America, how do I introduce Joyce?

EXERCISES

Some of the Issues

1. Why is it important to be able to talk to others about the person you are close to? What is the significance of having a name for that relationship?
2. How is the reference to the "progress" of the gay rights movement ironic (paragraph 3)?
3. What does it mean that gays and lesbians "live in the land of the gay euphemism" (paragraph 10)? What audience is included/excluded when one uses euphemisms?
4. In paragraph 22, Price says that in 1990 the Census Bureau began to count gay and lesbian couples as "unmarried partners." Who else would be included in this category? Do you agree with the Bureau's choice of categories? Why or why not? Are the categories important? Why or why not?
5. In paragraphs 23 through 26, Price talks about the problem of filling out official forms. What do you think are the psychological and political consequences of not having an official or legal status for her relationship?
6. How should Price introduce Joyce? Choose among the suggestions given in Price's essay or come up with one of your own. Defend your choice.

The Way We Are Told

7. What are the possible meanings of the title?

8. Examine the tone and use of humor in this essay. What effect does it have on the reader?
9. Who do you think is the audience for this essay? Does it include straights as well as gays and lesbians?

Some Subjects for Writing

10. What is your definition of family? Consider not only the current legal definition but other possible definitions based on closeness or commitment. Are Deb and Joyce a family? Explain your answer.
*11. Read Joshua Gamson's "Do Ask, Do Tell." Both he and Price argue for more open discussion of the lives of gays and lesbians. In what ways are gays and lesbians silenced or their affection for each other hidden? How might more visibility and discussion lead to equal rights and more acceptance for gays and lesbians?

Choosing a Mate

RUTH BREEN

Born in Israel, Ruth Breen is a student at Brooklyn College in New York. She came to the United States with her family as a teenager and was married shortly thereafter; she has five children.

Breen, a Hassidic Jew, tells the story of her marriage—arranged by her family when she was seventeen. Although, as Breen says, Americans typically think of arranged marriages as a thing of the past, they are still quite common in orthodox Jewish communities.

Breen argues in this essay that, though the view of marriage in her community seems at odds with the "modern world's" notion of marriage founded on romantic love, in reality her marriage and the ones she knows in her community are not so different from "love" marriages.

1   *Choice* is not one of the terms I would use to describe my marriage. This is not to say that I was forced into marrying my husband. It is just that I associate the word *choice* with some sort of selection. To choose is to select from among many, or at least, between two. It is pick out one's favorite: one's favorite pickle from the pickles in the jar, one's favorite dress, one's favorite man. But my husband was not picked out. I knew no other; I experienced no one else.

2   When people discuss arranged marriages, they usually refer to them as part of history, gone with the crinolines and hand-kissing. I don't usually volunteer the fact that my marriage was officially arranged—in New York, in the eighties. I keep silent because trying to explain my community's marriage rituals to those who are accustomed to modern notions of love is useless. The cultural gap is so great that I usually find no common ground to stand on. When it comes to love and marriage, Hassidic ideologies and values seem to be the very opposite of the modern world's view.

3   I was two weeks past my seventeenth birthday when I was engaged to be married. Before I met my husband, I had never spoken to "boys." My own brother was only four years old, and my male cousins were even younger. I went to an all-girls school. We discussed boys all the time, of course, but boys were truly as abstract and alien as Martians. Most of our information came from the "Romance" section in the public library.

4   One evening, while I was doing my homework, my father came into the room. He told me that a matchmaker had called and offered a *shiduch* (an arranged date). "Do you want to get married, Ruthic?" he asked.

Of course I wanted to get married. I also wanted to fly to the moon and to   5
be in a Hollywood motion picture. I was seventeen. I wanted adventure; I
wanted fun. A boy would definitely be an adventure.

And there would be whipped cream too: presents, a white gown, I, the cen-   6
ter of attraction, blossoming with youth, astonishing with beauty. I definitely
wanted to get married. I would have no more curfew. I would buy cases and cases
of orange soda. I would watch T.V. anytime, any channel that I wanted. I would
eat chocolates on the living room couch. I would be independent.

The "boy," whose name I couldn't remember, or was yet to know, was study-   7
ing in Israel. He would have to come to New York to meet me. But meeting me
would be a final step. Before that, for three weeks, my parents were busy investigating his background, his grades in school, his habits, his friends, his family's
history, his health—I even knew the names of his teachers in elementary
school—but I still had not seen him. There was an "executive conference"
between both sets of parents to discuss who would pay for what, and who would
support us, and for how long. Then there was an "exam" that I had to pass—
meeting his parents. Finally, the future bridegroom arrived.

When I saw my husband, Michael, for the first time, I thought, "So this is   8
the face I will see for the rest of my life; this is the father of my children." But
we still did not speak. Then we were left alone in the room. When we spoke, it
was no different than what one would expect. I told him a few jokes, he smiled.
We had some cake. I could have said that I didn't like him, but how could I
know? He was a stranger. I could have said that I needed more time, but my
mother was already cutting up cake for the party. I was not forced, but my
grandparents were already on the plane, coming to congratulate us.

I met my husband, Michael, on Saturday evening. Sunday, at noon, we were   9
engaged to be married. I received a diamond ring. We smiled a lot at each other.
I was in seventh heaven, but I didn't know him at all.

My story is not unique. Tens of thousands of boys and girls in Hassidic com-   10
munities are married that way. Did I expect love and passion? I don't remember.
Did I doubt that he was the "the one"? Maybe, for an hour. Am I happy? Yes,
we are both happy. We fell in love exactly five weeks after we were married. We
went through the same initial euphorias, the same first fight, the same delicious
reconciliation—but we were already married. We grew together. We practiced
everything on each other. Eleven years have passed, and I am the only woman
Michael has ever touched. I was always the only one.

My parents chose for me. I will probably choose for my children. Of the 32   11
girls in my class at school, all married by arrangement. Two are divorced. The
rest, still married, would probably fit any standard statistics of happy or miserable marriages.

Intellectually, arranged marriages may seem a prescription for failure. Emo-   12
tionally, arranged marriages may seem unfair, anti-love and anti-romance. In
spite of all, our couples find enough happiness to stick together. They learn to

love and desire, to bond and connect. They have candlelight dinners and secret silly jokes. They give cards to each other and buy flowers for Sabbath. They go on romantic vacations. They love, they lust, they fight, they leave. Their marriages are as strong and as weak as "love" marriages are. Love comes in different ways, yet people love the same all over the world, and against all odds.

EXERCISES

Some of the Issues

1. How does Breen define "choice" in the introductory paragraph? Why is it important that she define this word? How does her definition differ from others we might use?
2. In paragraph 2, why does the author not usually volunteer the fact that her marriage was officially arranged?
3. Looking at paragraphs 5 and 6, what does the author imagine marriage to be? Do you think her images of married life are different from or similar to those of most seventeen-year-olds?
4. What was your reaction to the authors' description of the marriage and courting process described in paragraphs 7 through 9?
5. Were you surprised to read that the author anticipates arranging marriages for her own children? Why or why not?
6. What claims does Breen make about the success of arranged marriages? Were her claims convincing to you?

The Way We Are Told

7. The thesis of this essay is implied rather than stated directly. If you were to develop a one-sentence thesis, what might it be?
8. Why does the author put the word *boys* in quotation marks? How do the quotes indicate her feelings?
9. Looking at paragraphs 4 though 7, how does the author build up anticipation about the marriage?
10. Analyze the tone of the writing. How does the author control the tone to indicate how she felt before, during, and after the marriage?
11. Consider possible audiences for this essay. What kinds of attitudes was the author anticipating on the part of her audience?

Some Subjects for Writing

12. What was your initial reaction to the essay? Taking into consideration both the author's and your own view of marriage, analyze both the benefits and drawbacks of arranged marriages.

13. What, in your opinion, is most important in a successful marriage: love, physical attraction, commitment, communication? Is marriage something one has to "work on"?

The Kitchen

ALFRED KAZIN

*Alfred Kazin was born in Brooklyn, New York, in 1915 to eastern
European parents. He has taught at several universities, most recently
at the City University of New York. He has held several distinguished
fellowships and is a member of the American Academy of Arts and
Sciences. His books include* On Native Grounds *(1942),* The Inmost
Leaf *(1955),* Starting Out in the Thirties *(1965),* New York Jew *(1978),
and* An American Procession *(1984). Selections from Kazin's journals
were published as* A Lifetime Burning in Every Moment: From the Journals of Alfred Kazin *(1996).*

In this selection from A Walker in the City *(1957) Kazin describes
the setting in which he grew up. It was not unusual for its time and
place: a tenement district in a large American city, peopled with immigrants from eastern Europe, working hard, struggling for a life for
themselves and, more importantly, for their children.*

*The large-scale immigration that brought as many as one million
new inhabitants annually from Europe to America lasted from the
1880s to the First World War. The majority of the immigrants in those
years came from eastern, southern, and central Europe. They included
large numbers of Jewish families like Kazin's, escaping not only the
stifling poverty of their regions but also the outright persecution to
which they were subjected in Czarist Russia.*

1 In Brownsville tenements the kitchen is always the largest room and the center
of the household. As a child I felt we lived in a kitchen to which four other
rooms were annexed. My mother, a "home" dressmaker, had her workshop in
the kitchen. She told me once that she had begun dressmaking in Poland at thirteen; as far back as I can remember, she was always making dresses for the local
women. She had an innate sense of design, a quick eye for all the subtleties in
the latest fashions, even when she despised them, and great boldness. For three
or four dollars she would study the fashion magazines with a customer, go with
the customer to the remnants store on Belmont Avenue to pick out the material,
argue the owner down—all remnants stores, for some reason, were supposed to
be shady, as if the owners dealt in stolen goods—and then for days would
patiently fit and baste and sew and fit again. Our apartment was always full of
women in their housedresses sitting around the kitchen table waiting for a fitting.

My little bedroom next to the kitchen was the fitting room. The sewing machine, an old nut-brown Singer with golden scrolls painted along the black arm and engraved along the two tiers of little drawers massed with needles and thread on each side of the treadle, stood next to the window and the great coal-black stove which up to my last year in college was our main source of heat. By December the two outer bedrooms were closed off, and used to chill bottles of milk and cream, cold borscht and jellied calves' feet.

The kitchen held our lives together. My mother worked in it all day long, we ate in it almost all meals except the Passover *seder*;[1] I did my homework and first writing at the kitchen table, and in winter I often had a bed made up for me on three kitchen chairs near the stove. On the wall just over the table hung a long horizontal mirror that sloped to a ship's prow at each end and was lined in cherry wood. It took up the whole wall, and drew every object in the kitchen to itself. The walls were a fiercely stippled whitewash, so often rewhitened by my father in slack seasons that the paint looked as if it had been squeezed and cracked into the walls. A large electric bulb hung down the center of the kitchen at the end of a chain that had been hooked into the ceiling; the old gas ring and key still jutted out of the wall like antlers. In the corner next to the toilet was the sink at which we washed, and the square tub in which my mother did our clothes. Above it, tacked to the shelf on which were pleasantly ranged square, blue bordered white sugar and spice jars, hung calendars from the Public National Bank on Pitkin Avenue and the Minsker Progressive Branch of the Workman's Circle; receipts for the payment of insurance premiums, and household bills on a spindle; two little boxes engraved with Hebrew letters. One of these was for the poor, the other to buy back the Land of Israel. Each spring a bearded little man would suddenly appear in our kitchen, salute us with a hurried Hebrew blessing, empty the boxes (sometimes with a sidelong look of disdain if they were not full), hurriedly bless us again for remembering our less fortunate Jewish brothers and sisters, and so take his departure until the next spring, after vainly trying to persuade my mother to take still another box. We did occasionally remember to drop coins in the boxes, but this was usually only on the dreaded morning of "mid-terms" and final examinations, because my mother thought it would bring me luck. She was extremely superstitious, but embarrassed about it, and always laughed at herself whenever, on the morning of an examination, she counseled me to leave the house on my right foot. "I know it's silly," her smile seemed to say, "but what harm can it do? It may calm God down."

The kitchen gave a special character to our lives; my mother's character. All my memories of that kitchen are dominated by the nearness of my mother sitting all day long at her sewing machine, by the clacking of the treadle against

2

3

[1]Jewish festival that commemorates the Israelites' exodus from Egypt.

the linoleum floor, by the patient twist of her right shoulder as she automatically pushed at the wheel with one hand or lifted the foot to free the needle where it had got stuck in a thick piece of material. The kitchen was her life. Year by year, as I began to take in her fantastic capacity for labor and her anxious zeal, I realized it was ourselves she kept stitched together. I can never remember a time when she was not working. She worked because the law of her life was work, work and anxiety; she worked because she would have found life meaningless without work. She read almost no English; she could read the Yiddish paper, but never felt she had time to. We were always talking of a time when I would teach her how to read, but somehow there was never time. When I awoke in the morning she was already at her machine, or in the great morning crowd of housewives at the grocery getting fresh rolls for breakfast. When I returned from school she was at her machine, or conferring over *McCall's* with some neighborhood woman who had come in pointing hopefully to an illustration— "Mrs. Kazin! Mrs. Kazin! Make me a dress like it shows here in the picture!" When my father came home from work she had somehow mysteriously interrupted herself to make supper for us, and the dishes cleared and washed, was back at her machine. When I went to bed at night, often she was still there, pounding away at the treadle, hunched over the wheel, her hands steering a piece of gauze under the needle with a finesse that always contrasted sharply with her swollen hands and broken nails. Her left hand had been pierced through when as a girl she had worked in the infamous Triangle Shirtwaist Factory on the East Side. A needle had gone straight through the palm, severing a large vein. They had sewn it up for her so clumsily that a tuft of flesh always lay folded over the palm.

4   The kitchen was the great machine that set our lives running; it whirred down a little only on Saturdays and holy days. From my mother's kitchen I gained my first picture of life as a white, overheated, starkly lit workshop redolent with Jewish cooking, crowded with women in housedresses, strewn with fashion magazines, patterns, dress material, spools of thread—and at whose center, so lashed to her machine that bolts of energy seemed to dance out of her hands and feet as she worked, my mother stamped the treadle hard against the floor, hard, hard, and silently, grimly at war, beat out the first rhythm of the world for me.

EXERCISES

Some of the Issues

1. Kazin writes about the kitchen in his childhood home. Is he writing from the point of view of a child or an adult? What indications do you have of one or the other?

2. In speaking of his mother, Kazin says, "The law of her life was work, work and anxiety." In an age in which many people's goal is self-fulfillment, this does not seem to be a happy life. Can you find any evidence as to whether Mrs. Kazin was happy or unhappy? What pleasures did she have?

3. What is the meaning of the first sentence in paragraph 4? Why does Kazin call the kitchen "the great machine"?

The Way We Are Told

4. The same two words are repeated in the first sentence of each paragraph. What purpose does that repetition serve?

5. Compare the first two paragraphs. How do they differ from each other in content and in the way they are written?

6. Kazin talks about the kitchen of his childhood home but does not describe it until the second paragraph. What would be the effect if he had started with that description?

7. Reread the second paragraph. What details does Kazin give? How are they arranged—in which kind of order? Could an artist draw a picture on the basis of Kazin's description? Could an architect draw a plan from it?

8. Kazin describes several items in detail—the sewing machine, aspects of the kitchen itself, and his mother's work. Find some adjectives that stand out because they are unusual or that add precision or feeling to his descriptions.

Some Subjects for Writing

9. Write a paragraph about a place of significance for you, using Kazin's second paragraph as your model. Try to show its significance by the way you describe it.

10. Consider the role of work in the life of Kazin's mother. If you know someone whose life seems completely tied up with some specific activity, describe that person through his or her activity.

*11. Read Arlene Skolnick's "The Paradox of Perfection." Examine the extent to which Kazin's family represents the kind of family Skolnick describes, particularly in paragraphs 23–27.

The Paradox of Perfection

ARLENE SKOLNICK

Arlene Skolnick is a research psychologist at the Institute of Human Development, University of California at Berkeley. Born in 1933, she received her undergraduate education at Queens College and her Ph.D. in psychology from Yale in 1962. She is the author of The Intimate Environment *(1973),* The Psychology of Human Development *(1986), and* Embattled Paradise: The American Family in an Age of Uncertainty *(1991).*

The article reprinted here first appeared in 1980 in the Wilson Quarterly. *In examining the development of the family from colonial times to the present, Skolnick finds that in recent times we have come to look upon the ideal as if it were the norm, making every state less than perfection seem like failure.*

In examining the myth of perfection, Skolnick makes reference to Brigadoon *(paragraph 8), a Broadway musical and Hollywood film. Brigadoon was an imaginary town that came to life every one hundred years, never changing from its idealized state. Dr. Benjamin Spock's (paragraph 31) advice to new parents, especially his best-selling book* Baby and Child Care, *shaped family life for a generation. Alexis de Tocqueville (1805–59), mentioned in paragraph 24, was a French aristocrat who traveled throughout America. Deeply impressed with what he saw as a new society, he published his observations and reflections in* Democracy in America.

1   The American Family, as even readers of *Popular Mechanics* must know by now, is in what Sean O'Casey would have called "a terrible state of chassis." Yet, there are certain ironies about the much-publicized crisis that give one pause.

2   True, the statistics seem alarming. The U.S. divorce rate, though it has reached something of a plateau in recent years, remains the highest in American history. The number of births out-of-wedlock among all races and ethnic groups continues to climb. The plight of many elderly Americans subsisting on low fixed incomes is well known.

What puzzles me is an ambiguity, not in the facts, but in what we are asked   3
to make of them. A series of opinion polls conducted in 1978 by Yankelovich,
Skelley, and White, for example, found that 38 percent of those surveyed had
recently witnessed one or more "destructive activities" (e.g., a divorce, a separation, a custody battle) within their own families or those of their parents or sib-
lings. At the same time, 92 percent of the respondents said the family was highly
important to them as a "personal value."

Can the family be at once a cherished "value" and a troubled institution? I   4
am inclined to think, in fact, that they go hand in hand. A recent "Talk of the
Town" report in *The New Yorker* illustrates what I mean:

> A few months ago word was heard from Billy Gray, who used to play
> brother Bud in "Father Knows Best," the 1950s television show about
> the nice Anderson family who lived in the white frame house on a side
> street in some mythical Springfield—the house at which the father
> arrived each night swinging open the front door and singing out "Mar-
> garet, I'm home!" Gray said he felt "ashamed" that he had ever had any-
> thing to do with the show. It was all "totally false," he said, and had
> caused many Americans to feel inadequate, because they thought that
> was the way life was supposed to be and that their own lives failed to
> measure up.

As Susan Sontag has noted in *On Photography*, mass-produced images have   5
"extraordinary powers to determine our demands upon reality." The family is
especially vulnerable to confusion between truth and illusion. What, after all, is
"normal"? All of us have a backstairs view of our own families, but we know The
Family, in the aggregate, only vicariously.

Like politics or athletics, the family has become a media event. Television   6
offers nightly portrayals of lump-in-the-throat family "normalcy" ("The Wal-
tons," "Little House on the Prairie") and, nowadays, even humorous "deviance"
("One Day at a Time," "The Odd Couple"). Family advisers sally forth in syndicated newspaper columns to uphold standards, mend relationships, suggest
counseling, and otherwise lead their readers back to the True Path. For commercial purposes, advertisers spend millions of dollars to create stirring
vignettes of glamorous-but-ordinary families, the kind of family most 11-year-
olds wish they had.

All Americans do not, of course, live in such a family, but most share an   7
intuitive sense of what the "ideal" family should be—reflected in the precepts of
religion, the conventions of etiquette, and the assumptions of law. And, charac-
teristically, Americans tend to project the ideal back into the past, the time when
virtues of all sorts are thought to have flourished.

We do not come off well by comparison with that golden age, nor could we,   8
for it is as elusive and mythical as Brigadoon. If Billy Gray shames too easily, he

has a valid point: While Americans view the family as the proper context for their own lives—9 out of 10 people live in one—they have no realistic context in which to view the family. Family history, until recently, was as neglected in academe as it still is in the press. The familiar, depressing charts of "leading family indicators"—marriage, divorce, illegitimacy—in newspapers and newsmagazines rarely survey the trends before World War II. The discussion, in short, lacks ballast.

9   Let us go back to before the American Revolution.

10   Perhaps what distinguishes the modern family most from its colonial counterpart is its newfound privacy. Throughout the 17th and 18th centuries, well over 90 percent of the American population lived in small rural communities. Unusual behavior rarely went unnoticed, and neighbors often intervened directly in a family's affairs, to help or to chastise.

11   The most dramatic example was the rural "charivari," prevalent in both Europe and the United States until the early 19th century. The purpose of these noisy gatherings was to censure community members for familial transgressions— unusual sexual behavior, marriages between persons of grossly discrepant ages, or "household disorder," to name but a few. As historian Edward Shorter describes it in *The Making of the Modern Family:*

> Sometimes the demonstration would consist of masked individuals circling somebody's house at night, screaming, beating on pans, and blowing cow horns…on other occasions, the offender would be seized and marched through the streets, seated perhaps backwards on a donkey or forced to wear a placard describing his sins.

12   The state itself had no qualms about intruding into a family's affairs by statute, if necessary. Consider 17th-century New England's "stubborn child" laws that, though never actually enforced, sanctioned the death penalty for chronic disobedience to one's parents.

13   If the boundaries between home and society seem blurred during the colonial era, it is because they were. People were neither very emotional nor very self-conscious about family life, and, as historian John Demos points out, family and community were "joined in a relation of profound reciprocity." In his *Of Domesticall Duties,* William Gouge, a 17th-century Puritan preacher, called the family "a little community." The home, like the larger community, was as much an economic as a social unit; all members of the family worked, be it on the farm, or in a shop, or in the home.

14   There was not much to idealize. Love was not considered the basis for marriage but one possible result of it. According to historian Carl Degler, it was easier to obtain a divorce in colonial New England than anywhere else in the Western world, and the divorce rate climbed steadily throughout the 18th century, though it remained low by contemporary standards. Romantic images to

the contrary, it was rare for more than two generations (parents and children) to share a household, for the simple reason that very few people lived beyond the age of 60. It is ironic that our nostalgia for the extended family—including grandparents and grandchildren—comes at a time when, thanks to improvements in health care, its existence is less threatened than ever before.

Infant mortality was high in colonial days, though not as high as we are   15
accustomed to believe, since food was plentiful and epidemics, owing to generally low population density, were few. In the mid-1700s, the average age of marriage was about 24 for men, 21 for women—not much different from what it is now. Households, on average, were larger, but not startlingly so: A typical household in 1790 included about 5.6 members, versus about 3.5 today. Illegitimacy was widespread. Premarital pregnancies reached a high in 18th-century America (10 percent of all first births) that was not equalled until the 1950s.

In simple demographic terms, then, the differences between the American   16
family in colonial times and today are not all that stark: the similarities are sometimes striking.

The chief contrast is psychological. While Western societies have always   17
idealized the family to some degree, the *most vivid* literary portrayals of family life before the 19th century were negative or, at best, ambivalent. In what might be called the "high tragic" tradition—including Sophocles, Shakespeare, and the Bible, as well as fairy tales and novels—the family was portrayed as a high-voltage emotional setting, laden with dark passions, sibling rivalries, and violence. There was also the "low comic" tradition—the world of hen-pecked husbands and tyrannical mothers-in-law.

It is unlikely that our 18th-century ancestors ever left the book of Genesis   18
or *Tom Jones* with the feeling that their own family lives were seriously flawed.

By the time of the Civil War, however, American attitudes toward the family   19
had changed profoundly. The early decades of the 19th century marked the beginnings of America's gradual transformation into an urban, industrial society. In 1820, less than 8 percent of the U.S. population lived in cities; by 1860, the urban concentration approached 20 percent, and by 1900 that proportion had doubled.

Structurally, the American family did not immediately undergo a compara-   20
ble transformation. Despite the large families of many immigrants and farmers, the size of the *average* family declined—slowly but steadily—as it had been doing since the 17th century. Infant mortality remained about the same, and may even have increased somewhat, owing to poor sanitation in crowded cities. Legal divorces were easier to obtain than they had been in colonial times. Indeed, the rise in the divorce rate was a matter of some concern during the 19th century, though death, not divorce, was the prime cause of one-parent families, as it was up to 1965.

Functionally, however, America's industrial revolution had a lasting effect   21
on the family. No longer was the household typically a group of interdependent

workers. Men went to offices and factories and became breadwinners; wives stayed home to mind the hearth; children went off to new public schools. The home was set apart from the dog-eat-dog arena of economic life; it came to be viewed as a utopian retreat or, in historian Christopher Lasch's phrase, a "haven in a heartless world." Marriage was now valued primarily for its emotional attractions. Above all, the family became something to worry about.

22   The earliest and most saccharine "sentimental model" of the family appeared in the new mass media that proliferated during the second quarter of the 19th century. Novels, tracts, newspaper articles, and ladies' magazines—there were variations for each class of society—elaborated a "Cult of True Womanhood" in which piety, submissiveness, and domesticity dominated the pantheon of desirable feminine qualities. This quotation from *The Ladies Book* (1830) is typical:

> See, she sits, she walks, she speaks, she looks—unutterable things!
> Inspiration springs up in her very paths—it follows her footsteps. A halo
> of glory encircles her, and illuminates her whole orbit. With her, man
> not only feels safe, but actually, renovated.

23   In the late 1800s, science came into the picture. The "professionalization" of the housewife took two different forms. One involved motherhood and child-rearing, according to the latest scientific understanding of children's special physical and emotional needs. (It is no accident that the publishing of children's books became a major industry during this period.) The other was the domestic science movement—"home economics," basically—which focused on the woman as full-time homemaker, applying "scientific" and "industrial" rationality to shopping, making meals, and housework.

24   The new ideal of the family prompted a cultural split that has endured, one that Tocqueville had glimpsed (and rather liked) in 1835. Society was divided more sharply into man's sphere and woman's sphere. Toughness, competition, and practicality were the masculine values that ruled the outside world. The softer values—affection, tranquility, piety—were worshiped in the home and the church. In contrast to the colonial view, the ideology of the "modern" family implied a critique of everything beyond the front door.

25   What is striking as one looks at the writings of the 19th-century "experts"—the physicians, clergymen, phrenologists, and "scribbling ladies"—is how little their essential message differs from that of the sociologists, psychiatrists, pediatricians, and women's magazine writers of the 20th century, particularly since World War II.

26   Instead of men's and women's spheres, of course, sociologists speak of "instrumental" and "expressive" roles. The notion of the family as a retreat from the harsh realities of the outside world crops up as "functional differentiation." And, like the 19th-century utopians who believed society could be regenerated

through the perfection of family life, 20th-century social scientists have looked at the failed family as the source of most American social problems.

None of those who promoted the sentimental model of the family—neither the popular writers nor the academics—considered the paradox of perfectionism: the ironic possibility that it would lead to trouble. Yet it has. The image of the perfect, happy family makes ordinary families seem like failures. Small problems loom as big problems if the "normal" family is thought to be one where there are no real problems at all.   27

One sees this phenomenon at work on the generation of Americans born and reared during the late 19th century, the first generation reared on the mother's milk of sentimental imagery. Between 1900 and 1920, the U.S. divorce rate doubled, from four to eight divorces annually per 1,000 married couples. The jump—comparable to the 100 percent increase in the divorce rate between 1960 and 1980—is not attributable to changes in divorce laws, which were not greatly liberalized. Rather, it would appear that, as historian Thomas O'Neill believes, Americans were simply more willing to dissolve marriages that did not conform to their ideal of domestic bliss—and perhaps try again.   28

If anything, family standards became even more demanding as the 20th century progressed. The new fields of psychology and sociology opened up whole new definitions of familial perfection. "Feelings"—fun, love, warmth, good orgasm—acquired heightened popular significance as the invisible glue of successful families.   29

Psychologist Martha Wolfenstein, in an analysis of several decades of government-sponsored infant care manuals, has documented the emergence of a "fun morality." In former days, being a good parent meant carrying out certain tasks with punctilio; if your child was clean and reasonably obedient, you had no cause to probe his psyche. Now, we are told, parents must commune with their own feelings and those of their children—an edict which has seeped into the ethos of education as well. The distinction is rather like that between religions of deed and religions of faith. It is one thing to make your child brush his teeth; it is quite another to transform the whole process into a joyous "learning experience."   30

The task of 20th-century parents has been further complicated by the advice offered them. The experts disagree with each other and often contradict themselves. The kindly Dr. Benjamin Spock, for, example, is full of contradictions. In a detailed analysis of *Baby and Child Care*, historian Michael Zuckerman observes that Spock tells mothers to relax ("trust yourself") yet warns them that they have an "ominous power" to destroy their children's innocence and make them discontented "for years" or even "forever."   31

Since the mid-1960s, there has been a youth rebellion of sorts, a new "sexual revolution," a revival of feminism, and the emergence of the two-worker family. The huge postwar Baby-Boom generation is pairing off, accounting in part for the upsurge in the divorce rate (half of all divorces occur within seven years of   32 a first marriage). Media images of the family have become more "realistic," reflecting new patterns of family life that are emerging (and old patterns that are re-emerging).

33   Among social scientists, "realism" is becoming something of an ideal in itself. For some of them, realism translates as pluralism: All forms of the family, by virtue of the fact that they happen to exist, are equally acceptable—from communes and cohabitation to one-parent households, homosexual marriages, and, come to think of it, the nuclear family. What was once labeled "deviant" is now merely "variant." In some college texts, "the family" has been replaced by "family systems." Yet, this new approach does not seem to have squelched perfectionist standards. Indeed, a palpable strain of perfectionism runs through the pop literature on "alternative" family lifestyles.

34   For the majority of scholars, realism means a more down-to-earth view of the American household. Rather than seeing the family as a haven of peace and tranquility, they have begun to recognize that even "normal" families are less than ideal, that intimate relations of any sort inevitably involve antagonism as well as love. Conflict and change are inherent in social life. If the family is now in a state of flux, such is the nature of resilient institutions; if it is beset by problems, so is life. The family will survive.

EXERCISES

Some of the Issues

1. Skolnick begins her analysis by saying that just about everyone knows that the family is in crisis. How does she support that assertion in the first three paragraphs?
2. Why is the family, according to Skolnick, "particularly vulnerable to confusion between truth and illusion"? How have the media increased that confusion?
3. In paragraph 8 Skolnick says: "While Americans view the family as the proper context for their own lives...they have no realistic context in which to view the family." What does she mean? How do Billy Gray's attitude (paragraph 4) and the examples drawn from the media (paragraphs 5–7) support her statement?
4. What reasons does Skolnick give for her decision to go back to before the American Revolution in tracing the history of the American family (paragraph 8)? What is the chief distinction she sees between the modern family and the family of 200 years ago? On the other hand, in what respects is the difference not very great?
5. What was the gradual effect on the family of the change from a predominantly rural society to an industrial, urban one (paragraphs 19–21)?

6. What were the causes for the increasing division of family roles into a man's sphere and a woman's sphere, according to Skolnick (paragraphs 21–24)? How do the two spheres differ?
7. In paragraph 27, Skolnick turns to the "paradox" she has referred to in her title. What is it? What is the irony in seeking perfectionism for the family?
8. What are the more demanding standards that modern social science has imposed on the family according to Skolnick (paragraphs 29–31)?
9. In the last two paragraphs (33 and 34) Skolnick speaks of a new realism. What does she mean?
*10. Compare and contrast the "realism" Skolnick talks about in the last two paragraphs to Jane Howard's view of what constitutes a good family in her essay "Families."

The Way We Are Told

11. In paragraph 1 Skolnick first states the commonly held view that the family is in a sorry state. In what way does the second sentence foreshadow the argument she will make?
12. Consider paragraph 8; how does Skolnick make a transition from her analysis of the contemporary family to the topic she introduces with her one-line paragraph 9?
13. Skolnick puts words or sentences in quotation marks, but these "quotes" are of two kinds. One is the regular kind, as for example those in paragraph 3. The other is used for some specific effect, such as "normalcy" (paragraph 6) or "ideal" (paragraph 7). Find further examples of the second kind and explain their effect.
14. Interview several friends and classmates on the subject of marriage and relationships. How many of them see marriage as a part of their future? What are the expectations people have about marriage? Is it realistic to expect a marriage to last a lifetime?
15. Analyze one or more songs about love and romance that have stuck in your mind. Do the lyrics give what is, in your opinion, a realistic view, or are they overly romantic?

Some Subjects for Writing

16. In her final paragraph Skolnick gives the reader a rather optimistic view of the future of the family. Evaluate whether her arguments based on history justify that conclusion, and why (or why not).
17. Skolnick claims that in 1980, when this essay was written, TV programs presenting family situations were becoming more realistic. Examine a current show that deals with family life. How realistic is the picture of family life, in terms of the situations, attitudes, and relationships presented?

My Papa's Waltz

THEODORE ROETHKE

Theodore Roethke (1908–63), a widely published and much honored American poet, received a Pulitzer Prize in 1953 and a Bollingen Prize in 1958, among other awards. Two of his collections of poems, Words for the Wind *(1958) and* The Far Field *(1964), received National Book Awards. His* Collected Poems *appeared in 1966. He taught at several universities, last as Poet in Residence at the University of Washington.*

This brief poem is like a snapshot—a recollection of a moment that sums up the relationship of father and son.

The whiskey on your breath
Could make a small boy dizzy;
But I hung on like death:
Such waltzing was not easy.

We romped until the pans
Slid from the kitchen shelf;
My mother's countenance
Could not unfrown itself.

The hand that held my wrist
Was battered on one knuckle;
At every step you missed
My right ear scraped a buckle.

You beat time on my head
With a palm caked hard by dirt,
Then waltzed me off to bed
Still clinging to your shirt.

EXERCISES

Some of the Issues

1. Read the poem aloud several times. The poem describes a waltz—a turning dance that is usually thought of as sedate and graceful but can be dizzyingly fast. How does the rhythm of the poem suggest the dance?
2. The poem is like a snapshot—a recollection of a moment that sums up the relationship of father and son. What indications are there that the relationship was a close one, despite difficulties?

Some Subjects for Writing

3. Describe an incident from your early childhood that you remember well. In your description, try to make the reader understand how you felt about the event.

4

Identities

Each of us carries a number of identities. We are identified as sons or daughters, as parents, as students, as members of clubs or teams, professions or unions, religious denominations, or social classes. In some cases our particular identities will not only associate us with specific groups of people, but also type us. In American society, as multiethnic and multiracial as it is, this attribution of identity is particularly complex and often carries with it, rightly or wrongly, certain notions about the members of a group.

To compound this complexity, Americans are also a very mobile people. They move physically from one part of the country to another, as well as socially. Young men or women who leave home to go to college may be moving not only a hundred or a thousand miles, but also away from high school friends, associations, and ideas about life. These changes may reshape their identities, the concepts that they and others have of them.

In the first selection, "Living in Two Worlds," Marcus Mabry, as a college junior, writes about the gap between his earlier and his present life. Returning home to his lower-class neighborhood in New Jersey from the prestigious Stanford University in California, he finds himself with two identities that are hard to reconcile. But the shift from one to the other may have already occurred: at home for spring break, he gets the one good bedroom in the house. He is already "different."

People trying to integrate two different identities must often make choices, and those choices may vary over a lifetime. Maria L. Muñiz struggled with her Cuban emigré parents to build a new life in America; 16 years later, she yearns to visit friends and relatives left behind in Cuba to preserve and renew "la Cubana" within herself. In "An Ethnic Trump," Gish Jen, a Chinese-American, and her husband, of Irish descent, consider whether to send their four-year-old son to Chinese day school. The debate centers around the questions of whether

┌─ **THINKING ABOUT THE THEME** *"Identities"* ─────────────────

1. Guess the ages of the young women in the photograph. What details are the basis for your answer? How do you read the expressions on their faces? What do the expressions tell you about their attitudes toward their appearance?

2. Looking in the mirror is a daily ritual for most people, a way of preparing oneself to face the rest of the world. Imagine you had to chose between a home with no mirrors and one with mirrors on every wall. Which home would you chose? Why?

3. How much emphasis do you think we place on appearance in our culture? Too much? Too little? How is the emphasis different for males and females? If you have lived in another place or country, compare the attitudes there about personal appearance with the attitudes of people where you live now.

4. How do you and your friends make choices about your clothing and hairstyles? Do you feel these choices say something about who you are? Explain.

5. Suppose you are going to have a portrait taken of yourself that will give the viewer a sense of your identity. What part(s) of your personality would you want to convey through that photograph? What clothing would you chose to wear? How would you arrange your hair? Describe the setting you would choose.

some identities are immutable and others are matters of choice. For Nicolette Toussaint, partially deaf since childhood, deafness is a part of her identity. She must decide whether to declare her disability to others to whom it may not be immediately apparent. If she does not, she risks being misunderstood; if she does, she risks being set aside as "other." Eva Hoffman feels the pain of nostalgia as she remembers the friends she left in Poland and the sense of strangeness and discomfort with her dual identity.

How do others understand one's identity? Sometimes understanding is clouded by myth. In "The Myth of the Latin Woman: I Just Met a Girl Named María," Judith Ortiz Cofer writes about the stereotypical, often demeaning images of Latinas generated by popular culture. A writer and professor raised alternately in Puerto Rico and in the United States, she has always balanced two identities, but to the outside world she is often taken to be the "María" of *West Side Story* or the "Evita" of the musical. Malcolm X describes how as a young boy in 1914 he sought to be more like the white majority by straightening his hair. Later in life he realizes how degrading the process was and decides to take pride in his African-American identity.

If identities can be multiple and can change over time, to what extent can they be chosen? In her article "Goin' Gangsta, Choosin' Cholita," Nell Bernstein examines teenagers in Northern California. Many of them claim an identity they were not born into or emphasize only one of several identities in their family heritage. At an age when it seems natural to "try on" identities in much the same way one might try on clothes, these teenagers may be reacting to social change by trying to join the group that they consider to be most powerful in their own world.

Gwendolyn Brooks's poem at the end of this section characterizes, in a very few lines, the identities of some who build a wall around themselves—or have others build one around them.

Living in Two Worlds

MARCUS MABRY

*Marcus Mabry was a junior at Stanford University when he wrote this
essay for the April 1988 issue of* Newsweek on Campus, *a supplement
to the popular newsmagazine distributed on college campuses. As he
himself tells it, he comes from a poor family in New Jersey whose lives
seem far removed from the life at Stanford, one of the most affluent
universities in the United States. It is this wide gap between home—
African American, poor—and college—white, mainstream, and
affluent—that Mabry discusses. His double identity attests to both the
mobility in American society and the tensions that it may create.*

Mabry is currently a Newsweek *bureau chief in South Africa and
is the author of* White Bucks and Black-Eyed Peas: Coming of Age
Black in White America *(1995).*

1   A round, green cardboard sign hangs from a string proclaiming, "We built a
proud new feeling," the slogan of a local supermarket. It is a souvenir from one
of my brother's last jobs. In addition to being a bagger, he's worked at a fast-food
restaurant, a gas station, a garage and a textile factory. Now, in the icy clutches
of the Northeastern winter, he is unemployed. He will soon be a father. He is
19 years old.

2   In mid-December I was at Stanford, among the palm trees and weighty
chores of academe. And all I wanted to do was get out. I joined the rest of the
undergrads in a chorus of excitement, singing the praises of Christmas break.
No classes, no midterms, no finals…and no freshmen! (I'm a resident assistant.)
Awesome! I was looking forward to escaping. I never gave a thought to what I
was escaping to.

3   Once I got home to New Jersey, reality returned. My dreaded freshmen had
been replaced by unemployed relatives; badgering professors had been replaced
by hard-working single mothers, and cold classrooms by dilapidated bedrooms
and kitchens. The room in which the "proud new feeling" sign hung contained
the belongings of myself, my mom and my brother. But for these two weeks it
was mine. They slept downstairs on couches.

4   Most students who travel between the universes of poverty and affluence during breaks experience similar conditions, as well as the guilt, the helplessness and,
sometimes, the embarrassment associated with them. Our friends are willing to
listen, but most of them are unable to imagine the pain of the impoverished lives

that we see every six months. Each time I return home I feel further away from the realities of poverty in America and more ashamed that they are allowed to persist. What frightens me most is not that the American socioeconomic system permits poverty to continue, but that by participating in that system I share some of the blame.

Last year I lived in an on-campus apartment, with a (relatively) modern bathroom, kitchen and two bedrooms. Using summer earnings, I added some expensive prints, a potted palm and some other plants, making the place look like the more-than-humble abode of a New York City Yuppie. I gave dinner parties, even a *soirée française.*[1]

For my roommate, a doctor's son, this kind of life was nothing extraordinary. But my mom was struggling to provide a life for herself and my brother. In addition to working 24-hour-a-day cases as a practical nurse, she was trying to ensure that my brother would graduate from high school and have a decent life. She knew that she had to compete for his attention with drugs and other potentially dangerous things that can look attractive to a young man when he sees no better future.

Living in my grandmother's house this Christmas break restored all the forgotten, and the never acknowledged, guilt. I had gone to boarding school on a full scholarship since the ninth grade, so being away from poverty was not new. But my own growing affluence has increased my distance. My friends say that I should not feel guilty: what could I do substantially for my family at this age, they ask. Even though I know that education is the right thing to do, I can't help but feel, sometimes, that I have it too good. There is no reason that I deserve security and warmth, while my brother has to cope with potential unemployment and prejudice. I, too, encounter prejudice, but it is softened by my status as a student in an affluent and intellectual community

More than my sense of guilt, my sense of helplessness increases each time I return home. As my success leads me further away for longer periods of time, poverty becomes harder to conceptualize and feels that much more oppressive when I visit with it. The first night of break, I lay in our bedroom, on a couch that let out into a bed that took up the whole room, except for a space heater. It was a little hard to sleep because the springs from the couch stuck through at inconvenient spots. But it would have been impossible to sleep anyway because of the groans coming from my grandmother's room next door. Only in her early 60s, she suffers from many chronic diseases and couldn't help but moan, then pray aloud, then moan, then pray aloud.

This wrenching of my heart was interrupted by the 3 A.M. entry of a relative who had been allowed to stay at the house despite rowdy behavior and threats toward the family in the past. As he came into the house, he slammed the door, and his heavy steps shook the second floor as he stomped into my grandmother's

[1]Elegant party in french style.

room to take his place, at the foot of her bed. There he slept, without blankets on a bare mattress. This was the first night. Later in the vacation, a Christmas turkey and a Christmas ham were stolen from my aunt's refrigerator on Christmas Eve. We think the thief was a relative. My mom and I decided not to exchange gifts that year because it just didn't seem festive.

10   A few days after New Year's I returned to California. The Northeast was soon hit by a blizzard. They were there, and I was here. That was the way it had to be, for now. I haven't forgotten; the ache of knowing their suffering is always there. It has to be kept deep down, or I can't find the logic in studying and partying while people, my people, are being killed by poverty. Ironically, success drives me away from those I most want to help by getting an education.

11   Somewhere in the midst of all that misery, my family has built, within me, "a proud feeling." As I travel between the two worlds it becomes harder to remember just how proud I should be—not just because of where I have come from and where I am going, but because of where they are. The fact that they survive in the world in which they live is something to be very proud of, indeed. It inspires within me a sense of tenacity and accomplishment that I hope every college graduate will someday possess.

EXERCISES

Some of the Issues

1. Describe the two worlds Mabry lives in.
2. Mabry looks forward to "escaping" from school (paragraph 2), not an unusual sentiment at the end of a semester. What is he escaping to? Considering the rest of what he tells the reader, what is the real direction of escape?
3. "Once I got home to New Jersey, reality returned" (paragraph 3). Why does Mabry refer to life in New Jersey as "reality"? Is life at Stanford not real?
4. In paragraph 8, Mabry says "More than my sense of guilt, my sense of helplessness increases each time I return home." What events does he describe that contribute to this feeling?
5. Why does Mabry say in paragraph 11 that his family built "a proud feeling" within him?

The Way We Are Told

6. Consider the order of the first two paragraphs. Why does Mabry start with his brother rather than himself? Is the reader likely to be more familiar with the brother's world or Mabry's?

7. In the opening and concluding paragraphs and again in paragraph 3, Mabry refers to the supermarket sign about a "proud new feeling." How does the reference change each time he uses it? How does the repetition of the phrase help him to unify the essay? Try to define the kind of pride he is talking about.

8. Account for Mabry's use of expressions like "weighty chores of academe," "awesome!" "more-than-humble abode," and "*soirée française.*" From which of Mabry's two worlds do these phrases come? What does he gain by including them?

Some Subjects for Writing

9. Many people have had the experience of living in two different worlds—perhaps not the same two as Mabry's. If you have had such an experience—in family life, as a result of a job, a vacation, or some other cause—discuss your worlds and your relation to them.

10. Most students experience some change when they go to college that distances them from their family or alters their family role. Describe a change that you have either gone through or that you see yourself going through in the future.

Back, but Not Home

MARIA L. MUÑIZ

Maria L. Muñiz was born in Cuba in 1958. A few months later, on January 1, 1959, after years of fighting, Fidel Castro led his followers into Havana, Cuba's capital, forcing the dictator Batista to flee the country. Many of Batista's followers left at that time. Later, others disillusioned with the new government joined them.

Muñiz arrived in the United States with her parents when she was five years old, leaving behind, as she explains in this essay, many members of her extended family—grandparents, aunts and uncles, and cousins. As she grew older she felt more keenly a wider sense of cultural loss, which led her to the views expressed here.

"Back, but Not Home" was written when the author was only 20 and first appeared in the New York Times *on July 13, 1979.*

1   With all the talk about resuming diplomatic relations with Cuba, and with the increasing number of Cuban exiles returning to visit friends and relatives, I am constantly being asked, "Would you ever go back?" In turn, I have asked myself, "Is there any reason for me to go?" I have had to think long and hard before finding my answer. Yes.

2   I came to the United States with my parents when I was almost five years old. We left behind grandparents, aunts, uncles and several cousins. I grew up in a very middle-class neighborhood in Brooklyn. With one exception, all my friends were Americans. Outside of my family, I do not know many Cubans. I often feel awkward visiting relatives in Miami because it is such a different world. The way of life in Cuban Miami seems very strange to me and I am accused of being too "Americanized." Yet, although I am now an American citizen, whenever anyone has asked me my nationality, I have always and unhesitatingly replied, "Cuban."

3   Outside American, inside Cuban.

4   I recently had a conversation with a man who generally sympathizes with the Castro regime. We talked of Cuban politics and although the discussion was very casual, I felt an old anger welling inside. After 16 years of living an "American" life, I am still unable to view the revolution with detachment or objectivity. I cannot interpret its results in social, political or economic terms. Too many memories stand in my way.

And as I listened to this man talk of the Cuban situation, I began to remember how as a little girl I would wake up crying because I had dreamed of my aunts and grandmothers and I missed them. I remembered my mother's trembling voice and the sad look on her face whenever she spoke to her mother over the phone. I thought of the many letters and photographs that somehow were always lost in transit. And as the conversation continued, I began to remember how difficult it often was to grow up Latina in an American world.

It meant going to kindergarten knowing little English. I'd been in this country only a few months and although I understood a good deal of what was said to me, I could not express myself very well. On the first day of school I remember one little girl's saying to the teacher: "But how can we play with her? She's so stupid she can't even talk!" I felt so helpless because inside I was crying, "Don't you know I can understand everything you're saying?" But I did not have words for my thoughts and my inability to communicate terrified me.

As I grew a little older, Latina meant being automatically relegated to the slowest reading classes in school. By now my English was fluent, but the teachers would always assume I was somewhat illiterate or slow. I recall one teacher's amazement at discovering I could read and write just as well as her American pupils. Her incredulity astounded me. As a child, I began to realize that Latina would always mean proving I was as good as the others. As I grew older, it became a matter of pride to prove I was better than the others.

As an adult I have come to terms with these memories and they don't hurt as much. I don't look or sound very Cuban. I don't speak with an accent and my English is far better than my Spanish. I am beginning my career and look forward to the many possibilities ahead of me.

But a persistent little voice is constantly saying, "There's something missing. It's not enough." And this is why when I am now asked, "Do you want to go back?" I say "yes" with conviction.

I do not say to Cubans, "It is time to lay aside the hurt and forgive and forget." It is impossible to forget an event that has altered and scarred all our lives so profoundly. But I find I am beginning to care less and less about politics. And I am beginning to remember and care more about the child (and how many others like her) who left her grandma behind. I have to return to Cuba one day because I want to know that little girl better.

When I try to review my life during the past 16 years, I almost feel as if I've walked into a theater right in the middle of a movie. And I'm afraid I won't fully understand or enjoy the rest of the movie unless I can see and understand the beginning. And for me, the beginning is Cuba. I don't want to go "home" again; the life and home we all left behind are long gone. My home is here and I am happy. But I need to talk to my family still in Cuba.

Like all immigrants, my family and I have had to build a new life from almost nothing. It was often difficult, but I believe the struggle made us strong. Most of my memories are good ones.

13   But I want to preserve and renew my cultural heritage. I want to keep "la Cubana" within me alive. I want to return because the journey back will also mean a journey within. Only then will I see the missing piece.

EXERCISES

Some of the Issues

1. In paragraph 1 Muñiz says "yes" when she asks herself if there is any reason to go back to Cuba. What does she say in paragraphs 2–5 that helps us to understand her response?
2. What were the difficulties Muñiz encountered in school (paragraphs 6 and 7)? What bearing do these experiences have on her wish to visit Cuba?
3. In paragraph 8, Muñiz, at 20, states that she has "come to terms" with her memories. How does she describe herself?
4. What does the "persistent little voice" (paragraph 9) tell Muñiz? What is missing? Why is it not enough?
5. What does Muñiz mean by saying in the final paragraph that "the journey back will also mean a journey within"?
*6. Read Elizabeth Wong's "The Struggle to Be an All-American Girl"; then consider Muñiz's characterization of herself as "Outside American, inside Cuban." Would a similar statement ("Outside American, inside Chinese") apply to Wong? Why or why not?

The Way We Are Told

7. Muñiz uses a common introductory technique: a question whose answer will be the focus of her essay. What are the advantages of this technique?
8. In paragraphs 1, 4, and 10 Muñiz interrupts her personal story with references to more general political issues. What does she gain by doing so?
9. Paragraph 3 consists of one striking statement. How does it sum up what Muñiz has said in the preceding paragraphs? How does it anticipate what she will say later?

Some Subjects for Writing

10. Muñiz was underestimated by teachers and later proved her ability. Recall a time when you or someone else doubted your ability. Describe the circumstances and the outcome.
11. Have you had the experience of returning to a place you knew as a young child? If so, describe that experience telling what you saw and what you felt.

12. Do you believe it is possible or advisable for a person exposed to two cultures to maintain the customs and language of both? You may want to examine other essays that refer to the bicultural experience, such as those by Kingston and Wong. You may also want to interview someone who has had that experience, or draw from your own.

An Ethnic Trump

GISH JEN

Born in 1956, Gish Jen grew up Chinese-American in predominantly Jewish suburbs of New York City. She graduated from Harvard College and received her master's degree in creative writing from the University of Iowa Writer's Workshop.

Jen is the author of two novels, Typical American *(1991) and, most recently,* Mona in the Promised Land *(1996)—both of which humorously chronicle the coming of age of young Chinese-Americans as they struggle with issues of family and ethnic identity.*

In this essay, Jen raises the question of why certain ethnicities "trump" others—why her son, for example, whose heritage is both Irish and Chinese, attends a Chinese culture school and not an Irish one. Jen concludes that one of the reasons might be "the relative distance of certain cultures from mainstream America." Most Irish-Americans today are descended from ancestors who came to the United States during the great wave of Irish immigration in the mid-1800s. Though Irish immigrants were seen as outsiders by mainstream American culture at the time, they have since become more accepted and assimilated. Though there have been Chinese immigrants to the United States since the Gold Rush of 1847, most Chinese-Americans trace their arrival to this country to much more recent times.

1   That my son, Luke, age 4, goes to Chinese-culture school seems inevitable to most people, even though his father is of Irish descent. For certain ethnicities trump others; Chinese, for example, trumps Irish. This has something to do with the relative distance of certain cultures from mainstream American culture, but it also has to do with race. For as we all know, it is not only certain ethnicities that trump others but certain colors: black trumps white, for example, always and forever; a mulatto is not a kind of white person, but a kind of black person.

2   And so it is, too, that my son is considered a kind of Asian person whose manifest destiny is to embrace Asian things. The Chinese language. Chinese food. Chinese New Year. No one cares whether he speaks Gaelic or wears green on St. Patrick's Day. For though Luke's skin is fair, and his features mixed, people see his straight black hair and "know" who he is.

3   But is this how we should define ourselves, by other people's perceptions? My husband, Dave, and I had originally hoped for Luke to grow up embracing

143

his whole complex ethnic heritage. We had hoped to pass on to him values and habits of mind that had actually survived in both of us.

Then one day, Luke combed his black hair and said he was turning it yellow. Another day, a fellow mother reported that her son had invited all blond-haired children like himself to his birthday party. And yet another day, Luke was happily scooting around the Cambridge Common playground when a pair of older boys, apparently brothers, blocked his way. "You're Chinese!" they shouted, leaning on the hood of Luke's scooter car. "You are! You're Chinese!" So brazen were these kids, that even when I, an adult, intervened, they continued to shout. Luke answered, "No, I'm not!"—to no avail; it was not clear if the boys even heard him. Then the boys' mother called to them from some distance away, outside the fence, and though her voice was no louder than Luke's, they left obediently. 4

Behind them opened a great, rippling quiet, like the wash of a battleship. 5

Luke and I immediately went over things he could say if anything like that ever happened again. I told him that he was 100 percent American, even though I knew from my own childhood in Yonkers that these words would be met only with derision. It was a sorry chore. Since then I have not asked him about the incident, hoping that he has forgotten about it, and wishing that I could, too. For I wish I could forget the sight of those kids' fingers on the hood of Luke's little car. I wish I could forget their loud attack, but also Luke's soft defense: *No, I'm not.* 6

Chinese-culture school. After dozens of phone calls, I was elated to discover the Greater Boston Chinese Cultural Association nearby in west Newton. The school takes children at 3, has a wonderful sense of community and is housed in a center paid for, in part, by great karaoke fund-raising events. (Never mind what the Japanese meant to the Chinese in the old world. In this world, people donate at least $200 each for a chance at the mike, and the singing goes on all night.) There are even vendors who bring home-style Chinese food to sell after class—stuff you can't get in a restaurant. Dave and I couldn't wait for the second class, and a chance to buy more *bao* for our freezer. 7

But in the car on the way to the second class, Luke announced that he didn't want to go to Chinese school anymore. He said that the teacher talked mostly about ducks and bears and that he wasn't interested in ducks and bears. And I knew this was true. I knew that Luke was interested only in whales and ships. And what's more, I knew we wouldn't push him to take swimming lessons if he didn't want to, or music. Chinese school was a wonderful thing, but there was a way in which we were accepting it as somehow non-optional. Was that right? Hadn't we always said that we didn't want our son to see himself as more essentially Chinese than Irish? 8

Yet we didn't want him to deny his Chinese heritage, either. And if there were going to be incidents on the playground, we wanted him to at least know what Chinese meant. So when Luke said again that he didn't want to go to Chinese school, I said, "Oh, really?" Later on we could try to teach him to define 9 himself irrespective of race. For now, though, he was going to Chinese school. I exchanged glances with Dave. And then together, in a most carefully casual manner, we squinted at the road and kept going.

EXERCISES

Some of the Issues

1. What does the author mean when she says that certain ethnicities trump others? Do you agree with this statement?
2. What incidents does the author describe in paragraph 4? Why are they significant and how do they relate to each other?
3. In the end, does the author come to see Chinese school as optional for her son?
4. What is both the literal and figurative meaning of the last line?
5. What are some of the issues Jen brings up concerning families with parents of different ethnic, religious, or racial groups? What are your feelings on this issue?

The Way We Are Told

6 What is the tone of the essay? Why might Jen have chosen this tone?
7. How does Jen use humor in paragraphs 7 and 8?
8. Throughout the essay, Jen uses direct quotations to emphasize certain points or ideas. Where does she use them, and are they effective?

Some Subjects for Writing

9. Jen concludes that, at least for now, Chinese school is not an option for Luke in the same way swimming and music lessons are. Were certain schools, events, or programs not optional for you as a child because they were highly significant to your family? Write a narrative in which you describe this experience. From your perspective as an adult, analyze its importance in your life.
10. Consider what it means to be multiracial or multiethnic. Is it important that people choose to identify more strongly with one aspect of their ethnic identity, or is it possible for people to see themselves as comprised of many identities, histories, and backgrounds?

Hearing the Sweetest Songs

NICOLETTE TOUSSAINT

Nicolette Toussaint is a writer, painter, and political activist who lives in San Francisco. This essay originally appeared in a 1994 issue of Newsweek.

Toussaint, who is hearing impaired, describes her experience of having a disability that "doesn't announce itself." Toussaint examines the advantages and disadvantages of choosing whether to "pass" as a nondisabled person or to announce her disability openly. In doing so she calls into question society's reactions to and acceptance of disability. As Toussaint concludes, "We're all just temporarily abled, and every one of us, if we live long enough, will become disabled in some way."

Every year when I was a child, a man brought a big, black, squeaking machine to school. When he discovered I couldn't hear all his peeps and squeaks, he would get very excited. The nurse would draw a chart with a deep canyon in it. Then I would listen to the squeaks two or three times, while the adults—who were all acting very, very nice—would watch me raise my hand. Sometimes I couldn't tell whether I heard the squeaks or just imagined them, but I liked being the center of attention.

My parents said I lost my hearing to pneumonia as a baby; but I knew I hadn't *lost* anything. None of my parts had dropped off. Nothing had changed: if I wanted to listen to Beethoven, I could put my head between the speakers and turn the dial up to 7, I could hear jets at the airport a block away. I could hear my mom when she was in the same room—if I wanted to. I could even hear my cat purr if I put my good ear right on top of him.

I wasn't aware of *not* hearing until I began to wear a hearing aid at the age of 30. It shattered my peace: shoes creaking, papers crackling, pencils tapping, phones ringing, refrigerators humming, people cracking knuckles, clearing throats and blowing noses! Cars, bikes, dogs, cats, kids all seemed to appear from nowhere and fly right at me.

I was constantly startled, unnerved, agitated—exhausted. I felt as though inquisitorial Nazis in an old World War II film were burning the side of my head with a merciless white spotlight. Under that onslaught, I had to break down and confess: I couldn't hear. Suddenly, I began to discover many things I couldn't do.

5   I couldn't identify sounds. One afternoon, while lying on my side watching a football game on TV, I kept hearing a noise that sounded like my cat playing with a flexible-spring doorstop. I checked, but the cat was asleep. Finally, I happened to lift my head as the noise occurred. Heard through my good ear, the metallic buzz turned out to be the referee's whistle.

6   I couldn't tell where sounds came from. I couldn't find my phone under the blizzard of papers on my desk. The more it rang, the deeper I dug, I shoveled mounds of paper onto the floor and finally had to track it down by following the cord from the wall.

7   When I lived alone, I felt helpless because I couldn't hear alarm clocks, vulnerable because I couldn't hear the front door open and frightened because I wouldn't hear a burglar until it was too late.

8   Then one day I missed a job interview because of the phone. I had gotten off the subway 20 minutes early, eager and dressed to the nines. But the address I had written down didn't exist! I must have misheard it: I searched the street, becoming overheated, late and frantic, knowing that if I confessed that I couldn't hear on the phone, I would make my odds of getting hired even worse.

9   For the first time, I felt unequal, disadvantaged and disabled. Now that I had something to compare, I knew that I *had* lost something; not just my hearing, but my independence and my sense of wholeness. I had always hated to be seen as inferior, so I never mentioned my lack of hearing. Unlike a wheelchair or a white cane, my disability doesn't announce itself. For most of my life, I chose to pass as abled, and I thought I did it quite well.

10   But after I got the hearing aid, a business friend said, "You know, Nicolette, you think you get away with not hearing, but you don't. Sometimes in meetings you answer the wrong question. People don't know you can't hear, so they think you're daydreaming, eccentric, stupid—or just plain rude. It would be better to just tell them."

11   I wondered about that then, and I still do. If I tell, I risk being seen as *un*able rather than *dis*abled. Sometimes, when I say I can't hear, the waiter will turn to my companion and say, "What does she want?" as though I have lost my power of speech.

12   If I tell, people may see *only* my disability. Once someone is labeled "deaf," "crippled," "mute" or "aged," that's too often all they are. I'm a writer, a painter, a slapdash housekeeper, a gardener who grows wondrous roses; my hearing is just part of the whole. It's a tender part, and you should handle it with care. But like most people with a disability, I don't mind if you ask about it.

13   In fact, you should ask, because it's an important part of me, something my friends see as part of my character. My friend Anne always rests a hand on my elbow in parking lots, since several times, drivers who assume that I hear them have nearly run me over. When I hold my head at a certain angle, my husband,

Mason, will say, 'It's a plane" or 'It's a siren." And my mother loves to laugh about the things I *thought* I heard: last week I was told that "the Minotaurs in the garden are getting out of hand." I imagined capering bullmen and I was disappointed to learn that all we had in the garden were overgrown "baby tears."

Not hearing can be funny, or frustrating. And once in a while, it can be the cause of something truly transcendent. One morning at the shore I was listening to the ocean when Mason said, "Hear the bird?" What bird? I listened hard until I heard a faint, unbirdlike, croaking sound. If he hadn't mentioned it, I would never have noticed it. As I listened, slowly I began to hear—or perhaps imagine—a distant song. Did I *really* hear it? Or just hear in my heart when he shared with me? I don't care. Songs imagined are as sweet as songs heard, and songs shared are sweeter still. 14

That sharing is what I want for all of us. We're all just temporarily abled, and every one of us, if we live long enough, will become disabled in some way. Those of us who have gotten there first can tell you how to cope with phones and alarm clocks. About ways of holding a book, opening a door and leaning on a crutch all at the same time. And what it's like to give up in despair on Thursday, then begin all over again on Friday, because there's no other choice—and because the roses are beginning to bud in the garden. 15

These are conversations we all should have, and it's not that hard to begin. Just let me see your lips when you speak. Stay in the same room. Don't shout. And ask what you want to know. 16

EXERCISES

Some of the Issues

1. In paragraphs 1 and 2 Toussaint talks about her childhood attitudes toward her loss of hearing. How did her attitudes differ from those of the adults around her?

2. In paragraphs 3 through 9 Toussaint tells what happened when she began wearing a hearing aid at age thirty. How did things change? How did she feel about the changes?

3. Why does Toussaint question whether she should tell people about her disability when they may not immediately notice it (paragraphs 11 and 12)? Having read the rest of the essay, what do you think her solution was?

4. In paragraph 14, Toussaint describes an important moment in her life—a bird's song that she may or may not have actually heard—and says "Songs imagined are as sweet as songs heard, and songs shared are sweeter still." What does she mean? Do you agree?

5. What, according to Toussaint, do all of us share (paragraph 15)?

6. Throughout the essay Toussaint mentions both positive and negative aspects of her disability. What are they?
7. Did Toussaint's essay influence how you consider and talk about either your own or others' disabilities? In what way?

The Way We Are Told

8. What do you think Toussaint gains by beginning her essay with a description of her childhood?
9. Many good writers use sensual details, describing what they see, hear, smell, or touch to add vividness to their writing. More often than not, the details writers provide are mostly visual. Give several examples of the sensual details Toussaint uses.
10. Toussaint gives several examples of sounds that she interprets differently than a person with normal hearing might. What does she gain by telling you of her "mistakes"?

Some Subjects for Writing

11. Toussaint is keenly aware of the sounds around her. Many of us with normal hearing block out some of the sounds around us. Increase your own awareness of sound by finding a place where you can close your eyes and listen for several minutes at a time. Concentrate on the sounds around you. Write a description of the place focusing on details of sound.
12. Toussaint tells how her hearing loss has had both positive and negative consequences. Many of us have experienced some physical challenge, whether genetic or caused by illness or injury. Some of these challenges, like poor eyesight, can be temporarily or permanently corrected; some cannot. Also, as Toussaint reminds us, we are all "temporarily abled" since our abilities will diminish with age. Write about how you, or someone you know, has coped with a loss of ability.
13. Research what your school or community does to provide for people with serious disabilities. If possible, interview people who are disabled or get information from groups that represent the disabled. Evaluate the effectiveness of current provisions.

Lost in Translation

EVA HOFFMAN

Eva (Ewa) Hoffman was born in Cracow, Poland, in 1945. In 1959 her family emigrated from postwar Poland to Canada. As an adult she has taught literature and written on a variety of cultural subjects. She is the author of a memoir, Lost in Translation, A Life in a New Language *(1989), and a book about eastern Europe,* Exit into History *(1994). In this excerpt from* Lost in Translation, *she describes the anguish of an adolescent with a bicultural identity growing up in the suburbs of Vancouver.*

The car is full of my new friends, or at least the crowd that has more or less accepted me as one of their own, the odd "greener" tag-along. They're as lively as a group of puppies, jostling each other with sharp elbows, crawling over each other to change seats, and expressing their well-being and amiability by trying to outshout each other. It's Saturday night, or rather Saturday Night, and party spirits are obligatory. We're on our way to the local White Spot, an early Canadian version of McDonald's, where we'll engage in the barbarous—as far as I'm concerned—rite of the "drive-in." This activity of sitting in your car in a large parking lot, and having sloppy, big hamburgers brought to you on a tray, accompanied by greasy french fries bounding out of their cardboard containers, mustard, spilly catsup, and sickly smelling relish, seems to fill these peers of mine with warm, monkeyish, groupy comfort. It fills me with a finicky distaste. I feel my lips tighten into an unaccustomed thinness—which, in turn, fills me with a small dislike for myself.

"Come on, foreign student, cheer up," one of the boys sporting a flowery Hawaiian shirt and a crew cut tells me, poking me in the ribs good-naturedly. "What's the matter, don't you like it here?" So as the car caroms off, I try to get in the mood. I try to giggle coyly as the girls exchange insinuating glances—though usually my titter comes a telling second too late. I try to join in the general hilarity, as somebody tells the latest elephant joke. Then—it's always a mistake to try too hard—I decide to show my goodwill by telling a joke myself. Finding some interruption in which to insert my uncertain voice, I launch into a translation of some slightly off-color anecdote I'd heard my father tell in Polish, no doubt hoping to get points for being risqué as well as a good sport. But as I hear my choked-up voice straining to assert itself, as I hear myself missing every beat and rhythm that would say "funny" and "punch line," I feel a hot flush

150

of embarrassment. I come to a lame ending. There's a silence. "I suppose that's supposed to be funny," somebody says. I recede into the car seat.

3   Ah, the humiliation, the misery of failing to amuse! The incident is as rankling to my amour propre[1] as being told I'm graceless or ugly. Telling a joke is like doing a linguistic pirouette. If you fall flat, it means not only that you don't have the wherewithal to do it well but also that you have misjudged your own skill, that you are fool enough to undertake something you can't finish—and that lack of self-control or self-knowledge is a lack of grace.

4   But these days, it takes all my will to impose any control on the words that emerge from me. I have to form entire sentences before uttering them; otherwise, I too easily get lost in the middle. My speech, I sense, sounds monotonous, deliberate, heavy—an aural mask that doesn't become me or express me at all. This willed self-control is the opposite of real mastery, which comes from a trust in your own verbal powers and allows for a free streaming of speech, for those bursts of spontaneity, the quickness of response that can rise into pleasure and overflow in humor. Laughter is the lightning rod of play, the eroticism of conversation; for now, I've lost the ability to make the sparks fly.

5   I've never been prim before, but that's how I am seen by my new peers. I don't try to tell jokes too often, I don't know the slang, I have no cool repartee. I love language too much to maul its beats, and my pride is too quick to risk the incomprehension that greets such forays. I become a very serious young person, missing the registers of wit and irony in my speech, though my mind sees ironies everywhere.

6   If primness is a small recoil of distaste at things that give others simple and hearty pleasure, then prim is what I'm really becoming. Although I'm not brave enough or hermit enough to stay home by myself every night, I'm a pretend teenager among the real stuff. There's too much in this car I don't like; I don't like the blue eye shadow on Cindy's eyelids, or the grease on Chuck's hair, or the way the car zooms off with a screech and then slows down as everyone plays we're-afraid-of-the-policeman. I don't like the way they laugh. I don't care for their "ugly" jokes, or their five-hundred-pound canary jokes, or their pickle jokes, or their elephant jokes either. And most of all, I hate having to pretend.

7   Perhaps the extra knot that strangles my voice is rage. I am enraged at the false persona I'm being stuffed into, as into some clumsy and overblown astronaut suit. I'm enraged at my adolescent friends because they can't see through the guise, can't recognize the light-footed dancer I really am. They only see this elephantine creature who too often sounds as if she's making pronouncements.

8   It will take years before I pick and choose, from the Babel[2] of American language, the style of wit that fits. It will take years of practice before its nuances

[1] Self-respect.
[2] Unintelligible language. In the Biblical story, the inhabitants of Babel attempt to build a tower to reach heaven. God frustrates their attempt by confusing the languages of the builders.

and patterns snap smartly into the synapses of my brain so they can generate verbal electricity. It will take years of observing the discreet sufferings of the corporate classes before I understand the equally discreet charm of *New Yorker* cartoons.

For now, when I come across a *New Yorker* issue, I stare at the drawings of well-heeled people expressing some dissatisfaction with their condition as yet another demonstration of the weirdness all around me. "What's funny about that?" my mother asks in puzzlement. "I don't know," I answer, and we both shrug and shake our heads. And, as the car veers through Vancouver's neatly shrubberied and sparsely populated streets, I know that, among my other faculties, I've lost my sense of humor. I am not about to convert my adolescent friends to anti-Russian jokes. I swallow my injury, and giggle falsely at the five-hundred-pound canary. 9

Happy as larks, we lurch toward the White Spot. 10

If you had stayed there, your hair would have been straight, and you would have worn a barrette on one side. 11

But maybe by now you would have grown it into a ponytail? Like the ones you saw on those sexy faces in the magazine you used to read? 12

I don't know. You would have been fifteen by now. Different from thirteen. 13

You would be going to the movies with Zbyszek, and maybe to a café after, where you would meet a group of friends and talk late into the night. 14

But maybe you would be having problems with Mother and Father. They wouldn't like your staying out late. 15

That would have been fun. Normal. Oh God, to be a young person trying to get away from her parents. 16

But you can't do that. You have to take care of them. Besides, with whom would you go out here? One of these churlish boys who play spin the bottle? You've become more serious than you used to be. 17

What jokes are your friends in Cracow exchanging? I can't imagine. What's Basia doing? Maybe she's beginning to act. Doing exactly what she wanted. She must be having fun. 18

But you might have become more serious even there. 19

Possible. 20

But you would have been different, very different. 21

No question. 22

And you prefer her, the Cracow Ewa. 23

Yes, I prefer her. But I can't be her. I'm losing track of her. In a few years, I'll have no idea what her hairdo would have been like. 24

But she's more real, anyway. 25

Yes, she's the real one. 26

For my birthday, Penny gives me a diary, complete with a little lock and key to keep what I write from the eyes of all intruders. It is that little lock—the visible 27 symbol of the privacy in which the diary is meant to exist—that creates my dilemma. If I am indeed to write something entirely for myself, in what language do I write? Several times, I open the diary and close it again. I can't decide. Writing in Polish at this point would be a little like resorting to Latin or ancient Greek—an eccentric thing to do in a diary, in which you're supposed to set down your most immediate experiences and unpremeditated thoughts in the most unmediated language. Polish is becoming a dead language, the language of the untranslatable past. But writing for nobody's eyes in English? That's like doing a school exercise, or performing in front of yourself, a slightly perverse act of self-voyeurism.

28   Because I have to choose something, I finally choose English. If I'm to write about the present, I have to write in the language of the present, even if it's not the language of the self. As a result, the diary becomes surely one of the more impersonal exercises of that sort produced by an adolescent girl. These are no sentimental effusions of rejected love, eruptions of familial anger, or consoling broodings about death. English is not the language of such emotions. Instead, I set down my reflections on the ugliness of wrestling; on the elegance of Mozart, and on how Dostoyevsky puts me in mind of El Greco. I write down Thoughts. I Write.

29   There is a certain pathos to this naïve snobbery, for the diary is an earnest attempt to create a part of my persona that I imagine I would have grown into in Polish. In the solitude of this most private act, I write, in my public language, in order to update what might have been my other self. The diary is about me and not about me at all. But on one level, it allows me to make the first jump. I learn English through writing, and, in turn, writing gives me a written self. Refracted through the double distance of English and writing, this self—my English self—becomes oddly objective; more than anything, it perceives. It exists more easily in the abstract sphere of thoughts and observations than in the world. For a while, this impersonal self, this cultural negative capability, becomes the truest thing about me. When I write, I have a real existence that is proper to the activity of writing—an existence that takes place midway between me and the sphere of artifice, art, pure language. This language is beginning to invent another me. However, I discover something odd. It seems that when I write (or, for that matter, think) in English, I am unable to use the word "I." I do not go as far as the schizophrenic "she"—but I am driven, as by a compulsion, to the double, the Siamese-twin "you."

EXERCISES

Some of the Issues

1. With what details does the author describe the "barbarous" Saturday Night at the White Spot? (paragraphs 1 and 2)?

2. Compare Hoffman's voice in the joke-telling (paragraph 2) with Maxine Hong Kingston's voice in the school recitation in "Girlhood among Ghosts" (paragraph 27). What stands out in each author's memory of voice?

3. What is Hoffman's definition of *prim* in paragraph 6? What do you think is the underlying reason for her primness?

4. In paragraph 8, what does Hoffman say is the key to understanding the humor in *New Yorker* cartoons? What can you infer about the author's appreciation of the cartoons today?

5. In what way does the little lock on her diary create a dilemma (paragraph 27)?

6. Describe Hoffman's "English self" (paragraph 29). How does that persona contrast with her "real self" (paragraphs 25 and 26)?

*7. What does Hoffman mean when she says she created herself through writing? You may want to read Lisel Mueller's poem "Why We Tell Stories" for another view of creating one's life through words.

The Way We Are Told

8. What analogy does the author use in paragraph 3 to describe telling a joke? Explain the comparison.

9. In paragraphs 11–26, there is a sudden shift in diction and in audience. What effect does this shift achieve?

Some Subjects for Writing

10. In this excerpt, Hoffman is nostalgic for her teenage friends in Cracow. Have you ever experienced a longing to go back to an earlier time or place? Describe a sound, a place, a smell, or a memory of a person that evokes nostalgic feelings for you.

11. Recount an experience from your adolescence and show what it revealed about your developing sense of self.

The Myth of the La ___ Woman: I Just Met a Girl Named María

JUDITH ORTIZ COFER

Judith Ortiz Cofer was born in 1952 in Hormigueros, Puerto Rico, and emigrated with her family to the United States in 1956 when her father joined the U.S. Navy and was assigned to a ship in Brooklyn Yard. Cofer's family returned frequently to Puerto Rico to stay with relatives while her father was away at sea.

Cofer has published several volumes of poetry and has said of her poems, "The 'infinite variety' and power of language interest me. I never cease to experiment with it. As a native Puerto Rican, my first language was Spanish. It was a challenge, not only to learn English, but to master it enough to teach it and—the ultimate goal—to write poetry in it."

Cofer is the author of Silent Dancing: A Partial Remembrance of a Puerto Rican Childhood *(1990). This essay is taken from* The Latin Deli: Telling the Lives of Barrio Women *(1993), a collection of stories, poems, and essays that describe the cultural duality of growing up both Puerto Rican and American. Her most recent book is* An Island Like You: Stories of the Barrio *(1995). She is currently professor of English at the University of Georgia.*

The song referred to in the title of this essay is from West Side Story, *a popular Broadway musical and film about two teenagers who fall in love despite their different ethnic backgrounds and allegiances to rival gangs.*

1   On a bus trip to London from Oxford University where I was earning some graduate credits one summer, a young man, obviously fresh from a pub, spotted me and as if struck by inspiration went down on his knees in the aisle. With both hands over his heart he broke into an Irish tenor's rendition of "María" from *West Side Story.* My politely amused fellow passengers gave his lovely voice the round of gentle applause it deserved. Though I was not quite as amused, I managed my version of an English smile: no show of teeth, no extreme contortions

of the facial muscles—I was at this time of my life practicing reserve and cool. Oh, that British control, how I coveted it. But María had followed me to London, reminding me of a prime fact of my life: you can leave the Island, master the English language, and travel as far as you can, but if you are a Latina, especially one like me who so obviously belongs to Rita Moreno's gene pool, the Island travels with you.

This is sometimes a very good thing—it may win you that extra minute of someone's attention. But with some people, the same things can make *you* an island—not so much a tropical paradise as an Alcatraz, a place nobody wants to visit. As a Puerto Rican girl growing up in the United States and wanting like most children to "belong," I resented the stereotype that my Hispanic appearance called forth from many people I met.

Our family lived in a large urban center in New Jersey during the sixties, where life was designed as a microcosm of my parents' casas on the island. We spoke in Spanish, we ate Puerto Rican food bought at the bodega, and we practiced strict Catholicism complete with Saturday confession and Sunday mass at a church where our parents were accommodated into a one-hour Spanish mass slot, performed by a Chinese priest trained as a missionary for Latin America.

As a girl I was kept under strict surveillance, since virtue and modesty were, by cultural equation, the same as family honor. As a teenager I was instructed on how to behave as a proper señorita. But it was a conflicting message girls got, since the Puerto Rican mothers also encouraged their daughters to look and act like women and to dress in clothes our Anglo friends and their mothers found too "mature" for our age. It was, and is, cultural, yet I often felt humiliated when I appeared at an American friend's party wearing a dress more suitable to a semi-formal than to a playroom birthday celebration. At Puerto Rican festivities, neither the music nor the colors we wore could be too loud. I still experience a vague sense of letdown when I'm invited to a "party" and it turns out to be a marathon conversation in hushed tones rather than a fiesta with salsa, laughter, and dancing—the kind of celebration I remember from my childhood.

I remember Career Day in our high school, when teachers told us to come dressed as if for a job interview. It quickly became obvious that to the barrio girls, "dressing up" sometimes meant wearing ornate jewelry and clothing that would be more appropriate (by mainstream standards) for the company Christmas party than as daily office attire. That morning I had agonized in front of my closet, trying to figure out what a "career girl" would wear because, essentially, except for Marlo Thomas on TV, I had no models on which to base my decision. I knew how to dress for school: at the Catholic school I attended we all wore uniforms; I knew how to dress for Sunday mass, and I knew what dresses to wear for parties at my relatives' homes. Though I do not recall the precise details of my Career Day outfit, it must have been a composite of the above choices. But I remember a comment my friend (an Italian-American) made in later years that coalesced my impressions of that day. She said that at the business school she was attending the Puerto Rican girls always stood out for wearing "everything at once." She meant, of course, too much jewelry, too many accessories. On that day at school, we were simply made the negative models by the nuns who were themselves not credible fashion experts to any of us. But it was painfully obvious to me that to the others, in their tailored skirts and silk blouses, we must have seemed "hopeless" and "vulgar." Though I now know that most adolescents feel out of step much of the time, I also know that for the Puerto Rican girls of my generation that sense was intensified. The way our teachers and classmates looked at us that day in school was just a taste of the culture clash that awaited us in the real world, where prospective employers and men on the street would often misinterpret our tight skirts and jingling bracelets as a come-on.

6   Mixed cultural signals have perpetuated certain stereotypes—for example, that of the Hispanic woman as the "Hot Tamale" or sexual firebrand. It is a one-dimensional view that the media have found easy to promote. In their special vocabulary, advertisers have designated "sizzling" and "smoldering" as the adjectives of choice for describing not only the foods but also the women of Latin America. From conversations in my house I recall hearing about the harassment that Puerto Rican women endured in factories where the "boss men" talked to them as if sexual innuendo was all they understood and, worse, often gave them the choice of submitting to advances or being fired.

7   It is custom, however, not chromosomes, that leads us to choose scarlet over pale pink. As young girls, we were influenced in our decisions about clothes and colors by the women—older sisters and mothers who had grown up on a tropical island where the natural environment was a riot of primary colors, where showing your skin was one way to keep cool as well as to look sexy. Most important of all, on the island, women perhaps felt freer to dress and move more provocatively, since, in most cases, they were protected by the traditions, mores, and laws of a Spanish/Catholic system of morality and machismo whose main rule was: *You may look at my sister, but if you touch her I will kill you.* The extended family and church structure could provide a young woman with a circle of safety in her small pueblo on the island; if a man "wronged" a girl, everyone would close in to save her family honor.

8   This is what I have gleaned from my discussions as an adult with older Puerto Rican women. They have told me about dressing in their best party clothes on Saturday nights and going to the town's plaza to promenade with their girlfriends in front of the boys they liked. The males were thus given an opportunity to admire the women and to express their admiration in the form of *piropos:* erotically charged street poems they composed on the spot. I have been subjected to a few piropos while visiting the Island, and they can be outrageous, although custom dictates that they must never cross into obscenity. This ritual, as I understand it, also entails a show of studied indifference on the woman's part; if she is "decent," she must not acknowledge the man's impas-

sioned words. So I do understand how things can be lost in translation. When a Puerto Rican girl dressed in her idea of what is attractive meets a man from the mainstream culture who has been trained to react to certain types of clothing as a sexual signal, a clash is likely to take place. The line I first heard based on this aspect of the myth happened when the boy who took me to my first formal dance leaned over to plant a sloppy overeager kiss painfully on my mouth, and when I didn't respond with sufficient passion said in a resentful tone: "I thought you Latin girls were supposed to mature early"—my first instance of being thought of as a fruit or vegetable—I was supposed to *ripen*, not just grow into womanhood like other girls.

It is surprising to some of my professional friends that some people, includ-   9
ing those who should know better, still put others "in their place." Though rarer, these incidents are still commonplace in my life. It happened to me most recently during a stay at a very classy metropolitan hotel favored by young professional couples for their weddings. Late one evening after the theater, as I walked toward my room with my new colleague (a woman with whom I was coordinating an arts program), a middle-aged man in a tuxedo, a young girl in satin and lace on his arm, stepped directly into our path. With his champagne glass extended toward me, he exclaimed, "Evita!"

Our way blocked, my companion and I listened as the man half-recited,   10
half-bellowed "Don't Cry for Me, Argentina." When he finished, the young girl said: "How about a round of applause for my daddy?" We complied, hoping this would bring the silly spectacle to a close. I was becoming aware that our little group was attracting the attention of the other guests. "Daddy" must have perceived this too, and he once more barred the way as we tried to walk past him. He began to shout-sing a ditty to the tune of "La Bamba"—except the lyrics were about a girl named María whose exploits all rhymed with her name and gonorrhea. The girl kept saying "Oh, Daddy" and looking at me with pleading eyes. She wanted me to laugh along with the others. My companion and I stood silently waiting for the man to end his offensive song. When he finished, I looked not at him but at his daughter. I advised her calmly never to ask her father what he had done in the army. Then I walked between them and to my room. My friend complimented me on my cool handling of the situation. I confessed to her that I really had wanted to push the jerk into the swimming pool. I knew that this same man—probably a corporate executive, well educated, even worldly by most standards—would not have been likely to regale a white woman with a dirty song in public. He would perhaps have checked his impulse by assuming that she could be somebody's wife or mother, or at least *somebody* who might take offense. But to him, I was just an Evita or a María: merely a character in his cartoon-populated universe.

Because of my education and my proficiency with the English language, I   11
have acquired many mechanisms for dealing with the anger I experience. This was not true for my parents, nor is it true for the many Latin women working

at menial jobs who must put up with stereotypes about our ethnic group such as: "They make good domestics." This is another facet of the myth of the Latin woman in the United States. Its origin is simple to deduce. Work as domestics, waitressing, and factory jobs are all that's available to women with little English and few skills. The myth of the Hispanic menial has been sustained by the same media phenomenon that made "Mammy" from *Gone with the Wind* America's idea of the black woman for generations; María, the housemaid or counter girl, is now indelibly etched into the national psyche. The big and the little screens have presented us with the picture of the funny Hispanic maid, mispronouncing words and cooking up a spicy storm in a shiny California kitchen.

12   This media-engendered image of the Latina in the United States has been documented by feminist Hispanic scholars, who claim that such portrayals are partially responsible for the denial of opportunities for upward mobility among Latinas in the professions. I have a Chicana friend working on a Ph.D. in philosophy at a major university. She says her doctor still shakes his head in puzzled amazement at all the "big words" she uses. Since I do not wear my diplomas around my neck for all to see, I too have on occasion been sent to that "kitchen," where some think I obviously belong.

13   One such incident that has stayed with me, though I recognize it as a minor offense, happened on the day of my first public poetry reading. It took place in Miami in a boat-restaurant where we were having lunch before the event. I was nervous and excited as I walked in with my notebook in my hand. An older woman motioned me to her table. Thinking (foolish me) that she wanted me to autograph a copy of my brand new slender volume of verse, I went over. She ordered a cup of coffee from me, assuming that I was the waitress. Easy enough to mistake my poems for menus, I suppose. I know that it wasn't an intentional act of cruelty, yet of all the good things that happened that day, I remember that scene most clearly, because it reminded me of what I had to overcome before anyone would take me seriously. In retrospect I understand that my anger gave my reading fire, that I have almost always taken doubts in my abilities as a challenge— and that the result is, most times, a feeling of satisfaction at having won a convert when I see the cold, appraising eyes warm to my words, the body language change, the smile that indicates that I have opened some avenue for communication. That day I read to that woman and her lowered eyes told me that she was embarrassed at her little faux pas, and when I willed her to look up at me, it was my victory, and she graciously allowed me to punish her with my full attention. We shook hands at the end of the reading, and I never saw her again. She has probably forgotten the whole thing but maybe not.

14   Yet I am one of the lucky ones. My parents made it possible for me to acquire a stronger footing in the mainstream culture by giving me the chance at an education. And,books and art have saved me from the harsher forms of ethnic and racial prejudice that many of my Hispanic *compañeras* have had to endure. I travel a lot around the United States, reading from my books of poetry and my

novel, and the reception I most often receive is one of positive interest by people who want to know more about my culture. There are, however, thousands of Latinas without the privilege of an education or the entrée into society that I have. For them life is a struggle against the misconceptions perpetuated by the myth of the Latina as whore, domestic or criminal. We cannot change this by legislating the way people look at us. The transformation, as I see it, has to occur at a much more individual level. My personal goal in my public life is to try to replace the old pervasive stereotypes and myths about Latinas with a much more interesting set of realities. Every time I give a reading, I hope the stories I tell, the dreams and fears I examine in my work, can achieve some universal truth which will get my audience past the particulars of my skin color, my accent, or my clothes.

I once wrote a poem in which I called us Latinas "God's brown daughters."   15 This poem is really a prayer of sorts, offered upward, but also, through the human-to-human channel of art, outward. It is a prayer for communication, and for respect. In it, Latin women pray "in Spanish to an Anglo God / with a Jewish heritage," and they are "fervently hoping / that if not omnipotent, / at least He be bilingual."

EXERCISES

Some of the Issues

1. How does Cofer react to the young man's serenade in paragraph 1?
2. In paragraphs 2 through 5, Cofer talks about her childhood in New Jersey where she received different cultural signals from her Puerto Rican family than from the Anglo world outside. What were these signals? How were they confusing to her?
3. What are the stereotypes of Latin women that the American media perpetuate (paragraph 6)? Can you think of others besides the ones Cofer mentions?
4. According to Cofer, what behaviors or customs are interpreted differently in Puerto Rico than in the United States? Why? Can you give other examples of behaviors that have different meanings in different cultures?
5. What role do stereotypes play in explaining the behavior of the man in the tuxedo (paragraphs 9–10) and the woman at the poetry reading (paragraph 13)? What is your own opinion of how stereotypes are formed in our culture?
*6. Cofer says that she is "one of the lucky ones" (paragraph 14). What does she believe her privileges allow her to do? You may want to compare her viewpoint with that expressed in Aurora Levins Morales's "Class Poem."

7. To what extent is the stereotyping Cofer experiences based on her being a woman? How are stereotypes about Latin men different? How are stereotypes about women in other cultures the same or different?

The Way We Are Told

8. Like many writers, Cofer begins with a story. How does this narrative help illustrate her point?
9. Cofer uses references to Latina and black women in popular culture (María, Evita, and Mammy in *Gone with the Wind*) to indicate stereotypical roles that mainstream culture assigns to minority women. Were you familiar with the references? If not, was it easy for you to associate Cofer's ideas with other stereotypical images in the media?

Some Subjects for Writing

10. In "The Myth of the Latin Woman" Cofer explores how that myth prevents people from seeing her as who see is. Analyze common stereotypes that are applied to people belonging to a particular group. These stereotypes can be based on race, ethnicity, gender, or sexual preference, but you can also use, for example, stereotypes about athletes, intellectuals, or lawyers.
11. What role do the media play in stereotyping? Find one or more examples of newspaper or magazine articles, television shows, or movies that you believe reinforce misconceptions about a particular group in American society. Explain in detail the nature of the misrepresentations.
*12. Gloria Naylor, in "The Meaning of a Word," writes about how the same word can be affectionate in the context of family but deeply hurtful when said by someone else. Cofer also talks about actions that can have different meanings in different contexts. Describe a situation in which you own behavior, or the behavior of someone toward you, was affected by context.

Hair

MALCOLM X

Malcolm X, born in Omaha, Nebraska, in 1925, changed his name from Malcolm Little when he joined Elijah Muhammad's Black Muslims, in which he eventually moved up to become second in command. He broke with the Muslims because of major differences in policy and established an organization of his own. Soon after that he was assassinated at a public meeting, on February 21, 1965. The Autobiography of Malcolm X, written with Alex Haley (later more widely known as the author of Roots*), was published in 1964. The selection reprinted here is from one of the early parts of the book and records an experience during Malcolm X's junior high school years in Michigan, in 1941. He gives the reader what amounts to a recipe, but a recipe on two levels: he describes in detail the painful process of "conking," straightening hair, that he as a boy subjected himself to. On a more fundamental level it was, as he says, a "big step toward self-degradation."*

Shorty soon decided that my hair was finally long enough to be conked. He had promised to school me in how to beat the barbershop's three- and four-dollar price by making up congolene, and then conking ourselves.

I took the little list of ingredients he had printed out for me, and went to a grocery store, where I got a can of Red Devil lye, two eggs, and two medium-sized white potatoes. Then at a drugstore near the poolroom, I asked for a large jar of vaseline, a large bar of soap, a large-toothed comb and a fine-toothed comb, one of those rubber hoses with a metal spray-head, a rubber apron and a pair of gloves.

"Going to lay on that first conk?" the drugstore man asked me. I proudly told him, grinning, "Right!"

Shorty paid six dollars a week for a room in his cousin's shabby apartment. His cousin wasn't at home. "It's like the pad's mine, he spends so much time with his woman," Shorty said. "Now, you watch me—"

He peeled the potatoes and thin-sliced them into a quart-sized Mason fruit jar, then started stirring them with a wooden spoon as he gradually poured in a little over half the can of lye. "Never use a metal spoon; the lye will turn it black," he told me.

6　　A jelly-like, starchy-looking glop resulted from the lye and potatoes, and Shorty broke in the two eggs, stirring real fast—his own conk and dark face bent down close. The congolene turned pale-yellowish. "Feel the jar," Shorty said. I cupped my hand against the outside, and snatched it away. "Damn right, it's hot, that's the lye," he said. "So you know it's going to burn when I comb it in—it burns *bad*. But the longer you can stand it, the straighter the hair."

7　　He made me sit down, and he tied the string of the new rubber apron tightly around my neck, and combed up my bush of hair. Then, from the big vaseline jar, he took a handful and massaged it hard all through my hair and into the scalp. He also thickly vaselined my neck, ears and forehead. "When I get to washing out your head, be sure to tell me anywhere you feel any little stinging," Shorty warned me, washing his hands, then pulling on the rubber gloves, and tying on his own rubber apron. "You always got to remember that any congolene left in burns a sore into your head."

8　　The congolene just felt warm when Shorty started combing it in. But then my head caught fire.

9　　I gritted my teeth and tried to pull the sides of the kitchen table together. The comb felt as if it was raking my skin off.

10　　My eyes watered, my nose was running. I couldn't stand it any longer; I bolted to the washbasin. I was cursing Shorty with every name I could think of when he got the spray going and started soap-lathering my head.

11　　He lathered and spray-rinsed, lathered and spray-rinsed, maybe ten or twelve times, each time gradually closing the hot-water faucet, until the rinse was cold, and that helped some.

12　　"You feel any stinging spots?"

13　　"No," I managed to say. My knees were trembling.

14　　"Sit back down, then. I think we got it all out okay."

15　　The flame came back as Shorty, with a thick towel, started drying my head, rubbing hard. *"Easy, man, easy"* I kept shouting.

16　　"The first time's always worst. You get used to it better before long. You took it real good, homeboy. You got a good conk."

17　　When Shorty let me stand up and see in the mirror, my hair hung down in limp, damp strings. My scalp still flamed, but not as badly; I could bear it. He draped the towel around my shoulders, over my rubber apron, and began again vaselining my hair.

18　　I could feel him combing, straight back, first the big comb, then the fine-tooth one.

19　　Then, he was using a razor, very delicately, on the back of my neck. Then, finally, shaping the sideburns.

20　　My first view in the mirror blotted out the hurting. I'd seen some pretty conks, but when it's the first time, on your *own* head, the transformation, after the lifetime of kinks, is staggering.

The mirror reflected Shorty behind me. We both were grinning and sweat-   21
ing. And on top of my head was this thick, smooth sheen of shining red hair—
real red—as straight as any white man's.

How ridiculous I was! Stupid enough to stand there simply lost in admira-   22
tion of my hair now looking "white," reflected in the mirror in Shorty's room.
I vowed that I'd never again be without a conk, and I never was for many years.

This was my first really big step toward self-degradation: when I endured   23
all of that pain, literally burning my flesh to have it look like a white man's hair.
I had joined that multitude of Negro men and women in America who are brain-
washed into believing that the black people are "inferior"—and white people
"superior"—that they will even violate and mutilate their God-created bodies to
try to look "pretty" by white standards.

EXERCISES

Some of the Issues

1. What is a conk and why did Malcolm X want it?
2. Why does Malcolm X describe the process of buying the ingredients and
   of applying them in such detail?
3. What is the thesis of this short selection? With what arguments, information, or assertions does Malcolm X support his thesis?

The Way We Are Told

4. The selection divides into two very different parts. What are they? How
   do they differ?
5. The main part of the selection is a description of a process. How is it
   arranged? What qualities of instruction, even of a recipe, has it? How and
   where does it differ from a recipe?

Some Subjects for Writing

6. Malcolm X describes a process that shows, among other things, that people
   will go to great lengths to conform. Develop a short essay describing, in a
   straightforward, neutral manner, some example of how people will subject
   themselves to pain, inconvenience, and embarrassment to conform to some
   fashion or idea.
7. Rewrite your previous essay, but take a strong stand indicating approval or
   disapproval of the process.
8. Write an essay examining the rewards American society offers for conforming, or the penalties for not conforming.

Goin' Gangsta, Choosin' Cholita: Teens Today "Claim" a Racial Identity

NELL BERNSTEIN

Nell Bernstein is a freelance journalist and the editor of YO! *(Youth Outlook), a San Francisco journal of teen life. This essay originally appeared in a 1994 issue of* West *magazine, the Sunday supplement to the* San Jose Mercury News.

In "Goin' Gangsta, Choosin' Cholita," Bernstein describes what she calls the "hybridization" of American teenagers, and explores the idea that among today's teenagers, identity is seen as a choice, not determined by what community, race, or heritage you were born into. For many of the Northern California teens interviewed in this essay, identity is seen as something as changeable as clothing, musical taste, or vocabulary; a lifestyle rather than a birthright.

1   Her lipstick is dark, the lip liner even darker, nearly black. In baggy pants, a blue plaid Pendleton, her bangs pulled back tight off her forehead, 15-year-old April is a perfect cholita, a Mexican gangsta girl.

2   But April Miller is Anglo. "And I don't like it!" she complains. "I'd rather be Mexican."

3   April's father wanders into the family room of their home in San Leandro, California, a suburb near Oakland. "Hey, cholita," he teases. "Go get a suntan. We'll put you in a barrio and see how much you like it."

4   A large, sandy-haired man with "April" tattooed on one arm and "Kelly"—the name of his older daughter—on the other, Miller spent 21 years working in a San Leandro glass factory that shut down and moved to Mexico a couple of years ago. He recently got a job in another factory, but he expects NAFTA to swallow that one, too.

5   "Sooner or later we'll all get nailed," he says. "Just another stab in the back of the American middle class."

6   Later, April gets her revenge: "Hey, Mr. White Man's Last Stand," she teases. "Wait till you see how well I manage my welfare check. You'll be asking me for money."

A once almost exclusively white, now increasingly Latin and black working-class suburb, San Leandro borders on predominantly black East Oakland. For decades, the boundary was strictly policed and practically impermeable. In 1970 April Miller's hometown was 97 percent white. By 1990 San Leandro was 65 percent white, 6 percent black, 15 percent Hispanic, and 13 percent Asian or Pacific Islander. With minorities moving into suburbs in growing numbers and cities becoming ever more diverse, the boundary between city and suburb is dissolving, and suburban teenagers are changing with the times.

In April's bedroom, her past and present selves lie in layers, the pink walls of girlhood almost obscured, Guns N' Roses and Pearl Jam posters overlaid by rappers Paris and Ice Cube. "I don't have a big enough attitude to be a black girl," says April, explaining her current choice of ethnic identification.

What matters is that she thinks the choice is hers. For April and her friends, identity is not a matter of where you come from, what you were born into, what color your skin is. It's what you wear, the music you listen to, the words you use—everything to which you pledge allegiance, no matter how fleetingly.

The hybridization of American teens has become talk show fodder, with "wiggers"—white kids who dress and talk "black"—appearing on TV in full gangsta regalia. In Indiana a group of white high school girls raised a national stir when they triggered an imitation race war at their virtually all white high school last fall simply by dressing "black."

In many parts of the country, it's television and radio, not neighbors, that introduce teens to the allure of ethnic difference. But in California, which demographers predict will be the first state with no racial majority by the year 2000, the influences are more immediate. The California public schools are the most diverse in the country: 42 percent white, 36 percent Hispanic, 9 percent black, 8 percent Asian.

Sometimes young people fight over their differences. Students at virtually any school in the Bay Area can recount the details of at least one "race riot" in which a conflict between individuals escalated into a battle between their clans. More often, though, teens would rather join than fight. Adolescence, after all, is the period when you're most inclined to mimic the power closest at hand, from stealing your older sister's clothes to copying the ruling clique at school.

White skaters and Mexican would-be gangbangers listen to gangsta rap and call each other "nigga" as term of endearment; white girls sometimes affect Spanish accents; blond cheerleaders claim Cherokee ancestors.

"Claiming" is the central concept here. A Vietnamese teen in Hayward, another Oakland suburb, "claims" Oakland—and by implication blackness—because he lived there as a child. A law-abiding white kid "claims" a Mexican gang he says he hangs with. A brown-skinned girl with a Mexican father and a white mother "claims" her Mexican side, while her fair-skinned sister "claims" white. The word comes up over and over, as if identity were territory, the self a kind of turf.

15   At a restaurant in a minimall in Hayward, Nicole Huffstutler, 13, sits with her friends and describes herself as "Indian, German, French, Welsh, and, um…American": "If somebody says anything like 'Yeah, you're just a pecker-wood,' I'll walk up and I'll say 'white pride!' 'Cause I'm proud of my race, and I wouldn't wanna be any other race."

16   "Claiming" white has become a matter of principle for Heather, too, who says she's "sick of the majority looking at us like we're less than them." (Hayward schools were 51 percent white in 1990, down from 77 percent in 1980, and whites are now the minority in many schools.)

17   Asked if she knows that nonwhites have not traditionally been referred to as "the majority" in America, Heather gets exasperated: "I hear that all the time, every day. They say, 'Well, you guys controlled us for many years, and it's time for us to control you.' Every day."

18   When Jennifer Vargas—a small, brown-skinned girl in purple jeans who quietly eats her salad while Heather talks—softly announces that she's "mostly Mexican," she gets in trouble with her friends.

19   "No, you're not!" scolds Heather.

20   "I'm mostly Indian and Mexican," Jennifer continues, flatly. "I'm very little…I'm mostly…"

21   "Your mom's white!" Nicole reminds her sharply. "She has blond hair."

22   "That's what I mean," Nicole adds. "People think that white is a bad thing. They think that white is a bad race. So she's trying to claim more Mexican than white."

23   "I have very little white in me," Jennifer repeats. "I have mostly my dad's side, 'cause I look like him and stuff. And most of my friends think that me and my brother and sister aren't related, 'cause they look more like my mom."

24   "But you guys are all the same race, you just look different," Nicole insists. She stops eating and frowns. "OK, you're half and half each what your parents have. So you're equal as your brother and sister, you just look different. And you should be proud of what you are—every little piece and bit of what you are. Even if you were Afghan or whatever, you should be proud of it."

25   Will Mosley, Heather's 17-year-old brother, says he and his friends listen to rap groups like Compton's Most Wanted, NWA, and Above the Law because they "sing about life"—that is, what happens in Oakland, Los Angeles, anyplace but where Will is sitting today, an empty Round Table Pizza in a minimall.

26   "No matter what race you are," Will says, "if you live like we do, then that's the kind of music you like."

27   And how do they live?

28   "We don't live bad or anything," Will admits. "We live in a pretty good neigh-borhood, there's no violence or crime. I was just…we're just city people, I guess."

29   Will and his friend Adolfo Garcia, 16, say they've outgrown trying to be something they're not. "When I was 11 or 12," Will says, "I thought I was

becoming a big gangsta and stuff. Because I liked that music, and thought it was the coolest, I wanted to become that. I wore big clothes, like you wear in jail. But then I kind of woke up. I looked at myself and thought, 'Who am I trying to be?'"

They may have outgrown blatant mimicry, but Will and his friends remain   30
convinced that they can live in a suburban tract house with a well-kept lawn on a tree-lined street in "not a bad neighborhood" and still call themselves "city" people on the basis of musical tastes. "City" for these young people means crime, graffiti, drugs. The kids are law-abiding, but these activities connote what Will admiringly calls "action." With pride in his voice, Will predicts that "in a couple of years, Hayward will be like Oakland. It's starting to get more known, because of crime and things. I think it'll be bigger, more things happening, more crime, more graffiti, stealing cars."

"That's good," chimes in 15-year-old Matt Jenkins whose new beeper—an   31
item that once connoted gangsta chic but now means little more than an active social life—goes off periodically. "More fun."

The three young men imagine with disdain life in a gangsta-free zone. "Too   32
bland, too boring," Adolfo says. "You have to have something going on. You can't just have everyday life."

"Mowing your lawn," Matt sneers.   33

"Like Beaver Cleaver's house," Adolfo adds. "It's too clean out here."   34

Not only white kids believe that identity is a matter of choice or taste, or   35
that the power of "claiming" can transcend ethnicity. The Manor Park Locos— a group of mostly Mexican-Americans who hang out in San Leandro's Manor Park—say they descend from the Manor Lords, tough white guys who ruled the neighborhood a generation ago.

They "are like our...uncles and dads, the older generation," says Jesse Mar-   36
tinez, 14. "We're what they were when they were around, except we're Mexican."

"There's three generations," says Oso, Jesse's younger brother. "There's   37
Manor Lords, Manor Park Locos, and Manor Park Pee Wees." The Pee Wees consist mainly of the Locos' younger brothers, eager kids who circle the older boys on bikes and brag about "punking people."

Unlike Will Mosley, the Locos find little glamour in city life. They survey the   38
changing suburban landscape and see not "action" or "more fun" but frightening decline. Though most of them are not yet 18, the Locos are already nostalgic, long-ing for a Beaver Cleaver past that white kids who mimic them would scoff at.

Walking through nearly empty Manor Park, with its eucalyptus stands, its   39
softball diamond and tennis courts, Jesse's friend Alex, the only Asian in the group, waves his arms in a gesture of futility. "A few years ago, every bench was filled," he says. "Now no one comes here. I guess it's because of everything that's going on. My parents paid a lot for this house, and I want it to be nice for them. I just hope this doesn't turn into Oakland."

Glancing across the park at April Miller's street, Jesse says he knows what   40
the white cholitas are about. "It's not a racial thing," he explains. "It's just all the

most popular people out here are Mexican. We're just the gangstas that everyone knows. I guess those girls wanna be known.'"

41 Not every young Californian embraces the new racial hybridism. Andrea Jones, 20, an African-American who grew up in the Bay Area suburbs of Union City and Hayward, is unimpressed by what she sees mainly as shallow mimicry. "It's full of posers out here," she says. "When *Boyz N the Hood* came out on video, it was sold out for weeks. The boys all wanna be black, the girls all wanna be Mexican. It's the glamour."

42 Driving down the quiet, shaded streets of her old neighborhood in Union City, Andrea spots two white preteen boys in Raiders jackets and hugely baggy pants strutting erratically down the empty sidewalk. "Look at them," she says. "Dislocated."

43 She knows why. "In a lot of these schools out here, it's hard being white," she says. "I don't think these kids were prepared for the backlash that is going on, all the pride now in people of color's ethnicity, and our boldness with it. They have nothing like that, no identity, nothing they can say they're proud of.

44 "So they latch onto their great-grandmother who's a Cherokee, or they take on the most stereotypical aspects of being black or Mexican. It's beautiful to appreciate different aspects of other people's culture—that's like the dream of what the 21st century should be. But to garnish yourself with pop culture stereotypes just to blend—that's really sad."

45 Roland Krevocheza, 18, graduated last year from Arroyo High School in San Leandro. He is Mexican on his mother's side, Eastern European on his father's. In the new hierarchies, it may be mixed kids like Roland who have the hardest time finding their place, even as their numbers grow. (One in five marriages in California is between people of different races.) They can always be called "wannabes," no matter what they claim.

46 "I'll state all my nationalities," Roland says. But he takes a greater interest in his father's side, his Ukrainian, Romanian, and Czech ancestors. "It's more unique," he explains. "Mexican culture is all around me. We eat Mexican food all the time, I hear stories from my grandmother. I see the low-riders and stuff. I'm already part of it. I'm not trying to be; I am."

47 His darker-skinned brother "says he's not proud to be white," Roland adds. "He calls me 'Mr. Nazi.'" In the room the two share, the American flags and the reproduction of the Bill of Rights are Roland's; the Public Enemy poster belongs to his brother.

48 Roland has good reason to mistrust gangsta attitudes. In his junior year in high school, he was one of several Arroyo students who were beaten up outside the school at lunchtime by a group of Samoans who came in cars from Oakland. Roland wound up with a split lip, a concussion, and a broken tailbone. Later he was told that the assault was "gang-related"—that the Samoans were beating up anyone wearing red.

"Rappers, I don't like them," Roland says. "I think they're a bad influence   49
on kids. It makes kids think they're all tough and bad."

Those who, like Roland, dismiss the gangsta and cholo styles as affectations   50
can point to the fact that several companies market overpriced knockoffs of
"ghetto wear" targeted at teens.

But there's also something going on out here that transcends adolescent fad-   51
dishness and pop culture exoticism. When white kids call their parents "racist"
for nagging them about their baggy pants; when they learn Spanish to talk to
their boyfriends; when Mexican-American boys feel themselves descended in
spirit from white "uncles"; when children of mixed marriages insist that they are
whatever race they say they are, all of them are more than just confused.

They're inching toward what Andrea Jones calls "the dream of what the 21st   52
century should be." In the ever more diverse communities of Northern California, they're also facing the complicated reality of what their 21st century will be.

Meanwhile, in the living room of the Miller family's San Leandro home, the   53
argument continues unabated. "You don't know what you are," April's father has
told her more than once. But she just keeps on telling him he doesn't know what
time it is.

EXERCISES

Some of the Issues

1. Paragraphs 1 through 9 describe April Miller's choice of identity. Given
   what you know about April's life, why do you think she makes the choice
   she does? Do you think her reasons are valid?
2. What is April's father's reaction to her choice? What might account for the
   differences in their feelings?
3. What are the demographic changes the author describes in paragraphs 7,
   11, and 16? How might these changes affect people's attitudes toward race
   and identity?
4. What does the author say about power in paragraph 12? How does her
   analysis relate to other ideas presented in the article?
5. Paragraphs 9 through 14 give other examples of teenagers "claiming" new
   racial or ethnic identities. Who claims what and why? How can "claiming"
   cause conflict?
6. Examine the discussion between Nicole, Heather, and Jennifer about claiming (paragraphs 15 through 24). On what basis does each young woman make
   her claim?
7. Paragraphs 25 through 34 recount the discussion between Heather's older
   brother and his friends about identity. How might you account for their
   attitudes? What is your reaction to them?

8. Paragraphs 35 through 40 look at "claiming" through the eyes of a group of young Mexican-Americans, Jesse and the others in "The Manor Park Locos." Compare and contrast their attitudes with those of the other teenagers in the essay. What is Jesse's explanation for white cholitas like April Miller?
9. Why is Andrea Jones critical (paragraphs 41 through 44)? Do you agree with her analysis?
10. Paragraphs 45 through 50 examine the views of Roland Krevocheza and his brother. How do they define themselves and why?
11. After examining the varying views of the Californians in Bernstein's article, do you agree with her that "there's something also going on here that transcends adolescent faddishness and pop culture exoticism"?
12. Do you see the changes Bernstein describes in your own part of the country? If so, describe what you think is happening.
13. Do you think April and her friends are inching toward "the dream of what the 21st century should be" (paragraphs 44 and 52)? Why or why not?

The Way We Are Told

14. Why do you think the author chose to begin and end with the story of April Miller and her father?
15. How does Bernstein use the various quotes and dialog to present different but often related perspectives?
16. What do you feel is the author's opinion of the teenagers she describes? How do you draw your conclusions?

Some Subjects for Writing

17. Choose one of the persons quoted in this article. Write a letter to that person either agreeing or disagreeing with the views he or she expresses and explaining why.
18. Each one of us chooses some aspects of our personalities to emphasize and present to the world as more "real" than others. Discuss your choice of clothes, music, and behavior. What do you want these choices to say about you and your character? If your ideas about your identity have changed over time, explain how and why.
19. Taking into consideration some of the issues brought up in the article, interview a group of teenagers about their views on identity. Develop a series of question beforehand and ask follow-up questions during the interview. You will probably want to use a tape recorder. Then, write an essay in which you analyze the opinions of the teenagers you interviewed.

The Pool Players: Seven at the Golden Shovel

GWENDOLYN BROOKS

Gwendolyn Brooks was born in Kansas in 1917 and has spent most of her life in Chicago. Her first volume of poetry, A Street in Bronzeville, *was published in 1945. Many of her poems concern conditions in the African-American community. In 1950 she won the Pulitzer Prize for poetry. In 1972 she published her autobiography,* Report from Part One. *Other works include* The Near Johannesburg Boy *(1991);* Winnie *(1991), and* Blacks *(1987) from which this poem was taken.*

The Pool Players
Seven at the Golden Shovel

We real cool. We
Left school. We

Lurk late. We
Strike straight. We

Sing sin. We
Thin gin. We

Jazz June. We
Die soon.

EXERCISES

Some of the Issues

1. Read the poem aloud several times. How do the short sentences and sharp rhythms help create the portrait of the seven players?
2. Every sentence in the poem begins with the pronoun "we." What does this suggest about the players' self-definition and individuality?
3. Why might the title of the pool hall, The Golden Shovel, be appropriate?

Some Subjects for Writing

4. Write a fictional portrait of someone you believe is not making the most of his or her life. Give your character a name and physical characteristics. Use dialog and descriptions of events. Like most writers of fiction, you may draw upon your own experience of people you know, but your portrait will be a composite of reality and imagination.

5

Encounters

In the past, the United States was often referred to as a "melting pot," the idea that America functions as one vast container into which different ingredients—people, in this case—are amalgamated. The image of the melting pot does not do justice to another American ideal: the mosaic, or the belief that our various nationalities and races contribute important, unique ingredients to the whole. More recently, there has been a shift toward recognition of and tolerance for our diversity.

We all know by the time we reach our teens, and sometimes much sooner, that difference is often viewed as threatening. Through ignorance and fear of the unknown, our worst selves can emerge. This section presents a variety of encounters that are the results of such fears. Some are simply personal; others occur as part of a historical event. Brent Staples, a tall African-American man, becomes a fearsome entity with whom pedestrians avoid making eye contact. Piri Thomas recalls being on "Alien Turf"—the new kid, a Puerto Rican—in an Italian neighborhood. Walter White describes how his family's house became a target of a mob during a race riot in Atlanta early in this century.

According to the traditional history books, the Pilgrims invited the Indians to our first Thanksgiving. Michael Dorris characterizes the account as an example of the conqueror's view of history, adding that later contacts between the two groups gave Native Americans no cause for any further giving of thanks. Jeanne Wakatsuki Houston, with her husband, records her own experience in a historical event: the internment of Japanese-Americans on the West Coast at the beginning of World War II. Likewise, in the poem at the end of the unit, Dwight Okita recalls the irrational fears foisted on other Americans to justify the Japanese-American relocation policy.

┌───┐

 THINKING ABOUT THE THEME *"Encounters"*

1. Examine the photo on the opposite page taken at a demonstration in Boston in 1996. Focusing on their gestures and postures, how would you describe the people sitting on the ground? What kind of discussion do you think they might be having? How would you describe the police standing behind them?

2. Photos, like essays, can work as commentaries. Does this photo function as a commentary on the scene or situation? Why or why not? If so, what kind of commentary is it making?

3. The right to free speech is protected in the Bill of Rights, although the issue is complicated because the courts draw the line at speech that incites violence or harmful action. With your classmates, consider one or more recent incidents in which free speech was an issue. What issues were raised by critics, courts, and the media? What issues were raised in your own mind?

4. Describe an incident in your own life in which you felt threatened or in danger, whether the threat was real or imagined.

5. There have been times when police have lashed out at demonstrators, such as at the 1968 Democratic Convention in Chicago, or stood by and let things happen when they should have intervened, as in the story Walter White recounts in this chapter. What role should the police play in protecting citizens or maintaining order?

└───┘

Night Walker

BRENT STAPLES

Brent Staples was born in 1951 in Chester, Pennsylvania. He holds a Ph.D. degree in psychology from the University of Chicago and is a member of the editorial board of the New York Times *and the author of* Parallel Time: A Memoir *(1991). The selection reprinted here appeared originally in* Ms. *magazine in September 1986. In it Staples describes repeated experiences he had when he was taking walks at night. A tall African-American man, he aroused the fear of other pedestrians as well as drivers who saw him as the stereotypical mugger.*

My first victim was a woman—white, well dressed, probably in her early twenties. I came upon her late one evening on a deserted street in Hyde Park, a relatively affluent neighborhood in an otherwise mean, impoverished section of Chicago. As I swung onto the avenue behind her, there seemed to be a discreet, uninflammatory distance between us. Not so. She cast back a worried glance. To her, the youngish black man—a broad six feet two inches with a beard and billowing hair, both hands shoved into the pockets of a bulky military jacket—seemed menacingly close. After a few more quick glimpses, she picked up her pace and was soon running in earnest. Within seconds she disappeared into a cross street.

That was more than a decade ago. I was 22 years old, a graduate student newly arrived at the University of Chicago. It was in the echo of that terrified woman's footfalls that I first began to know the unwieldy inheritance I'd come into—the ability to alter public space in ugly ways. It was clear that she thought herself the quarry of a mugger, a rapist, or worse. Suffering a bout of insomnia, however, I was stalking sleep, not defenseless wayfarers. As a softy who is scarcely able to take a knife to a raw chicken—let alone hold it to a person's throat—I was surprised, embarrassed, and dismayed all at once. Her flight made me feel like an accomplice in tyranny. It also made it clear that I was indistinguishable from the muggers who occasionally seeped into the area from the surrounding ghetto. That first encounter, and those that followed, signified that a vast, unnerving gulf lay between nighttime pedestrians—particularly women—and me. And I soon gathered that being perceived as dangerous is a hazard in itself. I only needed to turn a corner into a dicey situation, or crowd some frightened, armed person in a foyer somewhere, or make an errant move after being pulled over by a policeman. Where fear and weapons meet—and they often do in urban America—there is always the possibility of death.

3   In that first year, my first away from my hometown, I was to become thoroughly familiar with the language of fear. At dark, shadowy intersections in Chicago, I could cross in front of a car stopped at a traffic light and elicit the *thunk, thunk, thunk, thunk* of the driver—black, white, male, or female—hammering down the door locks. On less traveled streets after dark, I grew accustomed to but never comfortable with people who crossed to the other side of the street rather than pass me. Then there were the standard unpleasantries with police, doormen, bouncers, cab drivers, and others whose business it is to screen out troublesome individuals *before* there is any nastiness.

4   I moved to New York nearly two years ago and I have remained an avid night walker. In central Manhattan, the near-constant crowd cover minimizes tense one-on-one street encounters. Elsewhere—visiting friends in SoHo, where sidewalks are narrow and tightly spaced buildings shut out the sky—things can get very taut indeed.

5   After dark on the warrenlike streets of Brooklyn where I live, women seem to set their faces on neutral and, with their purse straps strung across their chests bandolier style, they forge ahead as though bracing themselves against being tackled. I understand, of course, that the danger they perceive is not a hallucination. Women are particularly vulnerable to street violence, and young black males are drastically overrepresented among the perpetrators of that violence. Yet these truths are no solace against the kind of alienation that comes of being ever the suspect, against being set apart, a fearsome entity with whom pedestrians avoid making eye contact.

6   It is not altogether clear to me how I reached the ripe old age of 22 without being conscious of the lethality nighttime pedestrians attributed to me. Perhaps it was because in Chester, Pennsylvania, the small, angry industrial town where I came of age in the 1960s, I was scarcely noticeable against a backdrop of gang warfare, street knifings, and murders. I grew up one of the good boys, had perhaps a half-dozen fist fights. In retrospect, my shyness of combat has clear sources.

7   Many things go into the making of a young thug. One of those things is the consummation of the male romance with the power to intimidate. An infant discovers that random flailings send the baby bottle flying out of the crib and crashing to the floor. Delighted, the joyful babe repeats those motions again and again, seeking to duplicate the feat. Just so, I recall the points at which some of my boyhood friends were finally seduced by the perception of themselves as tough guys. When a mark cowered and surrendered his money without resistance, myth and reality merged—and paid off. It is, after all, only manly to embrace the power to frighten and intimidate. We, as men, are not supposed to give an inch of our lane on the highway; we are to seize the fighter's edge in

work and in play and even in love; we are to be valiant in the face of hostile forces.

Unfortunately, poor and powerless young men seem to take all this nonsense literally. As a boy, I saw countless tough guys locked away; I have since buried several, too. They were babies, really—a teenage cousin, a brother of 22, a childhood friend in his mid-twenties—all gone down in episodes of bravado played out in the streets. I came to doubt the virtues of intimidation early on. I chose, perhaps even unconsciously, to remain a shadow—timid, but a survivor. 8

The fearsomeness mistakenly attributed to me in public places often has a perilous flavor. The most frightening of these confusions occurred in the late 1970s and early 1980s when I worked as a journalist in Chicago. One day, rushing into the office of a magazine I was writing for with a deadline story in hand, I was mistaken for a burglar. The office manager called security and, with an ad hoc posse, pursued me through the labyrinthine halls, nearly to my editor's door. I had no way of proving who I was. I could only move briskly toward the company of someone who knew me. 9

Another time I was on assignment for a local paper and killing time before an interview. I entered a jewelry store on the city's affluent Near North Side. The proprietor excused herself and returned with an enormous red Doberman pinscher straining at the end of a leash. She stood, the dog extended toward me, silent to my questions, her eyes bulging nearly out of her head. I took a cursory look around, nodded, and bade her good night. Relatively speaking, however, I never fared as badly as another black male journalist. He went to nearby Waukegan, Illinois, a couple of summers ago to work on a story about a murderer who was born there. Mistaking the reporter for the killer, police hauled him from his car at gunpoint and but for his press credentials would probably have tried to book him. Such episodes are not uncommon. Black men trade tales like this all the time. 10

In "My Negro Problem—And Ours" Podhoretz[1] writes that the hatred he feels for blacks makes itself known to him through a variety of avenues—one being his discomfort with that "special brand of paranoid touchiness" to which he says blacks are prone. No doubt he is speaking here of black men. In time, I learned to smother the rage I felt at so often being taken for a criminal. Not to do so would surely have led to madness—via that special "paranoid touchiness" that so annoyed Podhoretz at the time he wrote the essay. 11

I began to take precautions to make myself less threatening. I move about with care, particularly late in the evening. I give a wide berth to nervous people on subway platforms during the wee hours, particularly when I have exchanged 12

---

[1]This well-known essay by Norman Podhoretz was published in 1963 in *Commentary* magazine. The article recounts Podhoretz's experience growing up as a poor Jew in New York City and describes both his fear and envy of African-American youth, whom he felt held the power in his neighborhood.

business clothes for jeans. If I happen to be entering a building behind some people who appear skittish, I may walk by, letting them clear the lobby before I return, so as not to seem to be following them. I have been calm and extremely congenial on those rare occasions when I've been pulled over by the police.

13   And on late-evening constitutionals along streets less traveled by, I employ what has proved to be an excellent tension-reducing measure: I whistle melodies from Beethoven and Vivaldi and the more popular classical composers. Even steely New Yorkers hunching toward nighttime destinations seem to relax, and occasionally they even join in the tune. Virtually everybody seems to sense that a mugger wouldn't be warbling bright, sunny selections from Vivaldi's *Four Seasons*. It is my equivalent of the cowbell that hikers wear when they know they are in bear country.

EXERCISES

Some of the Issues

1. How does Staples first discover his "ability to alter public space" (paragraph 2)?
2. What is Staples's reaction to the way he is perceived by strangers on his nightly walks? Does he show that he understands the feelings of some of those who fear him? Does he also show anger? Where?
3. What does Staples tell us about himself? About his childhood? How does this knowledge emphasize the contrast between his real self and the way he is often perceived by strangers?
4. How does Staples respond to Norman Podhoretz's contention that black men have a "special brand of paranoid touchiness" (paragraph 11)?
5. What has Staples learned to do to reduce the tension of passersby? Why does he choose the music he does? Does it solve his problem?

The Way We Are Told

6. Staples starts with an anecdote. Why does he use the word "victim" in the first sentence? Is there really a "victim"?
7. Identify examples drawn from Staples's own experience. How are they used to support the generalizations he makes?

Some Subjects for Writing

8. Write about a time when someone misjudged you or something you did. What were the circumstances? How did you feel? What was the resolution? What did you learn from the experience?

9. Observe and reflect on your own neighborhood. Write an essay in which you examine to what extent "outsiders" are welcome in your community. You may want to focus on one incident or examine a particular public place in your area (for example, a bar frequented only by men).

10. In 1903 W. E. B. DuBois, one of the most prominent African-American intellectuals, predicted that the "problem of the Twentieth Century is the problem of the color line." To what extent do you believe he was right?

Alien Turf

PIRI THOMAS

Piri Thomas was born in Spanish Harlem in 1928 and grew up in its world of gangs, drugs, and petty crime. In his teens he became an addict, was convicted of attempted armed robbery, and served six years of a 15-year sentence. After his release, he began to work for drug rehabilitation programs in New York and Puerto Rico and developed a career as a writer. The autobiographical Down These Mean Streets *(1967), from which the following selection is taken, was his first book. A sequel,* Savior, Savior, Hold My Hand, *was published in 1972.*

Thomas tells the reader about an event in his childhood, one that many young people will have experienced: being the new kid on the block. But when the block is in a poor neighborhood and when, moreover, the new kid is from a background different from the prevailing culture, then the mix can turn explosive.

1   Sometimes you don't fit in. Like if you're a Puerto Rican on an Italian block. After my new baby brother, Ricardo, died of some kind of germs, Poppa moved us from 111th Street to Italian turf on 114th Street between Second and Third Avenue. I guess Poppa wanted to get Momma away from the hard memories of the old pad.

2   I sure missed 111th Street, where everybody acted, walked, and talked like me. But on 114th Street everything went all right for a while. There were a few dirty looks from the spaghetti-an'-sauce cats, but no big sweat. Till that one day I was on my way home from school and almost had reached my stoop when someone called: "Hey, you dirty fuckin' spic."

3   The words hit my ears and almost made me curse Poppa at the same time. I turned around real slow and found my face pushing in the finger of an Italian kid about my age. He had five or six of his friends with him.

4   "Hey, you," he said, "What nationality are ya?"

5   I looked at him and wondered which nationality to pick. And one of his friends said, "Ah, Rocky, he's black enuff to be a nigger. Ain't that what you is, kid?"

6   My voice was almost shy in its anger. "I'm Puerto Rican," I said. "I was born here." I wanted to shout it, but it came out like a whisper.

"Right here inna street?" Rocky sneered. "Ya mean right here inna middle   7
of da street?"

They all laughed. I hated them. I shook my head slowly from side to side.   8
"Uh-uh," I said softly. "I was born inna hospital—inna bed."   9
"Umm, *paisan*[1]—born inna bed," Rocky said.   10

I didn't like Rocky Italiano's voice. "Inna hospital," I whispered, and all the   11
time my eyes were trying to cut down the long distance from this trouble to my
stoop. But it was no good; I was hemmed in by Rocky's friends. I couldn't help
thinking about kids getting wasted for moving into a block belonging to other
people.

"What hospital, *paisan?*" Bad Rocky pushed.   12

"Harlem Hospital," I answered, wishing like all hell that it was 5 o'clock   13
instead of just 3 o'clock, 'cause Poppa came home at 5. I looked around for some
friendly faces belonging to grown-up people, but the elders were all busy yak-
king away in Italian. I couldn't help thinking how much like Spanish it sounded.
Shit, that should make us something like relatives.

"Harlem Hospital?" said a voice. "I knew he was a nigger."   14

"Yeah," said another voice from an expert on color. "That's the hospital   15
where all them black bastards get born at."

I dug three Italian elders looking at us from across the street and I felt saved.   16
But that went out the window when they just smiled and went on talking. I
couldn't decide whether they had smiled because this new whatever-he-was was
gonna get his ass kicked or because they were pleased that their kids were welcoming a new kid to their country. An older man nodded his head at Rocky, who
smiled back. I wondered if that was a signal for my funeral to begin.

"Ain't that right, kid?" Rocky pressed. "Ain't that where all black people get   17
born?"

I dug some of Rocky's boys grinding and pushing and punching closed fists   18
against open hands. I figured they were looking to shake me up, so I straightened
up my humble voice and made like proud. "There's all kinds of people born there.
Colored people, Puerto Ricans like me, an'—even spaghetti-benders like you."

"That's a dirty fuckin' lie"—*bash*, I felt Rocky's fist smack into my mouth—   19
"You dirty fuckin' spic."

I got dizzy and then more dizzy when fists started to fly from everywhere   20
and only toward me. I swung back, *splat, bish*—my fist hit some face and I wished
I hadn't, 'cause then I started getting kicked.

I heard people yelling in Italian and English and I wondered if maybe it was   21
'cause I hadn't fought fair in having hit that one guy. But it wasn't. The voices
were trying to help me.

"Whas'sa matta, you no-good kids, leeva da kid alone," a man said. I looked   22
through a swelling eye and dug some Italians pushing their kids off me with

[1]Buddy.

slaps. One even kicked a kid in the ass. I could have loved them if I didn't hate them so fuckin' much.

23   "You all right, kiddo?" asked the man.

24   "Where you live, boy?" said another one.

25   "Is the *bambino*[2] hurt?" asked a woman.

26   I didn't look at any of them. I felt dizzy. I didn't want to open my mouth to talk, 'cause I was fighting to keep from puking up. I just hoped my face was cool-looking. I walked away from the group of strangers. I reached my stoop and started to climb the steps.

27   "Hey, spic," came a shout from across the street. I started to turn to the voice and changed my mind. "Spic" wasn't my name. I knew that voice, though. It was Rocky's. "We'll see ya again, spic," he said.

28   I wanted to do something tough, like spitting in their direction. But you gotta have spit in your mouth in order to spit, and my mouth was hurt dry. I just stood there with my back to them.

29   "Hey, your old man just better be the janitor in that fuckin' building."

30   Another voice added, "Hey, you got any pretty sisters? We might let ya stay onna block."

31   Another voice mocked, "Aw, fer Chrissake, where ya ever hear of one of them black broads being pretty?"

32   I heard the laughter. I turned around and looked at them. Rocky made some kind of dirty sign by putting his left hand in the crook of his right arm while twisting his closed fist in the air.

33   Another voice said, "Fuck it, we'll just cover the bitch's face with the flag an' fuck'er for old glory."

34   All I could think of was how I'd like to kill each of them two or three times. I found some spit in my mouth and splattered it in their direction and went inside.

35   Momma was cooking, and the smell of rice and beans was beating the smell of Parmesan cheese from the other apartments. I let myself into our new pad. I tried to walk fast past Momma so I could wash up, but she saw me.

36   "My God, Piri, what happened?" she cried.

37   "Just a little fight in school, Momma. You know how it is, Momma, I'm new in school an'..." I made myself laugh. Then I made myself say, "But Moms, I whipped the living _____ outta two guys, an' one was bigger'n me."

38   "*Bendito*,[3] Piri, I raise my family in Christian way. Not to fight. Christ says to turn the other cheek."

39   "Sure, Momma." I smiled and went and showered, feeling sore at Poppa for bringing us into spaghetti country. I felt my face with easy fingers and thought about all the running back and forth from school that was in store for me.

[2]Child.
[3]Blessed.

I sat down to dinner and listened to Momma talk about Christian living   40
without really hearing her. All I could think of was that I hadda go out in that
street again. I made up my mind to go out right after I finished eating. I had to,
shook up or not; cats like me had to show heart.

"Be back, Moms," I said after dinner. "I'm going out on the stoop." I got   41
halfway to the stoop and turned and went back to our apartment. I knocked.

"Who is it?" Momma asked.   42

"Me, Momma."   43

She opened the door. "*¿Qué pasa?*"⁴ she asked.   44

"Nothing, Momma, I just forgot something," I said. I went into the bed-   45
room and fiddled around and finally copped a funny book and walked out the
door again. But this time I made sure the switch on the lock was open, just in
case I had to get back real quick. I walked out on that stoop as cool as could be,
feeling braver with the lock open.

There was no sign of Rocky and his killers. After awhile I saw Poppa coming   46
down the street. He walked like beat tired. Poppa hated his pick-and-shovel job
with the WPA. He couldn't even hear the name WPA without getting a fever.
Funny, I thought, *Poppa's the same like me, a stone Puerto Rican, and nobody in this
block even pays him a mind. Maybe older people get along better'n us kids.*

Poppa was climbing the stoop. "Hi, Poppa," I said.   47

"How's it going, son? Hey, you sure look a little lumped up. What happened?"   48

I looked at Poppa and started to talk it outta me all at once and stopped,   49
'cause I heard my voice start to sound scared, and that was no good.

"Slow down, son," Poppa said. "Take it easy." He sat down on the stoop and   50
made a motion for me to do the same. He listened and I talked. I gained confidence. I went from a tone of being shook up by the Italians to a tone of being
a better fighter than Joe Louis and Pedro Montanez lumped together, with Kid
Chocolate thrown in for extra.

"So that's what happened," I concluded. "And it looks like only the begin-   51
ning. Man, I ain't scared, Poppa, but like there's nothin' but Italianos on this
block and there's no me's like me except for me an' our family."

Poppa looked tight. He shook his head from side to side and mumbled   52
something about another Puerto Rican family that lived a coupla doors down
from us.

I thought, *What good would that do me, unless they prayed over my dead body in*   53
Spanish? But I said, "Man! That's great. Before ya know it, there'll be a whole
bunch of us moving in, huh?"

Poppa grunted something and got up. "Staying out here, son?"   54

"Yeah, Poppa, for a little while longer."   55

From that day on I grew eyes all over my head. Anytime I hit that street for   56
anything, I looked straight ahead, behind me and from side to side all at the

⁴What's happening?

same time. Sometimes I ran into Rocky and his boys—the cat was never without his boys—but they never made a move to snag me. They just grinned at me like a bunch of hungry alley cats that could get to their mouse anytime they wanted. That's what they made me feel like—a mouse. Not like a smart house mouse but like a white house pet that ain't got no business in the middle of cat country but don't know better 'cause he grew thinking he was a cat—which wasn't far from wrong 'cause he'd end up as part of the inside of some cat.

57   Rocky and his fellas got to playing a way-out game with me called "One-finger-across-the-neck-inna-slicing-motion," followed by such gentle words as "It won't be long, spico." I just looked at them blank and made it to wherever I was going.

58   I kept wishing those cats went to the same school I went to, a school that was on the border between their country and mine, and I had *amigos* there—and there I could count on them. But I couldn't ask two or three *amigos* to break into Rocky's block and help me mess up his boys. I knew 'cause I had asked them already. They had turned me down fast, and I couldn't blame them. It would have been murder, and I guess they figured one murder would be better than four.

59   I got through the days trying to play it cool and walk on by Rocky and his boys like they weren't there. One day I passed them and nothing was said. I started to let out my breath. I felt great; I hadn't been seen. Then someone yelled in a high, girlish voice, "Yoo-hoo…Hey, *paisan*…we see yoo…" And right behind that voice came a can of evaporated milk—whoosh, clatter. I walked cool for ten steps then started running like mad.

60   This crap kept up for a month. They tried to shake me up. Every time they threw something at me, it was just to see me jump. I decided that the next fucking time they threw something at me I was gonna play bad-o and not run. That next time came about a week later. Momma sent me off the stoop to the Italian market on 115th Street and First Avenue, deep in Italian country. Man, that was stompin' territory. But I went, walking in the style which I had copped from the colored cats I had seen, a swinging and stepping down hard at every step. Those cats were so down and cool that just walking made a way-out sound.

61   Ten minutes later I was on my way back with Momma's stuff. I got to the corner of First Avenue and 114th Street and crushed myself right into Rocky and his fellas.

62   "Well-l, fellas," Rocky said, "Lookee who's here."

63   I didn't like the sounds coming out of Rocky's fat mouth. And I didn't like the sameness of the shitty grins spreading all over the boys' faces. But I thought, *No more! No more! I ain't gonna run no more.* Even so, I looked around, like for some kind of Jesus miracle to happen. I was always looking for miracles to happen.

64   "Say, *paisan*," one guy said, "you even buying from us *paisans*, eh? Man, you must wantta be Italian."

Before I could bite that dopey tongue of mine, I said, "I wouldn't be a   65
guinea on a motherfucking bet."

"Wha-at?" said Rocky, really surprised. I didn't blame him; I was surprised   66
myself. His finger began digging a hole in his ear, like he hadn't heard me right.
"Wha-at? Say that again?"

I could feel a thin hot wetness cutting itself down my leg. I had been so   67
ashamed of being so damned scared that I had peed on myself. And then I wasn't
scared any more; I felt a fuck-it-all attitude. I looked real bad at Rocky and said,
"Ya heard me. I wouldn't be a guinea on a bet."

"Ya little sonavabitch, we'll kick the shit outta ya," said one guy, Tony, who   68
had made a habit of asking me if I had any sen-your-ritas for sisters.

"Kick the shit outta me yourself if you got any heart, you mother fuckin'   69
fucker," I screamed at him. I felt kind of happy, the kind of feeling that you get
only when you got heart.

Big-mouth Tony just swung out, and I swung back and heard all of   70
Momma's stuff plopping all over the street. My fist hit Tony smack dead in the
mouth. He was so mad he threw a fist at me from about three feet away. I faked
and jabbed and did fancy dance steps. Big-mouth put a stop to all that with a
punch in my mouth. I heard the home cheers of "Yea, yea, bust that spic wide
open!" Then I bloodied Tony's nose. He blinked and sniffed without putting his
hands to his nose, and I remembered Poppa telling me, "Son, if you're ever
fighting somebody an' you punch him in the nose, and he just blinks an' sniffs
without holding his nose, you can do one of two things: fight like hell or run
like hell—'cause that cat's a fighter."

Big-mouth came at me and we grabbed each other and pushed and pulled   71
and shoved. *Poppa,* I thought, *I ain't gonna cop out. I'm a fighter, too.* I pulled away
from Tony and blew my fist into his belly. He puffed and butted my nose with
his head. I sniffed back. *Poppa, I didn't put my hands to my nose.* I hit Tony again
in that same weak spot. He bent over in the middle and went down to his knees.

Big-mouth got up as fast as he could, and I was thinking how much heart   72
he had. But I ran toward him like my life depended on it; I wanted to cool him.
Too late. I saw his hand grab a fistful of ground asphalt which had been piled
nearby to fix a pothole in the street. I tried to duck; I should have closed my
eyes instead. The shitty-gritty stuff hit my face, and I felt the scrappy pain make
itself a part of my eyes. I screamed and grabbed for two eyes with one hand,
while the other I beat some kind of helpless tune on air that just couldn't be
hurt. I heard Rocky's voice shouting, "Ya scum bag, ya didn't have to fight the
spic dirty; you could've fucked him up fair and square!" I couldn't see. I heard a
fist hit a face, then Big-mouth's voice: "Whatta ya hittin' me for?" and then
Rocky's voice: "*Putana!*[5] I ought ta knock all your fuckin' teeth out."

[5]Whore.

73   I felt hands grabbing at me between my screams. I punched out. *I'm gonna get killed*, I thought. Then I heard many voices: "Hold it, kid." "We ain't gonna hurt ya." "Je-*sus*, don't rub your eyes." "Ooooohhhh, shit, his eyes is fulla that shit."

74   *You're fuckin' right*, I thought, *and it hurts like* coño.

75   I heard a woman's voice now: "Take him to a hospital." And an old man asked: "How did it happen?"

76   "Momma, Momma," I cried.

77   "Comon, kid," Rocky said, taking my hand. "Lemme take ya home." I fought for the right to rub my eyes. "Grab his other hand, Vincent," Rocky said. I tried to rub my eyes with my eyelids. I could feel hurt tears cutting down my cheeks. "Come on, kid, we ain't gonna hurt ya," Rocky tried to assure me. "Swear to our mudders. We just wanna take ya home."

78   I made myself believe him, and trying not to make pain noises, I let myself be led home. I wondered if I was gonna be blind like Mr. Silva, who went around from door to door selling dish towels and brooms, his son leading him around.

79   "You okay, kid?" Rocky asked.

80   "Yeah," what was left of me said.

81   "A-huh," mumbled Big-mouth.

82   "He got much heart for a nigger," somebody else said.

83   A *spic*, I thought.

84   "For anybody," Rocky said. "Here we are kid," he added. "Watch your step."

85   I was like carried up the steps. "What's your apartment number?" Rocky asked.

86   "One-B—inna back—ground floor," I said, and I was led there. Somebody knocked on Momma's door. Then I heard running feet and Rocky's voice yelling back, "Don't rat, huh, kid?" And I was alone.

87   I heard the door open and Momma say, "*Bueno*, Piri, come in." I didn't move. I couldn't. There was a long pause; I could hear Momma's fright. "My God," she said finally "What's happened?" Then she took a closer look. "Aieeee," she screamed. "¡Dios mío!"[6]

88   "I was playing with some kids, Momma," I said, "an' I got some dirt in my eyes." I tried to make my voice come out without the pain, like a man.

89   "*Dios eterno*[7]—your eyes!"

90   "What's the matter? What's the matter?" Poppa called from the bedroom.

91   "¡*Está ciego!*[8]" Momma screamed. "He is blind!"

92   I heard Poppa knocking things over as he came running. Sis began to cry. Blind, hurting tears were jumping out of my eyes. "Whattya mean, he's blind?"

---

[6]My God.
[7]Eternal God.
[8]He's blind!

Poppa said as he stormed into the kitchen. "What happened?" Poppa's voice was
both scared and mad.

"Playing, Poppa." 93

"Whatta ya mean, 'playing'?" Poppa's English sounded different when he 94
got warm.

"Just playing, Poppa." 95

"Playing? Playing got all that dirt in your eyes? I bet my ass. Them damn 96
Ee-ta-liano kids ganged up on you again." Poppa squeezed my head between the
fingers of one hand. "That settles it—we're moving outta this damn section,
outta this damn block, outta this damn shit."

Shit, I thought, *Poppa's sure cursin' up a storm.* I could hear him slapping the 97
side of his leg, like he always did when he got real mad.

"Son," he said, "you're gonna point them out to me." 98

"Point who out, Poppa? I was playin' an'—" 99

"Stop talkin' to him and take him to the hospital!" Momma screamed. 100

"*Pobrecito,*[9] poor Piri," cooed my little sister. 101

"You sure, son?" Poppa asked. "You was only playing?" 102

"Shit, Poppa, I said I was." 103

Smack—Poppa was so scared and mad, he let it out in the slap to the side of 104
my face.

"*¡Bestia!* ani-*mul!*" Momma cried. "He's blind, and you hit him!" 105

"I'm sorry, son, I'm sorry," Poppa said in a voice like almost crying. I heard 106
him running back into the bedroom yelling, "Where's my pants?"

Momma grabbed away fingers that were trying to wipe away the hurt in my 107
eyes. "*Caramba,* no rub, no rub," she said, kissing me. She told Sis to get a rag
and wet it with cold water.

Poppa came running back into the kitchen. "Let's go, son, let's go. Jesus! I 108
didn't mean to smack ya, I really didn't," he said, his big hand rubbing and grabbing my hair gently.

"Here's the rag, Momma," said Sis. 109

"What's that for?" asked Poppa. 110

"To put on his eyes," Momma said. 111

I heard the smack of a wet rag, *blapt,* against the kitchen wall. "We can't put 112
nothing on his eyes. It might make them worse. Come on, son," Poppa said nervously, lifting me up in his big arms. I felt like a little baby, like I didn't hurt so
bad. I wanted to stay there, but I said, "Let me down, Poppa, I ain't no kid."

"Shut up," Poppa said softly. "I know you ain't but it's faster this way." 113

"Which hospeetal are you taking him to?" Momma asked. 114

"Nearest one," Poppa answered as we went out the door. He carried me 115
through the hall and out into the street, where the bright sunlight made a red

---

[9]You poor boy.

hurting color through the crap in my eyes. I heard voices on the stoop and on the sidewalk: "Is that the boy?"

116   "A-huh. He's probably blinded."

117   "We'll get a cab, son," Poppa said. His voice loved me. I heard Rocky yelling from across the street, "We're pulling for ya, kid. Remember what we…" The rest was lost to Poppa's long legs running down to the corner of Third Avenue. He hailed a taxi and we zoomed off toward Harlem Hospital. I felt the cab make all kinds of sudden stops and turns.

118   "How do you feel, *hijo?*"[10] Poppa asked.

119   "It burns like hell."

120   "You'll be okay," he said, and as an afterthought added, "Don't curse, son."

121   I heard cars honking and the Third Avenue el roaring above us. I knew we were in Puerto Rican turf, 'cause I could hear our language.

122   "Son."

123   "Yeah, Poppa."

124   "Don't rub your eyes, fer Christ sake." He held my skinny wrists in his one hand, and everything got quiet between us.

125   The cab got to Harlem Hospital. I heard change being handled and the door opening and Poppa thanking the cabbie for getting here fast. "Hope the kid'll be okay," the driver said.

126   *I will be,* I thought, *I ain't gonna be like Mr. Silva.*

127   Poppa took me in his arms again and started running. "Where's emergency mister?" he asked someone.

128   "To your left and straight away," said a voice.

129   "Thanks a lot," Poppa said, and we were running again.

130   "Emergency?" Poppa said when we stopped.

131   "Yes, sir," said a girl's voice. "What's the matter?"

132   "My boy's got his eyes full of ground-up tar an'—"

133   "What's the matter?" said a man's voice.

134   "Youngster with ground tar in his eyes, doctor."

135   "We'll take him, mister. You just put him down here and go with the nurse. She'll take down the information. Uh, you the father?"

136   "That's right, doctor."

137   "Okay, just put him down here."

138   "Poppa, don't leave me," I cried.

139   "Sh, son, I ain't leaving you. I'm just going to fill out some papers, an' I'll be right back."

140   I nodded my head up and down and was wheeled away. When the rolling stretcher stopped, somebody stuck a needle in me and I got sleepy and started thinking about Rocky and his boys, and Poppa's slap, and how great Poppa was, and how my eyes didn't hurt no more…

[10]Son.

I woke up in a room blind with darkness. The only lights were the ones   141
inside my head. I put my fingers to my eyes and felt bandages. "Let them be,
sonny," said a woman's voice.

I wanted to ask the voice if they had taken my eyes out, but I didn't. I was   142
afraid the voice would say yes.

"Let them be, sonny," the nurse said, pulling my hand away from the ban-   143
dages. "You're all right. The doctor put the bandages on to keep the light out.
They'll be off real soon. Don't you worry none, sonny."

I wished she would stop calling me sonny. "Where's Poppa?" I asked cool   144
like.

"He's outside, sonny. Would you like me to send him in?"   145

I nodded. "Yeah." I heard walking-away shoes, a door opening, a whisper,   146
and shoes walking back toward me. "How do you feel, *hijo?*" Poppa asked.

"It hurts like shit, Poppa."   147

"It's just for awhile, son, and then off come the bandages. Everything's   148
gonna be all right."

I thought, *Poppa didn't tell me to stop cursing.*   149

"And son, I thought I told you to stop cursing," he added.   150

I smiled. Poppa hadn't forgotten. Suddenly I realized that all I had on was   151
a hospital gown. "Poppa, where's my clothes?" I asked.

"I got them. I'm taking them home an'—"   152

"Whatta ya mean, Poppa?" I said, like scared. "You ain't leavin' me here?   153
I'll be damned if I stay." I was already sitting up and feeling my way outta bed.
Poppa grabbed me and pushed me back. His voice wasn't mad or scared any
more. It was happy and soft, like Momma's.

"Hey," he said, "get your ass back in bed or they'll have to put a bandage   154
there too."

"Poppa," I pleaded. "I don't care, wallop me as much as you want, just take   155
me home."

"Hey, I thought you said you wasn't no kid. Hell, you ain't scared of being   156
alone?"

Inside my head there was a running of *Yeah, yeah, yeah,* but I answered,   157
"Naw, Poppa, it's just that Momma's gonna worry and she'll get sick an' everything, and—"

"Won't work, son," Poppa broke in with a laugh.   158

I kept quiet.   159

"It's only for a couple days. We'll come and see you an' everybody'll bring   160
you things."

I got interested but played it smooth. "What kinda things, Poppa?"   161

Poppa shrugged his shoulders and spread his big arms apart and answered   162
me like he was surprised that I should ask. "Uh…fruits and…candy and ice
cream. And Momma will probably bring you chicken soup."

I shook my head sadly, "Poppa, you know I don't like chicken soup."   163

164 "So we won't bring chicken soup. We'll bring what you like. Goddammit, whatta ya like?"

165 "I'd like the first things you talked about, Poppa," I said softly. "But instead of soup I'd like"—I held my breath back, then shot it out—"some roller skates!"

166 Poppa let out a whistle. Roller skates were about $1.50, and that was rice and beans for more than a few days. Then he said, "All right, son, soon as you get home, you got 'em."

167 But he had agreed too quickly. I shook my head from side to side. Shit, I was gonna push all the way for the roller skates. It wasn't every day you'd get hurt bad enough to ask for something so little like a pair of roller skates. I wanted them right away.

168 "Fer Christ sakes," Poppa protested, "you can't use 'em in here. Why, some kid will probably steal 'em on you." But Poppa's voice died out slowly in a "you win" tone as I just kept shaking my head from side to side. "Bring 'em tomorrow," he finally mumbled, "but that's it."

169 "Thanks, Poppa."

170 "Don't ask for no more."

171 My eyes were starting to hurt like mad again. The fun was starting to go outta the game between Poppa and me. I made a face.

172 "Does it hurt, son?"

173 "Naw, Poppa. I can take it." I thought how I was like a cat in a movie about Indians, taking it like a champ, tied to a stake and getting like burned toast.

174 Poppa sounded relieved. "Yeah, it's only at first it hurts." His hand touched my foot. "Well, I'll be going now…" Poppa rubbed my foot gently and then slapped me the same gentle way on the side of my leg. "Be good, son," he said and walked away. I heard the door open and the nurse telling him about how they were gonna move me to the ward 'cause I was out of danger. "Son," Poppa called back, "you're *un hombre*."[11]

175 I felt proud as hell.

176 "Poppa."

177 "Yeah, son?"

178 "You won't forget to bring the roller skates, huh?"

179 Poppa laughed, "Yeah, son."

180 I heard the door close.

---

[11]A man.

EXERCISES

Some of the Issues

1. How do the first two sentences set the scene?
2. Piri wants to project a certain self-image in front of the gang. Characterize it.
3. Until the climactic fight, the cat-and-mouse game that Rocky's gang plays goes through several stages. Determine what these stages are and how Piri reacts to them.
4. How do the adults (those in the street as well as Piri's parents) react to the situation at the various stages? How does Piri deal with his parents' reactions in particular?
5. How does Rocky's attitude toward Piri change after one of the gang members throws the asphalt? What causes the change?
6. What is the significance of Thomas calling himself a "spic" in paragraph 83?
7. Explain Piri's reaction to "spic" and "nigger." Is Piri's desire to be identified as a Puerto Rican a matter of pride or practicality?
8. What is the importance of being "*un hombre*," of having "heart"? How does Piri prove himself a man? By whose standards?

The Way We Are Told

9. There is almost no description in this selection; it is all action and dialog. Thomas nevertheless manages to convey some strong impressions of individuals and their attitudes. How does he do it? Cite some examples.
*10. Both Angelou ("Graduation") and Thomas tell their stories from an adolescent's point of view. Apart from the content, how do the two stories differ? What causes the differences?

Some Subjects for Writing

11. Write about a conflict that you have had. Set the scene and then use mostly dialog to tell your story. See if you can make the voices authentic.
*12. The term "rite of passage" is usually used to indicate the ceremony marking the formal change of a young person from childhood to adulthood, such as a confirmation or *bar mitzvah*, though it is not always a religious ceremony. Write an essay arguing that Angelou's graduation and Thomas's big fight (or one or the other) were such rites of passage.

I Learn What I Am

WALTER WHITE

*Walter White was born in Atlanta, Georgia, in 1893. He joined the
NAACP early in its development and served as its head from 1931
until his death in 1955. The following excerpt is taken from his autobiography, A Man Called White (1948).*

*The events White describes took place in his childhood, at the
beginning of the twentieth century. The year was 1906 and he was
living in Atlanta with his large family, near the line that separated the
white community from his own. His father, an employee of the U.S.
Postal Service, kept the house in immaculate repair, its white picket
fence symbolizing the American Dream. When a race riot erupted in
Atlanta, their house became a target of the mob. White tells the dramatic story of those two days.*

1   There were nine light-skinned Negroes in my family: mother, father, five sisters,
an older brother, George, and myself. The house in which I discovered what it
meant to be a Negro was located on Houston Street, three blocks from the Can-
dler Building, Atlanta's first skyscraper, which bore the name of the ex-drug
clerk who had become a millionaire from the sale of Coca-Cola. Below us lived
none but Negroes; toward town all but a very few were white. Ours was an eight
room, two-story frame house which stood out in its surroundings not because
of its opulence but by contrast with the drabness and unpaintedness of the other
dwellings in a deteriorating neighborhood.

2   Only Father kept his house painted, the picket fence repaired, the board
fence separating our place from those on either side whitewashed, the grass
neatly trimmed, and flower beds abloom. Mother's passion for neatness was even
more pronounced and it seemed to me that I was always the victim of her deter-
mination to see no single blade of grass longer than the others or any one of the
pickets in the front fence less shiny with paint than its mates. This spic-and-
spanness became increasingly apparent as the rest of the neighborhood became
more down-at-heel, and resulted, as we were to learn, in sullen envy among
some of our white neighbors. It was the violent expression of that resentment
against a Negro family neater than themselves which set the pattern of our lives.

3   On a day in September 1906, when I was thirteen, we were taught that there
is no isolation from life. The unseasonably oppressive heat of an Indian summer
day hung like a steaming blanket over Atlanta. My sisters and I had casually

commented upon the unusual quietness. It seemed to stay Mother's volubility and reduced Father, who was more taciturn, to monosyllables. But, as I remember it, no other sense of impending trouble impinged upon our consciousness.

I had read the inflammatory headlines in the *Atlanta News* and the more   4
restrained ones in the *Atlanta Constitution* which reported alleged rapes and other crimes committed by Negroes. But these were so standard and familiar that they made—as I look back on it now—little impression. The stories were more frequent, however, and consisted of eight-column streamers instead of the usual two- or four-column ones.

Father was a mail collector. His tour of duty was from three to eleven P.M.   5
He made his rounds in a little cart into which one climbed from a step in the rear. I used to drive the cart for him from two until seven, leaving him at the point nearest our home on Houston Street, to return home either for study or sleep. That day Father decided that I should not go with him. I appealed to Mother, who thought it might be all right, provided Father sent me home before dark because, she said, "I don't think they would dare start anything before nightfall." Father told me as we made the rounds that ominous rumors of a race riot that night were sweeping the town. But I was too young that morning to understand the background of the riot. I became much older during the next thirty-six hours, under circumstances which I now recognize as the inevitable outcome of what had preceded....

During the afternoon preceding the riot little bands of sullen, evil-looking   6
men talked excitedly on street corners all over downtown Atlanta. Around seven o'clock my father and I were driving toward a mail box at the corner of Peachtree and Houston Streets when there came from near-by Pryor Street a roar the like of which I had never heard before, but which sent a sensation of mingled fear and excitement coursing through my body. I asked permission of Father to go and see what the trouble was. He bluntly ordered me to stay in the cart. A little later we drove down Atlanta's main business thoroughfare, Peachtree Street. Again we heard the terrifying cries, this time near at hand and coming toward us. We saw a lame Negro bootblack from Herndon's barber shop pathetically trying to outrun a mob of whites. Less than a hundred yards from us the chase ended. We saw clubs and fists descending to the accompaniment of savage shouting and cursing. Suddenly a voice cried, "There goes another nigger!" Its work done, the mob went after the new prey. The body with the withered foot lay dead in a pool of blood on the street.

Father's apprehension and mine steadily increased during the evening,   7
although the fact that our skins were white kept us from attack. Another circumstance favored us—the mob had not yet grown violent enough to attack United States government property. But I could see Father's relief when he punched the time clock at eleven P.M. and got into the cart to go home. He wanted to go the back way down Forsyth Street, but I begged him, in my childish excitement and ignorance, to drive down Marietta to Five Points, the heart of Atlanta's business

district, where the crowds were densest and the yells loudest. No sooner had we turned into Marietta Street, however, than we saw careening toward us an undertaker's barouche. Crouched in the rear of the vehicle were three Negroes clinging to the sides of the carriage as it lunged and swerved. On the driver's seat crouched a white man, the reins held taut in his left hand. A huge whip was gripped in his right. Alternately he lashed the horses and, without looking backward, swung the whip in savage swoops in the faces of members of the mob as they lunged at the carriage determined to seize the three Negroes.

8   There was no time for us to get out of its path, so sudden and swift was the appearance of the vehicle. The hub cap of the right rear wheel of the barouche hit the right side of our much lighter wagon. Father and I instinctively threw our weight and kept the cart from turning completely over. Our mare was a Texas mustang which, frightened by the sudden blow, lunged in the air as Father clung to the reins. Good fortune was with us. The cart settled back on its four wheels as Father said in a voice which brooked no dissent, "We are going home the back way and not down Marietta."

9   But again on Pryor Street we heard the cry of the mob. Close to us and in our direction ran a stout and elderly woman who cooked at a downtown white hotel. Fifty yards behind, a mob which filled the street from curb to curb was closing in. Father handed the reins to me and, though he was of slight stature, reached down and lifted the woman into the cart. I did not need to be told to lash the mare to the fastest speed she could muster.

10   The church bells tolled the next morning for Sunday service. But no one in Atlanta believed for a moment that the hatred and lust for blood had been appeased. Like skulls on a cannibal's hut the hats and caps of victims of the mob of the night before had been hung on the iron hooks of telegraph poles. None could tell whether each hat represented a dead Negro. But we knew that some of those who had worn the hats would never again wear any.

11   Late in the afternoon friends of my father's came to warn of more trouble that night. They told us that plans had been perfected for a mob to form on Peachtree Street just after nightfall to march down Houston Street to what the white people called "Darktown," three blocks or so below our house, "to clean out the niggers." There had never been a firearm in our house before that day. Father was reluctant even in those circumstances to violate the law, but he at last gave in at Mother's insistence.

12   We turned out the lights early, as did all our neighbors. No one removed his clothes or thought of sleep. Apprehension was tangible. We could almost touch its cold and clammy surface. Toward midnight the unnatural quiet was broken by a roar that grew steadily in volume. Even today I grow tense in remembering it.

13   Father told mother to take my sisters, the youngest of them only six, to the rear of the house, which offered more protection from stones and bullets. My brother George was away, so Father and I, the only males in the house, took our

places at the front windows of the parlor. The windows opened on a porch along the front side of the house, which in turn gave onto a narrow lawn that sloped down to the street and a picket fence. There was a crash as Negroes smashed the street lamp at the corner of Houston and Piedmont Avenue down the street. In a very few minutes the vanguard of the mob, some of them bearing torches, appeared. A voice which we recognized as that of the son of the grocer with whom we had traded for many years yelled, "That's where that nigger mail carrier lives! Let's burn it down! It's too nice for a nigger to live in!" In the eerie light Father turned his drawn face toward me. In a voice as quiet as though he were asking me to pass him the sugar at the breakfast table, he said, "Son, don't shoot until the first man puts his foot on the lawn and then—don't you miss!"

In the flickering light the mob swayed, paused, and began to flow toward   14 us. In that instant there opened up within me a great awareness; I knew then who I was. I was a Negro, a human being with an invisible pigmentation which marked me a person to be hunted, hanged, abused, discriminated against, kept in poverty and ignorance, in order that those whose skin was white would have readily at hand a proof of their superiority, a proof patent and inclusive, accessible to the moron and the idiot as well as to the wise man and the genius. No matter how low a white man fell, he could always hold fast to the smug conviction that he was superior to two-thirds of the world's population, for those two-thirds were not white.

It made no difference how intelligent or talented my millions of brothers   15 and I were, or how virtuously we lived. A curse like that of Judas was upon us, a mark of degradation fashioned with heavenly authority. There were white men who said Negroes had no souls, and who proved it by the Bible. Some of these now were approaching us, intent upon burning our house.

Theirs was a world of contrasts in values: superior and inferior, profit and   16 loss, cooperative and noncooperative, civilized and aboriginal, white and black. If you were on the wrong end of the comparison, if you were inferior, if you were noncooperative, if you were aboriginal, if you were black, then you were marked for excision, expulsion, or extinction. I was a Negro; I was therefore that part of history which opposed the good, the just, and the enlightened. I was a Persian, falling before the hordes of Alexander. I was a Carthaginian, extinguished by the Legions of Rome. I was a Frenchman at Waterloo, an Anglo-Saxon at Hastings, a Confederate at Vicksburg. I was the defeated, wherever and whenever there was a defeat.

Yet as a boy there in the darkness amid the tightening fright, I knew the   17 inexplicable thing—that my skin was as white as the skin of those who were coming at me.

The mob moved toward the lawn. I tried to aim my gun, wondering what   18 it would feel like to kill a man. Suddenly there was a volley of shots. The mob hesitated, stopped. Some friends of my father's had barricaded themselves in a two-story brick building just below our house. It was they who had fired. Some

19   of the mobsmen, still blood-thirsty, shouted, "Let's go get the nigger." Others, afraid now for their safety, held back. Our friends, noting the hesitation, fired another volley. The mob broke and retreated up Houston Street.

19   In the quiet that followed I put my gun aside and tried to relax. But a tension different from anything I had ever known possessed me. I was gripped by the knowledge of my identity, and in the depths of my soul I was vaguely aware that I was glad of it. I was sick with loathing for the hatred which had flared before me that night and come so close to making me a killer; but I was glad I was not one of those who hated; I was glad I was not one of those made sick and murderous by pride. I was glad I was not one of those whose story is in the history of the world, a record of bloodshed, rapine, and pillage. I was glad my mind and spirit were part of the races that had not fully awakened, and who therefore had still before them the opportunity to write a record of virtue as a memorandum to Armageddon.[1]

20   It was all just a feeling then, inarticulate and melancholy, yet reassuring in the way that death and sleep are reassuring, and I have clung to it now for nearly half a century.

EXERCISES

Some of the Issues

1. In paragraph 1 White explains the location of his house in Atlanta. What is most important about the location?
2. In paragraph 2 White describes the appearance of the house and yard. Why is it important for him to stress the difference between it and its surroundings?
3. What does White mean when he says in paragraph 3, "we were taught that there is no isolation from life"?
4. In paragraph 4 White describes the headlines in the newspapers. How do they change in the days before the riot? Does he imply that his family believed what the papers said or not?
5. In paragraphs 5 through 13 there are indications that the riots are neither new nor isolated, unique occasions. Find these indicators.
6. In what ways do the actions of the mob differ between the first and second day of the rioting?
7. Where are the police?
8. In paragraphs 14 through 17 White interrupts his account of the mob's actions to describe his thoughts and feelings of bitterness. Contrast them to his thoughts in paragraphs 19 and 20, after the mob had fled and the danger was—temporarily—past.

[1]Biblical reference to the final battle between good and evil; total defeat. Generally refers to a massive conflict or slaughter.

The Way We Are Told

9. Why does White give his description of home and neighborhood in two paragraphs (1 and 2)? How do the paragraphs differ?
10. How does White begin to build suspense in paragraph 3? How do paragraphs 4 and 5 also prepare the reader for what is to come?
11. Paragraph 6 gives the first description of a specific event, using several words and phrases that have emotional impact. Cite four or five of these.
12. In paragraph 9 White describes another episode of rescue. See if there are any words here, like those in paragraph 6, that have emotional connotations.
13. How does White heighten the suspense in the final paragraphs of the essay?

Some Subjects for Writing

14. Have you ever felt yourself in real danger? If so, try to describe the circumstances in two ways: give an objective description of the events and then rewrite your essay, trying to heighten the effect by the careful use of emotionally effective words and phrases. (You will find that the overuse of emotional words diminishes rather than enhances the effect.)
15. White describes his experience in the Atlanta riots as a turning point in his life. Describe an experience in your own life that profoundly changed your values.
*16. Read Maya Angelou's "Graduation." Both she and White record bad experiences that turned into a kind of victory in the end; both indicate that the victory is not final but needs to be fought for again and again. Write an essay in which you compare these experiences and their meaning to White and Angelou.

For the Indians, No Thanksgiving

MICHAEL DORRIS

Michael Dorris, (1945–1997), taught anthropology for many years at Dartmouth College. He is author of several books, including the novels A Yellow Raft in Blue Water *(1987) and* Crown of Columbus *(1991), written with his wife, the novelist Louise Erdrich. He also published* Working Men *(1993), a collection of short stories, and* Paper Trail *(1994), a collection of essays, as well as several books for children.*

This essay originally appeared in the New York Times *in 1988. With bitter humor Dorris, a member of the Modoc tribe, explains why Indians have no reason to give thanks on that Thursday in November. He describes how mainstream Americans have shaped the image of the Native American to suit their purpose.*

King Philip's War, referred to in paragraph 2, was fought between the settlers in Massachusetts and the Wampanoags led by their chief Metacomet, who had taken the name Philip at a time when he befriended the colonists, and before he came to see them as enemies who would destroy his people. The Indians were defeated by the New England Confederation and Philip was killed.

1 Maybe those Pilgrims and Wampanoags actually got together for a November picnic, maybe not. It matters only as a facile, ironical footnote.

2 For the former group, it would have been a celebration of a precarious hurdle successfully crossed on the path to the political domination first of a continent and eventually of a planet. For the latter, it would have been, at best, a naïve extravaganza—the last meeting as equals with invaders who, within a few years, would win King Philip's War and decorate the city limits of their towns with rows of stakes, each topped with an Indian head.

3 The few aboriginal survivors of the ensuing violence were either sold into Caribbean slavery by their better armed, erstwhile hosts, or were ruthlessly driven from their Cape Cod homes. Despite the symbolic idealism of the first potluck, New England—from the emerging European point of view—simply wasn't big enough for two sets of societies.

An enduring benefit of success, when one culture clashes with another, is that the victorious group controls the record. It owns not only the immediate spoils but also the power to edit, embellish and concoct the facts of the original encounter for the generations to come. Events, once past, reside at the small end of the telescope, the vague and hazy antecedents to accepted reality. 4

Our collective modern fantasy of Thanksgiving is a case in point. It has evolved into a ritual pageant in which almost everyone of us, as children, either acted or were forced to watch a 17th century vision that we can conjure whole in the blink of an eye. 5

The cast of stock characters is as recognizable as those in any Macy's parade: long-faced Pilgrim men, pre-N.R.A.[1] muskets at their sides, sitting around a rude outdoor table while their wives, dressed in long dresses, aprons and linen caps, bustle about lifting the lids off steaming kettles—pater and materfamilias of New World hospitality. 6

They dish out the turkey to a scattering of shirtless Indian invitees. But there is no ambiguity as to who is in charge of the occasion, who could be asked to leave, whose protocol prevails. 7

Only good Indians are admitted into this tableau, of course: those who accept the manifest destiny[2] of a European presence and are prepared to adopt English dining customs and, by inference, English everything else. 8

These compliant Hollywood extras are, naturally enough, among the blessings the Pilgrims are thankful for—and why not? They're colorful, bring the food and vanish after dessert. They are something exotic to write home about, like a visit to Frontierland. In the sound bite of national folklore, they have metamorphosed into icons, totems of America as evocative, and ultimately as vapid, as a flag factory. 9

And these particular Indians did not all repair to the happy hunting grounds during the first Christmas rush. They lived on, smoking peace pipes and popping up at appropriate crowd-pleasing moments. 10

They lost mock battles from coast to coast in Wild West shows. In 19th century art, they sat bareback on their horses and watched a lot of sunsets. Whole professional teams of them take the home field every Sunday afternoon in Cleveland or Washington. 11

They are the sources of merit badges for Boy Scouts and the emblem of purity for imitation butter. They are, and have been from the beginning, predictable, manageable, domesticated cartoons, inventions without depth or reality apart from that bestowed by their creators. 12

These appreciative Indians, as opposed to the pesky flesh and blood native peoples on whom they are loosely modeled, did not question the enforced 13

---

[1]National Rifle Association; organization that supports gun ownership.
[2]Nineteenth-century American political philosophy that justified westward expansion.

exchange of their territories for a piece of pie. They did not protest when they died by the millions of European diseases.

14   They did not resist—except for the "bad" ones, the renegades—when solemn pacts made with them were broken or when their religions and customs were declared illegal. They did not make a fuss in courts in defense of their sovereignty. They never expected all the fixings anyway.

15   As for Thanksgiving 1988, the descendants of those first partygoers sit at increasingly distant tables, the pretense of equity all but abandoned. Against great odds, native Americans have maintained political identity—hundreds of tribes have Federal recognition as "domestic, dependent nations."

16   But, in a country so insecure about heterogeneity that it votes its dominant language as "official," this refusal to melt into the pot has been an expensive choice.

17   A majority of reservation Indians reside in among the most impoverished counties in the nation. They constitute the ethnic group at the wrong peak of every scale: most undernourished, most short-lived, least educated, least healthy.

18   For them, that long ago Thanksgiving was not a milestone, not a promise. It was the last full meal.

EXERCISES

Some of the Issues

1. What is the "November picnic"? If it did indeed take place, what does it signify for each group of participants?
2. What does Dorris mean by saying that the victor controls the record (paragraph 4)? How do the following paragraphs expand on that statement?
3. What, according to Dorris, is the definition of "good" Indians (paragraph 8)? What roles do they play? Who assigns them those roles?
4. In paragraphs 11–13 Dorris refers to various ways that the Indians' image has been used. What is his purpose?
5. What does Dorris mean in paragraph 15 when he says that the descendants of those first partygoers sit at increasingly distant tables?
6. Examine a calendar and see what days you get off from school or work, or days that state and federal offices are closed. Who do you think determines which holidays merit vacation? What criteria do you think they use? Which of these holidays have personal meaning to you? Are there holidays you celebrate that are not officially recognized? Should they be?
7. In paragraph 16, Dorris comments that the U.S. is "a country so insecure about heterogeneity that it votes its dominant language as 'official'." In your opinion, must a country have a single language or can it, like Canada, have two or, like South Africa, have eleven? Consider the role of language in promoting ethnic and national unity.

The Way We Are Told

8. What kind of tone does the first paragraph set for the essay?
9. Dorris calls Thanksgiving "our collective modern fantasy" (paragraph 5). What terms does he use in the following paragraphs that amplify that idea of fantasy?
10. Consider the tone of the entire essay. Would you call it funny? Bitter? Angry? How does Dorris's language create that tone? Cite examples.

Some Subjects for Writing

11. In recent years Native American groups have raised objections to the use of Indian names for sports teams (Cleveland Indians, Atlanta Braves) and the use of Indian symbols such as the tomahawk in advertising. Find examples and discuss whether the objections are justified.
*12. Read Jamaica Kincaid's "On Seeing England for the First Time." How does Dorris's statement that "the victorious group controls the record" relate to Kincaid's description and analysis of the effect of British rule on Antiguan culture? Drawing from both essays, analyze Dorris's claim.

Arrival at Manzanar

JEANNE WAKATSUKI HOUSTON
AND JAMES D. HOUSTON

Like Walter White in an earlier selection, Jeanne Wakatsuki was caught up in a historical event. The year was 1942, the place California. A few months before, the Japanese had attacked the United States, bombing Pearl Harbor and overrunning U.S. possessions in the Pacific. The war was going badly; the U.S. forces and those of its allies were in retreat all over the area. Popular anger and fear turned against the Japanese-Americans living on the West Coast. President Franklin D. Roosevelt signed an executive order to intern those thousands of U.S. citizens—men, women, and children. They were rounded up at short notice, had to leave their homes and businesses, either selling them or abandoning them outright. They were shipped off to internment camps; Manzanar was one of them. They had to spend the war years there, all except those men who volunteered for the army. The battalion formed by these Japanese-Americans, fighting in Italy, became the most decorated U.S. Army unit in the war.

The internment of Americans of Japanese descent increasingly became a subject of controversy and criticism in the decades following the war. In 1987 the U.S. Congress finally passed an act that made some restitution to the former internees; it acknowledged that what was done to them had been wrong and included a payment of $20,000 to each of the survivors of the camps, that is, to those who were still alive after more than 40 years.

Jean Wakatsuki, born in California in 1935, was seven years old when she, together with her family, was sent to the internment camp at Manzanar. She remained there until age eleven. After high school she studied sociology and journalism at San Jose State College, where she met her husband, James D. Houston, a novelist. Together they wrote Farewell to Manzanar, *published in 1973, as a record of life in the camp and of its impact on her and her family. The following is a selection from it.*

1   In December of 1941 Papa's disappearance didn't bother me nearly so much as the world I soon found myself in.

He had been a jack-of-all-trades. When I was born he was farming near   2
Inglewood. Later, when he started fishing, we moved to Ocean Park, near Santa
Monica, and until they picked him up, that's where we lived, in a big frame house
with a brick fireplace, a block back from the beach. We were the only Japanese
family in the neighborhood. Papa liked it that way. He didn't want to be labeled
or grouped by anyone. But with him gone and no way of knowing what to
expect, my mother moved all of us down to Terminal Island. Woody already
lived there, and one of my older sisters had married a Terminal Island boy.
Mama's first concern now was to keep the family together; and once the war
began, she felt safer there than isolated racially in Ocean Park. But for me, at
age seven, the island was a country as foreign as India or Arabia would have
been. It was the first time I had lived among other Japanese, or gone to school
with them, and I was terrified all the time.

This was partly Papa's fault. One of his threats to keep us younger kids in   3
line was "I'm going to sell you to the Chinaman." When I had entered kindergarten two years earlier, I was the only Oriental in the class. They sat me next
to a Caucasian girl who happened to have very slanted eyes. I looked at her and
began to scream, certain Papa had sold me out at last. My fear of her ran so deep
I could not speak of it, even to Mama, couldn't explain why I was screaming. For
two weeks I had nightmares about this girl, until the teachers finally moved me
to the other side of the room. And it was still with me, this fear of Oriental faces,
when we moved to Terminal Island.

In those days it was a company town, a ghetto owned and controlled by the   4
canneries. The men went after fish, and whenever the boats came back—day or
night—the women would be called to process the catch while it was fresh. One
in the afternoon or four in the morning, it made no difference. My mother had
to go to work right after we moved there. I can still hear the whistle—two toots
for French's, three for Van Camp's—and she and Chizu[1] would be out of bed in
the middle of the night, heading for the cannery.

The house we lived in was nothing more than a shack, a barracks with single   5
plank walls and rough wooden floors, like the cheapest kind of migrant workers'
housing. The people around us were hard-working, boisterous, a little proud of
their nickname, *yo-go-re*, which meant literally *uncouth one*, or roughneck, or
dead-end kid. They not only spoke Japanese exclusively, they spoke a dialect
peculiar to Kyushu, where their families had come from in Japan, a rough, fish-
erman's language, full of oaths and insults. Instead of saying *ba-ka-ta-re*, a common insult meaning *stupid*, Terminal Islanders would say *ba-ka-ya-ro*, a coarser
and exclusively masculine use of the word, which implies gross stupidity. They
would swagger and pick on outsiders and persecute anyone who didn't speak as
they did. That was what made my own time there so hateful. I had never spoken

---

[1]Woody's wife; the author's sister-in-law.

anything but English, and the other kids in the second grade despised me for it. They were tough and mean, like ghetto kids anywhere. Each day after school I dreaded their ambush. My brother Kiyo, three years older, would wait for me at the door, where we would decide whether to run straight home together, or split up, or try a new and unexpected route.

6 None of these kids ever actually attacked. It was the threat that frightened us, their fearful looks, and the noises they would make, like miniature Samurai,[2] in a language we couldn't understand.

7 At the time it seemed we had been living under this reign of fear for years. In fact, we lived there about two months. Late in February the navy decided to clear Terminal Island completely. Even though most of us were American-born, it was dangerous having that many Orientals so close to the Long Beach Naval Station, on the opposite end of the island. We had known something like this was coming. But, like Papa's arrest, not much could be done ahead of time. There were four of us kids still young enough to be living with Mama, plus Granny, her mother, sixty-five then, speaking no English, and nearly blind. Mama didn't know where else she could get work, and we had nowhere else to move *to*. On February 25 the choice was made for us. We were given forty-eight hours to clear out.

8 The secondhand dealers had been prowling around for weeks, like wolves, offering humiliating prices for goods and furniture they knew many of us would have to sell sooner or later. Mama had left all but her most valuable possessions in Ocean Park, simply because she had nowhere to put them. She had brought along her pottery, her silver, heirlooms like the kimonos Granny had brought from Japan, tea sets, lacquered tables, and one fine old set of china, blue and white porcelain, almost translucent. On the day we were leaving, Woody's car was so crammed with boxes and luggage and kids we had just run out of room. Mama had to sell this china.

9 One of the dealers offered her fifteen dollars for it. She said it was a full setting for twelve and worth at least two hundred. He said fifteen was his top price. Mama started to quiver. Her eyes blazed up at him. She had been packing all night and trying to calm down Granny, who didn't understand why we were moving again and what all the rush was about. Mama's nerves were shot, and now navy jeeps were patrolling the streets. She didn't say another word. She just glared at this man, all the rage and frustration channeled at him through her eyes.

10 He watched her for a moment and said he was sure he couldn't pay more than seventeen fifty for that china. She reached into the red velvet case, took out a dinner plate and hurled it at the floor right in front of his feet.

11 The man leaped back shouting, "Hey! Hey, don't do that! Those are valuable dishes!"

---

[2]Japanese warrior class from the twelfth to the end of the nineteenth century.

Mama took out another dinner plate and hurled it at the floor, then another   12
and another, never moving, never opening her mouth, just quivering and glaring
at the retreating dealer, with tears streaming down her cheeks. He finally turned
and scuttled out the door, heading for the next house. When he was gone she
stood there smashing cups and bowls and platters until the whole set lay in scattered blue and white fragments across the wooden floor.

The name Manzanar meant nothing to us when we left Boyle Heights. We   13
didn't know where it was or what it was. We went because the government
ordered us to. And, in the case of my older brothers and sisters, we went with
a certain amount of relief. They had all heard stories of Japanese homes being
attacked, of beatings in the streets of California towns. They were as frightened of the Caucasians as Caucasians were of us. Moving, under what appeared
to be government protection, to an area less directly threatened by the war
seemed not such a bad idea at all. For some it actually sounded like a fine
adventure.

Our pickup point was a Buddhist church in Los Angeles. It was very early,   14
and misty, when we got there with our luggage. Mama had bought heavy coats
for all of us. She grew up in eastern Washington and knew that anywhere inland
in early April would be cold. I was proud of my new coat, and I remember sitting
on a duffel bag trying to be friendly with the Greyhound driver. I smiled at him.
He didn't smile back. He was befriending no one. Someone tied a numbered tag
to my collar and to the duffel bag (each family was given a number, and that
became our official designation until the camps were closed), someone else
passed out box lunches for the trip, and we climbed aboard.

I had never been outside Los Angeles County, never traveled more than ten   15
miles from the coast, had never even ridden on a bus. I was full of excitement,
the way any kid would be, and wanted to look out the window. But for the first
few hours the shades were drawn. Around me other people played cards, read
magazines, dozed, waiting. I settled back, waiting too, and finally fell asleep.
The bus felt very secure to me. Almost half its passengers were immediate relatives. Mama and my older brothers had succeeded in keeping most of us
together, on the same bus, headed for the same camp. I didn't realize until much
later what a job that was. The strategy had been, first, to have everyone living
in the same district when the evacuation began, and then to get all of us included
under the same family number, even though names had been changed by marriage. Many families weren't as lucky as ours and suffered months of anguish
while trying to arrange transfers from one camp to another.

We rode all day. By the time we reached our destination, the shades were   16
up. It was late afternoon. The first thing I saw was a yellow swirl across a
blurred, reddish setting sun. The bus was being pelted by what sounded like
splattering rain. It wasn't rain. This was my first look at something I would soon
know very well, a billowing flurry of dust and sand churned up by the wind
through Owens Valley.

17   We drove past a barbed-wire fence, through a gate, and into an open space where trunks and sacks and packages had been dumped from the baggage trucks that drove out ahead of us. I could see a few tents set up, the first rows of black barracks, and beyond them, blurred by sand, rows of barracks that seemed to spread for miles across this plain. People were sitting on cartons or milling around, with their backs to the wind, waiting to see which friends or relatives might be on this bus. As we approached, they turned or stood up, and some moved toward us expectantly. But inside the bus no one stirred. No one waved or spoke. They just stared out the windows, ominously silent. I didn't understand this. Hadn't we finally arrived, our whole family intact? I opened a window, leaned out, and yelled happily "Hey! This whole bus is full of Wakatsukis!"

18   Outside, the greeters smiled. Inside there was an explosion of laughter, hysterical, tension-breaking laughter that left my brothers choking and whacking each other across the shoulders.

19   We had pulled up just in time for dinner. The mess halls weren't completed yet. An outdoor chow line snaked around a half-finished building that broke a good part of the wind. They issued us army mess kits, the round metal kind that fold over, and plopped in scoops of canned Vienna sausage, canned string beans, steamed rice that had been cooked too long, and on top of the rice a serving of canned apricots. The Caucasian servers were thinking the fruit poured over rice would make a good dessert. Among the Japanese, of course, rice is never eaten with sweet foods, only with salty or savory foods. Few of us could eat such a mixture. But at this point no one dared protest. It would have been impolite. I was horrified when I saw the apricot syrup seeping through my little mound of rice. I opened my mouth to complain. My mother jabbed me in the back to keep quiet. We moved on through the line and joined the others squatting in the lee of half-raised walls, dabbing courteously at what was, for almost everyone there, an inedible concoction.

20   After dinner we were taken to Block 16, a cluster of fifteen barracks that had just been finished a day or so earlier—although finished was hardly the word for it. The shacks were built of one thickness of pine planking covered with tarpaper. They sat on concrete footings, with about two feet of open space between the floorboards and the ground. Gaps showed between the planks, and as the weeks passed and the green wood dried out, the gaps widened. Knotholes gaped in the uncovered floor.

21   Each barracks was divided into six units, sixteen by twenty feet, about the size of a living room, with one bare bulb hanging from the ceiling and an oil stove for heat. We were assigned two of these for the twelve people in our family group; and our official family "number" was enlarged by three digits—16 plus the number of this barracks. We were issued steel army cots, two brown army blankets each, and some mattress covers, which my brothers stuffed with straw.

22   The first task was to divide up what space we had for sleeping. Bill and Woody contributed a blanket each and partitioned off the first room: one side

for Bill and Tomi, one side for Woody and Chizu and their baby girl. Woody also got the stove, for heating formulas.

The people who had it hardest during the first few months were young cou-   23
ples like these, many of whom had married just before the evacuation began, in order not to be separated and sent to different camps. Our two rooms were crowded, but at least it was all in the family. My oldest sister and her husband were shoved into one of those sixteen-by-twenty-foot compartments with six people they had never seen before—two other couples, one recently married like themselves, the other with two teenage boys. Partitioning off a room like that wasn't easy. It was bitter cold when we arrived, and the wind did not abate. All they had to use for room dividers were those army blankets, two of which were barely enough to keep one person warm. They argued over whose blanket should be sacrificed and later argued about noise at night—the parents wanted their boys asleep by 9:00 P.M.—and they continued arguing over matters like that for six months, until my sister and her husband left to harvest sugar beets in Idaho. It was grueling work up there, and wages were pitiful, but when the call came through camp for workers to alleviate the wartime labor shortage, it sounded better than their life at Manzanar. They knew they'd have, if nothing else, a room, perhaps a cabin of their own.

That first night in Block 16, the rest of us squeezed into the second room—   24
Granny, Lillian, age fourteen, Ray, thirteen, May, eleven, Kiyo, ten, Mama, and me. I didn't mind this at all at the time. Being youngest meant I got to sleep with Mama. And before we went to bed I had a great time jumping up and down on the mattress. The boys had stuffed so much straw into hers, we had to flatten it some so we wouldn't slide off. I slept with her every night after that until Papa came back.

EXERCISES

Some of the Issues

1. What do the first three paragraphs tell us about Houston's family?
2. Paragraphs 3 through 7 explain her fears. What are they? What would you imagine would be the mother's fears in this period?
3. What does the story about the secondhand dealer (paragraphs 8 through 12) tell us about the situation of Japanese-Americans at that time? What does it tell us about Houston's mother?
4. Examine the actions of the camp officials. To what extent can the authorities be said to be deliberately cruel? unthoughtful? or uninformed about cultural differences? Cite specific details to support your view.
*5. Read Maxine Hong Kingston's "Girlhood among Ghosts." Both Kingston and Houston grew up in California at about the same time. In what way are their two experiences similar? How do they differ?

The Way We Are Told

6. In paragraphs 20 through 24 Houston gives a detailed description of the barracks. Does her description contain any words or phrases that express emotions? Justify their presence or absence.

Some Subjects for Writing

7. Jeanne Houston describes the bus ride to Manzanar from a child's point of view, as an adventure, almost fun, and not as a tragedy. Recall an incident of your childhood that would look different to you now (a fire, getting lost in a strange neighborhood). Describe it from a child's point of view and end with a paragraph explaining how you view the same incident as an adult.
8. Write about a time you, or your family, experienced a challenge or unexpected change. How did you or others react to change at that time? Looking back on the experience, did it produce changes in individuals in your family or in the family structure as a whole?
9. At one point, all the members of Jeanne Wakatsuki's family had to live in one room along with five strangers. In an essay consider how important having your own space and privacy is to you. Describe your present arrangements and the extent to which you might like to change them.
*10. Jeanne Wakatsuki Houston (with James D. Houston) and Dwight Okita recount two experiences of Japanese-American children who were interned during World War II. With the help of your instructor, research and write a paper on the experience of Japanese-Americans during the war.

In Response to Executive Order 9066: All Americans of Japanese Descent Must Report to Relocation Centers

DWIGHT OKITA

*Dwight Okita was born in Chicago in 1958. A poet and playwright, he has had two plays—*The Salad Bowl Dance *and* The Rainy Season *produced. In 1992, he published a collection of poetry,* Crossing with the Light.*

Okita's mother was among the thousands of Japanese-Americans who were interned shortly after the United States entered World War II. This poem is written in his mother's voice.

Dear Sirs:
Of course I'll come. I've packed my galoshes
and three packets of tomato seeds. Janet calls them
"love apples." My father says where we're going
they won't grow.   5

I am a fourteen-year-old girl with bad spelling
and a messy room. If it helps any, I will tell you
I have always felt funny using chopsticks
and my favorite food is hot dogs.
My best friend is a white girl named Denise—   10
we look at boys together. She sat in front of me
all through grade school because of our names:
O'Connor, Ozawa. I know the back of Denise's head very well.
I tell her she's going bald. She tells me I copy on tests.
We are best friends.   15

I saw Denise today in Geography class.
She was sitting on the other side of the room.
"You're trying to start a war," she said, "giving secrets away
to the Enemy, Why can't you keep your big mouth shut?"
20   I didn't know what to say.
I gave her a packet of tomato seeds
and asked her to plant them for me, told her
when the first tomato ripened
she'd miss me.

EXERCISES

1. How do the tone and contents of the letter contrast with the title?
2. Okita's poem is written in the voice of a fourteen-year-old girl. What indications do we have that she sees the world as a "typical" American teenager? Why is this important to the ideas presented in the poem?
3. What does Denise say in lines 16 through 20? Does she make any sense? How do her comments reflect the government's policy toward Japanese-Americans?
4. What is the tone set by the opening lines of the letter? Does that tone change by the end of the poem?
5. What is the significance of the tomato seeds?
*6. Read Jeanne Wakatsuki Houston's account of her family's internment at Manzanar. What additional evidence does it give of how the government at that time misunderstood the "threat" posed by Japanese-Americans.

Some Subjects for Writing

*7. Read Jeanne Wakatsuki Houston and James D. Houston's "Arrival at Manzanar." Imagine yourself as a child or adolescent who is suddenly placed into a new and unfriendly environment. Write an imaginary journal entry for either the day before, or the day of, your arrival. Make sure your entry includes some indication of your age and your life before internment.

6

How We Live

We are, in many ways, defined by the world around us. Changes in technology, law, economics, and social custom alter the way we live our everyday lives. At the same time, our daily lives and decisions help shape and define social and political changes. Though the essays in this section deal with a variety of issues—from work issues to cable television—each addresses the relationship between our personal lives and our social and political environments. Taken together, these essays demonstrate that how we live is both a reflection of the world and a catalyst for changing it.

For most of us, work plays an important role in our day-to-day lives. In "One Man's Kids," Daniel Meier writes about his choice to be come a first-grade teacher and describes his day in the classroom. Having chosen a profession that has historically been regarded as "female," Meier questions the degree to which we are confined by our definitions of "traditional" male work. Barbara Brandt, in "Less is More: A Call for Shorter Work Hours," analyzes the American impulse toward overwork and advocates a change to a thirty-hour work week. According to Brandt, "Americans often assume that overwork is an inevitable fact of life," and we too easily accept this assumption without considering the sacrifices we make in terms of our families, communities, and personal leisure.

Looking at working conditions in developing countries, Barbara Ehrenreich and Annette Fuentes, in their 1981 article "Life on the Global Assembly Line," examine an issue that continues to be both disturbing and relevant. They challenge the assumption that foreign investment and industrialization of developing countries free the people of those countries from backbreaking labor in the fields by providing them with better jobs in factories and workshops. Their article examines substandard working conditions and the resultant social and cultural problems.

┌───┐

— **THINKING ABOUT THE THEME** *"How We Live"* ————————

1. The photographer juxtaposes two people in different circumstances. They occupy the same space, but they do not see each other. Describe the two persons pictured and their surroundings. What message do you think the photo is trying to convey?

2. Describe an encounter between two people from different social or economic circumstances. You may choose to draw from your own experience, or describe an event that you witnessed. In your narrative, concentrate on the contrasts between the people but also consider possible points of connection or similarity.

3. Imagine you were asked to prepare a photo essay under the title "American Life Today." Would you choose to include this photo? Why or why not? What other photos might you include?

4. What was your personal response the last few times you saw someone living in the street? What factors in the person's looks, dress, and behavior influenced your response? Is your response different when the person talks to you or asks you for money? Are you comfortable with your responses and the reasons for them?

5. What role do material goods play in your life? In considering present or future job opportunities, which is more important to you—salary, or factors such as the satisfaction you get from your work, its benefit to society, and the amount of leisure time it affords you?

└───┘

Other daily routines, which may or may not be defined as "work," may also reflect on or relate to larger social issues. Lars Eighner's description of "scavenging" in "On Dumpster Diving" becomes a commentary on both homelessness and on wastefulness in American society. Through his vivid and meticulous description of his daily dives into the dumpster, Eighner delivers a poignant commentary on consumer society and the irony of homelessness in a country of abundance.

Two of the authors in this section address the issue of how changes in technology impact our lives, identities, and our sense of home. In "Home Is Every Place," Pico Iyer describes his life as a member of a new breed of "transcontinental warriors," people for whom every place is equally familiar and strange. For Iyer, who sees himself living in an increasingly small and interconnected world, home can no longer be defined through our connection to place and nationality. In contrast to Iyer, Geraldine Brooks focuses on her town of Waterford, Virginia, and, using both irony and humor, recounts the story of how the townspeople fought back against the local cable company. In "Unplugged," she demonstrates that we, as individuals and communities, can make decisions that allow us to shape our environments regardless of larger changes in technology and communication.

This section ends with a poem that celebrates both everyday experience and personal identity. Through describing moments in the lives of friends and family that have touched upon her own life, Aurora Levins Morales, in "Class Poem," credits others for helping her define herself and allowing her to be proud of both her privilege and her heritage.

One Man's Kids

DANIEL MEIER

Daniel Meier teaches at a public elementary school in Boston and has published many essays about education and his personal experience. He received a bachelor's degree from Wesleyan University and a master's degree in education from Harvard University.

"One Man's Kids" originally appeared in the New York Times *"About Men" series in 1987. Meier begins his essay by describing part of his typical day as a first-grade teacher. He goes on to describe how, as a man who works with small children, his career choice sets him apart from other men he knows. Meier examines how concepts of gender influence both our choice of work, and how that work is perceived by others.*

1   I teach first graders. I live in a world of skinned knees, double-knotted shoelaces, riddles that I've heard a dozen times, stale birthday cakes, hurt feelings, wandering stories and one lost shoe ("and if you don't find it my mother'll kill me"). My work is dominated by 6-year-olds.

2   It's 10:45, the middle of snack, and I'm helping Emily open her milk carton. She has already tried the other end without success, and now there's so much paint and ink on the carton from her fingers that I'm not sure she should drink it at all. But I open it. Then I turn to help Scott clean up some milk he has just spilled onto Rebecca's whale crossword puzzle.

3   While I wipe my milk- and paint-covered hands, Jenny wants to know if I've seen that funny book about penguins that I read in class. As I hunt for it in a messy pile of books, Jason wants to know if there is a new seating arrangement for lunch tables. I find the book, turn to answer Jason, then face Maya, who is fast approaching with a new knock-knock joke. After what seems like the 10th "Who's there?" I laugh and Maya is pleased.

4   Then Andrew wants to know how to spell "flukes" for his crossword. As I get to "u," I give a hand signal for Sarah to take away the snack. But just as Sarah is almost out the door, two children complain that "we haven't even had ours yet." I stop the snack mid-flight, complying with their request for graham crackers. I then return to Andrew, noticing that he has put "flu" for 9 Down, rather than 9 Across. It's now 10:50.

5   My work is not traditional male work. It's not a singular pursuit. There is not a large pile of paper to get through or one deal to transact. I don't have one

219

area of expertise or knowledge. I don't have the singular power over language of a lawyer, the physical force of a construction worker, the command over fellow workers of a surgeon, the wheeling and dealing transactions of a businessman. My energy is not spent in pursuing, climbing, achieving, conquering or cornering some goal or object.

My energy is spent in encouraging, supporting, consoling and praising my   6
children. In teaching, the inner rewards come from without. On any given day, quite apart from teaching reading and spelling, I bandage a cut, dry a tear, erase a frown, tape a torn doll and locate a long-lost boot. The day is really won through matters of the heart. As my students groan, laugh, shudder, cry, exult and wonder, I do too. I have to be soft around the edges.

A few years ago, when I was interviewing for an elementary-school teaching   7
position, every principal told me with confidence that, as a male, I had an advantage over female applicants because of the lack of male teachers. But in the next breath, they asked with a hint of suspicion why I chose to work with young children. I told them that I wanted to observe and contribute to the intellectual growth of a maturing mind. What I really felt like saying, but didn't, was that I loved helping a child learn to write his name for the first time, finding someone a new friend, or sharing in the hilarity of reading about Winnie the Pooh getting so stuck in a hole that only his head and rear show.

I gave that answer to those principals, who were mostly male, because I   8
thought they wanted a "male" response. This meant talking about intellectual matters. If I had taken a different course and talked about my interest in helping children in their emotional development, it would have been seen as closer to a "female" answer. I even altered my language, not once mentioning the word "love" to describe what I do indeed love about teaching. My answer worked; every principal nodded approvingly.

Some of the principals also asked what I saw myself doing later in my career.   9
They wanted to know if I eventually wanted to go into educational administration. Becoming a dean of students or a principal has never been one of my goals, but they seemed to expect me, as a male, to want to climb higher on the career stepladder. So I mentioned that, at some point, I would be interested in working with teachers as a curriculum coordinator. Again, they nodded approvingly.

If those principals had been female instead of male, I wonder whether their   10
questions, and my answers, would have been different. My guess is that they would have been.

At other times, when I'm at a party or a dinner and tell someone that I teach   11
young children, I've found that men and women respond differently. Most men ask about the subjects I teach and the courses I took in my training. Then, unless they bring up an issue such as merit pay, the conversation stops. Most women, on the other hand, begin the conversation on a more immediate and personal level. They say things like "those kids must love having a male teacher" or "that age is just wonderful, you must love it." Then, more often than not, they'll talk

about their own kids or ask me specific questions about what I do. We're then off and talking shop.

12 Possibly, men would have more to say to me, and I to them, if my job had more of the trappings and benefits of more traditional male jobs. But my job has no bonuses or promotions. No complimentary box seats at the ball park. No cab fare home. No drinking buddies after work. No briefcase. No suit. (Ties get stuck in paint jars.) No power lunches. (I eat peanut butter and jelly, chips, milk and cookies with the kids.) No taking clients out for cocktails. The only place I take my kids is to the playground.

13 Although I could have pursued a career in law or business, as several of my friends did, I chose teaching instead. My job has benefits all its own. I'm able to bake cookies without getting them stuck together as they cool, buy cheap sewing materials, take out splinters, and search just the right trash cans for useful odds and ends. I'm sometimes called "Daddy" and even "Mommy" by my students, and if there's ever a lull in the conversation at a dinner party, I can always ask those assembled if they've heard the latest riddle about why the turkey crossed the road. (He thought he was a chicken.)

EXERCISES

Some of the Issues

1. Meier begins his essay by listing many specific things he does in his work as a first-grade teacher. What are they? In what way do they contribute to the children's lives?
2. How does Meier define "traditional male work" and how does he contrast it with his own work? Do you agree with his definition?
3. Meier tells us that he was not completely frank when he interviewed for his job. What reasons does he state for giving a "male" response to the principal's questions?
4. Meier claims that when he mentions his job to acquaintances, men and women respond differently. How does he characterize the different responses?
5. Do you think Meier's students are lucky to have a teacher like him? Why or why not?
6. Advertising and the media often reinforce, or call into question, gender stereotypes. Find two print advertisements, one focusing on male and one on female stereotypes. Working in groups of three to five, compare and discuss your advertisements with other students.

The Way We Are Told

7. Many writers believe that one can present an idea more effectively through description than through direct statements. Meier begins and ends his essay

by describing specific activities, showing rather than telling about his daily routine. What does he gain by starting with specific details?

8. Much of Meier's analysis depends on his use of comparison and contrast. What does he compare and how does this technique strengthen his argument?

Some Subjects for Writing

9. Describe the kind of work you would like to do in life and your reasons for choosing that work. In your essay, consider the factors that have influenced your choice.

10. Describe a job you have held or interview someone about his or her work. Begin with the details of a typical day's routine. Then establish your thesis about how the job is valuable (or not valuable) to society as a whole.

11. As Meier implies, the majority of primary school teachers are female, while the majority of principals are male. Work in small groups or brainstorm with the entire class to determine other jobs that are typically held by either men or women. Choose one of these jobs to write about, either justifying the present situation or arguing for change.

*12. In "Mother Tongue," Amy Tan speculates on why Asians often pursue careers in math or science. Clearly there are ways in which both culture and gender influence our career decisions, although those influences may be subtle at times. Consider the career choice of a family member or friend and write an essay in which you analyze the choice in relation to the person's gender and/or cultural background.

Unplugged

GERALDINE BROOKS

Geraldine Brooks is a native of Australia and a graduate of Sydney University and the Columbia University School of Journalism. She has spent extensive time in the Middle East, is a former foreign correspondent for the Wall Street Journal, *and is the author of* Nine Parts of Desire *(1995), a book about Arab women.*

In "Unplugged," Brooks reflects on the question of whether to bring cable television to Waterford, the small town in Virginia where she lives. The residents of Waterford are seen as eccentric because they choose to reject "more than seventy channels of the finest programming available" and question whether the information and entertainment brought to us by mass media expands our horizons or compromises our individuality.

1   Jake came to dinner a few weeks ago. We talked about the nine muses, and why tragedy is important in human storytelling. Jake has been reading a lot of Greek mythology lately. He's eight. A few nights later, Jake's dad, Mike, and I walked up the hill to the old schoolhouse for a Citizens' Association meeting about bringing cable TV to Waterford, a town of 250 people in the foothills of Virginia's Blue Ridge Mountains. The hills do terrible things to TV reception.

2   The president of the cable company had come to tell us that it probably wasn't a moneymaker for him to string the cable all the way out to our eighty-some houses, but he felt it was only right to give us the chance to partake of the rich offerings of his service. He passed around the latest full-color guide describing what we were missing that month. The cover featured Melanie Griffith. If we had cable, we would have been able to watch her in the movie *Milk Money.*

3   Mike's house on Main Street doesn't have a TV. But like most houses here, it has broad views of farmland rolling away to the wooded hillside, and big, old maples in the garden. From the high meadow behind town you can look at the Catoctin Creek as it wends through the valley, and see why the young Pennsylvania Quaker, Amos Janney, figured back in 1733 that this would be a fine place to build a mill.

4   The mill is still there, and like most buildings in town, it has American history written into the horsehair mortar holding up its walls. Just opposite, there's a stone house whose Quaker inhabitant found slaves a worse evil than war, even though fighting for the Union caused him to be read out of Meeting for violating

223

pacifist principles. The Baptist church on the High Street still has bullet holes in the bricks from the skirmish that took place there between the Confederates and Waterford's Loudoun Rangers, the only regiment raised in Virginia that fought on the Union side.

There aren't many Quakers here now, but they left behind a tradition of   5
stubborn singularity. The townspeople—farmers and carpenters who've always lived here, artists and software designers who've arrived more recently—like the fact that this place is different: always has been, always will.

At the Citizens' Association meeting, the cable guy brags about how his ser-   6
vice offers "more than seventy channels of the finest programming available." Mike, beside me, fidgets on his chair. Suddenly, he's speaking, softly and diffidently, as he always does.

"People here have time to talk to each other. I'm proud of our bad TV   7
reception because it gets us out of our houses, and I'd kind of hate that to change because there's nine different football games to watch. Personally, I'd rather go fishing than watch the fishing channel."

The cable man doesn't realize that this is one of those Martin Luther   8
moments, and that Mike has just nailed the theses to the door. His tone, when he replies, is unctuously patronizing.

"Well, that's your opinion and you're certainly entitled to it. But do you   9
have a child?" Mike nods. "Then you should think about his future. He's going to be at a disadvantage when he gets to college and has to compete with young people who've been exposed to all the marvelous information that cable can bring them."

People who know Mike's boy Jake burst into loud guffaws. "That's bullshit!"   10
shouts our neighbor Phil, sitting in back. And suddenly the tone of the meeting has changed, changed utterly. If Waterford could stand up to the Confederate States of America, it certainly can stand up to Cablevision of Loudoun County.

Someone who has just moved out here from a suburb that has Cablevision   11
is on her feet, saying what a bunch of crap the programs are, and how she had canceled her subscription after a couple of months.

"Haven't you ever heard of books?" someone else shouts. "There's more   12
'marvelous information' in the local library than's on seven hundred cable channels!" Last year, the county decided that Waterford was too small to warrant visits from the Bookmobile. We had a meeting about that, too. Our neighbors Casey and Jeff donated the front room of their house—a bay-windowed storefront that used to be the village milliner—so we'd have a place to put a cooperative library.

That meeting wasn't nearly as loud as this one. The decibels don't come   13
down until someone gets us off on a discussion of the life of Thomas Jefferson, and whether one could say it was impoverished for lack of television.

People barely notice when the cable man melts away. The next speaker is   14
our neighbor Mary, who wants to tell us about laying rumble strips to slow the

traffic through town. "Well," she says, raising an eyebrow, "I'm not sure I want to get up in front of *this* crowd!"

15   The next morning, when we meet up at the post office to pick up our mail, a few of us allow that we feel a bit sheepish about more or less running the cable man out of town. But then we look up at the ugly tangle of power lines—one of the few twentieth-century intrusions in town—and consider how one more big thick cable running along up there would make it even more unsightly, and less likely that we'll ever realize the village's long-standing dream of getting the things buried.

16   Marie, who lives right across from the post office, grows a morning glory vine every spring. She trains it up the power pole in front of her balcony, and lets the wires become a trellis for a cascade of royal blue blooms. In summer, a team from the power company came out intending to chop the vine down. Marie gave them each a cup of tea and a fresh-baked scone, then put them on the phone with the local agricultural extension agent, who explained that morning glory is a tender annual that will be gone with the first frost. The team finished their tea, and decided they'd leave the flowers be.

17   In less than a week, word of the Waterford Cable Rebellion filtered to the outside world. It seems we're the first town in the United States to resist it. Reporters from the *Washington Post*, CBS news, Fox network, and even South Korean TV showed up and filed bemused, "can-you-believe-it" features about the bunch of oddball hayseeds who don't want cable.

18   It's become eccentric not to want every place to be just like every other place. It isn't just the cable. Waterford is battling a new law that says the eighty buildings here, which have done just fine for 250 years without addresses, must now post three-inch-high, light-reflecting, five-digit street numbers to fit in with a county-wide grid system. One tiny lane has all of three cottages. But the first house will have to post a number that makes it 15545 Butchers Row.

19   Perhaps we'd have a better chance of holding on to what's here if the history it represented was linked with the museum-like grand estate of some long-ago rich man. But what's here isn't grand. These cottages and ice houses and root cellars are the templates of ordinary lives.

20   The old rooms have a way of slowly shaping you to fit them. You arrive here thinking you simply must have more built-in closets, but instead find yourself shedding your excess wardrobe. You open up the old stone-lined, hand-dug well so your arms can feel the effort of hauling a full water-bucket up thirty feet. I suppose, if we had cable, I could be watching *Body by Jake* on the Family Channel instead.

21   Down on Main Street, my neighbor Jake is toning his biceps by helping his dad stack the woodpile. I think I'll amble down there and have a word with him about a Corinthian king named Sisyphus.

EXERCISES

Some of the Issues

1. Brooks briefly describes two scenarios in her opening paragraph. How do they serve as introduction to the essay?
2. What historical events or moments does Brooks recount? How does she use this history to help her make her point?
3. Why is it ironic that the cable representative refers specifically to Mike's child in paragraph 9?
*4. Consider Brooks's statement: "It's become eccentric not to want every place to be just like every other place" (paragraph 18). For a different point of view, read Pico Iyer's "Home Is Every Place." What are the perspectives presented by each author? What are your own views on the subject?
5. Brooks presents a very positive view of Waterford. Some might see her as romantic or overly resistant to change. What do you think?

The Way We Are Told

6. Why do you suppose Brooks chose this title for the essay?
7. What tone does Brooks use to portray the cable representative in paragraph 2? Where else in the essay do you notice a similar tone?
8. Brooks's thesis is implied rather than directly stated. If you were to develop a thesis statement for her essay, what might it be?

Some Subjects for Writing

9. Brooks presents two different views of cable television: those of the cable representative and those of the townspeople and herself. Whose views come closest to your own? Write an essay in which you defend or criticize the role television plays in our society. Although you should present a strong defense of your opinion, make sure to consider other viewpoints.
*10. In Pico Iyer's "Home is Every Place," the author's sense of attachment to place clearly differs from Brooks's. Consider your own attachment to a place, or various places. How has it helped to shape your identity?

Home Is Every Place

PICO IYER

Pico Iyer was born in Oxford, England, in 1957 to Indian parents. The son of two college professors, he was educated in the elite British public school system and at Oxford and Harvard Universities. He later became an American citizen.

Iyer has written a novel, Cuba and the Night *(1995), and several volumes of travel literature. These chronicle his journeys through various parts of Asia, and include* Video Night in Kathmandu: And Other Reports from the Not-So-Far East *(1988) and* The Lady and the Monk: Four Seasons in Kyoto *(1991). Much of his writing focuses on the ways in which Western culture has infiltrated the Asian world.*

Iyer has said of his work, "Writing should be an act of communication more than of mere self-expression—a telling of a story rather than a flourishing of skills. The less conscious one is of being 'a writer,' the better the writing.... Writing, in fact, should ideally be as spontaneous and urgent as a letter to a lover, or a message to a friend who has just lost a parent. And because of the ways a writer is obliged to tap the private selves that even those closest to him never see, writing is, in the end, the oddest of anomalies; an intimate letter to a stranger."

This essay originally appeared in Homeground *(1996), an anthology of writings about the concept of "home." Iyer uses terms such as "transit loungers" and "privileged homeless" to describe a group of people, himself included, for whom the idea of home is not tied to a particular place, and who feel equally at home (or not at home) in many places. Iyer asserts that the modern world, with its blending of cultures and its distances shortened by fax, phone, and airplane, is increasingly made for people like him: "resident aliens of the world, impermanent residents of nowhere." Be describing himself as a member of this tribe of nomads who supposedly lack a specific national or cultural identity, Iyer, in a sense, claims a home for himself.*

1   By the time I was nine, I was already used to going to school by trans-Atlantic plane, to sleeping in airports, to shuttling back and forth, three times a year, between my parents' (Indian) home in California and my boarding school in England. Throughout the time I was growing up, I was never within 6,000 miles of the nearest relative—and came, therefore, to learn how to define relations in

non-familial ways. From the time I was a teenager, I took it for granted that I could take my budget vacations (as I did) in Bolivia and Tibet, China and Morocco. It never seemed strange to me that a girlfriend might be half a world (or 10 hours flying time) away, that my closest friends might be on the other side of a continent or sea.

It was only recently that I realized that all these habits of mind and life   2
would scarcely have been imaginable in my parents' youth; the very facts and facilities that shape my world are all distinctly new developments, and mark me as a modern type.

It was only recently, in fact, that I realized that I am an example, perhaps,   3
of an entirely new breed of people, a transcontinental tribe of wanderers that is multiplying as fast as international phone lines and Frequent Flyer programs. We are the Transit Loungers, forever heading to the Departure Gate, forever orbiting the world. We buy our interests duty-free, we eat our food on plastic plates, we watch the world through borrowed headphones. We pass through countries as through revolving doors, resident aliens of the world, impermanent residents of nowhere. Nothing is strange to us, and nowhere is foreign. We are visitors even in our own homes.

This is not, I think, a function of affluence so much as of simple circum-   4
stance. I am not, that is, a jet-setter pursuing vacations from Marbella[1] to Phuket;[2] I am simply a fairly typical product of a movable sensibility, living and working in a world that is itself increasingly small and increasingly mongrel. I am a multinational soul on a multicultural globe where more and more countries are as polyglot and restless as airports. Taking planes seems as natural to me as picking up the phone, or going to school; I fold up my self and carry it around with me as if it were an overnight case.

The modern world seems increasingly made for people like me. I can plop   5
myself down anywhere and find myself in the same relation of familiarity and strangeness: Lusaka,[3] after all, is scarcely more strange to me than the foreigners' England in which I was born; the America where I am registered as an "alien"; and the almost unvisited India that people tell me is my home. I can fly from London to San Francisco to Osaka and feel myself no more a foreigner in one place than another; all of them are just locations—pavilions in some intercontinental Expo—and I can work or live or love in any one of them. All have Holiday Inns, direct-dial phones, CNN, and DHL. All have sushi and Thai restaurants, Kentucky Fried Chicken and Coke. My office is as close as the nearest fax machine or modem. Roppongi is West Hollywood is Leblon.[4]

This kind of life offers an unprecedented sense of freedom and mobility: 6
tied down to nowhere, we can pick and choose among locations. Ours is the first

[1]Coastal town in southern Spain.
[2]Island off southern Thailand.
[3]Capital of Zambia.
[4]Entertainment districts in Tokyo, Los Angeles, and Rio de Janeiro, respectively.

generation that can go off to visit Tibet for a week, or meet Tibetans down the street; ours is the first generation to be able to go to Nigeria for a holiday to find our roots or to find they are not there. At the lowest level, this new internationalism also means that I can get on a plane in Los Angeles, get off a few hours later in Jakarta, check into a Hilton, order a cheeseburger in English, and pay for it all with an American Express card. At the next level, it means that I can meet, in the Hilton coffee shop, an Indonesian businessman who is as conversant as I am with Michael Kinsley and Magic Johnson and Madonna. At a deeper level, it means that I need never feel estranged. If all the world is alien to us, all the world is home.

7   I have learned, in fact, to love foreignness. In any place I visit, I have the privileges of an outsider: I am an object of interest, and even fascination; I am a person set apart, able to enjoy the benefits of the place without paying the taxes. And the places themselves seem glamorous to me, romantic, as seen through foreign eyes: distance on both sides lends enchantment. Policemen let me off speeding tickets, girls want to hear the stories of my life, pedestrians will gladly point me to the nearest Golden Arches. Perpetual foreigners in the transit lounge, we enjoy a kind of diplomatic immunity; and, living off room service in our hotel rooms, we are never obliged to grow up, or even, really, to be ourselves.

8   Thus, many of us learn to exult in the blessings of belonging to what feels like a whole new race. It is a race, as Salman Rushdie[5] says, of "people who root themselves in ideas rather than places, in memories as much as in material things; people who have been obliged to define themselves—because they are so defined by others—by their otherness; people in whose deepest selves strange fusions occur, unprecedented unions between what they were and where they find themselves." And when people argue that our very notion of wonder is eroded, that alienness itself is as seriously endangered as the wilderness, that more and more of the world is turning into a single synthetic monoculture, I am not worried: a Japanese version of a French fashion is something new, I say, not quite Japanese and not truly French. Comme des Garcons hybrids are the art form of the time.

9   And yet, sometimes, I stop myself and think. What kind of heart is being produced by these new changes? And must I always be a None of the Above? When the stewardess comes down the aisle with disembarkation forms, what do I fill in? My passport says one thing, my face another; my accent contradicts my eyes. Place of Residence, Final Destination, even Marital Status are not much easier to fill in; usually I just tick "Other."

10   And beneath all the boxes, where do we place ourselves? How does one fix a moving object on a map? I am not an exile, really, nor an immigrant; not

---

[5](1947–) Indian-born British novelist whose book, *The Satanic Verses* (1988), enraged many Muslims. He was forced into hiding by many death threats.

deracinated, I think, any more than I am rooted. I have not fled the oppression of war, nor found ostracism in the places where I do alight; I can scarcely feel severed from a home I have barely known. Yet is "citizen of the world" enough to comfort me? And does taking my home as every place make it easier to sleep at night?

Alienation, we are taught from kindergarten, is the condition of the time. This   11 is the century of exiles and refugees, of boat people and statelessness; the time when traditions have been abolished, and men become closer to machines. This is the century of estrangement: more than a third of all Afghans live outside Afghanistan; the second city of the Khmers is a refugee camp; the second tongue of Beverly Hills is Farsi. The very notion of nation-states is outdated; many of us are as crosshatched within as Beirut.

    We airport-hoppers can, in fact, go through the world as through a house of   12 wonders, picking up something at every stop, and taking the whole globe as our playpen, or our supermarket (and even if we don't go to the world, the world will increasingly come to us: just down the street, almost wherever we are, are nori[6] and salsa, tiramisu and *naan*[7]). We don't have a home, we have a hundred homes. And we can mix and match as the situation demands. "Nobody's history is my history," Kazuo Ishiguro, a great spokesman for the privileged homeless, once said to me, and then went on, "Whenever it was convenient for me to become very Japanese, I could become very Japanese, and then, when I wanted to drop it, I would just become this ordinary Englishman." Instantly, I felt a shock of recognition: I have a wardrobe of selves from which to choose. And I savor the luxury of being able to be an Indian in Cuba (where people are starving for yoga and Tagore[8]), or an American in Thailand, to be an Englishman in New York.

    And so we go on circling the world, six miles above the ground, displaced from   13 time, above the clouds, with all our needs attended to. We listen to announcements given in three languages. We confirm our reservations at every stop. We disembark at airports that are self-sufficient communities, with hotels, gymnasia, and places of worship. At customs we have nothing to declare but ourselves.

But what is the price we pay for all of this? I sometimes think that this mobile   14 way of life is as novel as high-rises, or the video monitors that are rewiring our consciousness. And even as we fret about the changes our progress wreaks in the air and on the airwaves, in forests and on streets, we hardly worry about the changes it is working in ourselves, the new kind of soul that is being born out of a new kind of life. Yet this could be the most dangerous development of all, and not only because it is the least examined.

---

[6]Japanese seaweed.
[7]Indian bread.
[8](1861–1941) Indian poet who won the Nobel prize for literature in 1913.

15   For us in the Transit Lounge, disorientation is as alien as affiliation. We become professional observers, able to see the merits and deficiencies of any-where, to balance our parents' viewpoints with their enemies' position. Yes, we say, of course it's terrible, but look at the situation from Saddam's point of view. I understand how you feel, but the Chinese had their own cultural reasons for Tiananmen Square.[9] Fervor comes to seem to us the most foreign place of all.

16   Seasoned experts at dispassion, we are less good at involvement, or suspen-sions of disbelief; at, in fact, the abolition of distance. We are masters of the aerial perspective, but touching down becomes more difficult. Unable to get stirred by the raising of a flag, we are sometimes unable to see how anyone could be stirred. I sometimes think that this is how Rushdie, the great analyst of this condition, somehow became its victim. He had juggled homes for so long, so adroitly, that he forgot how the world looks to someone who is rooted, in coun-try or belief. He had chosen to live so far from affiliation that he could no longer see why people choose affiliation in the first place. Besides, being part of no soci-ety means one is accountable to no one, and need respect no laws outside one's own. If single-nation people can be fanatical as terrorists, we can end up inef-fectual as peacekeepers.

17   We become, in fact, strangers to belief itself, unable to comprehend many of the rages and dogmas that animate (and unite) people. Conflict itself seems inexplicable to us sometimes, simply because partisanship is; we have the agnos-tic's inability to retrace the steps of faith. I could not begin to fathom why some Moslems would think of murder after hearing about *The Satanic Verses*; yet sometimes I force myself to recall that it is we, in our floating skepticism, who are the exceptions, that in China or Iran, in Korea or Peru, it is not so strange to give up one's life for a cause.

18   We end up, then, a little like nonaligned nations, confirming our reservations at every step. We tell ourselves, self-servingly, that nationalism breeds monsters, and choose to ignore the fact that internationalism breeds them too. Ours is the culpability not of the assassin, but of the bystander who takes a snapshot of the murder, Or, when the revolution catches fire, hops on the next plane out.

19   In any case, the issues in the Transit Lounge are passing; a few hours from now, they'll be a thousand miles away. Besides, this is a foreign country, we have no interests here. The only thing we have to fear are hijackers—passionate peo-ple with beliefs.

20   Sometimes, though, just sometimes, I am brought up short by symptoms of my condition. They are not major things, but they are peculiar ones, and ones that would not have been so common 50 years ago. I have never bought a house of any kind, and my ideal domestic environment, I sometimes tell my friends, is a hotel-room. I have never voted, or ever wanted to vote, and I eat in restaurants

[9]Student demonstrations in 1989 that were suppressed by the Chinese government.

three times a day. I have never supported a nation (in the Olympic Games, say), or represented "my country" in anything. Even my name is weirdly international, because my "real name' is one that makes sense only in the home where I have never lived.

I choose to live in America in part, I think, because it feels more alien the   21
longer I stay there. I love being in Japan because it reminds me, at every turn, of my foreignness. When I want to see if any place is home, I must subject the candidates to a battery of tests. Home is the place of which one has memories but no expectations.

If I have any deeper home, it is, I suppose, in English. My language is the   22
house I carry round with me as a snail his shell; and in my lesser moments I try to forget that mine is not the language spoken in America, or even, really, by any member of my family.

Yet even here, I find, I cannot place my accent, or reproduce it as I can the   23
tones of others. And I am so used to modifying my English inflections according to whom I am talking to—an American, an Englishman, a villager in Nepal, a receptionist in Paris—that I scarcely know what kind of voice I have.

I wonder, sometimes, if this new kind of non-affiliation may not be alien to   24
something fundamental in the human state. The refugee at least harbors passionate feelings about the world he has left—and generally seeks to return there; the exile at least is propelled by some kind of strong emotion away from the old country and towards the new—indifference is not an exile emotion. But what does the Transit Lounger feel? What are the issues that we would die for? What are the passions that we would live for?

Airports are among the only sites in public life where emotions are hugely   25
sanctioned, in block capitals. We see people weep, shout, kiss in airports; we see them at the furthest edges of excitement and exhaustion. Airports are privileged spaces where we can see the primal states writ large—fear, recognition, hope. But there are some of us, perhaps, sitting at the Departure Gate, boarding passes in hand, watching the destinations ticking over, who feel neither the pain of separation nor the exultation of wonder; who alight with the same emotions with which we embarked; who go down to the baggage carousel and watch our lives circling, circling, circling, waiting to be claimed.

EXERCISES

Some of the Issues

1. How does Iyer describe his life in paragraph 1?
2. In paragraph 3, Iyer defines himself as part of a new "breed" of people that he calls a "transcontinental tribe of wanderers"? Why does he use these terms? What other terms does he use to describe himself and others like him?

3. Iyer speculates that his situation is not "a function of affluence" (paragraph 4). To what extent do you agree with him?
4. Looking at paragraph 5, consider the extent to which chains, franchises, and modern technology affect the "smallness" of the world.
5. How does the perspective of the essay change in paragraph 9?
6. Viewing the essay as a whole, what does Iyer mean when he describes himself and those like him as "seasoned experts at dispassion" (paragraph 16)?
7. Looking at the whole essay, summarize what Iyer describes as both the benefits and drawbacks of being a "Transit Lounger."
8. How does Iyer define home throughout the essay? What role does language play in Iyer's conception of home?
*9. Read Anton Shammas's "Amérka, Amérka." What is the difference between Shammas's idea of a "portable" home (Shammas, paragraph 8) and Iyer's?
10. Working in small groups, use an atlas to find all the places Iyer mentions in his essay. On a blank map of the world, mark all of the places you find. Discuss what you know about these places or the images you have of them.

The Way We Are Told

11. Consider the title. How well does it describe the ideas discussed in the essay? What are some other titles Iyer might have used?
12. Paragraphs 9 and 10 offer a series of questions. What purpose do they serve? How do they help guide the reader?
13. The author uses descriptive language, but never describes one place in detail. Why is this appropriate to the essay?
14. What metaphor does Iyer use in his concluding paragraph? How does this metaphor help summarize his ideas?

Some Subjects for Writing

15. In paragraph 12, Iyer writes, "Even if we don't go to the world, the world will increasingly come to us." How true is this of the place you live now? Describe your city or town by painting a vivid picture of the various cultures and nationalities represented.
16. Reflecting on your relationship to your family, culture, nationality, and the place you were born, write an essay in which you provide your own definition of home.
*17. In Geraldine Brooks's "Unplugged," the argument of the cablevision man is that the media can broaden the town's perspective on the world. The townspeople reject his argument. Looking at both Iyer and Brooks, and thinking about your own perspective, write an essay in which you analyze how the media can influence our perceptions of community and identity.

On Dumpster Diving

LARS EIGHNER

Lars Eighner was born in 1948 in Corpus Christi, Texas. "On Dumpster Diving" is excerpted from Travels with Lizbeth, *a chronicle of Eighner's three years as a homeless person. Lizbeth is the author's dog and traveling companion. Typed on equipment found in the garbage,* Travels with Lizbeth *began as a series of letters to friends describing the events that took Eighner from a job in a mental institution to life as a homeless person. The book is written as a series of vignettes because, as the author says, "A homeless life has no story line."*

In a sober tone punctuated with sharp detail, Eighner describes, analyzes, and philosophizes about the things we as a society discard. Often these are things Eighner finds perfectly usable. Although the author doesn't directly draw conclusions for the reader, his careful descriptions of what we consider "garbage" make a statement about our "disposable" society and about what we value, whether we are homeless or not.

Eighner received much acclaim for Travels with Lizbeth *and its unique point of view. He is no longer homeless and lives in Austin, Texas. He has written several books of gay erotic fiction, and his most recent book is a novel,* Pawn to Queen Four *(1994).*

Long before I began Dumpster diving I was impressed with Dumpsters, enough so that I wrote the Merriam-Webster research service to discover what I could about the word *Dumpster.* I learned from them that it is a proprietary word belonging to the Dempster Dumpster company. Since then I have dutifully capitalized the word, although it was lowercased in almost all the citations Merriam-Webster photocopied for me. Dempster's word is too apt. I have never heard these things called anything but Dumpsters. I do not know anyone who knows the generic name for these objects. From time to time I have heard a wino or hobo give some corrupted credit to the original and call them Dipsy Dumpsters. 1

I began Dumpster diving about a year before I became homeless. 2

I prefer the word *scavenging* and use the word *scrounging* when I mean to be obscure. I have heard people, evidently meaning to be polite, use the word *foraging,* but I prefer to reserve that word for gathering nuts and berries and such, which I do also according to the season and the opportunity. *Dumpster diving* 3 seems to me to be a little too cute and, in my case, inaccurate because I lack the athletic ability to lower myself into the Dumpsters as the true divers do, much to their increased profit.

4   I like the frankness of the word *scavenging*, which I can hardly think of without picturing a big black snail on an aquarium wall. I live from the refuse of others. I am a scavenger. I think it a sound and honorable niche, although if I could I would naturally prefer to live the comfortable consumer life, perhaps—and only perhaps—as a slightly less wasteful consumer, owing to what I have learned as a scavenger.

5   While Lizbeth and I were still living in the shack on Avenue B as my savings ran out, I put almost all my sporadic income into rent. The necessities of daily life I began to extract from Dumpsters. Yes, we ate from them. Except for jeans, all my clothes came from Dumpsters. Boom boxes, candles, bedding, toilet paper, a virgin male love doll, medicine, books, a typewriter, dishes, furnishings, and change, sometimes amounting to many dollars—I acquired many things from the Dumpsters.

6   I have learned much as a scavenger. I mean to put some of what I have learned down here, beginning with the practical art of Dumpster diving and proceeding to the abstract.

7   What is safe to eat?

8   After all, the finding of objects is becoming something of an urban art. Even respectable employed people will sometimes find something tempting sticking out of a Dumpster or standing beside one. Quite a number of people, not all of them of the bohemian type, are willing to brag that they found this or that piece in the trash. But eating from Dumpsters is what separates the dilettanti from the professionals. Eating safely from the Dumpsters involves three principles: using the senses and common sense to evaluate the condition of the found materials, knowing the Dumpsters of a given area and checking them regularly, and seeking always to answer the question "Why was this discarded?"

9   Perhaps everyone who has a kitchen and a regular supply of groceries has, at one time or another, made a sandwich and eaten half of it before discovering mold on the bread or got a mouthful of milk before realizing the milk had turned. Nothing of the sort is likely to happen to a Dumpster diver because he is constantly reminded that most food is discarded for a reason. Yet a lot of perfectly good food can be found in Dumpsters.

10   Canned goods, for example, turn up fairly often in the Dumpsters I frequent. All except the most phobic people would be willing to eat from a can, even if it came from a Dumpster. Canned goods are among the safest of foods to be found in Dumpsters but are not utterly foolproof.

11   Although very rare with modern canning methods, botulism is a possibility. Most other forms of food poisoning seldom do lasting harm to a healthy person, but botulism is almost certainly fatal and often the first symptom is death.

Except for carbonated beverages, all canned goods should contain a slight vacuum and suck air when first punctured. Bulging, rusty, and dented cans and cans that spew when punctured should be avoided, especially when the contents are not very acidic or syrupy.

Heat can break down the botulin, but this requires much more cooking than   12
most people do to canned goods. To the extent that botulism occurs at all, of course, it can occur in cans on pantry shelves as well as in cans from Dumpsters. Need I say that home-canned goods are simply too risky to be recommended.

From time to time one of my companions, aware of the source of my pro-   13
visions, will ask, "Do you think these crackers are really safe to eat?" For some reason it is most often the crackers they ask about.

This question has always made me angry. Of course I would not offer my   14
companion anything I had doubts about. But more than that, I wonder why he cannot evaluate the condition of the crackers for himself. I have no special knowledge and I have been wrong before. Since he knows where the food comes from, it seems to me he ought to assume some of the responsibility for deciding what he will put in his mouth. For myself I have few qualms about dry foods such as crackers, cookies, cereal, chips, and pasta if they are free of visible contaminates and still dry and crisp. Most often such things are found in the original packaging, which is not so much a positive sign as it is the absence of a negative one.

Raw fruits and vegetables with intact skins seem perfectly safe to me,   15
excluding of course the obviously rotten. Many are discarded for minor imperfections that can be pared away. Leafy vegetables, grapes, cauliflower, broccoli, and similar things may be contaminated by liquids and may be impractical to wash.

Candy, especially hard candy, is usually safe if it has not drawn ants. Choc-   16
olate is often discarded only because it has become discolored as the cocoa butter de-emulsified. Candying, after all, is one method of food preservation because pathogens do not like very sugary substances.

All of these foods might be found in any Dumpster and can be evaluated   17
with some confidence largely on the basis of appearance. Beyond these are foods that cannot be correctly evaluated without additional information.

I began scavenging by pulling pizzas out of the Dumpster behind a pizza   18
delivery shop. In general, prepared food requires caution, but in this case I knew when the shop closed and went to the Dumpster as soon as the last of the help left.

Such shops often get prank orders; both the orders and the products made   19
to fill them are called *bogus*. Because help seldom stays long at these places, pizzas are often made with the wrong topping, refused on delivery for being cold, or baked incorrectly. The products to be discarded are boxed up because inventory is kept by counting boxes: A boxed pizza can be written off; an unboxed pizza does not exist.

20   I never placed a bogus order to increase the supply of pizzas and I believe no one else was scavenging in this Dumpster. But the people in the shop became suspicious and began to retain their garbage in the shop overnight. While it lasted I had a steady supply of fresh, sometimes warm pizza. Because I knew the Dumpster I knew the source of the pizza, and because I visited the Dumpster regularly I knew what was fresh and what was yesterday's.

21   The area I frequent is inhabited by many affluent college students. I am not here by chance; the Dumpsters in this area are very rich. Students throw out many good things, including food. In particular they tend to throw everything out when they move at the end of a semester, before and after breaks, and around midterm, when many of them despair of college. So I find it advantageous to keep an eye on the academic calendar.

22   Students throw food away around breaks because they do not know whether it has spoiled or will spoil before they return. A typical discard is a half jar of peanut butter. In fact, nonorganic peanut butter does not require refrigeration and is unlikely to spoil in any reasonable time. The student does not know that, and since it is Daddy's money, the student decides not to take a chance. Opened containers require caution and some attention to the question, "Why was this discarded?" But in the case of discards from student apartments, the answer may be that the item was thrown out through carelessness, ignorance, or wastefulness. This can sometimes be deduced when the item is found with many others, including some that are obviously perfectly good.

23   Some students, and others, approach defrosting a freezer by chucking out the whole lot. Not only do the circumstances of such a find tell the story, but also the mass of frozen goods stays cold for a long time and items may be found still frozen or freshly thawed.

24   Yogurt, cheese, and sour cream are items that are often thrown out while they are still good. Occasionally I find a cheese with a spot of mold, which of course I just pare off, and because it is obvious why such a cheese was discarded, I treat it with less suspicion than an apparently perfect cheese found in similar circumstances. Yogurt is often discarded, still sealed, only because the expiration date on the carton had passed. This is one of my favorite finds because yogurt will keep for several days, even in warm weather.

25   Students throw out canned goods and staples at the end of semesters and when they give up college at midterm. Drugs, pornography, spirits, and the like are often discarded when parents are expected—Dad's Day, for example. And spirits also turn up after big party weekends, presumably discarded by the newly reformed. Wine and spirits, of course, keep perfectly well even once opened, but the same cannot be said of beer.

26   My test for carbonated soft drinks is whether they still fizz vigorously. Many juices or other beverages are too acidic or too syrupy to cause much concern, provided they are not visibly contaminated. I have discovered nasty molds in vegetable juices, even when the product was found under its original seal; I recommend

that such products be decanted slowly into a clear glass. Liquids always require some care. One hot day I found a large jug of Pat O'Brien's Hurricane mix. The jug had been opened but was still ice cold. I drank three large glasses before it became apparent to me that someone had added the rum to the mix, and not a little rum. I never tasted the rum, and by the time I began to feel the effects I had already ingested a very large quantity of the beverage. Some divers would have considered this a boon, but being suddenly intoxicated in a public place in the early afternoon is not my idea of a good time.

I have heard of people maliciously contaminating discarded food and even   27
handouts, but mostly I have heard of this from people with vivid imaginations who have had no experience with the Dumpsters themselves. Just before the pizza shop stopped discarding its garbage at night, jalapeños began showing up on most of the thrown-out pizzas. If indeed this was meant to discourage me, it was a wasted effort because I am a native Texan.

For myself, I avoid game, poultry, pork, and egg-based foods, whether I find   28
them raw or cooked. I seldom have the means to cook what I find, but when I do I avail myself of plentiful supplies of beef, which is often in very good condition. I suppose fish becomes disagreeable before it becomes dangerous. Lizbeth is happy to have any such thing that is past its prime and, in fact, does not recognize fish as food until it is quite strong.

Home leftovers, as opposed to surpluses from restaurants, are very often   29
bad. Evidently, especially among students, there is a common type of personality that carefully wraps up even the smallest leftover and shoves it into the back of the refrigerator for six months or so before discarding it. Characteristic of this type are the reused jars and margarine tubs to which the remains are committed. I avoid ethnic foods I am unfamiliar with. If I do not know what it is supposed to look like when it is good, I cannot be certain I will be able to tell if it is bad.

No matter how careful I am I still get dysentery at least once a month,   30
oftener in warm weather. I do not want to paint too romantic a picture. Dumpster diving has serious drawbacks as a way of life.

I learned to scavenge gradually, on my own. Since then I have initiated several   31
companions into the trade. I have learned that there is a predictable series of stages a person goes through in learning to scavenge.

At first the new scavenger is filled with disgust and self-loathing. He is   32
ashamed of being seen and may lurk around, trying to duck behind things, or he may try to dive at night. (In fact, most people instinctively look away from a scavenger. By skulking around, the novice calls attention to himself and arouses suspicion. Diving at night is ineffective and needlessly messy.)

Every grain of rice seems to be a maggot. Everything seems to stink. He can   33
wipe the egg yolk off the found can, but he cannot erase from his mind the stigma of eating garbage.

34   That stage passes with experience. The scavenger finds a pair of running shoes that fit and look and smell brand-new. He finds a pocket calculator in perfect working order. He finds pristine ice cream, still frozen, more than he can eat or keep. He begins to understand: People throw away perfectly good stuff, a lot of perfectly good stuff.

35   At this stage, Dumpster shyness begins to dissipate. The diver, after all, has the last laugh. He is finding all manner of good things that are his for the taking. Those who disparage his profession are the fools, not he.

36   He may begin to hang on to some perfectly good things for which he has neither a use nor a market. Then he begins to take note of the things that are not perfectly good but are nearly so. He mates a Walkman with broken earphones and one that is missing a battery cover. He picks up things that he can repair.

37   At this stage he may become lost and never recover. Dumpsters are full of things of some potential value to someone and also of things that never have much intrinsic value but are interesting. All the Dumpster divers I have known come to the point of trying to acquire everything they touch. Why not take it, they reason, since it is all free? This is, of course, hopeless. Most divers come to realize that they must restrict themselves to items of relatively immediate utility. But in some cases the diver simply cannot control himself. I have met several of these pack-rat types. Their ideas of the values of various pieces of junk verge on the psychotic. Every bit of glass may be a diamond, they think, and all that glisters, gold.

38   I tend to gain weight when I am scavenging. Partly this is because I always find far more pizza and doughnuts than water-packed tuna, nonfat yogurt, and fresh vegetables. Also I have not developed much faith in the reliability of Dumpsters as a food source, although it has been proven to me many times. I tend to eat as if I have no idea where my next meal is coming from. But mostly I just hate to see food go to waste and so I eat much more than I should. Something like this drives the obsession to collect junk.

39   As for collecting objects, I usually restrict myself to collecting one kind of small object at a time, such as pocket calculators, sunglasses, or campaign buttons. To live on the street I must anticipate my needs to a certain extent: I must pick up and save warm bedding I find in August because it will not be found in Dumpsters in November. As I have no access to health care, I often hoard essential drugs, such as antibiotics and antihistamines. (This course can be recommended only to those with some grounding in pharmacology. Antibiotics, for example, even when indicated are worse than useless if taken in insufficient amounts.) But even if I had a home with extensive storage space, I could not save everything that might be valuable in some contingency.

40   I have proprietary feelings about my Dumpsters. As I have mentioned, it is no accident that I scavenge from ones where good finds are common. But my limited experience with Dumpsters in other areas suggests to me that even in

poorer areas, Dumpsters, if attended with sufficient diligence, can be made to yield a livelihood. The rich students discard perfectly good kiwifruit; poorer people discard perfectly good apples. Slacks and Polo shirts are found in the one place; jeans and T-shirts in the other. The population of competitors rather than the affluence of the dumpers most affects the feasibility of survival by scavenging. The large number of competitors is what puts me off the idea of trying to scavenge in places like Los Angeles.

Curiously, I do not mind my direct competition, other scavengers, so much as I hate the can scroungers.   41

People scrounge cans because they have to have a little cash. I have tried scrounging cans with an able-bodied companion. Afoot a can scrounger simply cannot make more than a few dollars a day. One can extract the necessities of life from the Dumpsters directly with far less effort than would be required to accumulate the equivalent value in cans. (These observations may not hold in places with container redemption laws.)   42

Can scroungers, then, are people who must have small amounts of cash. These are drug addicts and winos, mostly the latter because the amounts of cash are so small. Spirits and drugs do, like all other commodities, turn up in Dumpsters and the scavenger will from time to time have a half bottle of a rather good wine with his dinner. But the wino cannot survive on these occasional finds; he must have his daily dose to stave off the DTs. All the cans he can carry will buy about three bottles of Wild Irish Rose.   43

I do not begrudge them the cans, but can scroungers tend to tear up the Dumpsters, mixing the contents and littering the area. They become so specialized that they can see only cans. They earn my contempt by passing up change, canned goods, and readily hockable items.   44

There are precious few courtesies among scavengers. But it is common practice to set aside surplus items: pairs of shoes, clothing, canned goods, and such. A true scavenger hates to see good stuff go to waste, and what he cannot use he leaves in good condition in plain sight.   45

Can scroungers lay waste to everything in their path and will stir one of a pair of good shoes to the bottom of a Dumpster, to be lost or ruined in the muck. Can scroungers will even go through individual garbage cans, something I have never seen a scavenger do.   46

Individual garbage cans are set out on the public easement only on garbage days. On other days going through them requires trespassing close to a dwelling. Going through individual garbage cans without scattering litter is almost impossible. Litter is likely to reduce the public's tolerance of scavenging. Individual cans are simply not as productive as Dumpsters; people in houses and duplexes do not move so often and for some reason do not tend to discard as much useful material. Moreover, the time required to go through one garbage can that serves one household is not much less than the time required to go through a Dumpster that contains the refuse of twenty apartments.   47

48   But my strongest reservation about going through individual garbage cans is that this seems to me a very personal kind of invasion to which I would object if I were a householder. Although many things in Dumpsters are obviously meant never to come to light, a Dumpster is somehow less personal.

49   I avoid trying to draw conclusions about the people who dump in the Dumpsters I frequent. I think it would be unethical to do so, although I know many people will find the idea of scavenger ethics too funny for words.

50   Dumpsters contain bank statements, correspondence, and other documents, just as anyone might expect. But there are also less obvious sources of information. Pill bottles, for example. The labels bear the name of the patient, the name of the doctor, and the name of the drug. AIDS drugs and antipsychotic medicines, to name but two groups, are specific and are seldom prescribed for any other disorders. The plastic compacts for birth-control pills usually have complete label information.

51   Despite all of this sensitive information, I have had only one apartment resident object to my going through the Dumpster. In that case it turned out the resident was a university athlete who was taking bets and who was afraid I would turn up his wager slips.

52   Occasionally a find tells a story. I once found a small paper bag containing some unused condoms, several partial tubes of flavored sexual lubricants, a partially used compact of birth-control pills, and the torn pieces of a picture of a young man. Clearly she was through with him and planning to give up sex altogether.

53   Dumpster things are often sad—abandoned teddy bears, shredded wedding books, despaired-of sales kits. I find many pets lying in state in Dumpsters. Although I hope to get off the streets so that Lizbeth can have a long and comfortable old age, I know this hope is not very realistic. So I suppose when her time comes she too will go into a Dumpster. I will have no better place for her. And after all, it is fitting, since for most of her life her livelihood has come from the Dumpster. When she finds something I think is safe that has been spilled from a Dumpster, I let her have it. She already knows the route around the best ones. I like to think that if she survives me she will have a chance of evading the dog catcher and of finding her sustenance on the route.

54   Silly vanities also come to rest in the Dumpsters. I am a rather accomplished needleworker. I get a lot of material from the Dumpsters. Evidently sorority girls, hoping to impress someone, perhaps themselves, with their mastery of a womanly art, buy a lot of embroider-by-number kits, work a few stitches horribly, and eventually discard the whole mess. I pull out their stitches, turn the canvas over, and work an original design. Do not think I refrain from chuckling as I make gifts from these kits.

55   I find diaries and journals. I have often thought of compiling a book of literary found objects. And perhaps I will one day. But what I find is hopelessly

commonplace and bad without being, even unconsciously, camp. College students also discard their papers. I am horrified to discover the kind of paper that now merits an A in an undergraduate course. I am grateful, however, for the number of good books and magazines the students throw out.

In the area I know best I have never discovered vermin in the Dumpsters,   56
but there are two kinds of kitty surprise. One is alley cats whom I meet as they leap, claws first, out of Dumpsters. This is especially thrilling when I have Lizbeth in tow. The other kind of kitty surprise is a plastic garbage bag filled with some ponderous, amorphous mass. This always proves to be used cat litter.

City bees harvest doughnut glaze and this makes the Dumpster at the   57
doughnut shop more interesting. My faith in the instinctive wisdom of animals is always shaken when ever I see Lizbeth attempt to catch a bee in her mouth, which she does whenever bees are present. Evidently some birds find Dumpsters profitable, for birdie surprise is almost as common as kitty surprise of the first kind. In hunting season all kinds of small game turn up in Dumpsters, some of it, sadly, not entirely dead. Curiously, summer and winter, maggots are uncommon.

The worse of the living and near-living hazards of the Dumpsters are the   58
fire ants. The food they claim is not much of a loss, but they are vicious and aggressive. It is very easy to brush against some surface of the Dumpster and pick up half a dozen or more fire ants, usually in some sensitive area such as the underarm. One advantage of bringing Lizbeth along as I make Dumpster rounds is that, for obvious reasons, she is very alert to ground-based fire ants. When Lizbeth recognizes a fire-ant infestation around our feet, she does the Dance of the Zillion Fire Ants. I have learned not to ignore this warning from Lizbeth, whether I perceive the tiny ants or not, but to remove ourselves at Lizbeth's first pas de bourée. All the more so because the ants are the worst in the summer months when I wear flip-flops if I have them. (Perhaps someone will misunderstand this. Lizbeth does the Dance of the Zillion Fire Ants when she recognizes more fire ants than she cares to eat, not when she is being bitten. Since I have learned to react promptly, she does not get bitten at all. It is the isolated patrol of fire ants that falls in Lizbeth's range that deserves pity. She finds them quite tasty.)

By far the best way to go through a Dumpster is to lower yourself into it.   59
Most of the good stuff tends to settle at the bottom because it is usually weightier than the rubbish. My more athletic companions have often demonstrated to me that they can extract much good material from a Dumpster I have already been over.

To those psychologically or physically unprepared to enter a Dumpster, I   60
recommend a stout stick, preferably with some barb or hook at one end. The hook can be used to grab plastic garbage bags. When I find canned goods or other objects loose at the bottom of a Dumpster, I lower a bag into it, roll the

desired object into the bag, and then hoist the bag out—a procedure more easily described than executed. Much Dumpster diving is a matter of experience for which nothing will do except practice.

61　　Dumpster diving is outdoor work, often surprisingly pleasant. It is not entirely predictable; things of interest turn up every day and some days there are finds of great value. I am always very pleased when I can turn up exactly the thing I most wanted to find. Yet in spite of the element of chance, scavenging more than most other pursuits tends to yield returns in some proportion to the effort and intelligence brought to bear. It is very sweet to turn up a few dollars in change from a Dumpster that has just been gone over by a wino.

62　　The land is now covered with cities. The cities are full of Dumpsters. If a member of the canine race is ever able to know what it is doing, then Lizbeth knows that when we go around to the Dumpsters, we are hunting. I think of scavenging as a modern form of self-reliance. In any event, after having survived nearly ten years of government service, where everything is geared to the lowest common denominator, I find it refreshing to have work that rewards initiative and effort. Certainly I would be happy to have a sinecure again, but I am no longer heartbroken that I left one.

63　　I find from the experience of scavenging two rather deep lessons. The first is to take what you can use and let the rest go by. I have come to think that there is no value in the abstract. A thing I cannot use or make useful, perhaps by trading, has no value however rare or fine it may be. I mean useful in a broad sense—some art I would find useful and some otherwise.

64　　I was shocked to realize that some things are not worth acquiring, but now I think it is so. Some material things are white elephants that eat up the possessor's substance. The second lesson is the transience of material being. This has not quite converted me to a dualist, but it has made some headway in that direction. I do not suppose that ideas are immortal, but certainly mental things are longer lived than other material things.

65　　Once I was the sort of person who invests objects with sentimental value. Now I no longer have those objects, but I have the sentiments yet.

66　　Many times in our travels I have lost everything but the clothes I was wearing and Lizbeth. The things I find in Dumpsters, the love letters and rag dolls of so many lives, remind me of this lesson. Now I hardly pick up a thing without envisioning the time I will cast it aside. This I think is a healthy state of mind. Almost everything I have now has already been cast out at least once, proving that what I own is valueless to someone.

67　　Anyway, I find my desire to grab for the gaudy bauble has been largely sated. I think this is an attitude I share with the very wealthy—we both know there is plenty more where what we have came from. Between us are the rat-race millions who nightly scavenge the cable channels looking for they know not what.

68　　I am sorry for them.

EXERCISES

Some of the Issues

1. Why might Eighner begin his essay by defining words and terms?
2. In paragraphs 7 through 30, Eighner describes how to select safe food from Dumpsters. What information do you recall from his descriptions? How does Eighner establish his authority on the issue of Dumpster diving? What indications does he give that his judgment is not infallible?
3. What is Eighner's attitude toward the students in the neighborhood where he scavenges (paragraphs 21 through 25)? How did you, as a student, react to his comments?
4. What does Eighner say are the stages people go through as scavengers (paragraphs 31 through 37)?
5. Who are the scavengers Eighner disapproves of and why? Do you feel he is too judgmental?
6. What reasons does Eighner give for not scavenging in individual garbage cans? Can you think of a similar way in which you set boundaries for respecting the privacy of others?
7. What does Eighner feel he shares with the wealthy (paragraph 67)? How does he describe the "rat-race millions" and why does he feel sorry for them?
8. Eighner tells us in paragraph 4 that, as a scavenger, he has learned how wasteful consumers can be. Having finished his essay, summarize what he has learned about wastefulness, citing examples from throughout the text.
9. What are some of the ethical issues Eighner raises in this essay? What do you think of Eighner's sense of ethics?
10. What were your responses to this essay? Did it change your perceptions of the homeless in any way?

How We Are Told

11. "On Dumpster Diving" could be classified as a "process" essay, a type of writing that describes how to do something. How does Eighner use this form to tell us more than simply "how to" scavenge?
12. What is the tone of the essay? Does it vary?
13. Eighner gives detailed descriptions throughout the essay. What is their effect?

Some Subjects for Writing

14. Describe how to do something that you do well. Begin in a way that establishes your authority on the issue. If possible, choose something that is important to you, but whose value to others may not be obvious.

15. What provisions should be made for the homeless? Should they be allowed to share public buildings such as libraries, or sleep in sheltered areas of buildings, train, subway, or bus stations? Should churches open space for them? Write an essay explaining your views.

16. Do you feel there is too much wastefulness in American society? Give evidence based on personal experience and observations. For example, you may want to observe the habits of students in your school cafeteria, patrons in a local restaurant, or employees in your workplace.

17. Interview a homeless person about tactics for survival. You should talk to a person with whom you've already had contact or take the time to get to know the person you've chosen to interview. Write an essay in which you describe one or two routines in the person's daily life.

Less Is More: A Call for Shorter Work Hours

BARBARA BRANDT

Barbara Brandt is a community organizer and social change activist who lives in the Boston area and focuses her work on issues of gender, community, economics, and environment. She is the author of Whole Life Economics: Revaluing Daily Life *(1995). This essay was written in conjunction with a collective called the "Shorter Work Time Group," of which Brandt is a member, and appeared in the July-August issue of the* Utne Reader *as part of a section on work.*

Brandt argues that increases in technology such as computers and fax machines, while they initially seem to offer us more convenience, save us time, and decrease our workload, have actually increased the pace of our lives and raised our standards of productivity. Brandt makes the case that, while the typical American work week—8 hours a days, 40 hours a week—seems to most Americans like "the natural rhythm of the universe," we could all benefit from a conception of work that included more free time to care for families, explore hobbies and interests, and develop community.

America is suffering from overwork. Too many of us are too busy, trying to 1
squeeze more into each day while having less to show for it. Although our growing time crunch is often portrayed as a personal dilemma, it is in fact a major
social problem that has reached crisis proportions over the past 20 years.

The simple fact is that Americans today—both women and men—are 2
spending too much time at work, to the detriment of their homes, their families, their personal lives, and their communities. The American Dream promised that our individual hard work paired with the advances of modern
technology would bring about the good life for all. Glorious visions of the leisure society were touted throughout the '50s and '60s. But now most people
are working more than ever before, while still struggling to meet their economic commitments. Ironically, the many advances in technology, such as
computers and fax machines, rather than reducing our workload, seem to have
speeded up our lives at work. At the same time, technology has equipped us
with "conveniences" like microwave ovens and frozen dinners that merely

246

enable us to adopt a similar frantic pace in our home lives so we can cope with more hours at paid work.

3   A recent spate of articles in the mainstream media has focused on the new problems of overwork and lack of time. Unfortunately, overwork is often portrayed as a special problem of yuppies and professionals on the fast track. In reality, the unequal distribution of work and time in America today reflects the decline in both standard of living and quality of life for most Americans. Families whose members never see each other, women who work a double shift (first on the job, then at home), workers who need more flexible work schedules, and unemployed and underemployed people who need more work are all casualties of the crisis of overwork.

4   Americans often assume that overwork is an inevitable fact of life—like death and taxes. Yet a closer look at other times and other nations offers some startling surprises.

5   Anthropologists have observed that in pre-industrial (particularly hunting and gathering) societies, people generally spend 3 to 4 hours a day, 15 to 20 hours a week, doing the work necessary to maintain life. The rest of the time is spent in socializing, partying, playing, storytelling, and artistic or religious activities. The ancient Romans celebrated 175 public festivals a year in which everyone participated, and people in the Middle Ages had at least 115.

6   In our era, almost every other industrialized nation (except Japan) has fewer annual working hours and longer vacations than the United States. This includes all of Western Europe, where many nations enjoy thriving economies and standards of living equal to or higher than ours. Jeremy Brecher and Tim Costello, writing in *Z Magazine* (Oct. 1990), note that "European unions during the 1980s made a powerful and largely successful push to cut working hours. In 1987 German metalworkers struck and won a 37.5-hour week; many are now winning a 35-hour week. In 1990, hundreds of thousands of British workers have won a 37-hour week."

7   In an article about work-time in the *Boston Globe*, Suzanne Gordon notes that workers in other industrialized countries "enjoy—as a statutory right—longer vacations [than in the U.S.] from the moment they enter the work force. In Canada, workers are legally entitled to two weeks off their first year on the job.... After two or three years of employment, most get three weeks of vacation. After 10 years, it's up to four, and by 20 years, Canadian workers are off for five weeks. In Germany, statutes guarantee 18 days minimum for everyone, but most workers get five or six weeks. The same is true in Scandinavian countries, and in France."

8   In contrast to the extreme American emphasis on productivity and commitment, which results in many workers, especially in professional-level jobs, not taking the vacations coming to them, Gordon notes that "In countries that are America's most successful competitors in the global marketplace, all working

people, whether lawyers or teachers, CEOs or janitors, take the vacations to which they are entitled by law. 'No one in West Germany,' a West German embassy's officer explains, 'no matter how high up they are, would ever say they couldn't afford to take a vacation. Everyone takes their vacation.'"

And in Japan, where dedication to the job is legendary, Gordon notes that the Japanese themselves are beginning to consider their national workaholism a serious social problem leading to stress-related illnesses and even death. As a result, the Japanese government recently established a commission whose goal is to promote shorter working hours and more leisure time. 9

Most other industrialized nations also have better family-leave policies than the United States, and in a number of other countries workers benefit from innovative time-scheduling opportunities such as sabbaticals. 10

While the idea of a shorter workweek and longer vacations sounds appealing to most people, any movement to enact shorter work-time as a public policy will encounter surprising pockets of resistance, not just from business leaders but even from some workers. Perhaps the most formidable barrier to more free time for Americans is the widespread mind-set that the 40-hour workweek, 8 hours a day, 5 days a week, 50 weeks a year, is a natural rhythm of the universe. This view is reinforced by the media's complete silence regarding the shorter work-time and more favorable vacation and family-leave policies of other countries. This lack of information, and our leaders' reluctance to suggest that the United States can learn from any other nation (except workaholic Japan) is one reason why more Americans don't identify overwork as a major problem or clamor for fewer hours and more vacation. Monika Bauerlein, a journalist originally from Germany now living in Minneapolis, exclaims, "I can't believe that people here aren't rioting in the streets over having only two weeks of vacation a year." 11

A second obstacle to launching a powerful shorter work-time movement is America's deeply ingrained work ethic, or its modern incarnation, the workaholic syndrome. The work ethic fosters the widely held belief that people's work is their most important activity and that people who do not work long and hard are lazy, unproductive, and worthless. 12

For many Americans today, paid work is not just a way to make money but is a crucial source of their self-worth. Many of us identify ourselves almost entirely by the kind of work we do. Work still has a powerful psychological and spiritual hold over our lives—and talk of shorter work-time may seem somehow morally suspicious. 13

Because we are so deeply a work-oriented society, leisure-time activities— such as play, relaxation, engaging in cultural and artistic pursuits, or just quiet contemplation and "doing nothing"—are not looked on as essential and worthwhile components of life. Of course, for the majority of working women who must work a second shift at home, much of the time spent outside of paid work is not leisure anyway. Also much of our non-work time is spent not just in personal renewal, 14 but in building and maintaining essential social ties—with family, friends, and the larger community.

15   Today, as mothers and fathers spend more and more time on the job, we are beginning to recognize the deleterious effects—especially on our young people—of the breakdown of social ties and community in American life. But unfortunately, our nation reacts to these problems by calling for more paid professionals—more police, more psychiatrists, more experts—without recognizing the possibility that shorter work hours and more free time could enable us to do much of the necessary rebuilding and healing, with much more gratifying and longer-lasting results.

16   Of course, the stiffest opposition to cutting work hours comes not from citizens but from business. Employers are reluctant to alter the 8-hour day, 40-hour work-week, 50 weeks a year because it seems easier and more profitable for employers to hire fewer employees for longer hours rather than more employees—each of whom would also require health insurance and other benefits—with flexible schedules and work arrangements.

17   Harvard University economist Juliet B. Schor, who has been studying issues of work and leisure in America, reminds us that we cannot ignore the larger relationship between unemployment and overwork: While many of us work too much, others are unable to find paid work at all. Schor points out that "workers who work longer hours lose more income when they lose their jobs. The threat of job loss is an important determinant of management's power on the shop floor." A system that offers only two options—long work hours or unemployment—serves as both a carrot and a stick. Those lucky enough to get full-time jobs are bribed into docile compliance with the boss, while the spectre of unemployment always looms as the ultimate punishment for the unruly.

18   Some observers suggest that keeping people divided into "the employed" and "the unemployed" creates feelings of resentment and inferiority/superiority between the two groups, thus focusing their discontent and blame on each other rather than on the corporations and political figures who actually dictate our nation's economic policies.

19   Our role as consumers contributes to keeping the average work week from falling. In an economic system in which addictive buying is the basis of corporate profits, working a full 40 hours or more each week for 50 weeks a year gives us just enough time to stumble home and dazedly—almost automatically—shop; but not enough time to think about deeper issues or to work effectively for social change. From the point of view of corporations and policymakers, shorter work time may be bad for the economy, because people with enhanced free time may begin to find other things to do with it besides mindlessly buying products. It takes more free time to grow vegetables, cook meals from scratch, sew clothes, or repair broken items than it does to just buy these things at the mall.

Any serious proposal to give employed Americans a break by cutting into   20
the eight-hour work day is certain to be met with anguished cries about international competitiveness. The United States seems gripped by the fear that our
nation has lost its economic dominance, and pundits, policymakers, and business
leaders tell us that no sacrifice is too great if it puts America on top again.

As arguments like this are put forward (and we can expect them to increase   21
in the years to come), we need to remember two things. First, even if America
maintained its dominance (whatever that means) and the economy were boom-
ing again, this would be no guarantee that the gains—be they in wages, in
employment opportunities, or in leisure—would be distributed equitably between
upper management and everyone else. Second, the entire issue of competitiveness is suspect when it pits poorly treated workers in one country against poorly
treated workers in another; and when the vast majority of economic power, anyway, is in the control of enormous multinational corporations that have no loyalty to the people of any land.

EXERCISES

Some of the Issues

1. What was your immediate reaction to Brandt's first paragraph? Do you
   agree or disagree? Why or why not?
2. What does Brandt see as the irony of modern technology (paragraph 2)?
   How, in your opinion, has technology changed our commitments to work,
   family, and community?
3. According to Brandt, who in America suffers from overwork (paragraph 3)?
4. In paragraphs 4 through 10 Brandt contrasts the work habits or preindus-
   trial and other industrialized nations with those of the United States. Why
   does she make these comparisons?
5. In paragraphs 11 through 15, Brandt discusses two reasons why individuals
   resist a shorter workweek. What are they? Do you agree with her comments on the "work ethic"?
6. Why are employers reluctant to alter the 8-hour day (paragraph 16)?
7. According to Brandt and Juliet B. Schor, how does overwork divide us
   (paragraphs 16 through 19) and which groups are pitted against each other
   (paragraph 21)? What are the consequences of this division?
8. According to Brandt, what role do corporations play in encouraging con-
   sumption and keeping the workweek long (paragraph 19)? Do you agree
   with her analysis?

The Way We Are Told

9. Brandt makes certain points in her argument by first stating a common assumption and then presenting evidence against that assumption. Find places in the essay where she does this. Does it make her argument more effective?

10. How does Brandt use comparison and contrast to provide evidence for her argument?

Some Subjects for Writing

11. In a journal, document your own work habits for three or four days. Take note of how much time you devote to your work, school, leisure, family, and community. Using examples and descriptions from your journal, write an essay in which you define and examine your own work habits.

12. Interview three or four people from different social or cultural backgrounds about their work habits. Make sure to prepare a list of questions beforehand and ask follow-up questions during the interview. Write an essay in which you compare and contrast their attitudes toward both work and leisure.

13. Do you agree with Brandt that Americans overvalue the "work ethic" and undervalue leisure-time activities? Write an essay explaining your views.

14. In a section of the article not reprinted here, Brandt makes specific proposals for shortening the workweek to 30 hours. Write an essay explaining the benefits or drawbacks of either a 6-hour workday or a 4-day workweek.

Life on the Global
Assembly Line

BARBARA EHRENREICH AND ANNETTE FUENTES

Barbara Ehrenreich, born in 1941, is the author of several books of essays, including Fear of Falling *(1989),* The Worst Years of Our Lives *(1991) and* The Snarling Citizen *(1995). She is also the author of a novel,* Kipper's Game *(1993). She is a frequent contributor to* Time, The New York Times, *and* The Guardian, *among other publications. Annette Fuentes, also a journalist, is coauthor, with Barbara Ehrenreich, of* Women in the Global Factory *(1983).*

This selection, which first appeared in Ms. *magazine in January 1981, traces the consequences of large corporations shifting their production to Third World countries to take advantage of cheaper labor. Many of their new employees are women, lured by a promise of higher salaries and relative independence. The reality of these jobs for most Third World women is different from the promise. They perform tedious, often health-destroying tasks, at wages too low to accumulate savings. If the company moves, or a woman has exhausted her health, she is unlikely to find another job and is often unable to reintegrate herself into the traditional society she had left.*

In Ciudad Juárez, Mexico, Anna M. rises at 5 A.M. to feed her son before starting on the two-hour bus trip to the maquiladora (factory). He will spend the day along with four other children in a neighbor's one-room home. Anna's husband, frustrated by being unable to find work for himself, left for the United States six months ago. She wonders, as she carefully applies her new lip gloss, whether she ought to consider herself still married. It might be good to take a night course, become a secretary. But she seldom gets home before eight at night, and the factory, where she stitches brassieres that will be sold in the United States through J.C. Penney, pays only $48 a week. 1

In Penang, Malaysia, Julie K. is up before the three other young women with whom she shares a room, and starts heating the leftover rice from last night's supper. She looks good in the company's green-trimmed uniform, and she's proud to work in a modern, American-owned factory. Only not quite so proud as when she started working three years ago—she thinks as she squints out the door at a passing group of women. Her job involves peering all day through a microscope, bonding hair-thin gold wires to 2 *a silicon chip destined to end up inside a pocket calculator, and at 21, she is afraid she can no longer see very clearly.*

3   Every morning, between four and seven, thousands of women like Anna and Julie head out for the day shift. In Ciudad Juárez, they crowd into *ruteras* (run-down vans) for the trip from the slum neighborhoods to the industrial parks on the outskirts of the city. In Penang they squeeze, 60 or more at a time, into buses for the trip from the village to the low, modern factory buildings of the Bayan Lepas free trade zone. In Taiwan, they walk from the dormitories—where the night shift is already asleep in the still-warm beds—through the checkpoints in the high fence surrounding the factory zone.

4   This is the world's new industrial proletariat: young, female, Third World. Viewed from the "first world," they are still faceless, genderless "cheap labor," signaling their existence only through a label or tiny imprint—"made in Hong Kong," or Taiwan, Korea, the Dominican Republic, Mexico, the Philippines. But they may be one of the most strategic blocs of womanpower in the world of the 1980s. Conservatively, there are 2 million Third World female industrial workers employed now, millions more looking for work, and their numbers are rising every year. Anyone whose image of Third World women features picturesque peasants with babies slung on their backs should be prepared to update it. Just in the last decade, Third World women have become a critical element in the global economy and a key "resource" for expanding multinational corporations.

5   It doesn't take more than second-grade arithmetic to understand what's happening. In the United States, an assembly-line worker is likely to earn, depending on her length of employment, between $3.10 and $5 an hour. In many Third World countries, a woman doing the same work will earn $3 to $5 a *day*. According to the magazine *Business Asia*, in 1976 the average hourly wage for unskilled work (male or female) was 55 cents in Hong Kong, 52 cents in South Korea, 32 cents in the Philippines, and 17 cents in Indonesia. The logic of the situation is compelling: why pay someone in Massachusetts $5 an hour to do what someone in Manila will do for $2.50 a day? Or, as a corollary, why pay a male worker any-where to do what a female worker will do for 40 to 60 percent less?

6   And so, almost everything that can be packed up is being moved out to the Third World; not heavy industry, but just about anything light enough to travel—garment manufacture, textiles, toys, footwear, pharmaceuticals, wigs, appliance parts, tape decks, computer components, plastic goods. In some industries, like garment and textile, American jobs are lost in the process, and the biggest losers are women, often black and Hispanic. But what's going on is much more than a matter of runaway shops. Economists are talking about a "new international division of labor," in which the process of production is broken down and the fragments are dispersed to different parts of the world. In general, the low-skilled jobs are farmed out to the Third World, where labor costs are minuscule, while control over the overall process and technology remains safely

at company headquarters in "first world" countries like the United States and Japan.

The American electronics industry provides a classic example: circuits are   7
printed on silicon wafers and tested in California; then the wafers are shipped to Asia for the labor-intensive process by which they are cut into tiny chips and bonded to circuit boards; final assembly into products such as calculators or military equipment usually takes place in the United States. Garment manufacture too is often broken into geographically separated steps, with the most repetitive, labor-intensive jobs going to the poor countries of the southern hemisphere. Most Third World countries welcome whatever jobs come their way in the new division of labor, and the major international development agencies—like the World Bank and the United States Agency for International Development (AID)—encourage them to take what they can get.

So much any economist could tell you. What is less often noted is the *gender*   8
breakdown of the emerging international division of labor. Eighty to 90 percent of the low-skilled assembly jobs that go to the Third World are performed by women—in a remarkable switch from earlier patterns of foreign-dominated industrialization. Until now, "development" under the aegis of foreign corporations has usually meant more jobs for men and—compared to traditional agricultural society—a diminished economic status for women. But multinational corporations and Third World governments alike consider assembly-line work—whether the product is Barbie dolls or missile parts—to be "women's work."

One reason is that women can, in many countries, still be legally paid less   9
than men. But the sheer tedium of the jobs adds to the multinationals' preference for women workers—a preference made clear, for example, by this ad from a Mexican newspaper: *We need female workers; older than 17, younger than 30; single and without children: minimum education primary school, maximum education one year of preparatory school (high school): available for all shifts.*

It's an article of faith with management that only women can do, or will do,   10
the monotonous, painstaking work that American business is exporting to the Third World. Bill Mitchell, whose job is to attract United States businesses to the Bermudez Industrial Park in Ciudad Juárez told us with a certain macho pride: "A man just won't stay in this tedious kind of work. He'd walk out in a couple of hours." The personnel manager of a light assembly plant in Taiwan told anthropologist Linda Gail Arrigo: "Young male workers are too restless and impatient to do monotonous work with no career value. If displeased, they sabotage the machines and even threaten the foreman. But girls? At most, they cry a little."

In fact, the American businessmen we talked to claimed that Third World   11
women genuinely enjoy doing the very things that would drive a man to assault and sabotage. "You should watch these kids going into work," Bill Mitchell told us. "You don't have any sullenness here. They smile." A top level management

consultant who specializes in advising American companies on where to relocate their factories gave us this global generalization: "The [factory] girls genuinely enjoy themselves. They're away from their families. They have spending money. They can buy motorbikes, whatever. Of course it's a regulated experience too—with dormitories to live in—so its a healthful experience."

12   What is the real experience of the women in the emerging Third World industrial work force? The conventional Western stereotypes leap to mind: You can't really compare, the standards are so different.... Everything's easier in warm countries.... They really don't have any alternatives.... Commenting on the low wages his company pays its women workers in Singapore, a Hewlett-Packard vice-president said, "They live much differently here than we do...." But the differences are ultimately very simple. To start with, they have less money.

13   The great majority of the women in the new Third World work force live at or near the subsistence level for one person, whether they work for a multinational corporation or a locally owned factory. In the Philippines, for example, starting wages in U.S.-owned electronics plants are between $34 to $46 a month, compared to a cost of living of $37 a month; in Indonesia the starting wages are actually about $7 a month less than the cost of living. "Living," in these cases, should be interpreted minimally: a diet of rice, dried fish, and water—a Coke might cost a half-day's wages—lodging in a room occupied by four or more other people. Rachael Grossman, a researcher with the Southeast Asia Resource Center, found women employees of U.S. multinational firms in Malaysia and the Philippines living four to eight in a room in boardinghouses, or squeezing into tiny extensions built onto squatter huts near the factory. Where companies do provide dormitories for their employees, they are not of the "healthful," collegiate variety implied by our corporate informant. Staff from the American Friends Service Committee report that dormitory space is "likely to be crowded, with bed rotation paralleling shift rotation—while one shift works, another sleeps, as many as twenty to a room." In one case in Thailand, they found the dormitory "filthy," with workers forced to find their own place to sleep among "splintered floorboards, rusting sheets of metal, and scraps of dirty cloth."

14   Wages do increase with seniority, but the money does not go to pay for studio apartments or, very likely, motorbikes. A 1970 study of young women factory workers in Hong Kong found that 88 percent of them were turning more than half their earnings over to their parents. In areas that are still largely agricultural (such as parts of the Philippines and Malaysia), or places where male unemployment runs high (such as northern Mexico), a woman factory worker may be the sole source of cash income for an entire extended family

15   But wages on a par with what an 11-year-old American could earn on a paper route, and living conditions resembling what Engels found in 19th-century Manchester are only part of the story. The rest begins at the factory gate. The work that multinational corporations export to the Third World is not only the

most tedious, but often the most hazardous part of the production process. The countries they go to are, for the most part, those that will guarantee no interference from health and safety inspectors, trade unions, or even free-lance reformers. As a result, most Third World factory women work under conditions that already have broken or will break their health—or their nerves—within a few years, and often before they've worked long enough to earn any more than a subsistence wage.

Consider first the electronics industry, which is generally thought to be the safest and cleanest of the exported industries. The factory buildings are low and modern, like those one might find in a suburban American industrial park. Inside, rows of young women, neatly dressed in the company uniform or T-shirt, work quietly at their stations. There is air conditioning (not for the women's comfort, but to protect the delicate semiconductor parts they work with), and high-volume piped-in Bee Gees hits (not so much for entertainment, as to prevent talking).   16

For many Third World women, electronics is a prestige occupation, at least compared to other kinds of factory work. They are unlikely to know that in the United States the National Institute on Occupational Safety and Health (NIOSH) has placed electronics on its select list of "high health-risk industries using the greatest number of toxic substances." If electronics assembly work is risky here, it is doubly so in countries where there is no equivalent of NIOSH to even issue warnings. In many plants toxic chemicals and solvents sit in open containers, filling the work area with fumes that can literally knock you out. "We have been told of cases where ten to twelve women passed out at once," an AFSC field worker in northern Mexico told us, "and the newspapers report this as 'mass hysteria.'"   17

In one stage of the electronics assembly process, the workers have to dip the circuits into open vats of acid. According to Irene Johnson and Carol Bragg, who toured the National Semiconductor plant in Penang, Malaysia, the women who do the dipping "wear rubber gloves and boots, but these sometimes leak, and burns are common." Occasionally, whole fingers are lost. Most commonly, what electronics workers lose is the 20/20 vision they are required to have when they are hired. Most electronics workers spend seven to nine hours a day peering through microscopes, straining to meet their quotas.   18

One study in South Korea found that most electronics assembly workers developed severe eye problems after only one year of employment; 88 percent had chronic conjunctivitis; 44 percent became nearsighted, and 19 percent developed astigmatism. A manager for Hewlett-Packard's Malaysia plant, in an interview with Rachael Grossman, denied that there were any eye problems. "These girls are used to working with scopes. We've found no eye problems. But it sure makes me dizzy to look through those things."   19

Electronics, recall, is the "cleanest" of the exported industries. Conditions in the garment and textile industry rival those of any 19th-century (or 20th—   20 see below) sweatshop. The firms, generally local subcontractors to large American chains such as J.C. Penney and Sears, as well as smaller manufacturers, are usually even more indifferent to the health of their employees than the multinationals. Some of the worst conditions have been documented in South Korea, where the garment and textile industries have helped spark that country's "economic miracle." Workers are packed into poorly lit rooms, where summer temperatures rise above 100 degrees. Textile dust, which can cause permanent lung damage, fills the air. When there are rush orders, management may require forced overtime of as much as 48 hours at a stretch, and if that seems to go beyond the limits of human endurance, pep pills and amphetamine injections are thoughtfully provided. In her diary (originally published in a magazine now banned by the South Korean government) Min Chong Suk, 30, a sewing-machine operator, wrote of working from 7 A.M. to 11:30 P.M. in a garment factory. "When [the apprentices] shake the waste threads from the clothes, the whole room fills with dust, and it is hard to breathe. Since we've been working in such dusty air, there have been increasing numbers of people getting tuberculosis, bronchitis, and eye diseases. Since we are women, it makes us so sad when we have pale, unhealthy, wrinkled faces like dried-up spinach.... It seems to me that no one knows our blood dissolves into the threads and seams, with sighs and sorrow."

21   In all the exported industries, the most invidious, inescapable health hazard is stress. On their home ground United States corporations are not likely to sacrifice productivity for human comfort. On someone else's home ground, however, anything goes. Lunch breaks may be barely long enough for a woman to stand in line at the canteen or hawkers' stalls. Visits to the bathroom are treated as privilege; in some cases, workers must raise their hands for permission to use the toilet, and waits up to a half hour are common. Rotating shifts—the day shift one week, the night shift the next—wreak havoc with sleep patterns. Because inaccuracies or failure to meet production quotas can mean substantial pay losses, the pressures are quickly internalized; stomach ailments and nervous problems are not unusual in the multinationals' Third World female work force. In some situations, good work is as likely to be punished as slow or shoddy work. Correspondent Michael Flannery, writing for the AFL-CIO's *American Federationist*, tells the story of 23-year-old Basilia Altagracia, a seamstress who stitched collars onto ladies' blouses in the La Romana (Dominican Republic) free trade zone (a heavily guarded industrial zone owned by Gulf & Western industries, Inc.):

22   "A nimble veteran seamstress, Miss Altagracia eventually began to earn as much as $5.75 a day.... 'I was exceeding my piecework quota by a lot....' But then, Altagracia said, her plant supervisor, a Cuban emigré, called her into his office. 'He said I was doing a fine job, but that I and some other of the women were making too much money, and he was being forced to lower what we earned for each piece we sewed.' On the best days, she now can clear barely $3, she said.

'I was earning less, so I started working six and seven days a week. But I was tired and I could not work as fast as before.'" Within a few months, she was too ill to work at all.

As if poor health and the stress of factory life weren't enough to drive   23
women into early retirement, management actually encourages a high turn-over in many industries. "As you know, when seniority rises, wages rise," the management consultant to U.S. multinationals told us. He explained that it's cheaper to train a fresh supply of teenagers than to pay experienced women higher wages. "Older women, aged 23 or 24, are likely to be laid off and not rehired."

We estimate, based on fragmentary data from several sources, that the mul-   24
tinational corporations may already have used up (cast off) as many as 6 million Third World workers—women who are too ill, too old (30 is over the hill in most industries), or too exhausted to be useful any more. Few "retire" with any transferable skills or savings. The lucky ones find husbands.

The unlucky ones find themselves at the margins of society—as bar girls,   25
"hostesses," or prostitutes.

At 21, Julie's greatest fear is that she will never be able to find a husband. She knows   26
that just being a "factory girl" is enough to give anyone a bad reputation. When she
first started working at the electronics company, her father refused to speak to her for
three months. Now, every time she leaves Penang to go back to visit her home village
she has to put up with a lecture on morality from her older brother—not to mention a
barrage of lewd remarks from men outside her family. If they knew that she had actually
gone out on a few dates, that she had been to a discotheque, that she had once kissed a
young man who said he was a student.... Julie's stomach tightens as she imagines her
family's reaction. She tries to concentrate on the kind of man she would like to marry:
an engineer or technician of some sort, someone who had been to California, where the
company headquarters are located and where even the grandmothers wear tight pants
and lipstick—someone who had a good attitude about women. But if she ends up having
to wear glasses, like her cousin who worked three years at the "scopes," she might as well
forget about finding anyone to marry her.

One of the most serious occupational hazards that Julie and millions of   27
women like her may face is the lifelong stigma of having been a "factory girl." Most of the cultures favored by multinational corporations in their search for cheap labor are patriarchal in the grand old style: any young woman who is not under the wing of a father, husband, or older brother must be "loose." High levels of unemployment among men, as in Mexico, contribute to male resentment of working women. (Ironically, in some places the multinationals have increased male unemployment—for example, by paving over fishing and farming villages to make way for industrial parks.) Add to all this the fact that certain companies—American electronics firms are in the lead—actively promote

Western-style sexual objectification as a means of insuring employee loyalty: there are company-sponsored cosmetics classes, "guess whose legs these are" contests, and swimsuit-style beauty contests where the prize might be a free night *for two* in a fancy hotel. Corporate-promoted Westernization only heightens the hostility many men feel toward any independent working women—having a job is bad enough, wearing jeans and mascara to work is going too far.

28   Anthropologist Patricia Fernandez, who has worked in a *maquiladora* herself, believes that the stigmatization of working women serves, indirectly, to keep them in line. "You have to think of the kind of socialization that girls experience in a very Catholic—or, for that matter, Muslim—society. The fear of having a 'reputation' is enough to make a lot of women bend over backward to be 'respectable' and ladylike, which is just what management wants." She points out that in northern Mexico, the tabloids delight in playing up stories of alleged vice in the *maquiladoras*—indiscriminate sex on the job, epidemics of venereal disease, fetuses found in factory rest rooms. "I worry about this because there are those who treat you differently as soon as they know you have a job at a *maquiladora*," one woman told Fernandez. "Maybe they think that if you have to work, there is a chance you're a whore."

29   And there is always a chance you'll wind up as one. Probably only a small minority of Third World factory workers turn to prostitution when their working days come to an end. But it is, as for women everywhere, the employment of last resort, the only thing to do when the factories don't need you and traditional society won't—or, for economic reasons, can't—take you back. In the Philippines, the brothel business is expanding as fast as the factory system. If they can't use you one way, they can use you another.

EXERCISES

Some of the Issues

1. In paragraph 5, the authors discuss the wage differential between what Ehrenreich and Fuentes call the First and Third Worlds. What are its consequences? Who loses jobs as a result (paragraph 6)?
2. What do economists mean when they speak of a "new international division of labor"? How does this concept differ from the traditional meaning of the term "division of labor"?
3. How does the American electronics industry exemplify both that new division of labor and the consequences of wage differentials (paragraph 7)?
4. In paragraph 8 the authors begin to discuss in detail the "gender breakdown" of the new division of labor. What do they refer to? What are the reasons for the fact that 80–90 percent of the assembly-line jobs go to women?

5. What do the authors believe are the contradictions between the "conventional Western stereotypes" (paragraph 12) and the realities of women's work (paragraphs 13–14)?
6. In paragraphs 16–19 the authors describe the differences between appearance and reality in the electronics industry. What are the various hazards workers risk?
7. On what grounds do the authors assert that the garment industry is even worse than the electronics industry (paragraphs 20–22)?
8. What additional risks do women run when they rise in seniority?
9. Describe the conflicts that may arise in traditional societies between the young women who work in factories and their families.
10. What, according to the authors, is "the employment of last resort" (paragraph 29) and how are women driven to it?

The Way We Are Told

11. Three paragraphs of this essay (1, 2, and 26) are set in italics. What do you think is the reason?
12. The authors base their essay on different kinds of research. Cite examples of each kind and evaluate their effectiveness.
13. In a number of instances (paragraphs 11 and 12, for example) the authors cite what people in the industrialized world assume to be the case, and compare that view to reality. Cite some other instances and examine the effectiveness of the comparison.

Some Subjects for Writing

14. If you have any work experience, describe it. How did its reality differ from your expectations before starting?
15. Write an essay documenting discrimination in the workplace against one of the following groups: women, a racial or religious minority, the handicapped, the young worker, the older worker, or any other group of workers you believe is treated unjustly. Support your argument with evidence gained from library research.
16. Even though this article was written in 1981, many of the conditions the authors describe still exist. With the help of your instructor, research working conditions in one of the countries Ehrenreich and Fuentes describe.
17. Some activists have called for boycotts of products that are manufactured by workers who work under extremely poor conditions for very low wages. Do you agree with this strategy of protest? Would you boycott a product if you did not like the company's work policies?

Class Poem

AURORA LEVINS MORALES

*Aurora Levins Morales was born in 1954 in Indiera Baja, Puerto Rico,
the daughter of an American Jewish father and a Puerto Rican mother,
both Communists. She came to the United States at the age of thirteen.
Much of her work focuses on the many strands that, woven together,
make up her identity. This poem originally appeared in* Getting Home
Alive *(1986), a book of poetry she coauthored with her mother, Rosario Morales.*

*The author currently lives in the San Francisco Bay Area where
she works as a teacher, writer, and performer.*

This is my poem in celebration of my middle class privilege
This is my poem to say out loud
I'm glad I had food, and shelter, and shoes,
glad I had books and travel, glad there was air and light
5 and room for poetry.

This poem is for Tita, my best friend
who played in the dirt with me
and married at eighteen (which was late) and who was a scientist
but instead she bore six children and four of them died
10 Who wanted to know the exact location of color
in the hibiscus petal, and patiently peeled away the thinnest,
most translucent layers to find it
and who works in a douche bag factory in Maricao.

This poem is for the hunger of my mother
15 discovering books at thirteen in the New York Public Library
who taught me to read when I was five
and when we lived on a coffee farm
subscribed to a mail-order library,
who read the Blackwell's catalogue
20 like a menu of delights
and when we moved from Puerto Rico to the States
we packed 100 boxes of books and 40 of everything else.

This poem is for my father's immigrant Jewish family.
For my great-grandfather Abe Sackman
who worked in Bridgeport making nurse's uniforms   25
and came home only on weekends, for years, and who painted
on bits of old wooden crates, with housepaint,
birds and flowers for his great-grandchildren
and scenes of his old-country childhood.

This poem celebrates my father the scientist   30
who left the microscope within reach,
with whom I discovered the pomegranate eye of the fruitfly,
and yes, the exact location of color in a leaf.

This poem celebrates my brother the artist
who began to draw when he was two,   35
and so my parents bought him reams of paper
and when he used them up, bought him more,
and today it's a silkscreen workshop
and posters that travel around the world,
and I'm glad for him   and for Pop with his housepaints   40
and Tita staining the cement with crushed flowers
searching for color
and my mother shutting out the cries of her first-born
ten minutes at a time
to sketch the roofs and elevated tracks   45
in red-brown pastels.

This is for Norma
who died of parasites in her stomach when she was four
I remember because her mother wailed her name
screaming and sobbing   50
one whole afternoon in the road in front of our school
and for Angélica
who caught on fire while stealing kerosene for her family
and died in pain
because the hospital she was finally taken to   55
knew she was poor
and would not give her the oxygen she needed to live
but wrapped her in greased sheets
so that she suffocated.

This is a poem against the wrapped sheets,   60
against guilt.

This is a poem to say:
my choosing to suffer gives nothing
to Tita and Norma and Angélica
65 and that not to use the tongue, the self-confidence, the training
my privilege bought me
is to die again for people who are already dead
and who wanted to live.

And in case anyone here confuses the paraphernalia
70 with the thing itself
let me add that I lived with rats and termites
no carpet   no stereo   no TV
that the bath came in buckets and was heated on the stove
that I read by kerosene lamp and had Sears mail-order clothes
75 and that that has nothing to do
with the fact of my privilege.

Understand, I know exactly what I got: protection and choice
and I am through apologizing.
I am going to strip apology from my voice
80 my posture
my apartment
my clothing
my dreams
because the voice that says the only true puertorican
85 is a dead or dying puertorican
is the enemy's voice—
the voice that says
"How can you let yourself shine when Tita, when millions
are daily suffocating in those greased sheets…"
90 I refuse to join them there.
I will not suffocate.
I will not hold back.
Yes, I had books and food and shelter and medicine
and I intend to survive.

EXERCISES

Some of the Issues

1. Morales begins her poem by saying that she will be grateful "out loud" for her middle-class privilege. Why do you think it may have been difficult in the past for her to say some of the things she now says publicly?

2. In her poem, Morales celebrates several persons who have contributed to her life by deed or by example. How and why are they important to her?

3. In line 61 Morales mentions guilt. Why would anyone expect her to feel guilty? In Morales's view, or in your own, is there anything to be gained in feeling guilt?

4. What does Morales mean when she writes "in case anyone here confuses the paraphernalia with the thing itself" (lines 69–70)?

5. What is the "enemy's" voice in the last stanza of the poem? Why does she refuse to listen to it?

6. What are the possible meanings of the title?

Some Subjects for Writing

7. Write an essay (or a poem) in which you celebrate some aspect of your identity. You can even begin with the line "This essay is in celebration of...."

8. Who has influenced you in determining the values you now hold? Write about one or more persons whose ideas and/or actions have played an important role in your life. Be sure to cite specific actions or to quote things people have said.

9. Morales talks about a turning point in the way she views her experience— she is through apologizing. Was there a moment in your life when you changed the way you viewed things? What was the change? How did it change you?

7

New Worlds

The New World—that designation for America has had a wider meaning than simply the name of the continent that Columbus ran into on his way to find the western passage to Asia. America has been an idea, or rather different ideas at different times. To the Spaniards, who were the first arrivals nearly 500 years ago, it was a source of unimagined wealth. Large-scale Spanish expeditions searched prairies and deserts for El Dorado and the Fountain of Youth. In some of the early English descriptions, often by writers who had never laid eyes on the New World, it resembled the Lost World—the Garden of Eden, Paradise, or the closest approach to it. Continuing the metaphor into the present, Bette Bao Lord, in the first selection of this section, describes her first glimpse of the Golden Gate as "more like the portals to Heaven than the arches of a man-made bridge."

More than two hundred years earlier, Michel Guillaume St. Jean de Crèvecoeur had come as a young man to the New World and settled in the French colony of Louisiane. In his *Letters from an American Farmer* (1782), written in French, he defines the new creature, the American, as different in any number of ways from his classbound, traditional European ancestors. In defining "What is an American?", Crèvecoeur celebrates the creation of what he views as an almost classless society, in which persons can reach whatever position in life their abilities allow. A modern, and much lighter, view of what America "means" is found in the selection called "Recapture the Flag: 34 Reasons to Love America," reprinted from the Fourth of July edition of *City Pages*, an alternative newspaper.

Often, the "better life" in the New World proved to be less than a Garden of Eden. Anzia Yezierska, in a semiautobiographical story, recounts her struggle with those who had already "made it" in America and who tried to preserve their positions by keeping others out. In "Black Like Them" Malcolm Gladwell compares the lives of African-Americans and West Indian black immigrants to the United States. How does each group define itself? How are they perceived by

┌───┐

THINKING ABOUT THE THEME *"New Worlds"*

1. The picture shows two people taking an oath of allegiance as new citizens. Suppose you are organizing a ceremony to honor people who are being sworn in as new United States citizens. Write a letter to the immigration service describing your plans. Where would the ceremony be held? Who would speak and what subjects would be addressed? What music would be played?

2. The Oath of Allegiance that these new citizens are taking states: "I hereby declare, on oath, that I absolutely and entirely renounce and abjure all allegiance and fidelity to any foreign prince, potentate, state or sovereignty of whom or which I have heretofore been a subject or citizen; that I will support and defend the constitution and laws of the United States of America against all enemies, foreign and domestic; that I will bear true faith and allegiance to the same; that I will bear arms on behalf of the United States when required by law;... that I will perform work of national importance under civilian direction when required by the law; and that I take this obligation freely without any mental reservation or purpose of evasion: So help me God."

   Examine the oath. Does all of it seem reasonable to you? Are there things that might be objectionable to someone who would be a good citizen? Why or why not?

3. Interview someone who has recently become a citizen of the United States. What are their feelings about becoming a citizen? What difficulties did they encounter becoming a citizen? Why did they choose to become a citizen? Discuss the results of your interview with your classmates.

4. Some people declared themselves to be "citizens of the world" rather than citizens of a specific country. To what country, land, people, or place would you pledge allegiance (you may choose more than one, or none at all)? What aspects of citizenship do you think are important? Which do you think are unimportant?

5. Though not all of us have changed our citizenship, many of us have experienced turning points which are significant, points where we might feel that one door closes and another door opens in our lives. Some examples could be moving to a new place, starting a new job, getting married, divorced, or having a child. Describe such a turning point in your life and its significance for you.

└───┘

the white majority? In a complex essay, Gladwell uses his own family history and the work of scholars to reflect on the kinds of racism experienced by both groups.

At Ellis Island, Joseph Bruchac's Slavic grandparents were welcomed by a giant figure of a woman carrying a torch, cast in bronze weathered to green. However, the land that meant freedom and relief from poverty for them was also the land where Native Americans, Bruchac's other grandparents, had lived for centuries.

Walking in Lucky Shoes

BETTE BAO LORD

Bette Bao Lord was born on November 3, 1938, in Shanghai, China, where her father worked as an official of the Nationalist Chinese government. She immigrated to the United States in 1946, attended Tufts University, and completed a law degree at Fletcher School of Law and Diplomacy in 1960.

Lord was awarded the American Book Award for her first novel, Spring Moon *(1982). She originally planned the book as a nonfiction account of her 1973 journey to China. However, fearing that her family in China might suffer reprisals from leaders of the Cultural Revolution, she decided to write a historical novel instead. The novel chronicles five generations of the Chang family, whose lives witness the eradication of the traditional Chinese family structure and the disappearance of the upper-middle class. Lord is also the author of a memoir,* Legacies: A Chinese Mosaic *(1990) and another novel,* The Middle Heart *(1996).*

In the following Newsweek *guest editorial "My Turn," Lord emphasizes that multiculturalism is a national strength that has the potential both to make us proud of our diverse ancestries and to bind us together. She believes Americans can be different as individuals, but all members of the same family.*

I confess, Novelists have a fetish. We can't resist shoes. Indeed, we spend our 1
lives recalling the pairs we have shed and snatching others off unsuspecting
souls. We're not proud. We're not particular. Whether it's Air Jordans or the
clodhoppers of Frankenstein, Imelda's[1] gross collection or one glass slipper, we
covet them all. There's no cure for this affliction. To create characters, we must
traipse around and around in our heads sporting lost or stolen shoes.

At 8, I sailed for America from Shanghai without a passing acquaintance of 2
A, B or C, wearing scruffy brown oxfords. Little did I know then that they were
as magical as those glittering red pumps that propelled Dorothy down the yellow brick road.

Only yesterday, it seems, resting my chin on the rails of the SS Marylinx, I 3
peered into the mist for *Mei Guo*, Beautiful Country. It refused to appear. Then,

[1]Wife of former president/dictator of the Philippines, famous for her enormous shoe collection.

in a blink, there was the Golden Gate,[2] more like the portals to Heaven than the arches of a man-made bridge.

4   Only yesterday, standing at PS 8[3] in Brooklyn, I was bewitched—others, alas, were bothered and bewildered—when I proclaimed:

> *I pledge a lesson to the frog of*
> *   the United States of America.*
> *And to the wee puppet for witch's hands.*
> *   One Asian, in the vestibule,*
> *with little tea and just rice for all.*

5   Although I mangled the language, the message was not lost. Not on someone wearing immigrant shoes.

6   Only yesterday, rounding third base in galoshes, I swallowed a barrelful of tears wondering what wrong I had committed to anger my teammates so. Why were they all madly screaming at me to go home, go home?

7   Only yesterday, listening in pink cotton mules to Red Barber broadcasting from Ebbetts Field, I vaulted over the Milky Way as my hero, Jackie Robinson, stole home.

8   Only yesterday, enduring the pinch of new Mary Janes at my grammar-school graduation, I felt as tall as the Statue of Liberty, reciting Walt Whitman:[4] "I hear America singing, the varied carols I hear…Each singing what belongs to him or her and to none else…."

9   Today I cherish every unstylish pair of shoes that took me up a road cleared by the footfalls of millions of immigrants before me—to a room of my own. For America has granted me many a dream, even one that I never dared to dream— returning to the land of my birth in 1989 as the wife of the American ambassador. Citizens of Beijing were astounded to see that I was not a *yang guei ze*, foreign devil, with a tall nose and ghostly skin and bumpy hair colored in outlandish hues. I looked Chinese, I spoke Chinese, and after being in my company they accused me of being a fake, of being just another member of the clan.

10   I do not believe that the loss of one's native culture is the price one must pay for becoming an American. On the contrary, I feel doubly blessed. I can choose from two rich cultures those parts that suit my mood or the occasion best. And unbelievable as it may seem, shoes tinted red, white and blue go dandy with them all.

11   Recently I spoke at my alma mater. There were many more Asian faces in that one audience than there were enrolled at Tufts University when I cavorted in white suede shoes to cheer the Jumbos to victory. One asked, "Will you tell

[2]Long bridge at the entrance to San Francisco Bay.
[3]Public schools in New York City are designated by number.
[4](1819–92) American poet whose work celebrated both individual worth and human diversity.

us about your encounters with racial prejudice?" I had no ready answers. I thought hard. Sure, I had been roughed up at school. Sure, I had failed at work. Sure, I had at times felt powerless. But had prejudice against the shade of my skin and the shape of my eyes caused these woes? Unable to show off the wounds I had endured at the hands of racists, I could only cite a scene from my husband's 25th reunion at Yale eight years ago. Throughout that weekend, I sensed I was being watched. But even after the tall, burly man finally introduced himself, I did not recognize his face or name. He hemmed and hawed, then announced that he had flown from Colorado to apologize to me. I could not imagine why. Apparently at a party in the early '60s, he had hectored me to cease dating his WASP[5] classmate.

Someone else at Tufts asked, "How do you think of yourself? As a Chinese or as an American?" Without thinking, I blurted out the truth: "Bette Bao Lord." Did I imagine the collective sigh of relief that swept through the auditorium? I think not. Perhaps I am the exception that proves the rule. Perhaps I am blind to insult and injury. Perhaps I am not alone. No doubt I have been lucky. Others have not been as fortunate. They had little choice but to wear ill-fitting shoes warped by prejudice, to start down a less traveled road strewn with broken promises and littered with regrets, haunted by racism and awash with tears. Where could that road possibly lead? Nowhere but to a nation, divided, without liberty and no justice at all.   12

The Berlin wall[6] is down, but between East Harlem and West Hempstead, between the huddled masses of yesterday and today, the walls go up and up. Has the cold war ended abroad only to usher in heated racial and tribal conflicts at home? No, I believe we shall overcome. But only when: 13

We engage our diversity to yield a nation greater than the sum of its parts.   14

We can be different as sisters and brothers are, and belong to the same family.   15

We bless, not shame, America, our home.   16

A home, no doubt, where skeletons nest in closets and the roof leaks, where foundations must be shored and rooms added. But a home where legacies conceived by the forefathers are tendered from generation to generation to have and to hold. Legacies not of gold but as intangible and inalienable and invaluable as laughter and hope.   17

We the people can do just that—if we clear the smoke of ethnic chauvinism and fears by braving our journey to that "City Upon a Hill" in each other's shoes.   18

[5]White Anglo-Saxon Protestant.
[6]Built in 1961, it separated East and West Berlin until it was torn down in 1989.

EXERCISES

Some of the Issues

1. How do you characterize Lord's attitude and emotions toward America?
2. In paragraph 9, why did the Chinese accuse her of being a "a fake"? What point does she make by mentioning this experience?
3. In paragraph 11, what is significant about the man from Colorado's apology to her at her husband's 25th Yale reunion?
4. After she blurts out her name in the auditorium at Tufts University (paragraph 12) she perceives a "collective sigh of relief" from the audience. Why?

The Way We Are Told

5. The essay is structured chronologically. What stylistic device does Lord use to mark time transitions?
6. In paragraph 1, Lord introduces the shoe metaphor and then intersperses literal and figurative examples of shoes throughout the essay. Select instances of each use and show how they contribute to the thesis.
7. Give examples of Lord's uses of humor in paragraphs 4–6. Do you find them funny? believable?

Some Subjects for Writing

8. In your opinion, is Lord simply "walking in lucky shoes"? What role does luck play in her life? What other factors may have contributed to her success?
9. In the final paragraph, Lord is optimistic that Americans will overcome racial conflicts. Are you hopeful that this will be accomplished in the near future? Why or why not?

What Is an American?

MICHEL GUILLAUME ST. JEAN DE CRÈVECOEUR

Michel Guillaume St. Jean de Crèvecoeur (1735–1813) came as a young man to the New World, settling at first in the French colony of Louisiane, which at that time stretched in a huge arc from the mouth of the St. Lawrence River in the north to the mouth of the Mississippi in the south. In the Seven Years War (1756–1763), called the French and Indian Wars in America, he fought under Montcalm against the British. When the colonies passed into British hands, he remained and settled as a farmer in Vermont. The Revolutionary War found him on the side of the loyalists. Crèvecoeur returned to France permanently in 1790. His Letters from an American Farmer, *written in French, was published in 1782 and is among the earliest descriptions of life in America.*

Crèvecoeur defines and describes what he sees as the virtues and advantages America possesses as compared to the Europe of his day. He sees a prosperous agricultural society, virtually classless, in which persons can reach whatever position in life their abilities allow. He contrasts this to the Old World with its ingrained class structure, where a man (or woman) is born to wealth and high status or to poverty and lifelong drudgery, with no way to escape. He sees America as a young, mobile society in contrast to the static world from which the new man, the American, has made his escape.

I wish I could be acquainted with the feelings and thoughts which must agitate the heart and present themselves to the mind of an enlightened Englishman, when he first lands on this continent. He must greatly rejoice, that he lived at a time to see this fair country discovered and settled; he must necessarily feel a share of national pride, when he views the chain of settlements which embellishes these extended shores. When he says to himself, this is the work of my countrymen, who, when convulsed by factions, afflicted by a variety of miseries and wants, restless and impatient, took refuge here. They brought along with them their national genius, to which they principally owe what liberty they enjoy, and what substance they possess. Here he sees the industry of his native country, displayed in a new manner, and traces in their works the embryos of all the arts, sciences, and ingenuity which flourish in Europe. Here he beholds fair cities, substantial villages, extensive fields, an immense country filled with decent houses, good roads, orchards, meadows, and bridges, where an hundred years ago all was wild, woody, and uncultivated!

2   What a train of pleasing ideas this fair spectacle must suggest! It is a prospect which must inspire a good citizen with the most heartfelt pleasure. The difficulty consists in the manner of viewing so extensive a scene. He is arrived on a new continent; a modern society offers itself to his contemplation, different from what he had hitherto seen. It is not composed, as in Europe, of great lords who possess every thing, and of a herd of people who have nothing. Here are no aristocratical families, no courts, no kings, no bishops, no ecclesiastical dominion, no invisible power giving to a few a very visible one; no great manufacturers employing thousands, no great refinements of luxury. The rich and the poor are not so far removed from each other as they are in Europe.

3   Some few towns excepted, we are all tillers of the earth, from Nova Scotia to West Florida. We are a people of cultivators, scattered over an immense territory, communicating with each other by means of good roads and navigable rivers, united by the silken bands of mild government, all respecting the laws without dreading their power, because they are equitable. We are all animated with the spirit of industry, which is unfettered, and unrestrained, because each person works for himself. If he travels through our rural districts, he views not the hostile castle, and the haughty mansion, contrasted with the clay-built hut and miserable cabin, where cattle and men help to keep each other warm, and dwell in meanness, smoke, and indigence. A pleasing uniformity of decent competence appears throughout our habitations. The meanest of our log-houses is a dry and comfortable habitation. Lawyer or merchant are the fairest titles our towns afford; that of a farmer is the only appellation of the rural inhabitants of our country. It must take some time ere he can reconcile himself to our dictionary, which is but short in words of dignity, and names of honour. There, on a Sunday, he sees a congregation of respectable farmers and their wives, all clad in neat homespun, well mounted, or riding in their own humble waggons. There is not among them an esquire, saving the unlettered magistrate. There he sees a parson as simple as his flock, a farmer who does not riot on the labour of others. We have no princes, for whom we toil, starve, and bleed: we are the most perfect society now existing in the world. Here man is free as he ought to be; nor is this pleasing equality so transitory as many others are. Many ages will not see the shores of our great lakes replenished with inland nations, nor the unknown bounds of North America entirely peopled. Who can tell how far it extends? Who can tell the millions of men whom it will feed and contain? for no European foot has as yet travelled half the extent of this mighty continent?

4   The next wish of this traveller will be to know whence came all these people? They are a mixture of English, Scotch, Irish, Dutch, Germans, and Swedes. From this promiscuous breed, the race now called Americans have arisen. The eastern provinces must indeed be excepted, as being the unmixed descendants

of Englishmen. I have heard many wish they had been more intermixed also: for my part, I am no wisher; and think it much better as it has happened. They exhibit a most conspicuous figure in this great and variegated picture; they too enter for a great share in the pleasing perspective displayed in these thirteen provinces. I know it is fashionable to reflect on them; but I respect them for what they have done; for the accuracy and wisdom with which they have settled their territory; for the decency of their manners; for their early love of letters; their ancient college, the first in this hemisphere; for their industry, which to me, who am but a farmer, is the criterion of every thing. There never was a people, situated as they are, who, with so ungrateful a soil, have done more in so short a time. Do you think that the monarchical ingredients which are more prevalent in other governments, have purged them from all foul stains? Their histories assert the contrary.

In this great American asylum, the poor of Europe have by some means met together, and in consequence of various causes; to what purpose should they ask one another, what countrymen they are? Alas, two thirds of them had no country. Can a wretch who wanders about, who works and starves, whose life is a continual scene of sore affliction of pinching penury; can that man call England or any other kingdom his country? A country that had no bread for him, whose fields procured him no harvest, who met with nothing but the frowns of the rich, the severity of the laws, with jails and punishments; who owned not a single foot of the extensive surface of this planet? No! Urged by a variety of motives, here they came. Everything has tended to regenerate them; new laws, a new mode of living, a new social system; here they are become men: in Europe they were as so many useless plants, wanting vegetative mould, and refreshing showers; they withered, and were mowed down by want, hunger, and war: but now, by the power of transplantation, like all other plants, they have taken root and flourished! Formerly they were not numbered in any civil list of their country, except in those of the poor; here they rank as citizens. By what invisible power has this surprizing metamorphosis been performed? By that of the laws and that of their industry. The laws, the indulgent laws, protect them as they arrive, stamping on them the symbol of adoption; they receive ample rewards for their labours; these accumulated rewards procure them lands; those lands confer on them the title of freemen; and to that title every benefit is affixed which men can possibly require. This is the great operation daily performed by our laws. From whence proceed these laws? From our government. Whence that government? It is derived from the original genius and strong desire of the people, ratified and confirmed by government. This is the great chain which links us all, this is the picture which every province exhibits.

What attachment can a poor European emigrant have for a country where he had nothing? The knowledge of the language, the love of a few kindred as poor as himself, were the only cords that tied him: his country is now that which gives him land, bread, protection, and consequence: *Ubi panis ibi patria,*[1] is the motto of all emigrants. What then is the American, this new man? He is either an European, or the descendant of an European; hence that strange mixture of blood, which you will find in no other country. I could point out to you a man, whose grandfather was an Englishman, whose wife was Dutch, whose son married a French woman, and whose present four sons have now four wives of different nations. *He* is an American, who, leaving behind him all his ancient prejudices and manners, receives new ones from the new mode of life he has embraced, the new government he obeys, and the new rank he holds. He becomes an American by being received in the broad lap of our great *Alma Mater.*

7   Here individuals of all nations are melted into a new race of men, whose labours and posterity will one day cause great change in the world. Americans are the western pilgrims, who are carrying along with them that great mass of arts, sciences, vigour, and industry, which began long since in the east; they will finish the great circle. The Americans were once scattered all over Europe; here they are incorporated into one of the finest systems of population which has ever appeared, and which will hereafter become distinct by the power of the different climates they inhabit. The American ought, therefore, to love this country much better than that wherein either he or his forefathers were born. Here the rewards of his industry follow with equal steps the progress of his labour; his labour is founded on the basis of nature, *self-interest*; can it want a stronger allurement? Wives and children, who before in vain demanded of him a morsel of bread, now, fat and frolicsome, gladly help their father to clear those fields whence exuberant crops are to arise to feed and to clothe them all; without any part being claimed, either by a despotic prince, a rich abbot, or a mighty lord. Here religion demands but little of him; a small voluntary salary to the minister, and gratitude to God; can he refuse these? The American is a new man, who acts upon new principles; he must therefore entertain new ideas, and form new opinions. From involuntary idleness, servile dependence, penury, and useless labour, he has passed to toils of a very different nature, rewarded by ample subsistence.—This is an American.

EXERCISES

Some of the Issues

1. Why should the "enlightened Englishman" rejoice at landing in America?
2. What is the central idea of the second paragraph? How does it relate to the first? How does it carry Crèvecoeur's ideas beyond the first paragraph?
3. Consider the last sentence in paragraph 2 and explain how it is expanded on in paragraph 3.

---

[1]Where bread is, there is my country.

4. Paragraph 3 makes its point by means of contrasts. What are they?
5. Paragraphs 4 and 5 classify the people who came to America, but in two different ways. Paragraph 4 discusses national origins. How are Americans described in paragraph 5?
6. In paragraphs 6 and 7 Crèvecoeur asserts that these diverse Europeans are "melted into a new race of men"—Americans. How does that process take place? (Note the word "melted.")
7. Make a list of the contrasts Crèvecoeur makes or clearly implies between Europe and America. Then attempt to organize and classify them into major groupings.

The Way We Are Told

8. Why does Crèvecoeur create the character of the "enlightened Englishman" to report on America in paragraph 1, instead of continuing to use the first person singular, as he does in the opening sentence?
9. Crèvecoeur tries to convince the reader of the superiority of Americans and their institutions. Who, would you say, are his readers? What are their likely beliefs? How does Crèvecoeur respond to these beliefs?
10. Crèvecoeur uses rhetorical questions, exclamations, and repetition of words and phrases to strengthen his case. Find examples of each.

Some Subjects for Writing

11. Write an essay in praise of some institution that you admire. Select those aspects that seem important to you, organize them in some logical order, and write your description, stressing the favorable facts rather than giving your opinions.
12. Crèvecoeur presents the American as an ideal "new man," free of the shackles of history imposed on him in Europe. In an essay examine the extent to which the American can still be described in Crèvecoeur's terms today.
13. Crèvecoeur may have been the first to use the word *melt* to describe the fusion of people of different nationalities into a new "race of men"—Americans. The term *melting pot* has become a cliché representing that process. More recently some observers have cast doubts on the extent of that process and preferred the analogy of the salad bowl or mosaic to the melting pot. What are the implications of each of these terms? Write an essay discussing what term you might use to describe America and why.

Recapture the Flag: 34 Reasons to Love America

This list was selected from a longer one that appeared in the Minneapolis/St. Paul alternative weekly newspaper City Pages *on the day before Independence Day, July 3, 1991. Some of the items on the list might be considered traditional, whereas others are quite unconventional; together they attempt to capture the American mosaic.*

1. The hometown team on a winning streak
2. Pancakes (not crepes)
3. *Roe v. Wade*
4. Thurgood Marshall
5. American cranks—quirky thinkers with transformative visions: Gertrude Stein, William Burroughs, Howlin' Wolf, Henry Thoreau, R. Crumb, Charlie Parker, Abbie Hoffman, Charlotte Perkins Gilman, Lester Bangs, Jill Johnston, Dorothy Parker, Emma Goldman, Hunter S. Thompson, Josephine Baker, Walt Whitman, Lenny Bruce
6. Corn on the cob
7. The idea of the road as a place to reinvent yourself, a train of thought running from Robert Johnson through Kerouac to *Thelma & Louise*
8. Cool, dark bars where the bartender knows your name
9. Computer hackers
10. Dairy Queen
11. Soul food, po' boy sandwiches: Cuisine made from the cheap and unwanted
12. Elvis Presley. He had to invent himself first, because what he chased after—an amped-up fusion of black and white musics with deep, surreptitious roots—wasn't supposed to exist at all. When Elvis happened, the pitched reaction didn't portend only rock & roll; it foreshadowed a chain of events from the Selma marches to the Reagan backlash
13. Pioneers of social frontiers: Jackie Robinson, Queer Nation, AIM, Malcolm X, Angela Davis, Harriet Tubman, the Radical Faeries, Betty Friedan, Sojourner Truth, C.O.Y.O.T.E., Elizabeth Cady Stanton, Martin Luther King Jr.
14. The front porch or stoop: Gossip, swings, neighbor-spying, gin & tonics
15. The way immigration transforms the nation's eating habits: Wieners, potatoes, pizza, chow mein, spaghetti, tacos, egg rolls, curry, mock duck, pad thai

16. The phenomenal growth of popular literature written by women over the last 30 years: Adrienne Rich, Anne Tyler, Marge Piercy, Toni Morrison, Ursula LeGuin, Alice Hoffman, Maxine Hong Kingston, Audre Lorde, Gloria Naylor, Amy Tan, Kaye Gibbons, Louise Erdrich, Terry McMillan, Alice Walker, etc., etc., etc.

17. People who don't force you to love America

18. Blues, gospel, country & western, jazz, rock, bluegrass, soul, disco, rap, zydeco…strains from different cultures tossed together on the long, long road from Memphis to Chicago, Abilene to Hoboken, Detroit to L.A.

19. The land

20. Roadside diners with biscuits and gravy and bottomless glasses of iced tea

21. The richness of speech as you cross from state to state, region to region, sometimes city block to city block

22. All the highways in the Great Plains that curve into extravagant, sprawling space

23. The desperate courage of AIDS activists in the 1980s

24. Louis Armstrong, William Faulkner, Duke Ellington, Billie Holiday, Raymond Chandler, Ray Charles, John Ford and John Wayne, Alfred Stieglitz, Georgia O'Keeffe, Flannery O'Connor, Jimmie Rodgers, Aretha Franklin, Babe Ruth, Hank Williams, Muddy Waters, Robert Frank, Allen Ginsberg, Ishmael Reed, James Brown, Orson Welles, Jackson Pollock: While too much of white America still looked nervously to Europe, they helped shape a culture of breathtaking scope, vibrancy, and vulgar energy

25. Michael Jordan

26. The Vietnam War Memorial, for the lesson it takes to heart: Its egalitarianism, the air of loss, the way it ennobles war deaths without glorifying them

27. The verse of Woody Guthrie's "This Land Is Your Land" that most people never heard, which captured the spirit of the whole song: "Was a big high wall there that tried to stop me/A sign was painted said: Private Property/But on the back side it didn't say nothing/This land was made for you and me"

28. James Baldwin, the best thinker on race in the second half of this century, maybe the best essayist of his age, period: the writer most committed to working out his horrific ambivalence toward his motherland: America, not Africa

29. Earth First!

30. The Ramones: At a time when American rock & roll was becoming unbearably ponderous (Eagles, America, Jackson Browne), they melded '60s girl-group singing with Bay City Rollers pop chants, surf licks, and MC5 buzzsaw guitars, to create a whole new genre—cartoon rock. Gabba gabba hey

31. All-night grocery stores

32. Roadside monuments: Driving down the highway you spot something unusual on the horizon. It doesn't look like a tree exactly; it's definitely not a billboard. As you get closer, you figure it out—a 30-foot-high talking cow

33. Backyard barbecues: Swat the flies. Drop a burger in the dirt. Serve it anyway

34. Avon ladies, door-to-door encyclopedia salesmen, and Mary Kay pink Cadillacs

EXERCISES

Some of the Issues

1. Say which reasons are your favorites and why.
2. The title states that these are reasons to "love" America. Not everyone would agree that all 34 are positive qualities. What do you think?
3. Classify. Group similar reasons together and give a label to each category.
4. Meet with others in a small group and share your categories. Try to reach a consensus on at least three or four common categories.

The Way We Are Told

5. What can you infer about the composers of this list? What values and beliefs are inherent in their choices?
6. Do you think this list was generated by people your age? Justify your answer.

Some Topics for Writing

7. In a small group, brainstorm your own list of reasons to love (or not love) America. Discuss which categories you might add or expand on.
8. Use your own list or the one provided here to write about one representative trait that you think Americans can be proud of.

Soap and Water

ANZIA YEZIERSKA

Anzia Yezierska was born in Pinsk in the Russian-controlled part of Poland, circa 1885. At age 16, she immigrated to the United States with her family. Her father, a Talmudic scholar, depended on his wife and children to support the household. For three years Anzia worked as a seamstress, a domestic, and a factory worker before earning a scholarship to study at Columbia University. After graduation, she taught domestic science at an elementary school. In 1917 she met the American educator and philosopher John Dewey, who became her mentor and encouraged her literary pursuits. She published several novels, including Salome of the Tenements *(1923);* Bread Givers: A Struggle Between a Father of the Old World, and a Daughter of the New *(1925);* Arrogant Beggar *(1927); and an autobiographical novel* Red Ribbon on a White Horse *(1950). Some of her stories are collected in* How I Found America: Collected Stories of Anzia Yezierska *(1991). Much of her writing focuses on the Jewish immigrant experience seen from a woman's point of view.*

The following selection is taken from her first volume of stories, Hungry Hearts, *published in 1920. With the dream of America as a land of unlimited opportunities, the young immigrant struggles to find acceptance and self-expression in a hostile new world.*

What I so greatly feared, happened! Miss Whiteside, the dean of our college, withheld my diploma. When I came to her office, and asked her why she did not pass me, she said that she could not recommend me as a teacher because of my personal appearance.

She told me that my skin looked oily, my hair unkempt, and my fingernails sadly neglected. She told me that I was utterly unmindful of the little niceties of the well-groomed lady. She pointed out that my collar did not set evenly, my belt was awry, and there was a lack of freshness in my dress. And she ended with: "Soap and water are cheap. Anyone can be clean."

In those four years while I was under her supervision, I was always timid and diffident. I shrank and trembled when I had to come near her. When I had to say something to her, I mumbled and stuttered, and grew red and white in the face with fear.

4   Every time I had to come to the dean's office for a private conference, I prepared for the ordeal of her cold scrutiny, as a patient prepares for a surgical operation. I watched her gimlet eyes searching for a stray pin, for a spot on my dress, for my unpolished shoes, for my uncared-for fingernails, as one strapped on the operating table watches the surgeon approaching with his tray of sterilized knives.

5   She never looked into my eyes. She never perceived that I had a soul. She did not see how I longed for beauty and cleanliness. How I strained and struggled to lift myself from the dead toil and exhaustion that weighed me down. She could see nothing in people like me, except the dirt and the stains on the outside.

6   But this last time when she threatened to withhold my diploma, because of my appearance, this last time when she reminded me that "Soap and water are cheap. Anyone can be clean," this last time, something burst within me.

7   I felt the suppressed wrath of all the unwashed of the earth break loose within me. My eyes blazed fire. I didn't care for myself, nor the dean, nor the whole laundered world. I had suffered the cruelty of their cleanliness and the tyranny of their culture to the breaking point. I was too frenzied to know what I said or did. But I saw clean, immaculate, spotless Miss Whiteside shrivel and tremble and cower before me, as I had shriveled and trembled and cowered before her for so many years.

8   Why did she give me my diploma? Was it pity? Or can it be that in my outburst of fury, at the climax of indignities that I had suffered, the barriers broke, and she saw into the world below from where I came?

9   Miss Whiteside had no particular reason for hounding and persecuting me. Personally, she didn't give a hang if I was clean or dirty. She was merely one of the agents of clean society, delegated to judge who is fit and who is unfit to teach.

10   While they condemned me as unfit to be a teacher, because of my appearance, I was slaving to keep them clean. I was slaving in a laundry from five to eight in the morning, before going to college, and from six to eleven at night, after coming from college. Eight hours of work a day, outside my studies. Where was the time and the strength for the "little niceties of the well-groomed lady"?

11   At the time when they rose and took their morning bath, and put on their fresh-laundered linen that somebody had made ready for them, when they were being served with their breakfast, I had already toiled for three hours in a laundry.

12   When the college hours were over, they went for a walk in the fresh air. They had time to rest, and bathe again, and put on fresh clothes for dinner. But I, after college hours, had only time to bolt a soggy meal, and rush back to the grind of the laundry till eleven at night.

13   At the hour when they came from the theater or musicale, I came from the laundry. But I was so bathed in the sweat of exhaustion that I could not think of a bath of soap and water. I had only strength to drag myself home, and fall down

on the bed and sleep. Even if I had had the desire and the energy to take a bath, there were no such things as bathtubs in the house where I lived.

Often as I stood at my board at the laundry, I thought of Miss Whiteside, and 14 her clean world, clothed in the snowy shirtwaists I had ironed. I was thinking— I, soaking in the foul vapors of the steaming laundry, I, with my dirty, tired hands, I am ironing the clean, immaculate shirtwaists of clean, immaculate society. I, the unclean one, am actually fashioning the pedestal of their cleanliness, from which they reach down, hoping to lift me to the height that I have created for them.

I look back at my sweatshop[1] childhood. One day, when I was about sixteen, 15 someone gave me Rosenfeld's poem "The Machine" to read. Like a spark thrown among oil rags, it set my whole being aflame with longing for self-expression. But I was dumb. I had nothing but blind, aching feeling. For days I went about with agonies of feeling, yet utterly at sea how to fathom and voice those feelings—birth-throes of infinite worlds, and yet dumb.

Suddenly, there came upon me this inspiration. I can go to college! There 16 I shall learn to express myself, to voice my thoughts. But I was not prepared to go to college. The girl in the cigar factory, in the next block, had gone first to a preparatory school. Why shouldn't I find a way, too?

Going to college seemed as impossible for me, at that time, as for an igno- 17 rant Russian shop-girl to attempt to write poetry in English. But I was sixteen then, and the impossible was a magnet to draw the dreams that had no outlet. Besides, the actual was so barren, so narrow, so strangling, that the dream of the unattainable was the only air in which the soul could survive.

The ideal of going to college was like the birth of a new religion in my soul. 18 It put new fire in my eyes, and new strength in my tired arms and fingers.

For six years I worked daytimes and went at night to a preparatory school. 19 For six years I went about nursing the illusion that college was a place where I should find self-expression, and vague, pent-up feelings could live as thoughts and grow as ideas.

At last I came to college. I rushed for it with the outstretched arms of 20 youth's aching hunger to give and take of life's deepest and highest, and I came against the solid wall of the well-fed, well-dressed world—the frigid white-washed wall of cleanliness.

Until I came to college I had been unconscious of my clothes. Suddenly I 21 felt people looking at me at arm's length, as if I were crooked or crippled, as if I had come to a place where I didn't belong, and would never be taken in.

How I pinched, and scraped, and starved myself, to save enough to come to 22 college! Every cent of the tuition fee I paid was drops of sweat and blood from underpaid laundry work. And what did I get for it? A crushed spirit, a broken heart, a stinging sense of poverty that I never felt before.

[1]Small manufacturing establishments in which employees work long hours under poor conditions for low wages.

23   The courses of study I had to swallow to get my diploma were utterly barren of interest to me. I didn't come to college to get dull learning from dead books. I didn't come for that dry, inanimate stuff that can be hammered out in lectures. I came because I longed for the larger life, for the stimulus of intellectual associations. I came because my whole being clamored for more vision, more light. But everywhere I went I saw big fences put up against me, with the brutal signs: "No trespassing. Get off the grass."

24   I experienced at college the same feeling of years ago when I came to this country, when after months of shut-in-ness, in dark tenements and stifling sweatshops, I had come to Central Park for the first time. Like a bird just out from a cage, I stretched out my arms, and then flung myself in ecstatic abandon on the grass. Just as I began to breathe in the fresh-smelling earth, and lift up my eyes to the sky, a big, fat policeman with a club in his hand, seized me, with: "Can't you read the sign? Get off the grass!" Miss Whiteside, the dean of the college, the representative of the clean, the educated world, for all her external refinement, was to me like that big, brutal policeman, with the club in his hand, that drove me off the grass.

25   The death-blows to all aspiration began when I graduated from college and tried to get a start at the work for which I had struggled so hard to fit myself. I soon found other agents of clean society, who had the power of giving or withholding the positions I sought, judging me as Miss Whiteside judged me. One glance at my shabby clothes, the desperate anguish that glazed and dulled my eyes and I felt myself condemned by them before I opened my lips to speak.

26   Starvation forced me to accept the lowest-paid substitute position. And because my wages were so low and so unsteady, I could never get the money for the clothes to make an appearance to secure a position with better pay. I was tricked and foiled. I was considered unfit to get decent pay for my work because of my appearance, and it was to the advantage of those who used me that my appearance should damn me, so as to get me to work for the low wages I was forced to accept. It seemed to me the whole vicious circle of society's injustices was thrust like a noose around my neck to strangle me.

27   The insults and injuries I had suffered at college had so eaten into my flesh that I could not bear to get near it. I shuddered with horror whenever I had to pass the place blocks away. The hate which I felt for Miss Whiteside spread like poison inside my soul, into hate for all clean society. The whole clean world was massed against me. Whenever I met a well-dressed person, I felt the secret stab of a hidden enemy.

28   I was so obsessed and consumed with my grievances that I could not get away from myself and think things out in the light. I was in the grip of that blinding, destructive, terrible thing—righteous indignation. I could not rest. I wanted the whole world to know that the college was against democracy in education, that clothes form the basis of class distinctions, that after graduation the opportunities for the best positions are passed out to those who are best-dressed,

and the students too poor to put up a front are pigeon-holed and marked unfit and abandoned to the mercy of the wind.

A wild desire raged in the corner of my brain. I knew that the dean gave   29
dinners to the faculty at regular intervals. I longed to burst in at one of those feasts, in the midst of their grand speech-making, and tear down the fine clothes from these well-groomed ladies and gentlemen, and trample them under my feet, and scream like a lunatic: "Soap and water are cheap! Soap and water are cheap! Look at me! See how cheap it is!"

There seemed but three avenues of escape to the torments of my wasted life: 30
madness, suicide, or a heart-to-heart confession to someone who understood. I had not energy enough for suicide. Besides, in my darkest moments of despair, hope clamored loudest. Oh, I longed so to live, to dream my way up on the heights, above the unreal realities that ground me and dragged me down to earth.

Inside the ruin of my thwarted life, the *unlived* visionary immigrant hungered   31
and thirsted for America. I had come a refugee from the Russian pogroms,[2] aflame with dreams of America. I did not find America in the sweatshops, much less in the schools and colleges. But for hundreds of years the persecuted races all over the world were nurtured on hopes of America. When a little baby in my mother's arms, before I was old enough to speak, I saw all around me weary faces light up with thrilling tales of the far-off "golden country." And so, though my faith in this so-called America was shattered, yet underneath, in the sap and roots of my soul, burned the deathless faith that America is, must be, somehow, somewhere. In the midst of my bitterest hates and rebellions, visions of America rose over me, like songs of freedom of an oppressed people.

My body was worn to the bone from overwork, my footsteps dragged with   32
exhaustion, but my eyes still sought the sky, praying, ceaselessly praying, the dumb, inarticulate prayer of the lost immigrant: "America! Ach, America! Where is America?"

It seemed to me if I could only find some human being to whom I could   33
unburden my heart, I would have new strength to begin again my insatiable search for America.

But to whom could I speak? The people in the laundry? They never under-   34
stood me. They had a grudge against me because I left them when I tried to work myself up. Could I speak to the college people? What did these icebergs of convention know about the vital things of the heart?

And yet, I remembered, in the freshman year, in one of the courses in chem-   35
istry, there was an instructor, a woman, who drew me strangely. I felt she was the only real teacher among all the teachers and professors I met. I didn't care for the chemistry, but I liked to look at her. She gave me life, air, the unconscious emanation of her beautiful spirit. I had not spoken a word to her, outside the

---

[2]Organized massacres of Jews in turn-of-the-century Russia.

experiments in chemistry, but I knew her more than the people around her who were of her own class. I felt in the throb of her voice, in the subtle shading around the corner of her eyes, the color and texture of her dreams.

36 Often in the midst of our work in chemistry I felt like crying out to her: "Oh, please be my friend. I'm so lonely." But something choked me. I couldn't speak. The very intensity of my longing for her friendship made me run away from her in confusion the minute she approached me. I was so conscious of my shabbiness that I was afraid maybe she was only trying to be kind. I couldn't bear kindness. I wanted from her love, understanding, or nothing.

37 About ten years after I left college, as I walked the streets bowed and beaten with the shame of having to go around begging for work, I met Miss Van Ness. She not only recognized me, but stopped to ask how I was, and what I was doing.

38 I had begun to think that my only comrades in this world were the homeless and abandoned cats and dogs of the street, whom everybody gives another kick, as they slam the door on them. And here was one from the clean world human enough to be friendly. Here was one of the well-dressed, with a look in her eyes and a sound in her voice that was like healing oil over the bruises of my soul. The mere touch of that woman's hand in mine so overwhelmed me, that I burst out crying in the street.

39 The next morning I came to Miss Van Ness at her office. In those ten years she had risen to a professorship. But I was not in the least intimidated by her high office. I felt as natural in her presence as if she were my own sister. I heard myself telling her the whole story of my life, but I felt that even if I had not said a word she would have understood all I had to say as if I had spoken. It was all so unutterable, to find one from the other side of the world who was so simply and naturally that miraculous thing—a friend. Just as contact with Miss Whiteside had tied and bound all my thinking processes, so Miss Van Ness unbound and freed me and suffused me with light.

40 I felt the joy of one breathing on the mountain-tops for the first time. I looked down at the world below. I was changed and the world was changed. My past was the forgotten night. Sunrise was all around me.

41 I went out from Miss Van Ness's office, singing a song of new life: "America! I found America."

EXERCISES

Some of the Issues

1. "What I so greatly feared, happened!" says Anzia in the opening line. What made her suspect that she would not be given her diploma?
*2. In paragraph 7, Anzia protests against the tyranny of the dean and the "whole laundered world." Which social group in America is she referring

to? Compare Anzia's perceptions to Michael Novak's description of the "power elite" in "In Ethnic America" (paragraph 13).

3. What was the turning point that motivated her to seek a college education?
4. Do you think her hatred and "righteous indignation" (paragraph 28) are justified?
5. In paragraphs 37–40, the meeting with Miss Van Ness changes Anzia's outlook. How do you explain her sudden transformation?
6. In the last lines, Anzia exclaims that she has found America. What does she mean?

The Way We Are Told

7. Yezierska's style is characterized by language that is intended to provoke an emotional response. Can you find examples? Does the language seem overly dramatized or old-fashioned? If so, where?
8. Why is it ironic that Miss Whiteside points out to Anzia, "Soap and water are cheap. Anyone can be clean"?
9. How does Yezierska portray Miss Van Ness? Is the character convincing?

Some Subjects for Writing

10. After six years of hard work and anticipation, Anzia is disillusioned that college is not what she had expected. How does this compare with your own experience? Was there ever a time when you felt disenchanted or disappointed in your college education?
11. In paragraph 28, Anzia says "clothes form the basis of class distinctions." Do you agree that social class is reflected by a person's apparel? (To defend your view, you may want to include names of department stores; brand names; and descriptions of styles, colors, and fashions that Americans wear.)

Black Like Them

MALCOLM GLADWELL

*Malcolm Gladwell is a journalist living in New York City. He has writ-
ten for the* New Yorker, The New York Times, *and the* Los Angeles
Times. *His commentary has appeared on National Public Radio.
"Black Like Them" originally appeared in the* New Yorker *in 1996.*

*Gladwell begins his essay by telling the story of his cousins Rosie
and Noel, immigrants from Jamaica who have settled in New York
City. Gladwell explores the question of why West Indians and American blacks are treated differently in the United States, and why they
perceive themselves as fitting into American society in a different
way. Drawing from family experience, historical information, and
sociological studies, Gladwell uses the experience of West Indian
blacks to investigate both the roots and the pervasiveness of racism
in the U.S.*

1   My cousin Rosie and her husband, Noel, live in a two-bedroom bungalow on
Argyle Avenue, in Uniondale, on the west end of Long Island. When they came
to America, twelve years ago, they lived in a basement apartment a dozen or so
blocks away, next to their church. At the time, they were both taking classes at
the New York Institute of Technology, which was right nearby. But after they
graduated, and Rosie got a job managing a fast-food place and Noel got a job
in asbestos removal, they managed to save a little money and bought the house
on Argyle Avenue.

2   From the outside, their home looks fairly plain. It's in a part of Uniondale
that has a lot of tract housing from just after the war, and most of the houses are
alike—squat and square, with aluminum siding, maybe a dormer window in the
attic, and a small patch of lawn out front. But there is a beautiful park down the
street, the public schools are supposed to be good, and Rosie and Noel have
built a new garage and renovated the basement. Now that Noel has started his
own business, as an environmental engineer, he has his office down there—Suite
2B, it says on his stationery—and every morning he puts on his tie and goes
down the stairs to make calls and work on the computer. If Noel's business takes
off, Rosie says, she would like to move to a bigger house, in Garden City, which
is one town over. She says this even though Garden City is mostly white. In fact,
when she told one of her girlfriends, a black American, about this idea, her
friend said that she was crazy—that Garden City was no place for a black person.

But that is just the point. Rosie and Noel are from Jamaica. They don't consider themselves black at all.

This doesn't mean that my cousins haven't sometimes been lumped 3 together with American blacks. Noel had a job once removing asbestos at Kennedy Airport, and his boss there called him "nigger" and cut his hours. But Noel didn't take it personally. That boss, he says, didn't like women or Jews, either, or people with college degrees—or even himself, for that matter. Another time, Noel found out that a white guy working next to him in the same job and with the same qualifications was making ten thousand dollars a year more than he was. He quit the next day. Noel knows that racism is out there. It's just that he doesn't quite understand—or accept—the categories on which it depends.

To a West Indian, black is a literal description: you are black if your skin is 4 black. Noel's father, for example, is black. But his mother had a white father, and she herself was fair-skinned and could pass. As for Rosie, her mother and my mother, who are twins, thought of themselves while they were growing up as "middle-class brown," which is to say that they are about the same shade as Colin Powell. That's because our maternal grandfather was part Jewish, in addition to all kinds of other things, and Grandma, though she was a good deal darker than he was, had enough Scottish blood in her to have been born with straight hair. Rosie's mother married another brown Jamaican, and that makes Rosie a light chocolate. As for my mother, she married an Englishman, making everything that much more complicated, since by the racial categories of my own heritage I am one thing and by the racial categories of America I am another. Once, when Rosie and Noel came to visit me while I was living in Washington, D.C., Noel asked me to show him "where the black people lived," and I was confused for a moment until I realized that he was using "black" in the American sense, and so was asking in the same way that someone visiting Manhattan might ask where Chinatown was. That the people he wanted to see were in many cases racially indistinguishable from him didn't matter. The facts of his genealogy, of his nationality, of his status as an immigrant made him, in his own eyes, different.

This question of who West Indians are and how they define themselves may 5 seem trivial, like racial hairsplitting. But it is not trivial. In the past twenty years, the number of West Indians in America has exploded. There are now half a million in the New York area alone and, despite their recent arrival, they make substantially more money than American blacks. They live in better neighborhoods. Their families are stronger. In the New York area, in fact, West Indians fare about as well as Chinese and Korean immigrants. That is why the Caribbean invasion and the issue of West Indian identity have become such controversial issues. What does it say about the nature of racism that another group of blacks, who have the same legacy of slavery as their American counterparts and are physically indistinguishable from them, can come here and succeed as well as the Chinese and the Koreans do? Is overcoming racism as simple as doing what Noel does, which is to dismiss it, to hold himself above it, to brave it and move on?

6   These are difficult questions, not merely for what they imply about American blacks but for the ways in which they appear to contradict conventional views of what prejudice is. Racism, after all, is supposed to be indiscriminate. For example, sociologists have observed that the more blacks there are in a community the more negative the whites' attitudes will be. Blacks in Denver have a far easier time than blacks in, say, Cleveland. Lynchings in the South at the turn of this century, to give another example, were far more common in counties where there was a large black population than in areas where whites were in the majority. Prejudice is the crudest of weapons, a reaction against blacks in the aggregate that grows as the perception of black threat grows. If that is the case, however, the addition of hundreds of thousands of new black immigrants to the New York area should have made things worse for people like Rosie and Noel, not better. And, if racism is so indiscriminate in its application, why is one group of blacks flourishing and the other not?

7   The implication of West Indian success is that racism does not really exist at all—at least, not in the form that we have assumed it does. The implication is that the key factor in understanding racial prejudice is not the behavior and attitudes of whites but the behavior and attitudes of blacks—not white discrimination but black culture. It implies that when the conservatives in Congress say the responsibility for ending urban poverty lies not with collective action but with the poor themselves they are right.

8   I think of this sometimes when I go with Rosie and Noel to their church, which is in Hempstead, just a mile away. It was once a white church, but in the past decade or so it has been taken over by immigrants from the Caribbean. They have so swelled its membership that the church has bought much of the surrounding property and is about to add a hundred seats to its sanctuary. The pastor, though, is white, and when the band up front is playing and the congregation is in full West Indian form the pastor sometimes seems out of place, as if he cannot move in time with the music. I always wonder how long the white minister at Rosie and Noel's church will last—whether there won't be some kind of groundswell among the congregation to replace him with one of their own. But Noel tells me the issue has never really come up. Noel says, in fact, that he's happier with a white minister, for the same reasons that he's happy with his neighborhood, where the people across the way are Polish and another neighbor is Hispanic and still another is a black American. He doesn't want to be shut off from everyone else, isolated within the narrow confines of his race. He wants to be part of the world, and when he says these things it is awfully tempting to credit that attitude with what he and Rosie have accomplished.

9   Is this confidence, this optimism, this equanimity all that separates the poorest of American blacks from a house on Argyle Avenue?

* * * * *

In 1994, Philip Kasinitz, a sociologist at Manhattan's Hunter College, and Jan   10
Rosenberg, who teaches at Long Island University, conducted a study of the Red
Hook area of Brooklyn, a neighborhood of around thirteen or fourteen thousand
which lies between the waterfront and the Gowanus Expressway. Red Hook has
a large public-housing project at its center, and around the project, in the streets
that line the waterfront, are several hundred thriving blue-collar businesses—
warehouses, shipping companies, small manufacturers, and contractors. The
object of the study was to resolve what Kasinitz and Rosenberg saw as the paradox of Red Hook: despite Red Hooks seemingly fortuitous conjunction of
unskilled labor and blue-collar jobs, very few of the Puerto Ricans and African-
Americans from the neighborhood ever found work in the bustling economy of
their own back yard.

After dozens of interviews with local employers, the two researchers uncov-   11
ered a persistent pattern of what they call positive discrimination. It was not that
the employers did not like blacks and Hispanics. It was that they had developed
an elaborate mechanism for distinguishing between those they felt were "good"
blacks and those they felt were "bad" blacks, between those they judged to be
"good" Hispanics and those they considered "bad" Hispanics. "Good" meant
that you came from outside the neighborhood, because employers identified
locals with the crime and dissipation they saw on the streets around them.
"Good" also meant that you were an immigrant, because employers felt that
being an immigrant implied a loyalty and a willingness to work and learn not
found among the native-born. In Red Hook, the good Hispanics are Mexican
and South American, not Puerto Rican. And the good blacks are West Indian.

The Harvard sociologist Mary C. Waters conducted a similar study, in 1993,   12
which looked at a food-service company in Manhattan where West Indian workers have steadily displaced African-Americans in the past few years. The tran-
scripts of her interviews with the company managers make fascinating reading,
providing an intimate view of the perceptions that govern the urban workplace.
Listen to one forty-year-old white male manager on the subject of West Indians:

> They tend more to shy away from doing all of the illegal things because
> they have such strict rules down in their countries and jails. And they're
> nothing like here. So like, they're like really paranoid to do something
> wrong. They seem to be very, very self-conscious of it. No matter what
> they have to do, if they have to try and work three jobs, they do. They
> won't go into drugs or anything like that.

Or listen to this, from a fifty-three-year-old white female manager: 13

> I work closely with this one girl who's from Trinidad. And she told me
> when she first came here to live with her sister and cousin, she had two

children. And she said I'm here four years and we've reached our goals. And what was your goal? For her two children to each have their own bedroom. Now she has a three bedroom apartment and she said that's one of the goals she was shooting for.... If that was an American, they would say, I reached my goal. I bought a Cadillac.

14   This idea of the West Indian as a kind of superior black is not a new one. When the first wave of Caribbean immigrants came to New York and Boston, in the early nineteen-hundreds, other blacks dubbed them Jewmaicans, in derisive reference to the emphasis they placed on hard work and education. In the nineteen-eighties, the economist Thomas Sowell gave the idea a serious intellectual imprimatur by arguing that the West Indian advantage was a historical legacy of Caribbean slave culture. According to Sowell, in the American South slaveowners tended to hire managers who were married, in order to limit the problems created by sexual relations between overseers and slave women. But the West Indies were a hardship post, without a large and settled white population. There the overseers tended to be bachelors, and, with white women scarce, there was far more commingling of the races. The resulting large group of coloreds soon formed a kind of proto-middle class, performing various kinds of skilled and sophisticated tasks that there were not enough whites around to do, as there were in the American South. They were carpenters, masons, plumbers, and small businessmen, many years in advance of their American counterparts, developing skills that required education and initiative.

15   My mother and Rosie's mother came from this colored class. Their parents were schoolteachers in a tiny village buried in the hills of central Jamaica. My grandmother's and grandfather's salaries combined put them, at best, on the lower rungs of the middle class. But their expectations went well beyond that. In my grandfather's library were Dickens and Maupassant. My mother and her sister were pushed to win scholarships to a proper English-style boarding school at the other end of the island; and later, when my mother graduated, it was taken for granted that she would attend university in England, even though the cost of tuition and passage meant that my grandmother had to borrow a small fortune from the Chinese grocer down the road.

16   My grandparents had ambitions for their children, but it was a special kind of ambition, born of a certainty that American blacks did not have—that their values were the same as those of society as a whole, and that hard work and talent could actually be rewarded. In my mother's first year at boarding school, she looked up "Negro" in the eleventh edition of the Encyclopedia Britannica. "In certain...characteristics...the negro would appear to stand on a lower evolutionary plane than the white man," she read. And the entry continued:

The mental constitution of the negro is very similar to that of a child, normally good-natured and cheerful, but subject to sudden fits of emotion and passion during which he is capable of performing acts of singular atrocity, impressionable, vain, but often exhibiting in the capacity of servant a dog-like fidelity which has stood the supreme test.

All black people of my mother's generation—and of generations before and since—have necessarily faced a moment like this, when they are confronted for the first time with the allegation of their inferiority. But, at least in my mother's case, her school was integrated, and that meant she knew black girls who were more intelligent than white girls, and she knew how she measured against the world around her. At least she lived in a country that had blacks and browns in every position of authority, so her personal experience gave the lie to what she read in the encyclopedia. This, I think, is what Noel means when he says that he cannot quite appreciate what it is that weighs black Americans down, because he encountered the debilitating effects of racism late, when he was much stronger. He came of age in a country where he belonged to the majority.   17

When I was growing up, my mother sometimes read to my brothers and me from the work of Louise Bennett, the great Jamaican poet of my mother's generation. The poem I remember best is about two women—one black and one white—in a hair salon, the black woman getting her hair straightened and, next to her, the white woman getting her hair curled: 18

> same time me mind start 'tink
> 'bout me and de white woman
> how me tek out me natural perm
> and she put in false one

There is no anger or resentment here, only irony and playfulness—the two races captured in a shared moment of absurdity. Then comes the twist. The black woman is paying less to look white than the white woman is to look black: 19

> de two a we da tek a risk
> what rain or shine will bring
> but fe har risk is t're poun'
> fi me onle five shillin'

In the nineteen-twenties, the garment trade in New York was first integrated by West Indian women, because, the legend goes, they would see the sign on the door saying "No blacks need apply" and simply walk on in. When I look back on Bennett's poem, I think I understand how they found the courage to do that.   20

It is tempting to use the West Indian story as evidence that discrimination doesn't really exist—as proof that the only thing inner-city African-Americans have to do to be welcomed as warmly as West Indians in places like Red Hook   21 is to make the necessary cultural adjustments. If West Indians are different, as they clearly are, then it is easy to imagine that those differences are the reason for their success—that their refusal to be bowed is what lets them walk on by the signs that prohibit them or move to neighborhoods that black Americans would shy away from. It also seems hard to see how the West Indian story is in any way consistent with the idea of racism as an indiscriminate, pernicious threat aimed at all black people.

22   But here is where things become more difficult, and where what seems obvious about West Indian achievement turns out not to be obvious at all. One of the striking things in the Red Hook study, for example, is the emphasis that the employers appeared to place on hiring outsiders—Irish or Russian or Mexican or West Indian immigrants from places far from Red Hook. The reason for this was not, the researchers argue, that the employers had any great familiarity with the cultures of those immigrants. They had none, and that was the point. They were drawn to the unfamiliar because what was familiar to them—the projects of Red Hook—was anathema. The Columbia University anthropologist Katherine Newman makes the same observation in a recent study of two fast-food restaurants in Harlem. She compared the hundreds of people who applied for jobs at those restaurants with the few people who were actually hired, and found, among other things, that how far an applicant lived from the job site made a huge difference. Of those applicants who lived less than two miles from the restaurant, ten per cent were hired. Of those who lived more than two miles from the restaurant, nearly forty per cent were hired. As Newman puts it, employers preferred the ghetto they didn't know to the ghetto they did.

23   Neither study describes a workplace where individual attitudes make a big difference, or where the clunky and impersonal prejudices that characterize traditional racism have been discarded. They sound like places where old-style racism and appreciation of immigrant values are somehow bound up together. Listen to another white manager who was interviewed by Mary Waters:

> Island blacks who come over, they're immigrant. They may not have such a good life where they are so they gonna try to strive to better themselves and I think there's a lot of American blacks out there who feel we owe them. And enough is enough already. You know, this is something that happened to their ancestors, not now. I mean, we've done so much for the black people in America now that it's time that they got off their butts.

24   Here, then, are the two competing ideas about racism side by side: the manager issues a blanket condemnation of American blacks even as he holds West Indians up as a cultural ideal. The example of West Indians as "good" blacks makes the old blanket prejudice against American blacks all the easier to express. The manager can tell black Americans to get off their butts without fear of

sounding, in his own ears, like a racist, because he has simultaneously celebrated island blacks for their work ethic. The success of West Indians is not proof that discrimination against American blacks does not exist. Rather, it is the means by which discrimination against American blacks is given one last, vicious twist: I am not so shallow as to despise you for the color of your skin, because I have found people your color that I like. Now I can despise you for who you are.

This is racism's newest mutation—multicultural racism, where one ethnic   25
group can be played off against another. But it is wrong to call West Indians the victors in this competition, in anything but the narrowest sense. In American history, immigrants have always profited from assimilation: as they have adopted the language and customs of this country, they have sped their passage into the mainstream. The new racism means that West Indians are the first group of people for whom that has not been true. Their advantage depends on their remaining outsiders, on remaining unfamiliar, on being distinct by custom, culture, and language from the American blacks they would otherwise resemble. There is already some evidence that the considerable economic and social advantages that West Indians hold over American blacks begin to dissipate by the second generation, when the island accent has faded, and those in positions of power who draw distinctions between good blacks and bad blacks begin to lump West Indians with everyone else. For West Indians, assimilation is tantamount to suicide. This is a cruel fate for any immigrant group, but it is especially so for West Indians, whose history and literature are already redolent with the themes of dispossession and loss, with the long search for identity and belonging. In the nineteen-twenties, Marcus Garvey[1] sought community in the idea of Africa. Bob Marley, the Jamaican reggae singer, yearned for Zion. In "Rites of Passage" the Barbadian poet Edward Kamau Brathwaite writes:

Where, then, is the nigger's
home?

In Paris Brixton Kingston
Rome?

Here?
Or in Heaven?

America might have been home. But it is not: not Red Hook, anyway; not   26
Harlem; not even Argyle Avenue.

There is also no small measure of guilt here, for West Indians cannot escape   27
the fact that their success has come, to some extent, at the expense of American

---

[1](1887–1940) Black nationalist who was born in Jamaica and lived in the United States after 1916.

blacks, and that as they have noisily differentiated themselves from African-Americans—promoting the stereotype of themselves as the good blacks—they have made it easier for whites to join in. It does not help matters that the same kinds of distinctions between good and bad blacks which govern the immigrant experience here have always lurked just below the surface of life in the West Indies as well. It was the infusion of white blood that gave the colored class its status in the Caribbean, and the members of this class have never forgotten that, nor have they failed, in a thousand subtle ways, to distance themselves from those around them who experienced a darker and less privileged past.

28   In my mother's house, in Harewood, the family often passed around a pencilled drawing of two of my great-grandparents; she was part Jewish, and he was part Scottish. The other side—the African side—was never mentioned. My grandmother was the ringleader in this. She prized my grandfather's light skin, but she also suffered as a result of this standard. "She's nice, you know, but she's too dark," her mother-in-law would say of her. The most telling story of all, though, is the story of one of my mother's relatives, whom I'll call Aunt Joan, who was as fair as my great-grandmother was. Aunt Joan married what in Jamaica is called an Injun—a man with a dark complexion that is redeemed from pure Africanness by straight, fine black hair. She had two daughters by him—handsome girls with dark complexions. But he died young, and one day, while she was travelling on a train to visit her daughter, she met and took an interest in a light-skinned man in the same railway car. What happened next is something that Aunt Joan told only my mother, years later, with the greatest of shame. When she got off the train, she walked right by her daughter, disowning her own flesh and blood, because she did not want a man so light-skinned and desirable to know that she had borne a daughter so dark.

29   My mother, in the nineteen-sixties, wrote a book about her experiences. It was entitled *Brown Face, Big Master*, the brown face referring to her and the big master, in the Jamaican dialect, referring to God. Sons, of course, are hardly objective on the achievements of their mothers, but there is one passage in the book that I find unforgettable, because it is such an eloquent testimony to the moral precariousness of the Jamaican colored class—to the mixture of confusion and guilt that attends its position as beneficiary of racism's distinctions. The passage describes a time just after my mother and father were married, when they were living in London and my eldest brother was still a baby. They were looking for an apartment, and after a long search my father found one in a London suburb. On the day after they moved in, however, the landlady ordered them out. "You didn't tell me your wife was colored," she told my father, in a rage.

30   In her book my mother describes her long struggle to make sense of this humiliation, to reconcile her experience with her faith. In the end, she was forced to acknowledge that anger was not an option—that as a Jamaican "middle-class brown," and a descendant of Aunt Joan, she could hardly reproach another for the impulse to divide good black from bad black:

I complained to God in so many words: "Here I was, the wounded representative of the negro race in our struggle to be accounted free and equal with the dominating whites!" And God was amused; my prayer did not ring true with Him. I would try again. And then God said, "Have you not done the same thing? Remember this one and that one, people whom you have slighted or avoided or treated less considerately than others because they were different superficially, and you were ashamed to be identified with them. Have you not been glad that you are not more colored than you are? Grateful that you are not black?" My anger and hate against the landlady melted. I was no better than she was, nor worse for that matter.... We were both guilty of the sin of self-regard, the pride and the exclusiveness by which we cut some people off from ourselves.

I grew up in Canada, in a little farming town an hour and a half outside of Toronto. My father teaches mathematics at a nearby university, and my mother is a therapist. For many years, she was the only black person in town, but I cannot remember wondering or worrying, or even thinking, about this fact. Back then, color meant only good things. It meant my cousins in Jamaica. It meant the graduate students from Africa and India my father would bring home from the university. My own color was not something I ever thought much about, either, because it seemed such a stray fact. Blacks knew what I was. They could discern the hint of Africa beneath my fair skin. But it was a kind of secret—something that they would ask me about quietly when no one else was around. ("Where you from?" an older black man once asked me. "Ontario," I said, not thinking. "No," he replied. "Where you *from*?" And then I understood and told him, and he nodded as if he had already known. "We was speculatin' about your heritage," he said.) But whites never guessed, and even after I informed them it never seemed to make a difference. Why would it? In a town that is ninety-nine per cent white, one modest alleged splash of color hardly amounts to a threat. 31

But things changed when I left for Toronto to attend college. This was during the early nineteen-eighties, when West Indians were immigrating to Canada in droves, and Toronto had become second only to New York as the Jamaican expatriates' capital in North America. At school, in the dining hall, I was served by Jamaicans. The infamous Jane-Finch projects, in northern Toronto, were considered the Jamaican projects. The drug trade then taking off was said to be the Jamaican drug trade. In the popular imagination, Jamaicans were—and are—welfare queens and gun-toting gangsters and dissolute youths. In Ontario, blacks accused of crimes are released by the police eighteen per cent of the time; whites are released twenty-nine per cent of the time. In drug-trafficking and importing cases, blacks are twenty-seven times as likely as whites to be jailed before their trial takes place, and twenty times as likely to be imprisoned on drug-possession charges. 32

33   After I had moved to the United States, I puzzled over this seeming contradiction—how West Indians celebrated in New York for their industry and drive could represent, just five hundred miles northwest, crime and dissipation. Didn't Torontonians see what was special and different in West Indian culture? But that was a naïve question. The West Indians were the first significant brush with blackness that white, smug, comfortable Torontonians had ever had. They had no bad blacks to contrast with the newcomers, no African-Americans to serve as a safety valve for their prejudices, no way to perform America's crude racial triage.

34   Not long ago, I sat in a coffee shop with someone I knew vaguely from college, who, like me, had moved to New York from Toronto. He began to speak of the threat that he felt Toronto now faced. It was the Jamaicans, he said. They were a bad seed. He was, of course, oblivious of my background. I said nothing, though, and he launched into a long explanation of how, in slave times, Jamaica was the island where all the most troublesome and obstreperous slaves were sent, and how that accounted for their particularly nasty disposition today.

35   I have told that story many times since, usually as a joke, because it was funny in an appalling way—particularly when I informed him much, much later that my mother was Jamaican. I tell the story that way because otherwise it is too painful. There must be people in Toronto just like Rosie and Noel, with the same attitudes and aspirations, who want to live in a neighborhood as nice as Argyle Avenue, who want to build a new garage and renovate their basement and set up their own business downstairs. But it is not completely up to them, is it? What has happened to Jamaicans in Toronto is proof that what has happened to Jamaicans here is not the end of racism, or even the beginning of the end of racism, but an accident of history and geography. In America, there is someone else to despise. In Canada, there is not. In the new racism, as in the old, somebody always has to be the nigger.

EXERCISES

Some of the Issues

1. Examine the description of Rosie and Noel's house and office in paragraph 2. What is your image of Rosie and Noel? How do the beginning paragraphs serve as an introduction to the ideas presented in the article?

2. According to the author, what are some of the reasons behind Noel's response to racism (paragraph 3)?

3. Summarize the differences the author describes between the West Indian definition of black and the American definition (paragraph 4).

4. Reread paragraphs 5 through 7. What are some of the other immigrant groups to which the author compares West Indians? Why are some of the questions raised by Gladwell "difficult"?

5. What are the conclusions of each of the studies Gladwell discusses in paragraphs 10 through 13 and 22 through 24? How does he use these conclusions to support his ideas?

6. What are the differences between the history and culture of American blacks and those of West Indians, particularly Gladwell's family (paragraphs 14 and 15)?

7. What happened when Gladwell's mother looked up the word "Negro" in the encyclopedia? How did her personal experience give "the lie to what she read" (paragraph 16)?

8. In paragraph 21, the author writes, "It is tempting to use the West Indian story as evidence that discrimination doesn't really exist." How does the author go on to question this "evidence"?

9. How does the author define "multicultural racism" in paragraph 25? Why are West Indians not "the victims in this competition, in anything but the narrowest sense"?

10. In paragraphs 31 through 35, Gladwell compares the history and treatment of Canadian West Indians to that of American West Indians. What is Gladwell trying to point out through these comparisons?

The Way We Are Told

11. Why does the author wait until the end of paragraph 2 to tell us that Rosie and Noel are from Jamaica?

12. How does Gladwell combine the use of personal and family history with more objective sources? Do you find the mixture effective?

13. Gladwell concludes his essay with a strong statement. How does he build his evidence for this statement throughout the essay? Why might he have chosen not to make this statement toward the beginning?

14. We are not absolutely sure of Gladwell's point until the middle or even the end of his essay. In fact, we might initially suspect that Gladwell is making an opposite point to the one he finally makes. Why would he structure his essay this way?

Some Subjects for Writing

15. Interview two or more relatives or friends who either immigrated to the United States or identify with a specific ethnic or racial group. Keeping in mind some of the issues Gladwell raises, focus on both their self-image and identify as well as how they perceive themselves to be treated by others. Make sure you develop a series of quesitons beforehand and, as you are interviewing, ask follow-up questions that might help your subjects elaborate on, explain, or analyze their experience. Write an essay in which you recount their stories and compare their experiences.

Ellis Island

JOSEPH BRUCHAC

Joseph Bruchac, born in 1942, is of mixed immigrant and Native American ancestry. He has written poetry and fiction and translated West African and Iroquois literature. He is the editor of Survival This Way: Interviews with Native American Poets *(1990) and* Roots of Survival: Native American Storytelling and the Sacred *(1996). He is also the author of several books for children.*

Ellis Island in New York harbor became the main point of entry for immigrants to the United States in 1892. As many as a million people a year passed through its vast sheds in the early twentieth century; up to fifteen thousand were herded through in one day. Finally closed in 1954, it was abandoned and allowed to decay. In 1965 Ellis Island was declared a national landmark, but it was not until the 1980s that interest in its place in history became sufficiently strong to encourage moves toward its restoration. Work on it was begun in earnest at the time the Statue of Liberty, its neighbor, was being restored. In 1990 Ellis Island, partially restored as a museum of immigration and a national monument, was reopened to the public.

In his poem Joseph Bruchac concerns himself not only with the waves of immigration but with one of its results: the displacement of Native Americans from their ancestral lands.

Beyond the red brick of Ellis Island
Where the two Slovak children
who became my grandparents
waited the long days of quarantine,
5   after leaving the sickness,
the old Empires of Europe,
a Circle Line ship slips easily
on its way to the island
of the tall woman, green
10   as dreams of forests and meadows
waiting for those who'd worked
a thousand years
yet never owned their own.

Like millions of others,
I too come to this island,   15
nine decades the answerer
of dreams.

Yet only one part of my blood loves that memory.
another voice speaks
of native lands   20
within this nation.
Lands invaded
when the earth became owned.
Lands of those who followed
The changing Moon,   25
knowledge of the season
in their veins.

EXERCISES

Some of the Issues

1. Who is the tall, green woman Bruchac's European grandparents saw? What does Bruchac suggest she represents to them?
2. Why does Bruchac's memory of his other ancestors keep him from fully sharing the feelings of his immigrant grandparents?
3. How is the ownership of land significant to both grandparents? Why is this theme important to the poem?

Some Subjects for Writing

4. Explore the meaning of heritage or multiple heritages in your own life, going back to your grandparents or great-grandparents if you can. If you have children, or intend to, you might also want to examine what part of that heritage you want to pass on to them.

8

Other Worlds

The selections in Part Eight take the reader to other parts of the globe. Knowledge of widely varied cultures can sharpen our awareness and appreciation of cultural differences. Unfortunately, it is too often the case that people will tolerate the *idea* of cultural difference as long as it remains an idea. Americans may not mind, for example, the fact that some people in France consider horses desirable to eat. Eating horses, defined as a custom, may seem strange, even offensive, but not of central concern as long as one is not obliged to participate. However, when cultural differences touch on values we consider central, we may find them harder to accept. We are likely to judge another culture as simple or backward simply because we do not know very much about it. Further, we are likely to believe that our way of looking at the world is the right way and the only way. These attitudes are forms of ethnocentricity—the view that our culture is at the center of things. A more enlightened view respects cultural differences out of a concern for a more harmonious world and, ultimately, for the future survival of our planet. All nations need to understand that different cultures may have different answers to the same questions and that these answers may be as logical as the ones they are accustomed to hearing.

The first selection, by Margaret Atwood, humorously debunks the notion that Canada is a country almost identical to the United States and reveals that many Canadians are concerned about economic and cultural dominance by their much more powerful neighbor.

Other selections illustrate the knowledge that can be gained by encountering a culture whose values are very different from those of one's own. Mark Salzman, a young American teaching English in China, discovers that his students have a different view of the "truth" about the role of their country and his in world affairs. Although the differences in worldview keep communication with the students on a friendly but superficial level, Salzman gains a deeper under-

┌───┐

— THINKING ABOUT THE THEME *"Other Worlds"* —————

This photo was taken at the opening of a McDonalds in Tiananmen Square, a historic spot in Beijing, China. Tiananmen Square is both the site of the declaration of the government of Mao Tse-Tung, and the scene of the rebellion put down by Chinese government forces in 1989.

1. How do the two figures in the photograph relate to each other? What are the similarities and differences in expression, dress, gestures? What ideas(s) do you think the photographer was trying to convey?

2. What are your feelings about the pervasiveness of McDonalds and other large fast-food chains throughout the United States and in countries around the world? What do you think is the reason for their popularity? Does the uniformity they introduce endanger regional and national eating habits and lifestyles? How nutritious is the food they provide? What effects do fast food and its packaging have on the environment?

3. Advertising for children and adults often uses mythical characters such as Ronald McDonald, or real celebrities who have obtained mythic status. Examine some of the print and television advertisements that use symbolic figures. How is the figure connected to the product? How convincing is the connection? Do you see a difference in advertisements addressed specifically to children?

4. At your local library or at a large bookstore, examine popular magazines from another country, focusing on advertisements. Even if you can't read the language the magazines are written in, try to deduce some of the similarities and differences you see between U.S. popular culture and popular culture in other countries.

   In some communities McDonalds has been forced to modify its golden arches symbol to be less conspicuous, or more true to the communities' traditions or architecture.

└───┘

standing of life in China through his meeting with a young woman doctor. Their immediate sympathy for one another bridges the cultural gap between them. John David Morley's story about an Englishman living in Japan builds on the two cultures' different uses of space to present two different views of privacy, and concept of self. Laura Bohannan, an anthropologist, addresses the question of differences in cultural interpretation and proves that no story is universal. The western values enshrined in Shakespeare's *Hamlet* are apparently obvious, but only to westerners. The prince of Denmark's behavior is seen in a completely different way by the tribe she observes in Africa.

Several pieces in this chapter reflect on the colonial experience. In an essay written 250 years ago, Jonathan Swift makes a proposal that is more outrageous than "modest" to convince the English to rethink the way they treat the Irish. George Orwell, a British colonial officer in Burma, discovers, as he says, "the real motives for which despotic governments act." Jamaica Kincaid, in "On Seeing England for the First Time," writes about her childhood in Antigua, then a British colony. For Kincaid, colonial rule meant that her own culture and the surroundings of a tropical island were forcibly replaced by an alien and "colder" culture. In school she was so immersed in study of English geography, English history, and the lives and customs of the people of England that she could not "see" her own island. When she actually travels to England as an adult, her resentment at the culture foisted upon her and other colonials bursts out.

In the poem that ends the section, Gloria Anzaldúa explores living with several different and perhaps warring identities, crossing categories of race, ethnicity, and gender roles that others consider fixed. To live in the borderlands between cultures is to live in a dangerous place, but it is the only place that Anzaldúa feels she can be free.

Canadians: What Do They Want?

MARGARET ATWOOD

Margaret Atwood is one of Canada's foremost contemporary writers. She was born in Ottawa in 1939 and holds a B.A. degree from the University of Toronto and an M.A. from Radcliffe (Harvard). She has served as writer in residence at several universities and has received a number of honorary degrees and prizes for her writing. Poet, novelist, and essayist, she is best known for her novels, among them The Edible Woman *(1970),* Lady Oracle *(1976),* Life Before Man *(1980),* The Handmaid's Tale *(1985),* Cat's Eye *(1988),* The Robber Bride *(1994), and* Alias Grace *(1996).*

With its 10 provinces and vast Northern and Yukon Territories stretching toward the North Pole, Canada is larger than the United States. But with some 24 million inhabitants, the size of its population is just 10 percent of that of its southern (and only) neighbor, and the vast majority of Canadians live within 100 miles of the U.S. border. Canadians often complain that Americans know far too little about Canada, taking it for granted as an ally, a trading partner, and a fellow democracy. Canadians are concerned about dominance by their much more powerful neighbor, not only economic but cultural dominance as well.

About one in four Canadians is French-speaking, most of them living in the province of Quebec, north of New York State and New England. Just as Canadians in general are concerned about being dominated by the United States, so French Canadians are concerned about being deprived of their culture by the English-speaking majority, which has led to a separatist movement and some legislation restricting the use of English in Quebec.

1 Last month, during a poetry reading, I tried out a short prose poem called "How to Like Men." It began by suggesting that one start with the feet. Unfortunately, the question of jackboots soon arose, and things went on from there. After the reading I had a conversation with a young man who thought I had been unfair to men. He wanted men to be liked totally, not just from the heels to the knees,

305

and not just as individuals but as a group; and he thought it negative and inegalitarian of me to have alluded to war and rape. I pointed out that as far as any of us knew these were two activities not widely engaged in by women, but he was still upset. "We're both in this together," he protested. I admitted that this was so; but could he, maybe, see that our relative positions might be a little different.

This is the conversation one has with Americans, even, uh, *good* Americans, 2
when the dinner-table conversation veers round to Canadian-American relations. "We're in this together," they like to say, especially when it comes to continental energy reserves. How do you *explain* to them, as delicately as possible, why they are not categorically beloved? It gets like the old Lifebuoy ads: even their best friends won't tell them. And Canadians are supposed to be their best friends, right? Members of the family?

Well, sort of. Across the river from Michigan, so near and yet so far, there 3
I was at the age of eight, reading *their* Donald Duck comic books (originated however by one of *ours*; yes, Walt Disney's parents were Canadian) and coming at the end to Popsicle Pete, who promised me the earth if only I would save wrappers, but took it all away from me again with a single asterisk: Offer Good Only in the United States. Some cynical members of the world community may be forgiven for thinking that the same asterisk is there, in invisible ink, on the Constitution and the Bill of Rights.

But quibbles like that aside, and good will assumed, how does one go about 4
liking Americans? Where does one begin? Or, to put it another way, why did the Canadian women lock themselves in the john during a '70s "international" feminist conference being held in Toronto? Because the American sisters were being "imperialist," that's why.

But then, it's always a little naive of Canadians to expect that Americans, of 5
whatever political stamp, should stop being imperious. How can they? The fact is that the United States is an empire and Canada is to it as Gaul[1] was to Rome.

It's hard to explain to Americans what it feels like to be a Canadian. Pessi- 6
mists among us would say that one has to translate the experience into their own terms and that this is necessary because Americans are incapable of thinking in any other terms—and this in itself is part of the problem. (Witness all those draft dodgers[2] who went into culture shock when they discovered to their horror that Toronto was not Syracuse.)

Here is a translation: Picture a Mexico with a population ten times larger 7
than that of the United States. That would put it at about two billion. Now suppose that the official American language is Spanish, that 75 percent of the books Americans buy and 90 percent of the movies they see are Mexican, and that the profits flow across the border to Mexico. If an American does scrape it together

---

[1]The Roman name for the part of Western Europe (now France) conquered by Julius Caesar.
[2]Atwood is referring to American men who opposed the Vietnam war and fled to Canada to avoid the draft.

to make a movie, the Mexicans won't let him show it in the States, because they own the distribution outlets. If anyone tries to change this ratio, not only the Mexicans but many fellow Americans cry "National chauvinism," or, even more effectively, "National socialism." After all, the American public prefers the Mexican product. It's what they're used to.

8   Retranslate and you have the current American-Canadian picture. It's changed a little recently, not only on the cultural front. For instance, Canada, some think a trifle late, is attempting to regain control of its own petroleum industry. Americans are predictably angry. They think of Canadian oil as *theirs*.

9   "What's mine is yours," they have said for years, meaning exports: "What's yours is mine" means ownership and profits. Canadians are supposed to do retail buying, not controlling, or what's an empire for? One could always refer Americans to history, particularly that of their own revolution. They objected to the colonial situation when they themselves were a colony; but then, revolution is considered one of a very few homegrown American products that definitely are not for export.

10   Objectively, one cannot become too self-righteous about this state of affairs. Canadians owned lots of things, including their souls, before World War II. After that they sold, some say because they had put too much into financing the war, which created a capital vacuum (a position they would not have been forced into if the Americans hadn't kept out of the fighting for so long, say the sore losers). But for whatever reason, capital flowed across the border in the '50s, and Canadians, traditionally sock-under-the-mattress hoarders, were reluctant to invest in their own country. Americans did it for them and ended up with a large part of it, which they retain to this day. In every sellout there's a seller as well as a buyer, and the Canadians did a thorough job of trading their birthright for a mess.

11   That's on the capitalist end, but when you turn to the trade union side of things you find much the same story, except that the sellout happened in the '30s under the banner of the United Front. Now Canadian workers are finding that in any empire the colonial branch plants are the first to close, and what could be a truly progressive labor movement has been weakened by compromised bargains made in international union headquarters south of the border.

12   Canadians are sometimes snippy to Americans at cocktail parties. They don't like to feel owned and they don't like having been sold. But what really bothers them—and it's at this point that the United States and Rome part company—is the wide-eyed innocence with which their snippiness is greeted.

13   Innocence becomes ignorance when seen in the light of international affairs, and though ignorance is one of the spoils of conquest—the Gauls always knew more about the Romans than the Romans knew about them—the world can no longer afford America's ignorance. Its ignorance of Canada, though it makes Canadians bristle, is a minor and relatively harmless example. More dangerous is the fact that individual Americans seem not to know that the United States is an imperial power and is behaving like one. They don't want to admit that

empires dominate, invade and subjugate—and live on the proceeds—or, if they do admit it, they believe in their divine right to do so. The export of divine right is much more harmful than the export of Coca-Cola, though they may turn out to be much the same thing in the end.

Other empires have behaved similarly (the British somewhat better, Genghis Khan[3] decidedly worse); but they have not expected to be *liked* for it. It's the final Americanism, this passion for being liked. Alas, many Americans are indeed likable; they are often more generous, more welcoming, more enthusiastic, less picky and sardonic than Canadians, and it's not enough to say it's only because they can afford it. Some of that revolutionary spirit still remains: the optimism, the 18th-century belief in the fixability of almost anything, the conviction of the possibility of change. However, at cocktail parties and elsewhere one must be able to tell the difference between an individual and a foreign policy. Canadians can no longer afford to think of Americans as only a spectator sport. If Reagan blows up the world, we will unfortunately be doing more than watching it on television. "No annihilation without representation" sounds good as a slogan, but if we run it up the flagpole, who's going to salute? 14

We *are* all in this together. For Canadians, the question is how to survive it. For Americans there is no question, because there does not have to be. Canada is just that vague, cold place where their uncle used to go fishing, before the lakes went dead from acid rain.[4] 15

How do you like Americans? Individually, it's easier. Your average American is no more responsible for the state of affairs than your average man is for war and rape. Any Canadian who is so narrow-minded as to dislike Americans merely on principle is missing out on one of the good things in life. The same might be said, to women, of men. As a group, as a foreign policy, it's harder. But if you like men, you can like Americans. Cautiously. Selectively. Beginning with the feet. One at a time. 16

EXERCISES

Some of the Issues

1. How does Atwood answer the young man who asserts that men and women are "in this together"? How does she respond as a Canadian when Americans tell her the same thing?
2. Why is it hard to explain to Americans what it feels like to be Canadian?

---

[3](1167?–1227) Mongol ruler and warrior who controlled a vast empire from China to Russia and was known for his brutality and thirst for power.
[4]Acid precipitation formed in the atmosphere from industrial waste gases that falls as rain. Canadians have protested pollution in the United States that affects Canada.

3. Atwood accuses Americans of being imperialists. Does she support that claim? How? Do you think most Americans would be surprised by her accusation? Do you agree with it? Why or why not?

4. Explain the analogy Atwood makes (paragraphs 7 and 8) to help Americans understand Canada's attitudes toward American dominance.

5. What according to Atwood is "one of a very few homegrown American products that definitely are not for export"?

6. In paragraphs 10 and 11 Atwood concedes that Canadians must share some blame for American domination. What specific examples does she give?

7. Atwood accuses Americans of ignorance. Of what in particular? What, according to Atwood, accounts for this ignorance?

8. Atwood admits that many Americans are likeable as individuals. Why is this not enough for her?

The Way We Are Told

9. Who is Atwood's audience? Can she afford to be critical of it? Does she make any concessions to her audience's sense of patriotism?

10. Consider Atwood's style. Does it often resemble speech? Make note of the use of italics, the phrase "even, uh, *good* Americans," and the choice of vocabulary.

11. How would you characterize the tone of Atwood's article? How does she use humor? Does humor help her to disarm the reader?

12. Atwood makes several references to slogans; for example, "even their best friends won't tell them" (paragraph 2). What is the effect? What is she referring to when she says "No annihilation without representation"?

13. In the last paragraph Atwood returns to a comment she made at the very beginning of the essay. What is the advantage of beginning and ending in this way?

Some Subjects for Writing

14. Atwood accuses the United States of being an imperialist power in certain ways. Examine her claim. Do you agree or disagree?

*15. Read Jamaica Kincaid's "On Seeing England for the First Time." Both Atwood and Kincaid are concerned with the way in which their cultures have been dominated by more powerful ones. Contrast both the tone of their writing and the situation they describe. Try to come up with reasons for both the differences and similarities.

Teacher Mark

MARK SALZMAN

Mark Salzman, scholar of Chinese language and literature, screen-writer, actor, and martial arts expert, was born in Greenwich, Connect-icut, in 1959. Not long after his graduation from Yale University in 1982, he took a job teaching English in Changsha, the capital of Hunan province in China. The following selection is taken from his memoir of that experience, Iron and Silk: A Young American Encounters Swordsmen, Bureaucrats, and Other Citizens of Contemporary China *(1987). He is also the author of two novels,* The Laughing Sutra *(1991) and* The Soloist *(1994), and a memoir,* Lost in Place: Growing Up Absurd in Suburbia *(1995).*

The early and mid-1980s were marked by rapid changes in the People's Republic of China. The country, with more than one billion people—by far the most populous on earth—was rapidly opening up to the outside world, particularly the industrialized West. Tens of thousands of Chinese university students were coming to study in Western countries, including the United States. Western corporations were encouraged to develop commerce and industry with, and in, China. The communist government that had ruled the country since the revolution in 1949 was experimenting with capitalist incentives for economic development. The country seemed to be moving from a rigidly socialist system under a dictatorial regime to an intellectual opening up that promised changes in a democratic direction. In 1989 the impatience with the slow pace of that opening-up process, as well as anger about corruption and favoritism in the government, led to huge protest demonstrations led by hundreds of thousands of students. In the late spring of 1989 these movements were harshly suppressed.

Mark Salzman describes a time when the opening up seemed in full flower and likely to continue. The Cultural Revolution referred to in paragraph 41 was a time of great upheaval and destruction in the 1960s. Bands of young women and men, called the Red Guards, roamed the country out of control, dispensing what they considered justice. Education came to a standstill as millions of teachers, students, and professionals were sent to work as peasants in the countryside under the harshest conditions.

The Gulag Archipelago *(paragraph 50) by the Russian novelist*

Aleksandr Solzhenitsyn is a description—and severe indictment—of the concentration camps in the Soviet Union under Josef Stalin, in which millions of people lived and died.

1   In 1982, I graduated from Yale University as a Chinese literature major. I was fluent in Mandarin and nearly so in Cantonese, had struggled through a fair amount of classical Chinese and had translated the works of Huang Po-Fei, a modern poet. Oddly, though, I had no real desire to go to China; it sounded like a giant penal colony to me, and besides, I have never liked traveling much. I applied to the Yale-China Association because I needed a job, and was assigned to teach English at Hunan Medical College in Changsha, a sooty, industrial city of more than a million people and the capital of the southern province of Hunan.

2   When I arrived in Changsha, the temperature was above 100 degrees. I was 22 years old and homesick. The college assigned three classes to me: 26 doctors and teachers of medicine; four men and one woman identified as "the Middle-Aged English Teachers," and 25 medical students, ages 22 to 28. I was entirely unsure what to expect from them; the reverse, I would learn, was also true.

3   Their English ability ranged from nearly fluent to practically hopeless. At the end of the first week the Class Monitor for the class of doctors read aloud the results of their "Suggestions for Better Study" meeting: "Dear Teacher Mark. You are an active boy! Your lessons are very humorous and very wonderful. To improve our class, may we suggest that in the future, we (1) spend more time reading (2) spend more time listening (3) spend more time writing, and (4) spend more time speaking. Also, some students feel you are moving too quickly through the book. However, some students request that you speed up a little, because the material is too elementary. We hope we can struggle together to overcome these contradictions! Thank you, our dear teacher."

4   On the first day of class, when I asked the Middle-Aged English Teachers to introduce themselves to me, each chose instead to introduce the person sitting next to him. Teacher Xu began: "Teacher Cai was a wonderful dancer when he was a young man. He is famous in our college because he has a beautiful wife." Teacher Cai hit Teacher Xu and said, "Teacher Xu is always late to class, and he is afraid of his wife!"

5   "I am not!"

6   "Oh, but you are!"

7   Teacher Zhang pointed to Teacher Zhu. "Teacher Zhu was a navy man," he said. "But he can't swim! And Teacher Du is very fat. So we call her Fatty Du—she has the most powerful voice in our college!" Fatty Du beamed with pride and said, "And Teacher Zhang's special characteristic is that he is afraid of me!"

8   "I am not!"

9   "Oh, but you are!"

On an afternoon some weeks later, I asked them to open their textbooks to a 10 chapter entitled "War," which contained photographs of World War II, including one of the atomic bomb explosion over Hiroshima.

"Teacher Zhu," I said, "Can you tell us something about your experiences 11 during the war?"

Teacher Zhu, an aspiring Communist Party member, stood up and smiled. 12 "Yes," he said. Then he hesitated. "This is a picture of the atom bomb, isn't it?" 13 "Yes." 14

He smiled stiffly. "Teacher Mark—how do you feel, knowing your country 15 dropped an atom bomb on innocent people?"

My face turned red with embarrassment at having the question put so per- 16 sonally, but I tried to remain detached.

"This is a good question, Teacher Zhu. I can tell you that in America, many 17 people disagree about this. Not everyone thinks it was the right thing to do, although most people think that it saved lives."

"How did it save lives?" 18

"Well, by ending the war quickly." 19

Here, Teacher Zhu looked around the room at his classmates. 20

"But Teacher Mark. It is a fact that the Japanese had already surrendered to 21 the Communist Eighth Route Army of China. America put the bomb on Japan to make the world think America was the…"

"The victor!" shouted Fatty Du. 22

"Yes, the victor," said Teacher Zhu. 23

I must have stood gaping for a long time, for the other students began to laugh. 24

"Teacher Zhu," I asked, "how do you know this is a fact?" 25

"Because that is what our newspapers say!" 26

"I see. But our newspapers tell a different story. How can we know which 27 newspaper has told the truth?"

Here he seemed relieved. 28

"That is easy! Our newspapers are controlled by the people, but your news- 29 papers are owned by capitalist organizations, so of course they make things up to support themselves."

My mouth opened and closed a few times. Fatty Du, apparently believing 30 that the truth had been too much for me, came to my aid.

"It doesn't matter! Any capitalist country would do that. It is not just your 31 country!"

My head swimming, I asked her if she thought only capitalist countries lied 32 in the papers.

"Oh, of course not! The Russians do it, too. But here in China, we have no 33 reason to lie in the papers. When we make a mistake, we admit it! As for war, there is nothing to lie about. China has never attacked a nation. It has only defended its borders. We love peace. If we were the most powerful country in the world, think how peaceful the world would be!"

34   I agreed that war was a terrible thing and said I was glad that China and the United States had become friendly. The class applauded my speech.

35   "Teacher Mark—can I trouble you? I have a relative. She is my wife's cousin. She is a doctor visiting from Harbin. She speaks very good English and is very interested in learning more. Could I take her here to practice with you? It would only be once or twice."

36   Because of the overwhelming number of relatives and friends of students, not to mention perfect strangers, who wanted to learn English, I had to be protective of my time. I explained this to my student and apologized for not being able to help him.

37   "This is terrible," he said, smiling sheepishly.

38   "Why?" I asked.

39   "Because…I already told her you would."

40   I tried to let my annoyance show, but the harder I frowned, the more broadly he smiled, so at last I agreed to meet with her once.

41   "Her name is Little Mi," he said, much relieved. "She is very smart and strong-willed. She was always the leader of her class and was even the head of the Communist Youth League in her school. During the Cultural Revolution, she volunteered to go to the countryside. There she almost starved to death. At last she had a chance to go to medical school. She was the smartest in her class."

42   Little Mi sounded like a terrific bore; I cleared my throat, hoping that my student would simply arrange a time and let me be, but he continued. "Her specialty was pediatrics. She wanted to work with children. When the time came for job assignments after graduation, though, some people started a rumor that she and some of the other English students read Western literature in their spare time instead of studying medicine. They were accused of *fang yang pi!*"—imitating Westerners.

43   "So instead of being sent to a good hospital, she was sent to a small family planning clinic outside of the city. There she mostly assists doctors with abortions. That is how she works with children. But saddest of all, she has leukemia. Truly, she has eaten bitter all her life. When can I bring her?"

44   I told him they could come to my office in the Foreign Languages Building that evening. He thanked me extravagantly and withdrew.

45   At the appointed time someone knocked. I braced myself for an hour of grammar questions and opened the door. There stood Little Mi, who could not have been much older than I, with a purple scarf wrapped around her head like a Russian peasant woman. She was petite, unsmiling and beautiful. She looked at me without blinking.

46   "Are you Teacher Mark?" she asked in an even, low voice.

47   "Yes—please come in." She walked in, sat down and said in fluent English, "My cousin's husband apologizes for not being able to come. His adviser called him in for a meeting. Do you mind that I came alone?"

"Not at all. What can I do for you?" 48

"Well," she said, looking at the bookshelf next to her, "I love to read, but it 49
is difficult to find good books in English. I wonder if you would be so kind as
to lend me a book or two, which I can send back to you from Harbin as soon as
I finish them." I told her to pick whatever she liked from my shelf. As she went
through the books she talked about the foreign novels she had enjoyed; "Of
Mice and Men," "From Here To Eternity" and "The Gulag Archipelago."

"How did you get 'The Gulag Archipelago'?" I asked her. 50

"It wasn't easy," she answered. "I hear that Americans are shocked by what 51
they read in it. Is that true?"

"Yes, weren't you?" 52

"Not really," she answered quietly. 53

I remembered the story of her life my student had told. "You are a pretty 54
tough girl, aren't you?" I said.

She looked up from the magazine she had been leafing through with a sur- 55
prised expression, then covered her mouth with her hand and giggled nervously.
"How terrible! I'm not like that at all!"

We talked for over an hour, and she picked a few books to take with her. 56
When she got up to leave, I asked her when she would return to Harbin.

"The day after tomorrow." 57

Against all better judgment I asked her to come visit me again the next 58
evening. She eyed me closely, said "Thank you—I will," then disappeared into
the unlit hallway. I listened to her footsteps as she made her way down the stairs
and out of the deserted building. Then from the window I watched her shadowy
figure cross the athletic field.

She came the next night at exactly the same time. I had brought for her a 59
few books of photographs of the United States, and she marveled at the color
pictures taken in New England during the fall: "How beautiful," she said. "Just
like a dream."

I could not openly stare at her, so I gazed at her hand as she turned the pages 60
of the book, listened to her voice, and occasionally glanced at her face when she
asked me something.

We talked and talked, then she seemed to remember something and looked 61
at her watch. It was after 10 o'clock—nearly two hours had passed. She gasped,
suddenly worried. "I've missed the last bus!"

She was staying in a hospital on the other side of the river, at least a two-hour 62
walk. It was a bitter cold night. On foot, she would get back after midnight and
arouse considerable suspicion. The only thing to do was put her on the back of a
bicycle and ride her. That in itself would not attract attention, since that is how
most Chinese families travel around town. I had seen families of five on one bicycle many times, and young couples ride this way for want of anything else to do
at night. The woman usually rides sidesaddle on the rack over the rear wheel with
her arms around the man's waist, leaning her shoulder and face against his back.

63   A Chinese woman riding that way on a bicycle powered by a Caucasian male would attract attention, however. I put on my thick padded Red Army coat, tucked my hair under a Mao hat, wore a surgical mask (as many Chinese do, to keep dust out of their lungs), and put on a pair of Chinese sunglasses, the kind that *liumang*—young punks—wear. Little Mi wrapped her scarf around her head and left the building first.

64   Five minutes later, I went out, rode fast through the gate of our college, and saw her down the street, shrouded in the haze of dust kicked up by a coal truck. I pulled alongside her and she jumped on before I stopped.

65   The street was crowded. Neither of us said a word. Trucks, buses and jeeps flung themselves madly through the streets, bicycles wove around us, and pedestrians darted in front of us, cursing the *liumang*. Finally I turned onto the road that ran along the river, and the crowd thinned out. It was a horrible road, with potholes everywhere that I could not see in time to avoid. She, too shy to put her arms around my waist, had been balancing herself across the rack, but when we hit an especially deep rut I heard her yelp and felt her grab on to me. Regaining her balance, she began to loosen her grip, but I quickly steered into another pothole and told her to hold on. Very slowly, I felt her leaning her shoulder against my back. When at last her face touched my coat, I could feel her cheek through it.

66   We reached the steep bridge and I started the climb. About halfway up she told me to stop riding, that we could walk up the bridge to give me a rest. At the top, we stopped to lean against the rail and look at the lights of the city. Trucks and jeeps were our only company.

67   "Does this remind you of America?" she asked, gesturing toward the city lights with her chin.

68   "Yes, a little."

69   'Do you miss home?"

70   "Very much. But I'll be home very soon. And when I get home, I will miss Changsha."

71   "Really? But China is so…no you tell me—what is China like?"

72   "The lights are dimmer here."

73   "Yes," she said quietly, "and we are boring people, aren't we?" Only her eyes showed above the scarf wrapped around her face. I asked her if she thought she was boring, and her eyes wrinkled with laughter.

74   "I am not boring. I believe I am a very interesting girl. Do you think so?"

75   "Yes, I think so." She had pale skin, and I could see her eyelids blush.

76   "When you go back to America, will you live with your parents?"

77   "No."

78   "Why not?"

79   "I'm too old! They would think it was strange if I didn't live on my own."

80   "How wonderful! I wish my parents felt that way. I will have to live with them forever."

"Forever?"

81

"Of course! Chinese parents love their children, but they also think that children are like furniture. They own you, and you must make them comfortable until they decide to let you go. I cannot marry, so I will have to take care of them forever. I am almost 30 years old, and I must do whatever they say. So I sit in my room and dream. In my imagination I am free, and I can do wonder things!"

82

"Like what?"

83

She cocked her head to one side and raised one eyebrow.

84

"Do you tell people your dreams?"

85

"Yes, sometimes."

86

She laughed and said, "I'm not going to tell you my dreams."

87

We were silent awhile, then she suddenly asked me if I was a sad man or a happy man.

88

"That's hard to say—sometimes I'm happy, sometimes I'm sad. Mostly, I just worry."

89

"Worry? What do you worry about?"

90

"I don't know—everything, I guess. Mostly about wasting time."

91

"How strange! My cousin's husband says that you work very hard."

92

"I like to keep busy. That way I don't have time to worry."

93

"I can't understand that. You are such a free man—you can travel all over the world as you like, make friends everywhere. You are a fool not to be happy, especially when so many people depend on it."

94

"What do you mean?"

95

"My relative says that your nickname in the college is *huoshenxian*—an immortal in human form—because you are so...different. Your lectures make everyone laugh, and you make people feel happy all the time. This is very unusual."

96

I asked her if she was happy or sad. She raised one eyebrow again, looking not quite at me.

97

"I don't have as many reasons to be happy as you." She looked at her watch and shook her head. "I must get back—we have to hurry." As I turned toward the bicycle she leaned very close to me, almost touching her face against mine, looking straight into my eyes, and said, "I have an idea."

98

I could feel her breath against my throat.

99

"Let's coast down the bridge," she said. "Fast! No brakes!"

100

I got on the bicycle.

101

"Are you getting on?" I asked her.

102

"Just a minute. At the bottom I'll get off, so I'll say goodbye now."

103

"I should at least take you to the gate of the hospital."

104

"No, that wouldn't be a good idea. Someone might see me and ask who you were. At the bottom of the bridge I'll hop off, and you turn around. I won't see you again, so thank you. It was fun meeting you. You should stop worrying." She jumped on, pressed her face against my back, held me like a vice, and said, "Now—go! As fast as you can!"

105

EXERCISES

Some of the Issues

1. How did Salzman feel about going to China before traveling there? What was his preparation for the job of teaching English?
2. Describe Salzman's English classes. How appropriate are the doctors' suggestions? How did the middle-aged English teachers introduce one another?
3. What differing views of history are revealed in paragraphs 13–34?
4. What impression did Salzman have of Little Mi before meeting her? What do you learn about her past? About the effects of the Cultural Revolution?
5. What is Salzman's reaction when he finds out that Little Mi has read *The Gulag Archipelago?*
6. How is Little Mi's personality revealed to us? What indications are there of a change in Salzman's feelings?
7. The final conversation between Salzman and Little Mi reveals many differences in their lives and attitudes toward living. What are they? Do you think Salzman and Little Mi understand each other in spite of their differences?

The Way We Are Told

8. At first sight Salzman seems simply to be recording his conversations and impressions. Yet, in doing so, he lets the reader know quite clearly what he feels. How does Salzman express his point of view? Try to find some examples.
9. In paragraph 15 Teacher Zhu confronts Salzman with a question about dropping the atom bomb on Hiroshima. Examine the rest of the discussion between Salzman and the teachers. How does Salzman show that they, far from wanting a confrontation on that topic, go out of their way to "help" him understand?

Some Subjects for Writing

10. Salzman and Little Mi lead lives that are very far apart. Before their meeting Salzman expects her to be a bore. Yet, in the few hours they spend together, they bridge the wide gap between them. Describe a situation in which your own anticipation or first impression of someone turned out to be wrong.
11. Write about a meeting with someone that led to a turning point in your life. Try to convey the importance of the meeting mostly through the use of dialogue. Since you will probably not remember the exact words that were said, you may, like all writers, invent words as long as they are true to the experience.

Living in a Japanese Home

JOHN DAVID MORLEY

John David Morley was born in Singapore in 1948, of British parents, and educated at Oxford University. His earliest job was as tutor to the children of Elizabeth Taylor and Richard Burton when they were filming in Mexico. His interest in theater led him to Japanese theater and eventually to Japanese culture in general. He taught himself Japanese, studied at the Language Research Institute at Waseda University in Tokyo, and then went to work for Japanese Television as liaison officer, interpreter, and researcher, stationed in Munich, Germany. In 1985 he published a novel, Pictures from the Water Trade: Adventures of a Westerner in Japan, *from which the present selection is taken. The novel is based on some of his own experiences.*

The Japanese island empire successfully managed to isolate itself from foreign influences until the middle of the nineteenth century. Once that isolation had been breached, however, Japan moved rapidly to catch up with the Western world, not only by industrializing but also by following the major powers' expansionist policies. Japan fought a successful war with Russia (1905), occupied and eventually annexed Korea (1910), and, in the 1930s, occupied Manchuria and large parts of China. After its surprise attack on Pearl Harbor (December 7, 1941), Japan had spectacular initial successes in World War II, occupying the Philippines, Indochina, Indonesia, Burma, and Singapore. Defeated and virtually destroyed in the later phases of the war, Japan was occupied by the U.S. Army under General Douglas Mac-Arthur, whose administration of the islands is primarily responsible for converting Japan into a constitutional monarchy with a parliamentary government. Japan's economic recovery has been spectacular—today the country is the second most powerful industrial nation in the world. Japan's success is all the more remarkable when one considers that the country has almost no natural resources of its own on its crowded islands. With its size smaller than California, it has 122 million inhabitants, half as many as the United States. Japanese society is highly homogeneous, has a very low crime rate, a very high level of literacy, and is considered very hard-working.

1   The introduction was arranged through a mutual acquaintance, Yoshida, at the private university where Boon was taking language courses and where Sugama was employed on the administrative staff. They met one afternoon in the office of their acquaintance and inspected each other warily for ten minutes.

2   "Nice weather," said Boon facetiously as he shook hands with Sugama. Outside it was pouring with rain.

3   "Nice weather?" repeated Sugama doubtfully, glancing out of the window. "But it's raining."

4   It was not a good start.

5   Sugama had just moved into a new apartment. It was large enough for two, he said, but he was looking for someone to share the expenses. This straightforward information arrived laboriously, in bits and pieces, sandwiched between snippets of Sugama's personal history and vague professions of friendship, irritating to Boon, because at the time he felt they sounded merely sententious. All this passed back and forth between Sugama and Boon through the mouth of their mutual friend, as Boon understood almost no Japanese and Sugama's English, though well-intentioned, was for the most part impenetrable.

6   It made no odds to Boon where he lived or with whom. All he wanted was a Japanese-speaking environment in order to absorb the language as quickly as possible. He had asked for a family, but none was available.

7   One windy afternoon in mid-October the three of them met outside the gates of the university and set off to have a look at Sugama's new apartment. It was explained to Boon that cheap apartments in Tokyo were very hard to come by, the only reasonable accommodation available being confined to housing estates subsidized by the government. Boon wondered how a relatively prosperous bachelor like Sugama managed to qualify for government-subsidized housing. Sugama admitted that this was in fact only possible because his grandfather would also be living there. It was the first Boon had heard of the matter and he was rather taken aback.

8   It turned out, however, that the grandfather would "very seldom" be there—in fact, that he wouldn't live there at all. He would only be there on paper, he and his grandson constituting a "family." That was the point. "You must *say* he is there," said Sugama emphatically.

9   The grandfather lived a couple of hundred miles away, and although he never once during the next two years set foot in the apartment he still managed to be the bane of Boon's life. A constant stream of representatives from charities, government agencies and old people's clubs, on average one or two a month, came knocking on the door, asking to speak to grandfather. At first grandfather was simply "not in" or had "gone for a walk," but as time passed and the flow of visitors never faltered, Boon found himself having to resort to more drastic measures. Grandfather began to make long visits to his home in the country; he had not yet returned because he didn't feel up to making the journey; his health gradually deteriorated. Finally Boon decided to have him invalided, and for a

long time his condition remained "grave." On grandfather's behalf Boon received the condolences of all these visitors, and occasionally even presents.

Two years later grandfather did in fact die. Boon was thus exonerated, but   10
in the meantime he had got to know grandfather well and had become rather fond of him. He attended his funeral with mixed feelings.

Sugama had acquired tenure of his government-subsidized apartment by a   11
stroke of luck. He had won a ticket in a lottery. These apartments were much sought after, and in true Japanese style their distribution among hundreds of thousands of applicants was discreetly left to fate. The typical tenant was a young couple with one or two children, who would occupy the apartment for ten or fifteen years, often under conditions of bleak frugality, in order to save money to buy a house. Although the rent was not immoderate, prices generally in Tokyo were high, and it was a mystery to Boon how such people managed to live at all. Among the lottery winners there were inevitably also those people for whom the acquisition of an apartment was just a prize, an unexpected bonus, to be exploited as a financial investment. It was no problem for these nominal tenants to sub-let their apartments at prices well above the going rate.

Boon had never lived on a housing estate and his first view of the tall con-   12
crete compound where over fifty thousand people lived did little to reassure him. Thousands of winner families were accommodated in about a dozen rectangular blocks, each between ten and fifteen stories high, apparently in no way different (which disappointed Boon most of all) from similar housing compounds in Birmingham or Berlin. He had naively expected Japanese concrete to be different, to have a different colour, perhaps, or a more exotic shape.

But when Sugama let them into the apartment and Boon saw the interior   13
he immediately took heart: this was unmistakably Japanese. Taking off their shoes in the tiny box-like hall, the three of them padded reverently through the kitchen into the *tatami*[1] rooms.

"Smell of fresh *tatami*," pronounced Sugama, wrinkling his nose.   14

Boon was ecstatic. Over the close-woven pale gold straw matting lay a very   15
faint greenish shimmer, sometimes perceptible and sometimes not, apparently in response to infinitesimal shifts in the texture of the falling light. The *tatami* was quite unlike a carpet or any other form of floor-covering he had ever seen. It seemed to be alive, humming with colours he could sense rather than see, like a greening tree in the brief interval between winter and spring. He stepped on to it and felt the fibres recoil, sinking under the weight of his feet, slowly and softly.

"You can see green?" asked Sugama, squatting down.   16
"Yes indeed."   17
"Fresh *tatami*. Smell of grass, green colour. But not for long, few weeks only."   18
"What exactly is it?"   19
"Yes."   20

[1]Woven straw matting used as a floor covering in Japanese homes.

21   Boon turned to Yoshida and repeated the question, who in turn asked Sugama and conferred with him at length.

22   "*Tatami* comes from *oritatamu*, which means to fold up. So it's a kind of matting you can fold up."

23   "Made of straw."

24   "Yes."

25   "How long does it last?"

26   Long consultation.

27   "He says this is not so good quality. Last maybe four, five years."

28   "And then what?"

29   "New *tatami*. Quite expensive, you see. But very practical."

30   The three *tatami* rooms were divided by a series of *fusuma*, sliding screens made of paper and light wood. These screens were decorated at the base with simple grass and flower motifs; a natural extension, it occurred to Boon, of the grass-like *tatami* laid out in-between. Sugama explained that the *fusuma* were usually kept closed in winter, and in summer, in order to have "nice breeze," they could be removed altogether. He also showed Boon the *shoji*, a type of sliding screen similar to the *fusuma* but more simple: an open wooden grid covered on one side with semi-transparent paper, primitive but rather beautiful. There was only one small section of *shoji* in the whole apartment; almost as a token, thought Boon, and he wondered why.

31   With the exception of a few one- and two-room apartments every house that Boon ever visited in Japan was designed to incorporate these three common elements: *tatami, fusuma* and *shoji*. In the houses of rich people the *tatami* might last longer, the *fusuma* decorations might be more costly, but the basic concept was the same. The interior design of all houses being much the same, it was not surprising to find certain similarities in the behavior and attitudes of the people who lived in them.

32   The most striking feature of the Japanese house was lack of privacy: the lack of individual, inviolable space. In winter, when the *fusuma* were kept closed, any sound above a whisper was clearly audible on the other side, and of course in summer they were usually removed altogether. It is impossible to live under such conditions for very long without a common household identity emerging which naturally takes precedence over individual wishes. This enforced family unity was still held up to Boon as an ideal, but in practice it was ambivalent, as much a yoke as a bond.

33   There was no such thing as the individual's private room, no bedroom, dining- or sitting-room as such, since in the traditional Japanese house there was no furniture determining that a room should be reserved for any particular function. A person slept in a room, for example, without thinking of it as a bedroom or as his room. In the morning his bedding would be rolled up and stored away in a cupboard; a small table known as the *kotatsu*, which could also be plugged into the mains to provide heating, was moved back into the centre of the room and

here the family ate, drank, worked and relaxed for the rest of the day. Although it was becoming standard practice in modern Japan for children to have their own rooms, many middle-aged and nearly all older Japanese still lived this way. They regarded themselves as "one flesh," their property as common to all; the *uchi* (household, home) was constituted according to a principle of indivisibility. The system of moveable screens meant that the rooms could be used by all the family and for all purposes: walls were built round the *uchi*, not inside it.

Boon later discovered analogies between this concept of house and the Japanese concept of self. The Japanese carried his house around in his mouth and produced it in everyday conversation, using the word *uchi* to mean "I," the representative of my house in the world outside. His self-awareness was naturally expressed as corporate individuality, hazy about quite what that included, very clear about what it did not.   34

Ittaikan, the traditional view of the corporate *uchi* as one flesh, had unmistakably passed into decline in modern Japan. A watery sentiment remained, lacking the conviction that had once made the communal *uchi* as self-evident in practice as it was in principle. This was probably why people had become acutely aware of the problem of space, although they did not necessarily have less space now than they had had before. A tendency to restrict the spatial requirements of daily life quite voluntarily had been evident in Japan long before land became scarce. When the tea-room was first introduced during the Muromachi period (early fourteenth to late sixteenth century) the specification of its size was four and a half mats, but in the course of time this was reduced to one mat (two square metres). The reasons for this kind of scaling down were purely aesthetic. It was believed that only within a space as modest as this could the spirit of *wabi*, a taste for the simple and quiet, be truly cultivated.   35

The almost wearying sameness about all the homes which Boon visited, despite differences in the wealth and status of their owners, prompted a rather unexpected conclusion: the classlessness of the Japanese house. The widespread use of traditional materials, the preservation of traditional structures, even if in such contracted forms as to have become merely symbolic, suggested a consensus about the basic requirements of daily life which was very remarkable, and which presumably held implications for Japanese society as a whole. Boon's insight into that society was acquired very slowly, after he had spent a great deal of time sitting on the *tatami* mats and looking through the sliding *fusuma* doors which had struck him as no more than pleasing curiosities on his first visit to a Japanese-style home.   36

EXERCISES

Some of the Issues

1. Describe the first meeting of Boon and Sugama. Why did Boon consider it "not a good start"?

2. Describe the selection process for government-subsidized housing in Japan—very different from Western practices. Can you find a rationale for the Japanese system?
3. On entering the new apartment Sugama wrinkles his nose while Boon is ecstatic. What accounts for their difference in attitude?
4. What are the key elements of the Japanese home? What are the advantages of this mode of living? What disadvantages does it have?
5. How does the arrangement condition the lives of the people who live in it? How does it reflect Japanese values?
6. Morley says that the most striking feature of the Japanese house is lack of privacy. Later he speaks of the classlessness of the Japanese home. How does he illustrate his two points?
*7. Read Marcus Mabry's "Living in Two Worlds." Both Morley (through Boon) and Mabry are concerned with privacy, Boon when he joins Sugama and Mabry when he goes home to New Jersey. How and why are their attitudes different?

The Way We Are Told

8. The author does not at any time refer to Western conditions and attitudes; yet they are constantly implied in his discussion of events, contacts with people, and descriptions of living conditions. Give some examples.
9. What does the author achieve by his gradual revelation of the truth about Sugama's grandfather?
10. The story is told by Boon, a fictional British visitor, but the experiences presumably reflect Morley's own. What does the author gain by creating Boon to tell his story?

Some Subjects for Writing

11. How important is privacy to you? How did the physical environment in which you grew up shape your attitudes?
12. Compare and contrast the Western or American concept of privacy to the Japanese view as described by Morley. How does the physical environment of the Japanese home support Japanese notions of privacy? In describing the American living space, you might think of the "ideal" American family home, a bedroom for each child, preferably with a private bath, and a kitchen and family room as places for the family to gather.

Shakespeare in the Bush

LAURA BOHANNAN

Laura Bohannan, born in New York City in 1922, was a professor of anthropology at the University of Illinois in Chicago. She received her doctorate from Oxford University and later did field work with various peoples in Africa, including the Tiv, a tribe in central Nigeria, with whom this story is concerned. Under the pseudonym Elenore Smith Bowen, she has published a novel about anthropological field work, Return to Laughter.

The Tiv, who have a tradition of storytelling (accompanied by beer drinking) during the rainy season, asked their visitor to tell a story. She chose Shakespeare's Hamlet, *believing that its universality would make it comprehensible, even in a culture very different from the one in which it was originally conceived. This assumption turned out to be quite wrong.*

Just before I left Oxford for the Tiv in West Africa, conversation turned to the 1 season at Stratford. "You Americans," said a friend, "often have difficulty with Shakespeare. He was, after all, a very English poet, and one can easily misinterpret the universal by misunderstanding the particular."

I protested that human nature is pretty much the same the whole world 2 over; at least the general plot and motivation of the greater tragedies would always be clear—everywhere—although some details of custom might have to be explained and difficulties of translation might produce other slight changes. To end an argument we could not conclude, my friend gave me a copy of *Hamlet* to study in the African bush: it would, he hoped, lift my mind above its primitive surroundings, and possibly I might, by prolonged meditation, achieve the grace of correct interpretation.

It was my second field trip to that African tribe, and I thought myself ready 3 to live in one of its remote sections—an area difficult to cross even on foot. I eventually settled on the hillock of a very knowledgeable old man, the head of a homestead of some hundred and forty people, all of whom were either his close relatives or their wives and children. Like the other elders of the vicinity, the old man spent most of his time performing ceremonies seldom seen these days in the more accessible parts of the tribe. I was delighted. Soon there would be three months of enforced isolation and leisure, between the harvest that takes place just before the rising of the swamps and the clearing of new farms when the water goes down. Then, I thought, they would have even more time to perform ceremonies and explain them to me.

4 I was quite mistaken, Most of the ceremonies demanded the presence of elders from several homesteads. As the swamps rose, the old men found it too difficult to walk from one homestead to the next, and the ceremonies gradually ceased. As the swamps rose even higher, all activities but one came to an end. The women brewed beer from maize and millet. Men, women, and children sat on their hillocks and drank it.

5 People began to drink at dawn. By midmorning the whole homestead was singing, dancing, and drumming. When it rained, people had to sit inside their huts: there they drank and sang or they drank and told stories. In any case, by noon or before, I either had to join the party or retire to my own hut and my books. "One does not discuss serious matters when there is beer. Come, drink with us." Since I lacked their capacity for the thick native beer, I spent more and more time with *Hamlet*. Before the end of the second month, grace descended on me. I was quite sure that *Hamlet* had only one possible interpretation, and that one universally obvious.

6 Early every morning, in the hope of having some serious talk before the beer party, I used to call on the old man at his reception hut—a circle of posts supporting a thatched roof above a low mud wall to keep out wind and rain. One day I crawled through the low doorway and found most of the men of the homestead sitting huddled in their ragged cloths on stools, low plank beds, and reclining chairs, warming themselves against the chill of the rain around a smoky fire. In the center were three pots of beer. The party, had started.

7 The old man greeted me cordially, "Sit down and drink." I accepted a large calabash full of beer, poured some into a small drinking gourd, and tossed it down. Then I poured some more into the same gourd for the man second in seniority to my host before I handed my calabash over to a young man for further distribution. Important people shouldn't ladle beer themselves.

8 "It is better like this," the old man said, looking at me approvingly, and plucking at the thatch that had caught in my hair. "You should sit and drink with us more often. Your servants tell me that when you are not with us, you sit inside your hut looking at a paper."

9 The old man was acquainted with four kinds of "papers": tax receipts, bride price receipts, court fee receipts, and letters. The messenger who brought him letters from the chief used them mainly as a badge of office, for he always knew what was in them and told the old man. Personal letters for the few who had relatives in the government or mission stations were kept until someone went to a large market where there was a letter writer and reader. Since my arrival, letters were brought to me to be read. A few men also brought me bride price receipts, privately, with requests to change the figures to a higher sum. I found moral arguments were of no avail, since in-laws are fair game, and the technical hazards of forgery difficult to explain to an illiterate people. I did not wish them

to think me silly enough to look at any such paper for days on end, and I hastily explained that my "paper" was one of the "things of long ago" of my country.

"Ah," said the old man. "Tell us."   10

I protested that I was not a storyteller. Storytelling is a skilled art among   11 them; their standards are high, and the audiences critical—and vocal in their criticism. I protested in vain. This morning they wanted to hear a story while they drank. They threatened to tell me no more stories until I told them one of mine. Finally, the old man promised that no one would criticize my style "for we know you are struggling with our language." "But," put in one of the elders, "you must explain what we do not understand, as we do when we tell you our stories." Realizing that here was my chance to prove *Hamlet* universally intelligible, I agreed.

The old man handed me some more beer to help me on with my storytell-   12 ing. Men filled their long wooden pipes and knocked coals from the fire to place in the pipe bowls; then, puffing contentedly, they sat back to listen. I began in the proper style.

"Not yesterday, not yesterday, but long ago, a thing occurred. One night   13 three men were keeping watch outside the homestead of the great chief, when suddenly they saw the former chief approach them."

"Why was he no longer the chief?"   14

"He was dead," I explained. "That is why they were troubled and afraid   15 when they saw him."

"Impossible," began one of the elders, handing his pipe on to his neighbor,   16 who interrupted, "Of course it wasn't the dead chief. It was an omen sent by a witch. Go on."

Slightly shaken, I continued. "One of these three was a man who knew   17 things"—the closest translation for scholar, but unfortunately it also meant witch. The second elder looked triumphantly at the first. "So he spoke to the dead chief saying, 'Tell us what we must do so you may rest in your grave,' but the dead chief did not answer. He vanished, and they could see him no more. Then the man who knew things—his name was Horatio—said this event was the affair of the dead chief's son, Hamlet."

There was a general shaking of heads round the circle. "Had the dead chief no   18 living brothers? Or was this son the chief?"

"No," I replied. "That is, he had one living brother who became the chief   19 when the elder brother died."

The old men muttered: such omens were matters for chiefs and elders, not   20 for youngsters; no good could come of going behind a chief's back; clearly Horatio was not a man who knew things.

"Yes, he was," I insisted, shooing a chicken away from my beer. "In our   21 country the son is next to the father. The dead chief's younger brother had become the great chief. He had also married his elder brother's widow only about a month after the funeral."

22   "He did well," the old man beamed and announced to the others, "I told you that if we knew more about Europeans, we would find they really were very like us. In our country also," he added to me, "the younger brother marries the elder brother's widow and becomes the father of his children. Now, if your uncle, who married your widowed mother, is your father's full brother, then he will be a real father to you. Did Hamlet's father and uncle have one mother?"

23   His question barely penetrated my mind; I was too upset and thrown too far off balance by having one of the most important elements of *Hamlet* knocked straight out of the picture. Rather uncertainly I said that I thought they had the same mother, but I wasn't sure—the story didn't say. The old man told me severely that these genealogical details made all the difference and that when I got home I must ask the elders about it. He shouted out the door to one of his younger wives to bring his goatskin bag.

24   Determined to save what I could of the mother motif, I took a deep breath and began again. "The son Hamlet was very sad because his mother had married again so quickly. There was no need for her to do so, and it is our custom for a widow not to go to her next husband until she has mourned for two years."

25   "Two years is too long," objected the wife, who had appeared with the old man's battered goatskin bag. "Who will hoe your farms for you while you have no husband?"

26   "Hamlet," I retorted without thinking, "was old enough to hoe his mother's farms himself. There was no need for her to remarry." No one looked convinced. I gave up. "His mother and the great chief told Hamlet not to be sad, for the great chief himself would be a father to Hamlet. Furthermore, Hamlet would be the next chief: therefore he must stay to learn the things of a chief. Hamlet agreed to remain, and all the rest went off to drink beer."

27   While I paused, perplexed at how to render Hamlet's disgusted soliloquy to an audience convinced that Claudius and Gertrude had behaved in the best possible manner, one of the younger men asked me who had married the other wives of the dead chief.

28   "He had no other wives," I told him.

29   "But a chief must have many wives! How else can he brew beer and prepare food for all his guests?"

30   I said firmly that in our country even chiefs had only one wife, that they had servants to do their work, and that they paid them from tax money.

31   It was better, they returned, for a chief to have many wives and sons who would help him hoe his farms and feed his people; then everyone loved the chief who gave much and took nothing—taxes were a bad thing.

32   I agreed with the last comment, but for the rest fell back on their favorite way of fobbing off my questions: "That is the way it is done, so that is how we do it."

33   I decided to skip the soliloquy. Even if Claudius was here thought quite right to marry his brother's widow, there remained the poison motif, and I knew

they would disapprove of fratricide. More hopefully I resumed, "That night Hamlet kept watch with the three who had seen his dead father. The dead chief again appeared, and although the others were afraid, Hamlet followed his dead father off to one side. When they were alone, Hamlet's dead father spoke."

"Omens can't talk!" The old man was emphatic.   34

"Hamlet's dead father wasn't an omen. Seeing him might have been an   35
omen, but he was not." My audience looked as confused as I sounded. "It *was* Hamlet's dead father. It was a thing we call a 'ghost.'" I had to use the English word, for unlike many of the neighboring tribes, these people didn't believe in the survival after death of any individuating part of the personality.

"What is a 'ghost'? An omen?"   36

"No, a 'ghost' is someone who is dead but who walks around and can talk,   37
and people can hear him and see him but not touch him."

They objected. "One can touch zombis."   38

"No, no! It was not a dead body the witches had animated to sacrifice and   39
eat. No one else made Hamlet's dead father walk. He did it himself."

"Dead men can't walk," protested my audience as one man.   40

I was quite willing to compromise. "A 'ghost' is the dead man's shadow."   41

But again they objected. "Dead men cast no shadows."   42

"They do in my country," I snapped.   43

The old man quelled the babble of disbelief that arose immediately and told   44
me with that insincere, but courteous, agreement one extends to the fancies of the young, ignorant, and superstitious, "No doubt in your country the dead can also walk without being zombis." From the depths of his bag he produced a withered fragment of kola nut, bit off one end to show it wasn't poisoned, and handed me the rest as a peace offering.

"Anyhow," I resumed, "Hamlet's dead father said that his own brother, the   45
one who became chief, had poisoned him. He wanted Hamlet to avenge him. Hamlet believed this in his heart, for he did not like his father's brother." I took another swallow of beer. "In the country of the great chief, living in the same homestead, for it was a very large one, was an important elder who was often with the chief to advise and help him. His name was Polonius. Hamlet was courting his daughter, but her father and her brother...[I cast hastily about for some tribal analogy] warned her not to let Hamlet visit her when she was alone on her farm, for he would be a great chief and so could not marry her."

"Why not?" asked the wife, who had settled down on the edge of the old   46
man's chair. He frowned at her for asking stupid questions and growled, "They live in the same homestead."

"That was not the reason," I informed them. "Polonius was a stranger who   47
lived in the homestead because he helped the chief, not because he was a relative."

"Then why couldn't Hamlet marry her?"   48

"He could have," I explained, "But Polonius didn't think he would. After all, 49
Hamlet was a man of great importance who ought to marry a chief's daughter,

for in his country a man could have only one wife. Polonius was afraid that if Hamlet made love to his daughter, then no one else would give a high price for her."

50   "That might be true," remarked one of the shrewder elders, "but a chief's son would give his mistress's father enough presents and patronage to more than make up the difference. Polonius sounds like a fool to me."

51   "Many people think he was," I agreed. "Meanwhile Polonius sent his son Laertes off to Paris to learn the things of that country, for it was the homestead of a very great chief indeed. Because he was afraid that Laertes might waste a lot of money on beer and women and gambling, or get into trouble by fighting, he sent one of his servants to Paris secretly, to spy out what Laertes was doing. One day Hamlet came upon Polonius's daughter Ophelia. He behaved so oddly he frightened her. Indeed"—I was fumbling for words to express the dubious quality of Hamlet's madness—"the chief and many others had also noticed that when Hamlet talked one could understand the words but not what they meant. Many people thought that he had become mad." My audience suddenly became much more attentive. "The great chief wanted to know what was wrong with Hamlet, so he sent for two of Hamlet's age mates [school friends would have taken long explanation] to talk to Hamlet and find out what troubled his heart. Hamlet, seeing that they had been bribed by the chief to betray him, told them nothing. Polonius, however, insisted that Hamlet was mad because he had been forbidden to see Ophelia, whom he loved."

52   "Why," inquired a bewildered voice, "should anyone bewitch Hamlet on that account?"

53   "Bewitch him?"

54   "Yes, only witchcraft can make anyone mad, unless, of course, one sees the beings that lurk in the forest."

55   I stopped being a storyteller, took out my notebook and demanded to be told more about these two causes of madness. Even while they spoke and I jotted notes, I tried to calculate the effect of this new factor on the plot. Hamlet had not been exposed to the beings that lurk in the forests. Only his relatives in the male line could bewitch him. Barring relatives not mentioned by Shakespeare, it had to be Claudius who was attempting to harm him. And, of course, it was.

56   For the moment I staved off questions by saying that the great chief also refused to believe that Hamlet was mad for the love of Ophelia and nothing else. "He was sure that something much more important was troubling Hamlet's heart."

57   "Now Hamlet's age mates," I continued, "had brought with them a famous storyteller. Hamlet decided to have this man tell the chief and all his homestead a story about a man who had poisoned his brother because he desired his brother's wife and wished to be chief himself. Hamlet was sure the great chief could not hear the story without making a sign if he was indeed guilty, and then he would discover whether his dead father had told him the truth."

The old man interrupted, with deep cunning, "Why should a father lie to   58
his son?" he asked.

I hedged: "Hamlet wasn't sure that it really was his dead father." It was   59
impossible to say anything, in that language, about devil-inspired visions.

"You mean," he said, "it actually was an omen, and he knew witches some-   60
times send false ones. Hamlet was a fool not to go to one skilled in reading omens
and divining the truth in the first place. A man-who-sees-the-truth could have
told him how his father died, if he really had been poisoned, and if there was
witchcraft in it; then Hamlet could have called the elders to settle the matter."

The shrewd elder ventured to disagree. "Because his father's brother was a   61
great chief, one-who-sees-the-truth might therefore have been afraid to tell it.
I think it was for that reason that a friend of Hamlet's father—a witch and an
elder—sent an omen so his friend's son would know. Was the omen true?"

"Yes," I said, abandoning ghosts and the devil; a witch-sent omen it would   62
have to be. "It was true, for when the storyteller was telling his tale before all
the homestead, the great chief rose in fear. Afraid that Hamlet knew his secret
he planned to have him killed."

The stage set of the next bit presented some difficulties of translation. I   63
began cautiously. "The great chief told Hamlet's mother to find out from her
son what he knew. But because a woman's children are always first in her heart,
he had the important elder Polonius hide behind a cloth that hung against the
wall of Hamlet's mother's sleeping hut. Hamlet started to scold his mother for
what she had done."

There was a shocked murmur from everyone. A man should never scold his   64
mother.

"She called out in fear, and Polonius moved behind the cloth. Shouting, 'A   65
rat!' Hamlet took his machete and slashed through the cloth." I paused for dramatic effect. "He had killed Polonius!"

The old men looked at each other in supreme disgust. "That Polonius truly   66
was a fool and a man who knew nothing! What child would not know enough
to shout, 'It's me!'" With a pang, I remembered that these people are ardent
hunters, always armed with bow, arrow, and machete; at the first rustle in the
grass an arrow is aimed and ready, and the hunter shouts "Game!" If no human
voice answers immediately, the arrow speeds on its way. Like a good hunter
Hamlet had shouted, "A rat!"

I rushed in to save Polonius's reputation. "Polonius did speak. Hamlet heard   67
him. But he thought it was the chief and wished to kill him to avenge his father.
He had meant to kill him earlier that evening...." I broke down, unable to
describe to these pagans, who had no belief in individual afterlife, the difference
between dying at one's prayers and dying "unhousell'd, disappointed, unaneled."

This time I had shocked my audience seriously. "For a man to raise his hand   68
against his father's brother and the one who had become his father—that is a
terrible thing. The elders ought to let such a man be bewitched."

69   I nibbled at my kola nut in some perplexity, then pointed out that after all the man had killed Hamlet's father.

70   "No," pronounced the old man, speaking less to me than to the young men sitting behind the elders. "If your father's brother has killed your father, you must appeal to your father's age mates; *they* may avenge him. No man may use violence against his senior relatives." Another thought struck him. "But if his father's brother had indeed been wicked enough to bewitch Hamlet and make him mad that would be a good story indeed, for it would be his fault that Hamlet, being mad, no longer had any sense and thus was ready to kill his father's brother."

71   There was a murmur of applause. *Hamlet* was again a good story to them, but it no longer seemed quite the same story to me. As I thought over the coming complications of plot and motive, I lost courage and decided to skim over dangerous ground quickly.

72   "The great chief," I went on, "was not sorry that Hamlet had killed Polonius. It gave him a reason to send Hamlet away, with his two treacherous age mates, with letters to a chief of a far country, saying that Hamlet should be killed. But Hamlet changed the writing on their papers, so that the chief killed his age mates instead." I encountered a reproachful glare from one of the men whom I had told undetectable forgery was not merely immoral but beyond human skill. I looked the other way.

73   "Before Hamlet could return, Laertes came back for his father's funeral. The great chief told him Hamlet had killed Polonius. Laertes swore to kill Hamlet because of this, and because his sister Ophelia, hearing her father had been killed by the man she loved, went mad and drowned in the river."

74   "Have you already forgotten what we told you?" The old man was reproachful. "One cannot take vengeance on a madman; Hamlet killed Polonius in his madness. As for the girl, she not only went mad, she was drowned. Only witches can make people drown. Water itself can't hurt anything. It is merely something one drinks and bathes in."

75   I began to get cross. "If you don't like the story, I'll stop."

76   The old man made soothing noises and himself poured me some more beer. "You tell the story well, and we are listening. But it is clear that the elders of your country have never told you what the story really means. No, don't interrupt! We believe you when you say your marriage customs are different, or your clothes and weapons. But people are the same everywhere; therefore, there are always witches and it is we, the elders, who know how witches work. We told you it was the great chief who wished to kill Hamlet, and now your own words have proved us right. Who were Ophelia's male relatives?"

77   "There were only her father and her brother." Hamlet was clearly out of my hands.

78   "There must have been many more; this also you must ask of your elders when you get back to your country. From what you tell us, since Polonius was

dead, it must have been Laertes who killed Ophelia, although I do not see the reason for it."

We had emptied one pot of beer, and the old men argued the point with 79 slightly tipsy interest. Finally one of them demanded of me, "What did the servant of Polonius say on his return?"

With difficulty I recollected Reynaldo and his mission. "I don't think he did 80 return before Polonius was killed."

"Listen," said the elder, "and I will tell you how it was and how your story 81 will go, then you may tell me if I am right. Polonius knew his son would get into trouble, and so he did. He had many fines to pay for fighting, and debts from gambling. But he had only two ways of getting money quickly. One was to marry off his sister at once, but it is difficult to find a man who will marry a woman desired by the son of a chief. For if the chief's heir commits adultery with your wife, what can you do? Only a fool calls a case against a man who will someday be his judge. Therefore Laertes had to take the second way: he killed his sister by witchcraft, drowning her so he could secretly sell her body to the witches."

I raised an objection. "They found her body and buried it. Indeed Laertes 82 jumped into the grave to see his sister once more—so, you see, the body was truly there. Hamlet, who had just come back, jumped in after him."

"What did I tell you?" The elder appealed to the others. "Laertes was up to 83 no good with his sister's body. Hamlet prevented him, because the chief's heir, like a chief, does not wish any other man to grow rich and powerful. Laertes would be angry, because he would have killed his sister without benefit to himself. In our country he would try to kill Hamlet for that reason. Is this not what happened?"

"More or less," I admitted. "When the great chief found Hamlet was still 84 alive, he encouraged Laertes to try to kill Hamlet and arranged a fight with machetes between them. In the fight both the young men were wounded to death. Hamlet's mother drank the poisoned beer that the chief meant for Hamlet in case he won the fight. When he saw his mother die of poison, Hamlet, dying, managed to kill his father's brother with his machete."

"You see, I was right!" exclaimed the elder. 85

"That was a very good story," added the old man, "and you told it with very 86 few mistakes. There was just one more error, at the very end. The poison Hamlet's mother drank was obviously meant for the survivor of the fight, whichever it was. If Laertes had won, the great chief would have poisoned him, for no one would know that he arranged Hamlet's death. Then, too, he need not fear Laertes' witchcraft; it takes a strong heart to kill one's only sister by witchcraft."

"Sometime," concluded the old man, gathering his ragged toga about him, 87 "you must tell us some more stories of your country. We, who are elders, will instruct you in their true meaning, so that when you return to your own land your elders will see that you have not been sitting in the bush, but among those who know things and who have taught you wisdom."

EXERCISES

Some of the Issues

1. In paragraphs 1 and 2 Bohannan and a friend discuss human nature in relation to Shakespeare's *Hamlet*. What are their opinions?
2. Read paragraphs 3–6. What were Bohannan's expectations for her second field trip to the Tiv, and why were they mistaken? How do her plans change?
3. What is the significance of the discussion about "papers" in paragraphs 8 and 9? How does it foretell that the Tiv's interpretation of *Hamlet* may differ from Bohannan's (and ours)?
4. In a number of instances, Bohannan shows that she is knowledgeable about the social customs of the Tiv and is trying to conform to them. Give some specific instances.
5. In paragraphs 24–32 two differences between the Tiv and Western cultural presumptions are made clear: they relate to the period of mourning for the dead and to the number of wives a chief may have. In what way does the Tiv's view on these matters differ from Western views? Does their view have any advantages for their culture?
6. The Tiv elders are shocked—morally upset—at several parts of the story of *Hamlet*. What specific instances can you cite? Do their moral perceptions differ from ours in those instances?
7. Bohannan makes several efforts to make *Hamlet* more intelligible or acceptable to the Tiv. What are some of these? Does she succeed?
8. Both Bohannan (paragraph 2) and the chief (paragraph 76) say that human nature is much the same everywhere. What evidence do you find in the essay to support or contradict these assertions?

The Way We Are Told

9. Why does Bohannan begin her essay with the conversation with a friend at Oxford?
10. Several times in her essay Bohannan expresses surprise at the Tiv's reaction to her story. Is it possible that she was in reality not as surprised as she indicates?

Some Subjects for Writing

11. Bohannan does her best to adapt the story of Hamlet to the experiences, customs, and feelings of the Tiv. Have you ever had the experience of having to adapt yourself in some way to a situation in which the rules and assumptions differed greatly from your own? Tell the story.

12. Describe a particular American event or activity to someone who has never experienced it. Topics might be Thanksgiving, a rock concert, a barbeque, a commencement exercise.

*13. Read "A Modest Proposal" by Jonathan Swift. In an essay demonstrate that both Bohannan and Swift adopt poses in order to make their arguments effectively.

A Modest Proposal

JONATHAN SWIFT

Jonathan Swift (1667–1745) is the author of Gulliver's Travels *(1726).
Born in Dublin of a Protestant family in a Catholic country, he was
educated at Trinity College, Dublin, and Oxford University. He was
ordained in the Anglican Church and eventually became Dean of St.
Patrick's Cathedral in Dublin. One of the great satirists of English literature, he attacked religious as well as social and educational corruption in his books* A Tale of a Tub *and* Gulliver's Travels. *In his
"Modest Proposal" Swift addresses himself to the English absentee rul-
ers of Ireland.*

*"This great town" in the first paragraph refers to Dublin. The last
sentence of paragraph 1 refers to the practice of poor people commit-
ting themselves, usually for a fixed number of years, to service in a
military enterprise or in a colony (including the American colonies).*

A MODEST PROPOSAL

For Preventing the Children of Poor People in Ireland from Being a
Burden to Their Parents or Country, and for Making Them Beneficial
to the Public

1   It is a melancholy object to those who walk through this great town or travel in
the country, when they see the streets, the roads, and cabin doors, crowded with
beggars of the female sex, followed by three, four, or six children, all in rags and
importuning every passenger for an alms. These mothers, instead of being able
to work for their honest livelihood, are forced to employ all their time in stroll-
ing to beg sustenance for their helpless infants, who, as they grow up, either turn
thieves for want of work, or leave their dear native country to fight for the
Pretender[1] in Spain, or sell themselves to the Barbadoes.[2]

2   I think it is agreed by all parties that this prodigious number of children in
the arms, or on the backs, or at the heels of their mothers, and frequently of their
fathers, is in the present deplorable state of the kingdom a very great additional

[1]Reference to James Edward Stuart (1688–1766)—known as "the Old Pretender"—a Catholic
who laid claim to the British throne though he was exiled in France.
[2]Irish often sailed to Barbados and exchanged labor for their passage.

grievance; and therefore whoever could find out a fair, cheap, and easy method of making these children sound, useful members of the commonwealth would deserve so well of the public as to have his statue set up for a preserver of the nation.

But my intention is very far from being confined to provide only for the children of professed beggars; it is of a much greater extent, and shall take in the whole number of infants at a certain age who are born of parents in effect as little able to support them as those who demand our charity in the streets.

As to my own part, having turned my thoughts for many years upon this important subject, and maturely weighed the several schemes of other projectors, I have always found them grossly mistaken in their computation. It is true, a child just dropped from its dam may be supported by her milk for a solar year, with little other nourishment; at most not above the value of two shillings, which the mother may certainly get, or the value in scraps, by her lawful occupation of begging; and it is exactly at one year old that I propose to provide for them in such a manner as instead of being a charge upon their parents or the parish, or wanting food and raiment for the rest of their lives, they shall on the contrary contribute to the feeding, and partly to the clothing, of many thousands.

There is likewise another great advantage in my scheme, that it will prevent those voluntary abortions, and that horrid practice of women murdering their bastard children, alas, too frequent among us, sacrificing the poor innocent babes, I doubt, more to avoid the expense than the shame, which would move tears and pity in the most savage and inhuman breast.

The number of souls in this kingdom being usually reckoned one million and a half, of these I calculate there may be about two hundred thousand couples whose wives are breeders; from which number I subtract thirty thousand couples who are able to maintain their own children, although I apprehend there cannot be so many under the present distress of the kingdom; but this being granted, there will remain an hundred and seventy thousand breeders. I again subtract fifty thousand for those women who miscarry, or whose children die by accident or disease within the year. There only remain an hundred and twenty thousand children of poor parents annually born. The question therefore is, how this number shall be reared and provided for, which, as I have already said, under the present situation of affairs, is utterly impossible by all the methods hitherto proposed. For we can neither employ them in handicraft nor agriculture; we neither build houses (I mean in the country) nor cultivate land. They can very seldom pick up a livelihood by stealing till they arrive at six years old, except where they are of towardly parts; although I confess they learn the rudiments much earlier, during which time they can however be looked upon only as probationers, as I have been informed by a principal gentleman in the country of Cavan, who protested to me that he never knew above one or two instances under the age of six, even in a part of the kingdom so renowned for the quickest proficiency in that art.

7   I am assured by our merchants that a boy or a girl before twelve years old is no salable commodity; and even when they come to this age, they will not yield above three pounds, or three pounds and half a crown at most on the Exchange; which cannot turn to account either to the parents or the kingdom, the charge of nutriment and rags having been at least four times that value.

8   I shall now therefore humbly propose my own thoughts, which I hope will not be liable to the least objection.

9   I have been assured by a very knowing American of my acquaintance in London, that a young healthy child well nursed is at a year old a most delicious, nourishing, and wholesome food, whether stewed, roasted, baked, or boiled; and I make not doubt that it will equally serve in a fricassee or a ragout.

10   I do therefore humbly offer it to public consideration that of the hundred and twenty thousand children, already computed, twenty thousand may be reserved for breed, whereof only one fourth part to be males, which is more than we allow to sheep, black cattle, or swine; and my reason is that these children are seldom the fruits of marriage, a circumstance not much regarded by our savages, therefore one male will be sufficient to serve four females. That the remaining hundred thousand may at a year old be offered in sale to the persons of quality and fortune through the kingdom, always advising the mother to let them suck plentifully in the last month, so as to render them plump and fat for a good table. A child will make two dishes at an entertainment for friends; and when the family dines alone, the fore or hind quarter will make a reasonable dish, and seasoned with a little pepper or salt will be very good boiled on the fourth day, especially in winter.

11   I have reckoned upon a medium that a child just born will weigh twelve pounds, and in a solar year if tolerably nursed increaseth to twenty-eight pounds.

12   I grant this food will be somewhat dear, and therefore very proper for land-lords, who, as they have already devoured most of the parents, seem to have the best title to the children.

13   Infant's flesh will be in season throughout the year, but more plentiful in March, and a little before and after. For we are told by a grave author, an eminent French physician, that fish being a prolific diet, there are more children born in Roman Catholic countries about nine months after Lent, than at any other season; therefore, reckoning a year after Lent, the markets will be more glutted than usual, because the number of popish infants is at least three to one in this kingdom; and therefore it will have one other collateral advantage, by lessening the number of Papists among us.

14   I have already computed the charge of nursing a beggar's child (in which list I reckon all cottagers, laborers, and four fifths of the farmers) to be about two shillings per annum, rags included; and I believe no gentleman would repine to give ten shillings for the carcass of a good fat child, which, as I have said, will make four dishes of excellent nutritive meat, when he hath only some particular friend or his own family to dine with him. Thus the squire will learn to be a

good landlord, and grow popular among the tenants; the mother will have eight shillings net profit, and be fit for work till she produces another child.

Those who are more thrifty (as I must confess the times require) may flay   15 the carcass; the skin of which artificially dressed will make admirable gloves for ladies, and summer boots for fine gentlemen.

As to our city of Dublin, shambles[3] may be appointed for this purpose in   16 the most convenient parts of it, and butchers we may be assured will not be wanting; although I rather recommend buying the children alive, and dressing them hot from the knife as we do roasting pigs.

A very worthy person, a true lover of this country, and whose virtues I   17 highly esteem, was lately pleased in discoursing on this matter to offer a refinement upon my scheme. He said that many gentlemen of his kingdom, having of late destroyed their deer, he conceived that the want of venison might be well supplied by the bodies of young lads and maidens, not exceeding fourteen years of age nor under twelve, so great a number of both sexes in every county being now ready to starve for want of work and service; and these to be disposed of by their parents, if alive, or otherwise by their nearest relations. But with due deference to so excellent a friend and so deserving a patriot, I cannot be altogether in his sentiments; for as to the males, my American acquaintance assured me from frequent experience that their flesh was generally tough and lean, like that of our schoolboys, by continual exercise, and their taste disagreeable; and to fatten them would not answer the charge. Then as to the females, it would, I think with humble submission, be a loss to the public, because they soon would become breeders themselves; and besides, it is not improbable that some scrupulous people might be apt to censure such a practice (although indeed very unjustly) as a little bordering upon cruelty; which, I confess, hath always been with me the strongest objection against any project, how well soever intended.

But in order to justify my friend, he confessed that this expedient was put   18 into his head by the famous Psalmanazar, a native of the island Formosa, who came from thence to London above twenty years ago, and in conversation told my friend that in his country when any young person happened to be put to death, the executioner sold the carcass to the persons of quality as a prime dainty; and that in his time the body of a plump girl of fifteen, who was crucified for an attempt to poison the emperor, was sold to his Imperial Majesty's prime minister of state, and other great mandarins of the court, in joints from the gibbet, at four hundred crowns. Neither indeed can I deny that if the same use were made of several plump young girls in this town, who without one single groat to their fortunes cannot stir abroad without a chair,[4] and appear at the playhouse and assemblies in foreign fineries which they never will pay for, the kingdom would not be the worse.

---

[3] Slaughterhouses.
[4] A portable chair carried by two people on foot.

19   Some persons of a desponding spirit are in great concern about that vast number of poor people who are aged, diseased, or maimed, and I have been desired to employ my thoughts what course may be taken to ease the nation of so grievous an encumbrance. But I am not in the least pain upon that matter, because it is very well known that they are every day dying and rotting by cold and famine, and filth and vermin, as fast as can be reasonably expected. And as to the younger laborers, they are now in almost as hopeful a condition. They cannot get work, and consequently pine away for want of nourishment to a degree that if any time they are accidentally hired to common labor, they have not strength to perform it; and thus the country and themselves are happily delivered from the evils to come.

20   I have too long digressed, and therefore shall return to my subject. I think the advantages by the proposal which I have made are obvious and many, as well as of the highest importance.

21   For first, as I have already observed, it would greatly lessen the number of Papists, with whom we are yearly overrun, being the principal breeders of the nation as well as our most dangerous enemies; and who stay at home on purpose to deliver the kingdom to the Pretender, hoping to take their advantage by the absence of so many good Protestants, who have chosen rather to leave their country than to stay at home and pay tithes against their conscience to an Episcopal curate.

22   Secondly, the poorer tenants will have something valuable of their own, which by law may be made liable to distress, and help to pay their landlord's rent, their corn and cattle being already seized and money a thing unknown.

23   Thirdly, whereas the maintenance of an hundred thousand children, from two years old and upwards, cannot be computed at less than ten shillings a piece per annum, the nation's stock will be thereby increased fifty thousand pounds per annum, besides the profit of a new dish introduced to the tables of all gentlemen of fortune in the kingdom who have any refinement in taste. And the money will circulate among ourselves, the goods being entirely of our own growth and manufacture.

24   Fourthly, the constant breeders, besides the gain of eight shillings sterling per annum by the sale of their children, will be rid of the charge for maintaining them after the first year.

25   Fifthly, this food would likewise bring great custom to taverns, where the vintners will certainly be so prudent as to procure the best receipts for dressing it to perfection, and consequently have their houses frequented by all the fine gentlemen, who justly value themselves upon their knowledge in good eating; and a skillful cook, who understands how to oblige his guests, will contrive to make it as expensive as they please.

26   Sixthly, this would be a great inducement to marriage, which all wise nations have either encouraged by rewards or enforced by laws and penalties. it would increase the care and tenderness of mothers toward their children, when they

were sure of a settlement for life to the poor babes, provided in some sort by the public, to their annual profit instead of expense. We should see an honest emulation among the married women, which of them could bring the fattest child to the market. Men would become as fond of their wives during the time of their pregnancy as they are now of their mares in foal, their cows in calf, or sows when they are ready to farrow; nor offer to beat or kick them (as is too frequent a practice) for fear of a miscarriage.

Many other advantages might be enumerated. For instance, the addition of some thousand carcasses in our exportation of barreled beef, the propagation of swine's flesh, and improvements in the art of making good bacon, so much wanted among us by the great destruction of pigs, too frequent at our tables, which are no way comparable in taste or magnificence to a well-grown, fat, yearling child, which roasted whole will make a considerable figure at a lord mayor's feast or any other public entertainment. But this and many others I omit, being studious of brevity.   27

Supposing that one thousand families in this city would be constant customers for infants' flesh, besides others who might have it at merry meetings, particularly weddings and christenings, I compute that Dublin would take off annually about twenty thousand carcasses, and the rest of the kingdom (where probably they will be sold somewhat cheaper) the remaining eighty thousand.   28

I can think of no one objection that will possibly be raised against this proposal, unless it should be urged that the number of people will be thereby much lessened in the kingdom. This I freely own, and it was indeed one principal design in offering it to the world. I desire the reader will observe, and I calculate my remedy for this one individual kingdom of Ireland and for no other that ever was, is, or I think ever can be upon earth. Therefore, let no man talk to me of other expedients: of taxing our absentees at five shillings a pound: of using neither clothes nor household furniture except what is of our own growth and manufacture: of utterly rejecting the materials and instruments that promote foreign luxury: of curing the expensiveness of pride, vanity, idleness, and gaming in our women: of introducing a vein of parsimony, prudence, and temperance: of learning to love our country, in the want of which we differ even from Laplanders and the inhabitants of Topinamboo: of quitting our animosities and factions, nor acting any longer like the Jews, who were murdering one another at the very moment their city was taken: of being a little cautious not to sell our country and conscience for nothing: of teaching landlords to have at least one degree of mercy toward their tenants: lastly, of putting a spirit of honesty, industry, and skill into our shopkeepers; who, if a resolution could not be taken to buy only our native goods, would immediately unite to cheat and exact upon us in the price, the measure, and the goodness, nor could ever yet be brought to make one fair proposal of just dealing, though often and earnestly invited to it.   29

Therefore, I repeat, let no man talk to me of these and the like expedients, til he hath at least some glimpse of hope that there will ever be some hearty and sincere attempt to put them in practice.   30

31   But as to myself, having been wearied out for many years with offering vain, idle, visionary thoughts, and at length utterly despairing of success, I fortunately fell upon this proposal, which, as it is wholly new, so it hath something solid and real, of no expense and little trouble, full in our own power, and whereby we can incur no danger in disobliging England. For this kind of commodity will not bear exportation, the flesh being of too tender a consistence to admit a long continuance in salt, although perhaps I could name a country which would be glad to eat up our whole nation without it.

32   After all, I am not so violently bent upon my own opinion as to reject any offer proposed by wise men, which shall be found equally innocent, cheap, easy, and effectual. But before something of that kind shall be advanced in contradiction to my scheme, and offering a better, I desire the author or authors will be pleased maturely to consider two points. First, as things now stand, how they will be able to find food and raiment for an hundred thousand useless mouths and backs. And secondly, there being a round million of creatures in human figure throughout this kingdom, whose sole subsistence put into a common stock would leave them in debt two millions of pounds sterling, adding those who are beggars by profession to the bulk of farmers, cottagers, and laborers, with their wives and children who are beggars in effect; I desire those politicians who dislike my overture, and may perhaps be so bold to attempt an answer, that they will first ask the parents of these mortals whether they would not at this day think it a great happiness to have been sold for food at a year old in this manner I prescribe, and thereby have avoided such a perpetual scene of misfortunes as they have since gone through by the oppression of landlords, the impossibility of paying rent without money or trade, the want of common sustenance, with neither house nor clothes to cover them from the inclemencies of the weather, and the most inevitable prospect of entailing the like or greater miseries upon their breed forever.

33   I profess, in the sincerity of my heart, that I have not the least personal interest in endeavoring to promote this necessary work, having no other motive than the public good of my country, by advancing our trade, providing for infants, relieving the poor, and giving some pleasure to the rich. I have no children by which I can propose to get a single penny; the youngest being nine years old, and my wife past childbearing.

EXERCISES

Some of the Issues

1. Paragraphs 1–6 are an introduction. What is the main point the author wants to make?
2. Paragraph 7 is a transition. Before you have read the rest, what might it foretell?

3. The short paragraph 8 is the beginning of the real proposal; and paragraph 9, its central idea. Explain that idea.
4. Paragraph 10 expands the proposal in 9. It relates in particular to paragraph 6. Why are all these statistical calculations important? What do they contribute to the impact of the essay?
5. Look back to paragraph 5. What hints of the idea to come do you now find in it?
6. Paragraphs 15 through 17 offer refinements on the main theme. What are they?
7. Examine the logic of each of the advantages of the proposal, as listed in paragraphs 21 through 26. Why is the lessening of the number of Papists a particular advantage?
8. In paragraph 29, when the essay turns to possible objections, which are the ones that are omitted completely? Why? Why does the narrator so vehemently concentrate on Ireland in this paragraph?
9. In paragraph 29 other remedies are also proposed for solving the plight of Ireland. What distinguishes them from the one the narrator is advocating?

The Way We Are Told

10. Readers of this essay will for a time take Swift's observations at face value. At what point in the essay are they likely to change their minds?
11. Swift creates a narrator whose modest proposal this is. Try to imagine him: What kind of person might he be? What might be his profession? Consider some of the phrases he uses, his obsession with statistics and the financial aspects of the problem, and his attention to detail.
12. In paragraph 4, in the narrator's choice of words, you find the first hint of what is to come. Locate it. Do you find an echo in paragraph 6?
13. Having made his proposal boldly in paragraph 9, the narrator develops it in paragraphs 10 through 14. Paragraphs 15 through 17 heighten the effect. Consider the choice of images in these paragraphs.

Some Subjects for Writing

14. Do you have any modest proposals as to what to do with teachers, younger brothers or sisters, former boyfriends or girlfriends, or anyone else?
15. Write an essay in which you attempt to change somebody's mind. You may use irony, as Swift does, exaggerating the consequences of the other side's position. Or you may write more objectively, proposing a real solution to the problem. Your challenge, a difficult one, is to get a person who disagrees with you to take your argument seriously.

Shooting an Elephant

GEORGE ORWELL

George Orwell (the pseudonym of Eric Arthur Blair) was an English journalist, critic, and novelist. Born in 1903 in India, he was educated in England at Eton College. He served with the Indian Imperial Police in Burma from 1922 to 1927. This essay is based on his experience there.

Orwell returned to England in 1927 and turned to writing but with little success. He lived in great poverty for some time, as described in his first published book, Down and Out in Paris and London *(1933). In the mid-1930s he fought on the side of the Republic in the Spanish Civil War, was wounded and wrote of his experience in* Homage to Catalonia *(1938). Success finally came late in his life with* Animal Farm *(1945) and* 1984, *both of which expressed his concerns about totalitarian governments.* 1984 *was published in 1949, the year before his death from tuberculosis.*

In Orwell's time, Burma was a part of the Indian Empire under British rule. When India gained independence in 1947, Burma became a separate, sovereign state. About the size of Texas with a population of 40 million, this country, now called Myanmar, is ruled by a heavy-handed military dictatorship, and is largely closed off from the rest of the world.

In 1988, under international pressure, free elections were held, but the party winning 80 percent of the vote was not allowed to take power. The following year a pro-democracy uprising was brutally put down. One of the leaders of the uprising was Aung San Suu Kyi, winner of the Nobel Peace Prize in 1991.

1   In Moulmein, in lower Burma, I was hated by large numbers of people—the only time in my life that I have been important enough for this to happen to me. I was sub-divisional police officer of the town, and in an aimless, petty kind of way anti-European feeling was very bitter. No one had the guts to raise a riot, but if a European woman went through the bazaars alone somebody would probably spit betel juice over her dress. As a police officer I was an obvious target and was baited whenever it seemed safe to do so. When a nimble Burman tripped me up on the football field and the referee (another Burman) looked the other way, the crowd yelled with hideous laughter. This happened more than

once. In the end the sneering yellow faces of young men that met me every-where, the insults hooted after me when I was at a safe distance, got badly on my nerves. The young Buddhist priests were the worst of all. There were several thousands of them in the town and none of them seemed to have anything to do except stand on street corners and jeer at Europeans.

All this was perplexing and upsetting. For at that time I had already made   2
up my mind that imperialism was an evil thing and the sooner I chucked up my job and got out of it the better. Theoretically—and secretly, of course—I was all for the Burmese and all against their oppressors, the British. As for the job I was doing, I hated it more bitterly than I can perhaps make clear. In a job like that you see the dirty work of Empire at close quarters. The wretched prisoners hud-dling in the stinking cages of the lockups, the grey, cowed faces of the long-term convicts, the scarred buttocks of the men who had been flogged with bamboos—all these oppressed me with an intolerable sense of guilt. But I could get nothing into perspective. I was young and ill-educated and I had had to think out my problems in the utter silence that is imposed on every Englishman in the East. I did not even know that the British Empire is dying, still less did I know that it is a great deal better than the younger empires that are going to supplant it. All I knew was that I was stuck between my hatred of the empire I served and my rage against the evil-spirited little beasts who tried to make my job impos-sible. With one part of my mind I thought of the British Raj[1] as an unbreakable tyranny, as something clamped down, in *saecula saeculorum,*[2] upon the will of prostrate peoples; with another part I thought that the greatest joy in the world would be to drive a bayonet into a Buddhist priest's guts. Feelings like these are the normal by-products of imperialism; ask any Anglo-Indian official, if you can catch him off duty.

One day something happened which in a roundabout way was enlightening.   3
It was a tiny incident in itself, but it gave me a better glimpse than I had had before of the real nature of imperialism—the real motives for which despotic governments act. Early one morning the sub-inspector at a police station the other end of the town rang me up on the 'phone and said that an elephant was ravaging the bazaar. Would I please come and do something about it? I did not know what I could do, but I wanted to see what was happening and I got on to a pony and started out. I took my rifle, an old .44 Winchester and much too small to kill an elephant, but I thought the noise might be useful *in terrorem.*[3] Various Burmans stopped me on the way and told me about the elephant's doings. It was not, of course, a wild elephant, but a tame one which had gone "must." It had been chained up, as tame elephants always are when their attack of "must" is due, but on the previous night it had broken its chain and escaped.

[1]British rule over India, Pakistan, and Burma until 1947. (Raj is the Hindi word for reign.)
[2]For all time.
[3]To spread terror.

Its mahout,[4] the only person who could manage it when it was in that state, had set out in pursuit, but had taken the wrong direction and was now twelve hours' journey away, and in the morning the elephant had suddenly reappeared in the town. The Burmese population had no weapons and were quite helpless against it. It had already destroyed somebody's bamboo hut, killed a cow and raided some fruit-stalls and devoured the stock; also it had met the municipal rubbish van and, when the driver jumped out and took to his heels, had turned the van over and inflicted violences upon it.

4   The Burmese sub-inspector and some Indian constables were waiting for me in the quarter where the elephant had been seen. It was a very poor quarter, a labyrinth of squalid bamboo huts, thatched with palm-leaf, winding all over a steep hillside. I remember that it was a cloudy, stuffy morning at the beginning of the rains. We began questioning the people as to where the elephant had gone and, as usual, failed to get any definite information. That is invariably the case in the East; a story always sounds clear enough at a distance, but the nearer you get to the scene of events the vaguer it becomes. Some of the people said that the elephant had gone in one direction, some said that he had gone in another, some professed not even to have heard of any elephant. I had almost made up my mind that the whole story was a pack of lies, when we heard yells a little distance away. There was a loud, scandalized cry of "Go away, child! Go away this instant!" and an old woman with a switch in her hand came round the corner of a hut, violently shooing away a crowd of naked children. Some more women followed, clicking their tongues and exclaiming; evidently there was something that the children ought not to have seen. I rounded the hut and saw a man's dead body sprawling in the mud. He was an Indian, a black Dravidian coolie,[5] almost naked, and he could not have been dead many minutes. The people said that the elephant had come suddenly upon him round the corner of the hut, caught him with its trunk, put its foot on his back and ground him into the earth. This was the rainy season and the ground was soft; and his face had scored a trench a foot deep and a couple yards long. He was lying on his belly with arms crucified and head sharply twisted to one side. His face was coated with mud, the eyes wide open, the teeth bared and grinning with an expression of unendurable agony. (Never tell me, by the way, that the dead look peaceful. Most of the corpses I have seen looked devilish.) The friction of the great beast's foot had stripped the skin from his back as neatly as one skins a rabbit. As soon as I saw the dead man I sent an orderly to a friend's house nearby to borrow an elephant rifle. I had already sent back the pony, not wanting it to go mad with fright and throw me if it smelt the elephant.

5   The orderly came back in a few minutes with a rifle and five cartridges, and meanwhile some Burmans had arrived and told us that the elephant was in the

[4]Elephant keeper and driver.
[5]Native laborer of south India.

paddy fields below, only a few hundred yards away. As I started forward practically the whole population of the quarter flocked out of the houses and followed me. They had seen the rifle and were all shouting excitedly that I was going to shoot the elephant. They had not shown much interest in the elephant when he was merely ravaging their homes, but it was different now that he was going to be shot. It was a bit of fun to them, as it would be to an English crowd; besides they wanted the meat. It made me vaguely uneasy. I had no intention of shooting the elephant—I had merely sent for the rifle to defend myself if necessary—and it is always unnerving to have a crowd following you. I marched down the hill, looking and feeling a fool, with the rifle over my shoulder and an ever-growing army of people jostling at my heels. At the bottom, when you got away from the huts, there was a metalled road and beyond that a miry waste of paddy fields a thousand yards across, not yet ploughed but soggy from the first rains and dotted with coarse grass. The elephant was standing eight yards from the road, his left side towards us. He took not the slightest notice of the crowd's approach. He was tearing up bunches of grass, beating them against his knees to clean them and stuffing them into his mouth.

I had halted on the road. As soon as I saw the elephant I knew with perfect certainty that I ought not to shoot him. It is a serious matter to shoot a working elephant—it is comparable to destroying a huge and costly piece of machinery—and obviously one ought not to do it if it can possibly be avoided. And at that distance, peacefully eating, the elephant looked no more dangerous than a cow. I thought then and I think now that his attack of "must" was already passing off; in which case he would merely wander harmlessly about until the mahout came back and caught him. Moreover, I did not in the least want to shoot him. I decided that I would watch him for a little while to make sure that he did not turn savage again, and then go home. 6

But at that moment I glanced round at the crowd that had followed me. It was an immense crowd, two thousand at the least and growing every minute. It blocked the road for a long distance on either side. I looked at the sea of yellow faces above the garish clothes—faces all happy and excited over this bit of fun, all certain that the elephant was going to be shot. They were watching me as they would watch a conjurer about to perform a trick. They did not like me, but with the magical rifle in my hands I was momentarily worth watching. And suddenly I realized that I should have to shoot the elephant after all. The people expected it of me and I had got to do it; I could feel their two thousand wills pressing me forward, irresistibly. And it was at this moment, as I stood there with the rifle in my hands, that I first grasped the hollowness, the futility of the white man's dominion in the East. Here was I, the white man with his gun, standing in front of the unarmed native crowd—seemingly the leading actor of the piece; but in reality I was only an absurd puppet pushed to and fro by the will of those yellow faces behind. I perceived in this moment that when the white man turns tyrant it is his own freedom that he destroys. He becomes a 7 sort of hollow, posing dummy, the conventionalized figure of a sahib.[6] For it is the condition of his rule that he shall spend his life in trying to impress the "natives," and so in every crisis he has got to do what the "natives" expect of him. He wears a mask, and his face grows to fit it. I had got to shoot the elephant. I had committed myself to doing it when I sent for the rifle. A sahib has got to act like a sahib; he has got to appear resolute, to know his own mind and do definite things. To come all that way, rifle in hand, with two thousand people marching at my heels, and then to trail feebly away, having done nothing—no, that was impossible. The crowd would laugh at me. And my whole life, every white man's life in the East, was one long struggle not to be laughed at.

8   But I did not want to shoot the elephant. I watched him beating his bunch of grass against his knees, with that preoccupied grandmotherly air that elephants have. It seemed to me that it would be murder to shoot him. At that age I was not squeamish about killing animals, but I had never shot an elephant and never wanted to. (Somehow it always seems worse to kill a *large* animal.) Besides, there was the beast's owner to be considered. Alive, the elephant was worth at least a hundred pounds; dead, he would only be worth the value of his tusks, five pounds, possibly. But I had got to act quickly. I turned to some experienced-looking Burmans who had been there when we arrived, and asked them how the elephant had been behaving. They all said the same thing: he took no notice of you if you left him alone, but he might charge if you went too close to him.

9   It was perfectly clear to me what I ought to do. I ought to walk up to within, say, twenty-five yards of the elephant and test his behavior. If he charged, I could shoot; if he took no notice of me, it would be safe to leave him until the mahout came back. But also I knew that I was going to do no such thing. I was a poor shot with a rifle and the ground was soft mud into which one would sink at every step. If the elephant charged and I missed him, I should have about as much chance as a toad under a steam-roller. But even then I was not thinking particularly of my own skin, only of the watchful yellow faces behind. For at that moment, with the crowd watching me, I was not afraid in the ordinary sense, as I would have been if I had been alone. A white man mustn't be frightened in front of "natives"; and so, in general, he isn't frightened. The sole thought in my mind was that if anything went wrong those two thousand Burmans would see me pursued, caught, trampled on and reduced to a grinning corpse like that Indian up the hill. And if that happened it was quite probable that some of them would laugh. That would never do. There was only one alternative. I shoved the cartridges into the magazine and lay down on the road to get a better aim.

10   The crowd grew very still, and a deep, low, happy sigh, as of people who see the theatre curtain go up at last, breathed from innumerable throats. They were going to have their bit of fun after all. The rifle was a beautiful German thing with cross-hair sights. I did not then know that in shooting an elephant one

[6]Term formerly used by inhabitants of colonial India to address Europeans.

would shoot to cut an imaginary bar running from ear-hole to ear-hole. I ought, therefore, as the elephant was sideways on, to have aimed straight at his ear-hole; actually I aimed several inches in front of this, thinking the brain would be further forward.

When I pulled the trigger I did not hear the bang or feel the kick—one 11 never does when a shot goes home—but I heard the devilish roar of glee that went up from the crowd. In that instant, in too short a time, one would have thought, even for the bullet to get there, a mysterious, terrible change had come over the elephant. He neither stirred nor fell, but every line of his body had altered. He looked suddenly stricken, shrunken, immensely old, as though the frightful impact of the bullet had paralysed him without knocking him down. At last, after what seemed a long time—it might have been five seconds, I dare say—he sagged flabbily to his knees. His mouth slobbered. An enormous senility seemed to have settled upon him. One could have imagined him thousands of years old. I fired again into the same spot. At the second shot he did not collapse but climbed with desperate slowness to his feet and stood weakly upright, with legs sagging and head drooping. I fired a third time. That was the shot that did for him. You could see the agony of it jolt his whole body and knock the last remnant of strength from his legs. But in falling he seemed for a moment to rise, for as his hind legs collapsed beneath him he seemed to tower upward like a huge rock toppling, his trunk reaching skywards like a tree. He trumpeted, for the first and only time. And then down he came, his belly towards me, with a crash that seemed to shake the ground even where I lay.

I got up. The Burmans were already racing past me across the mud. It was 12 obvious that the elephant would never rise again, but he was not dead. He was breathing very rhythmically with long rattling gasps, his great mound of a side painfully rising and falling. His mouth was wide open—I could see far down into caverns of pale pink throat. I waited a long time for him to die, but his breathing did not weaken. Finally I fired my two remaining shots into the spot where I thought his heart must be. The thick blood welled out of him like red velvet, but still he did not die. His body did not even jerk when the shots hit him, the tortured breathing continued without a pause. He was dying, very slowly and in great agony, but in some world remote from me where not even a bullet could damage him further. I felt that I had got to put an end to that dreadful noise. It seemed dreadful to see the great beast lying there, powerless to move and yet powerless to die, and not even to be able to finish him. I send back for my small rifle and poured shot after shot into his heart and down his throat. They seemed to make no impression. The tortured gasps continued as steadily as the ticking of a clock.

In the end I could not stand it any longer and went away. I heard later that 13 it took him half an hour to die. Burmans were bringing dahs[7] and baskets even

---

[7]Large heavy knives used in Burma.

before I left, and I was told they had stripped his body almost to the bones by the afternoon.

14   Afterwards, of course, there were endless discussions about the shooting of the elephant. The owner was furious, but he was only an Indian and could do nothing. Besides, legally I had done the right thing, for a mad elephant has to be killed, like a mad dog, if its owner fails to control it. Among the Europeans opinion was divided. The older men said I was right, the younger men said it was a damn shame to shoot an elephant for killing a coolie, because an elephant was worth more than any damn Coringhee coolie. And afterwards I was very glad that the coolie had been killed; it put me legally in the right and it gave me a sufficient pretext for shooting the elephant. I often wondered whether any of the others grasped that I had done it solely to avoid looking a fool.

EXERCISES

Some of the Issues

1. Before Orwell begins to tell the story of the shooting of the elephant, he uses two paragraphs to talk about feelings: the feelings of the Burmese toward him as a colonial officer, and his own "perplexing and upsetting" feelings toward the Burmese. Why are Orwell's feelings complex and contradictory? How does this discussion of attitudes set the scene for the narrative that follows?

2. The main topic or theme of the essay is stated in the first few sentences of paragraph 3. After reading the whole essay, explain why the incident Orwell describes gave him "a better glimpse…of the real nature of imperialism." What, according to Orwell, are "the real motives for which despotic governments act"?

3. In paragraph 7 Orwell says, "I perceived in this moment that when the white man turns tyrant it is his own freedom that he destroys." Explain the meaning of this sentence; how does it apply to the story Orwell tells?

The Way We Are Told

4. When Orwell begins to tell the story of the elephant, in paragraph 3, he continues to reveal his attitude toward the Burmese in various indirect ways. Try to show how he does this.

5. In paragraph 4 Orwell describes the dead coolie in considerable detail. Later, in paragraphs 11 and 12, he goes on to describe the elephant's death in even greater detail. Compare the two descriptions.

6. In paragraphs 5–9 Orwell discusses his plans and options regarding the elephant. Paragraphs 5 and 6, however, differ greatly from 7, 8, and 9, in both content and treatment. Characterize the difference.

7. The largest section of Orwell's essay describes an event that takes place within a short period of time. Estimate the time lapse from the moment Orwell sent for the rifle (end of paragraph 4) to the moment he turns away (paragraph 13).
8. Consider Orwell's tone in the last paragraph. What evidence is there that he is being ironic?

Some Subjects for Writing

9. In paragraphs 11 and 12 Orwell describes in detail an event that took only a few minutes. The abundance of sensory detail about the incident brings us closer to seeing it as Orwell did. Recall a dramatic moment in your life, a time when you needed to act quickly. Recreate that moment in writing by giving details about what you saw, heard, felt, and smelled. Try to bring the reader there.
10. Have you ever been placed in a situation in which you were forced to do something that you did not entirely agree with? For example, an employee must often carry out the policies of his or her employer even while disagreeing with them. Write an essay describing such an incident and detail your feelings before, during, and after.
11. Orwell is placed in a position of authority but finds that it restricts his scope of action rather than expands it. Write an essay that asserts the truth of this apparent contradiction. Try to find examples of other situations in which the possession of power limits the possessor.

On Seeing England for the First Time

JAMAICA KINCAID

Jamaica Kincaid was born Elaine Potter Richardson in St. Johns, Antigua, in 1949; she left that country at seventeen to become an au pair (a live-in babysitter) in New York City. She did not return to Antigua to visit until almost twenty years later.

Kincaid is the author of three novels: Annie John *(1985),* Lucy *(1990), and* Autobiography of My Mother *(1996), and a book of short stories,* At the Bottom of the River. *She is also the author of* A Small Place *(1988), a long essay about Antigua in which she explores the effects of colonialism and how the rule of the British Empire has shaped the identity of her native country and its people.*

Antigua is an independent island state in the eastern Caribbean. The country was colonized in 1632, when the British established a settlement there. It remained a British colony until it became an internally self-governing state in association with Great Britain in 1967, and declared its independence in 1981.

Like A Small Place, *"On Seeing England for the First Time" explores the moral, psychological, cultural, and economic devastation brought on by the rule of a colonial power. The essay describes Kincaid's experience of first visiting England as an adult, comparing her experience of that country to the familiarity she had consciously or unconsciously absorbed by growing up under British rule.*

1   When I saw England for the first time, I was a child in school sitting at a desk. The England I was looking at was laid out on a map gently, beautifully, delicately, a very special jewel; it lay on a bed of sky blue—the background of the map—its yellow form mysterious, because though it looked like a leg of mutton, it could not really look like anything so familiar as a leg of mutton because it was England—with shadings of pink and green, unlike any shadings of pink and green I had seen before, squiggly veins of red running in every direction. England was a special jewel all right, and only special people got to wear it. The people who got to wear England were English people. They wore it well and they wore it everywhere: in jungles, in deserts, on plains, on top of the highest

mountains, on all the oceans, on all the seas, in places where they were not welcome, in places they should not have been. When my teacher had pinned this map up on the blackboard, she said, "This is England"—and she said it with authority, seriousness, and adoration, and we all sat up. It was as if she had said, "This is Jerusalem, the place you will go to when you die but only if you have been good." We understood then—we were meant to understand then—that England was to be our source of myth and the source from which we got our sense of reality, our sense of what was meaningful, our sense of what was meaningless—and much about our own lives and much about the very idea of us headed that last list.

At the time I was a child sitting at my desk seeing England for the first time,   2 I was already very familiar with the greatness of it. Each morning before I left for school, I ate a breakfast of half a grapefruit, an egg, bread and butter and a slice of cheese, and a cup of cocoa; or half a grapefruit, a bowl of oat porridge, bread and butter and a slice of cheese, and a cup of cocoa. The can of cocoa was often left on the table in front of me. It had written on it the name of the company, the year the company was established, and the words "Made in England." Those words, "Made in England," were written on the box the oats came in too. They would also have been written on the box the shoes I was wearing came in; a bolt of gray linen cloth lying on the shelf of a store from which my mother had bought three yards to make the uniform that I was wearing had written along its edge those three words. The shoes I wore were made in England; so were my socks and cotton undergarments and the satin ribbons I wore tied at the end of two plaits of my hair. My father, who might have sat next to me at breakfast, was a carpenter and cabinet maker. The shoes he wore to work would have been made in England, as were his khaki shirt and trousers, his underpants and undershirt, his socks and brown felt hat. Felt was not the proper material from which a hat that was expected to provide shade from the hot sun should be made, but my father must have seen and admired a picture of an Englishman wearing such a hat in England, and this picture that he saw must have been so compelling that it caused him to wear the wrong hat for a hot climate most of his long life. And this hat—a brown felt hat—became so central to his character that it was the first thing he put on in the morning as he stepped out of bed and the last thing he took off before he stepped back into bed at night. As we sat at breakfast a car might go by. The car, a Hillman or a Zephyr, was made in England. The very idea of the meal itself, breakfast, and its substantial quality and quantity was an idea from England; we somehow knew that in England they began the day with this meal called breakfast and a proper breakfast was a big breakfast. No one I knew liked eating so much food so early in the day; it made us feel sleepy, tired. But this breakfast business was Made in England like almost everything else that surrounded us, the exceptions being the sea, the sky, and the air we breathed.

At the time I saw this map—seeing England for the first time—I did not say   3 to myself, "Ah, so that's what it looks like," because there was no longing in me to put a shape to those three words that ran through every part of my life, no matter how small; for me to have had such a longing would have meant that I lived in a certain atmosphere, an atmosphere in which those three words were felt as a burden. But I did not live in such an atmosphere. My father's brown felt hat would develop a hole in its crown, the lining would separate from the hat itself, and six weeks before he thought that he could not be seen wearing it—he was a very vain man—he would order another hat from England. And my mother taught me to eat my food in the English way: the knife in the right hand, the fork in the left, my elbows held still close to my side, the food carefully balanced on my fork and then brought up to my mouth. When I had finally mastered it, I overheard her saying to a friend, "Did you see how nicely she can eat?" But I knew then that I enjoyed my food more when I ate it with my bare hands, and I continued to do so when she wasn't looking. And when my teacher showed us the map, she asked us to study it carefully, because no test we would ever take would be complete without this statement: "Draw a map of England."

4   I did not know then that the statement "Draw a map of England" was something far worse than a declaration of war, for in fact a flat-out declaration of war would have put me on alert, and again in fact, there was no need for war—I had long ago been conquered. I did not know then that this statement was part of a process that would result in my erasure, not my physical erasure, but my erasure all the same. I did not know then that this statement was meant to make me feel in awe and small whenever I heard the word "England": awe at its existence, small because I was not from it. I did not know very much of anything then—certainly not what a blessing it was that I was unable to draw a map of England correctly.

5   After that there were many times of seeing England for the first time. I saw England in history. I knew the names of all the kings of England. I knew the names of their children, their wives, their disappointments, their triumphs, the names of people who betrayed them, I knew the dates on which they were born and the dates they died. I knew their conquests and was made to feel glad if I figured in them; I knew their defeats. I knew the details of the year 1066 (the Battle of Hastings, the end of the reign of the Anglo-Saxon kings) before I knew the details of the year 1832 (the year slavery was abolished). It wasn't as bad as I make it sound now; it was worse. I did like so much hearing again and again how Alfred the Great, traveling in disguise, had been left to watch cakes, and because he wasn't used to this the cakes got burned, and Alfred burned his hands pulling them out of the fire, and the woman who had left him to watch the cakes screamed at him. I loved King Alfred. My grandfather was named after him; his son, my uncle, was named after King Alfred; my brother is named after King Alfred. And so there are three people in my family named after a man they have never met, a man who died over ten centuries ago. The first view I got of England then was not unlike the first view received by the person who named my grandfather.

This view, though—the naming of the kings, their deeds, their disappoint- 6
ments—was the vivid view, the forceful view. There were other views, subtler
ones, softer, almost not there—but these were the ones that made the most lasting impression on me, these were the ones that made me really feel like nothing.
"When morning touched the sky" was one phrase, for no morning touched the
sky where I lived. The mornings where I lived came on abruptly, with a shock
of heat and loud noises. "Evening approaches" was another, but the evenings
where I lived did not approach; in fact, I had no evening—I had night and I had
day and they came and went in a mechanical way: on, off; on, off. And then there
were gentle mountains and low blue skies and moors over which people took
walks for nothing but pleasure, when where I lived a walk was an act of labor, a
burden, something only death or the automobile could relieve. And there were
things that a small turn of a head could convey—entire worlds, whole lives
would depend on this thing, a certain turn of a head. Everyday life could be quite
tiring, more tiring than anything I was told not to do. I was told not to gossip,
but they did that all the time. And they ate so much food, violating another of
those rules they taught me: do not indulge in gluttony. And the foods they ate
actually: if only sometime I could eat cold cuts after theater, cold cuts of lamb
and mint sauce, and Yorkshire pudding and scones, and clotted cream, and sau-
sages that came from up-country (imagine, "up-country"). And having troubling
thoughts at twilight, a good time to have troubling thoughts, apparently; and
servants who stole and left in the middle of a crisis, who were born with a limp
or some other kind of deformity, not nourished properly in their mother's womb
(that last part I figured out for myself; the point was, oh to have an untrustwor-
thy servant); and wonderful cobbled streets onto which solid front doors
opened; and people whose eyes were blue and who had fair skins and who
smelled only of lavender, or sometimes sweet pea or primrose. And those flowers
with those names: delphiniums, foxgloves, tulips, daffodils, floribunda, peonies;
in bloom, a striking display, being cut and placed in large glass bowls, crystal,
decorating rooms so large twenty families the size of mine could fit in comfortably but used only for passing through. And the weather was so remarkable
because the rain fell gently always, only occasionally in deep gusts, and it colored
the air various shades of gray, each an appealing shade for a dress to be worn
when a portrait was being painted; and when it rained at twilight, wonderful
things happened: people bumped into each other unexpectedly and that would
lead to all sorts of turns of events—a plot, the mere weather caused plots. I saw
that people rushed: they rushed to catch trains, they rushed toward each other
and away from each other; they rushed and rushed and rushed. That word:
rushed! I did not know what it was to do that. It was too hot to do that, and so
I came to envy people who would rush, even though it had no meaning to me
to do such a thing. But there they are again. They loved their children; their
children were sent to their own rooms as a punishment, rooms larger than my
entire house. They were special, everything about them said so, even their

clothes; their clothes rustled, swished, soothed. The world was theirs, not mine; everything told me so.

7   If now as I speak of all this I give the impression of someone on the outside looking in, nose pressed up against a glass window, that is wrong. My nose was pressed up against a glass window all right, but there was an iron vise at the back of my neck forcing my head to stay in place. To avert my gaze was to fall back into something from which I had been rescued, a hole filled with nothing, and that was the word for everything about me, nothing. The reality of my life was conquests, subjugation, humiliation, enforced amnesia. I was forced to forget. Just for instance, this: I lived in a part of St. John's, Antigua, called Ovals. Ovals was made up of five streets, each of them named after a famous English seaman—to be quite frank, an officially sanctioned criminal: Rodney Street (after George Rodney), Nelson Street (after Horatio Nelson), Drake Street (after Francis Drake), Hood Street, and Hawkins Street (after John Hawkins). But John Hawkins was knighted after a trip he made to Africa, opening up a new trade, the slave trade. He was then entitled to wear as his crest a Negro bound with a cord. Every single person living on Hawkins Street was descended from a slave. John Hawkins's ship, the one in which he transported the people he had bought and kidnapped, was called *The Jesus*. He later became the treasurer of the Royal Navy and rear admiral.

8   Again, the reality of my life, the life I led at the time I was being shown these views of England for the first time, for the second time, for the one-hundred-dred-millionth time, was this: the sun shone with what sometimes seemed to be a deliberate cruelty; we must have done something to deserve that. My dresses did not rustle in the evening air as I strolled to the theater (I had no evening, I had no theater; my dresses were made of a cheap cotton, the weave of which would give way after not too many washings). I got up in the morning, I did my chores (fetched water from the public pipe for my mother, swept the yard), I washed myself, I went to a woman to have my hair combed freshly every day (because before we were allowed into our classroom our teachers would inspect us, and children who had not bathed that day, or had dirt under their fingernails, or whose hair had not been combed anew that day, might not be allowed to attend class). I ate that breakfast. I walked to school. At school we gathered in an auditorium and sang a hymn, "All Things Bright and Beautiful," and looking down on us as we sang were portraits of the Queen of England and her husband; they wore jewels and medals and they smiled. I was a Brownie. At each meeting we would form a little group around a flagpole, and after raising the Union Jack, we would say, "I promise to do my best, to do my duty to God and the Queen, to help other people every day and obey the scouts' law."

9   Who were these people and why had I never seen them, I mean really seen them, in the place where they lived? I had never been to England. No one I knew had ever been to England, or I should say, no one I knew had ever been and returned to tell me about it. All the people I knew who had gone to England

had stayed there. Sometimes they left behind them their small children, never to see them again. England! I had seen England's representatives. I had seen the governor general at the public grounds at a ceremony celebrating the Queen's birthday. I had seen an old princess and I had seen a young princess. They had both been extremely not beautiful, but who of us would have told them that? I had never seen England, really seen it, I had only met a representative, seen a picture, read books, memorized its history. I had never set foot, my own foot, in it.

The space between the idea of something and its reality is always wide and deep 10
and dark. The longer they are kept apart—idea of thing, reality of thing—the wider the width, the deeper the depth, the thicker and darker the darkness. This space starts out empty, there is nothing in it, but it rapidly becomes filled up with obsession or desire or hatred or love—sometimes all of these things, sometimes some of these things, sometimes only one of these things. The existence of the world as I came to know it was a result of this: idea of thing over here, reality of thing way, way over there. There was Christopher Columbus, an unlikable man, an unpleasant man, a liar (and so, of course, a thief) surrounded by maps and schemes and plans, and there was the reality on the other side of that width, that depth, that darkness. He became obsessed, he became filled with desire, the hatred came later, love was never a part of it. Eventually, his idea met the longed for reality. That the idea of something and its reality are often two completely different things is something no one ever remembers; and so when they meet and find that they are not compatible, the weaker of the two, idea or reality, dies. That idea Christopher Columbus had was more powerful than the reality he met, and so the reality he met died.

And so finally, when I was a grown-up woman, the mother of two children, 11
the wife of someone, a person who resides in a powerful country that takes up more than its fair share of a continent, the owner of a house with many rooms in it and of two automobiles, with the desire and will (which I very much act upon) to take from the world more than I give back to it, more than I deserve, more than I need, finally then, I saw England, the real England, not a picture, not a painting, not through a story in a book, but England, for the first time. In me, the space between the idea of it and its reality had become filled with hatred, and so when at last I saw it I wanted to take it into my hands and tear it into little pieces and then crumble it up as if it were clay, child's clay. That was impossible, and so I could only indulge in not-favorable opinions.

There were monuments everywhere; they commemorated victories, battles 12
fought between them and the people who lived across the sea from them, all vile people, fought over which of them would have dominion over the people who looked like me. The monuments were useless to them now, people sat on them and ate their lunch. They were like markers on an old useless trail, like a piece of old string tied to a finger to jog the memory, like old decoration in an old

house, dirty, useless, in the way. Their skins were so pale, it made them look so fragile, so weak, so ugly. What if I had the power to simply banish them from their land, send boat after boatload of them on a voyage that in fact had no destination, force them to live in a place where the sun's presence was a constant? This would rid them of their pale complexion and make them look more like me, make them look more like the people I love and treasure and hold dear, and more like the people who occupy the near and far reaches of my imagination, my history, my geography, and reduce them and everything they have ever known to figurines as evidence that I was in divine favor, what if all this was in my power? Could I resist it? No one ever has.

13   And they were rude, they were rude to each other. They didn't like each other very much. They didn't like each other in the way they didn't like me, and it occurred to me that their dislike for me was one of the few things they agreed on.

14   I was on a train in England with a friend, an English woman. Before we were in England she liked me very much. In England she didn't like me at all. She didn't like the claim I said I had on England, she didn't like the views I had of England. I didn't like England, she didn't like England, but she didn't like me not liking it too. She said, "I want to show you my England, I want to show you the England that I know and love." I had told her many times before that I knew England and I didn't want to love it anyway. She no longer lived in England; it was her own country, but it had not been kind to her, so she left. On the train, the conductor was rude to her; she asked something, and he responded in a rude way. She became ashamed. She was ashamed at the way he treated her; she was ashamed at the way he behaved. "This is the new England," she said. But I liked the conductor being rude; his behavior seemed quite appropriate. Earlier this had happened: we had gone to a store to buy a shirt for my husband; it was meant to be a special present, a special shirt to wear on special occasions. This was a store where the Prince of Wales has his shirts made, but the shirts sold in this store are beautiful all the same. I found a shirt I thought my husband would like and I wanted to buy him a tie to go with it. When I couldn't decide which one to choose, the salesman showed me a new set. He was very pleased with these, he said, because they bore the crest of the Prince of Wales, and the Prince of Wales had never allowed his crest to decorate an article of clothing before. There was something in the way he said it; his tone was slavish, reverential, awed. It made me feel angry; I wanted to hit him. I didn't do that. I said, my husband and I hate princes, my husband would never wear anything that had a prince's anything on it. My friend stiffened. The salesman stiffened. They both drew themselves in, away from me. My friend told me that the prince was a symbol of her Englishness, and I could see that I had caused offense. I looked at her. She was an English person, the sort of English person I used to know at home, the sort who was nobody in England but somebody when they came to live among the people like me. There were many people I could have seen England

with; that I was seeing it with this particular person, a person who reminded me of the people who showed me England long ago as I sat in church or at my desk, made me feel silent and afraid, for I wondered if, all these years of our friendship, I had had a friend or had been in the thrall of a racial memory.

I went to Bath—we, my friend and I, did this, but though we were together, 15 I was no longer with her. The landscape was almost as familiar as my own hand, but I had never been in this place before, so how could that be again? And the streets of Bath were familiar, too, but I had never walked on them before. It was all those years of reading, starting with Roman Britain. Why did I have to know about Roman Britain? It was of no real use to me, a person living on a hot, drought-ridden island, and it is of no use to me now, and yet my head is filled with this nonsense, Roman Britain. In Bath, I drank tea in a room I had read about in a novel written in the eighteenth century. In this very same room, young women wearing those dresses that rustled and so on danced and flirted and sometimes disgraced themselves with young men, soldiers, sailors, who were on their way to Bristol or someplace like that, so many places like that where so many adventures, the outcome of which was not good for me, began. Bristol, England. A sentence that began "That night the ship sailed from Bristol, England" would end not so good for me. And then I was driving through the countryside in an English motorcar, on narrow winding roads, and they were so familiar, though I had never been on them before; and through little villages the names of which I somehow knew so well though I had never been there before. And the countryside did have all those hedges and hedges, fields hedged in. I was marveling at all the toil of it, the planting of the hedges to begin with and then the care of it, all that clipping, year after year of clipping, and I wondered at the lives of the people who would have to do this, because wherever I see and feel the hands that hold up the world, I see and feel myself and all the people who look like me. And I said, "Those hedges" and my friend said that someone, a woman named Mrs. Rothchild, worried that the hedges weren't being taken care of properly; the farmers couldn't afford or find the help to keep up the hedges, and often they replaced them with wire fencing. I might have said to that, well if Mrs. Rothchild doesn't like the wire fencing, why doesn't she take care of the hedges herself, but I didn't. And then in those fields that were now hemmed in by wire fencing that a privileged woman didn't like was planted a vile yellow flowering bush that produced an oil, and my friend said that Mrs. Rothchild didn't like this either; it ruined the English countryside, it ruined the traditional look of the English countryside.

It was not at that moment that I wished every sentence, everything I knew, 16 that began with England would end with "and then it all died; we don't know how, it just all died." At that moment, I was thinking, who are these people who forced me to think of them all the time, who forced me to think that the world I knew was incomplete, or without substance, or did not measure up because it was not England; that I was incomplete, or without substance, and did not measure up because I was not English. Who were these people? The person sitting next to me couldn't give me a clue; no one person could. In any case, if I had said to her, I find England ugly, I hate England; the weather is like a jail sentence, the English are a very ugly people, the food in England is like a jail sentence, the hair of English people is so straight, so dead looking, the English have an unbearable smell so different from the smell of people I know, real people of course, she would have said that I was a person full of prejudice. Apart from the fact that it is I—that is, the people who look like me—who made her aware of the unpleasantness of such a thing, the idea of such a thing, prejudice, she would have been only partly right, sort of right: I may be capable of prejudice, but my prejudices have no weight to them, my prejudices have no force behind them, my prejudices remain opinions, my prejudices remain my personal opinion. And a great feeling of rage and disappointment came over me as I looked at England, my head full of personal opinions that could not have public, my public, approval. The people I come from are powerless to do evil on grand scale.

17   The moment I wished every sentence, everything I knew, that began with England would end with "and then it all died, we don't know how, it just all died" was when I saw the white cliffs of Dover. I had sung hymns and recited poems that were about a longing to see the white cliffs of Dover again. At the time I sang the hymns and recited the poems, I could really long to see them again because I had never seen them at all, nor had anyone around me at the time. But there we were, groups of people longing for something we had never seen. And so there they were, the white cliffs, but they were not that pearly majestic thing I used to sing about, that thing that created such a feeling in these people that when they died in the place where I lived they had themselves buried facing a direction that would allow them to see the white cliffs of Dover when they were resurrected, as surely they would be. The white cliffs of Dover, when finally I saw them, were cliffs, but they were not white; you would only call them that if the word "white" meant something special to you; they were dirty and they were steep; they were so steep, the correct height from which all my views of England, starting with the map before me in my classroom and ending with the trip I had just taken, should jump and die and disappear forever.

EXERCISES

Some of the Issues

1. The first paragraph describes the way Kincaid, as a child, first "saw" England. What was she supposed to feel? What indications are there of what she actually did feel?
2. Cite several examples of how Antiguans adopted English dress, food, and customs even when clearly inappropriate for their own needs. What would account for these practices?

3. Why is the teacher's command to draw a map of England "far worse than a declaration of war" (paragraph 4)?

4. In paragraphs 5 and 6, Kincaid tells of all the facts she learned in school about England. Why doesn't she mention learning anything about Antigua in school?

5. In paragraph 7, why does Kincaid think that she would fall into a "hole filled with nothing" if she were to avert her gaze from the glass window?

6. How can a "famous" English seaman and the officially sanctioned criminal (paragraph 7) be the same person?

7. In paragraph 10 Kincaid talks about the idea versus the reality of Columbus. How, according to Kincaid, did ideas overpower reality?

8. When Kincaid finally travels to England, how has she changed from her childhood self? How has she remained the same?

9. In paragraphs 14 and 16, how do Kincaid's feelings differ from those of her English friend? Why do those feelings become literally "unspeakable"?

10. In the final two paragraphs, Kincaid expresses anger so strong that she wishes England and the English were dead. Trace the development of that anger and its sources. Do you think her anger is justified? Why or why not?

The Way We Are Told

11. How does Kincaid make use of the multiple meanings of "see" in the title and throughout the essay?

12. Kincaid's essay uses multiple contrasts: between imported customs and everyday life; between history written by the conquerors and by the conquered; between what she feels about England and what she is expected to feel. How does the structure of the essay help to underline those contrasts?

13. Why is it important that the white cliffs of Dover are not really white?

14. Kincaid's last sentence refers back to the map described in her beginning paragraph. Is this an effective conclusion?

Some Subjects for Writing

15. Write about an experience in your own life that was radically different from what you had been led to expect. Compare your expectations with the reality you found.

16. Describe a current or historical event from two radically different points of view: that of those who have benefited from it and that of those who have not.

17. In the library, gather basic information about Antigua or a country that is now or has recently been a colony. Then with your instructor plan a research project that explores some aspect of the history of colonialism in that country.

To live in the Borderlands means you...

GLORIA ANZALDÚA

Gloria Anzaldúa describes herself as a "Chicana tejana lesbian-feminist poet and fiction writer." She has taught Chicana studies, feminist studies, and creative writing at various universities, and has conducted writing workshops around the country.

She is editor of Making Face Making Soul/Haciendo Caras: Creative and Critical Perspectives by Women of Color *(1990) and coeditor of* This Bridge Called My Back: Writings by Radical Women of Color *(1981). This poem is taken from* Borderlands/La Frontera: The New Mestiza *(1987), a collection of prose and poetry that describes the author's childhood along the Texas-Mexico border, growing up between two cultures, Anglo and Mexican, equally at home and alien in both. Anzaldúa speaks of an actual physical border, but expands her metaphor to include the psychological "borderlands" that occur whenever two or more cultures coexist together.*

To live in the Borderlands means you...

are neither *hispana india negra española*
ni gabacha, eres mestiza, mulata,[1] half-breed
caught in the crossfire between camps
while carrying all five races on your back
5 not knowing which side to turn to, run from;

To live in the Borderlands means knowing
that the *india* in you, betrayed for 500 years,
is no longer speaking to you,
that *mexicanas* call you *rajetas,*[2]
10 that denying the Anglo inside you
is as bad as having denied the Indian or Black;

[1]Hispanic, Indian (Native American), black, Spanish nor white (*gabacha* is the Hispanic term for a white woman), you are of mixed blood, mulatto.
[2]Split.

Cuando vives en la frontera[3]
people walk through you, the wind steals your voice,
you're a *burra, buey,*[4] scapegoat,
forerunner of a new race,
half and half—both woman and man, neither—   15
a new gender;

To live in the Borderlands means to
put *chile* in the borscht,
eat whole wheat *tortillas,*   20
speak Tex-Mex with a Brooklyn accent;
be stopped by *la migra*[5] at the border checkpoints;

Living in the Borderlands means you fight hard to
resist the gold elixir beckoning from the bottle,
the pull of the gun barrel,   25
the rope crushing the hollow of your throat;

In the Borderlands
you are the battleground
where enemies are kin to each other;
you are at home, a stranger,   30
the border disputes have been settled
the volley of shots have shattered the truce
you are wounded, lost in action
dead, fighting back;

To live in the Borderlands means   35
the mill with the razor white teeth wants to shred off
your olive-red skin, crush out the kernel, your heart
pound you pinch you roll you out
smelling like white bread but dead;

To survive the Borderlands   40
you must live *sin fronteras*[6]
be a crossroads.

---

[3]When you live in the borderlands.
[4]Donkey, ox.
[5]Immigration officials—specifically U.S. immigration officials.
[6]Without borders.

EXERCISES

Some of the Issues

1. The title of Anzaldúa's poem is also its beginning line and is repeated, with some variation, again and again. What is the effect of the near repetition and of the changes?
2. What might Anzaldúa gain by her use of Spanish words?
3. Throughout the poem, Anzaldúa speaks of borders within herself, and borders imposed by the outside world. What are these? Why is it sometimes difficult to tell the difference?
4. Anzaldúa often uses contradictory images in her poem. For example, in the third stanza she is both "a scapegoat" and the "forerunner of a new race." Find other pairs of opposing images. What is their effect?
5. What is "the mill with the razor white teeth" (line 36) and what is its danger?
6. What is Anzaldúa's suggestion for survival? What does she mean by it?
7. Although the author speaks of the difficulty of living in the borderlands, there are also indications of optimism. Which do you see as the principal message of the poem?
*8. Read Aurora Levins Morales's "Class Poem." Like Anzaldúa, she writes about her various heritages and their relationship to her current identity. What similarities and differences do you see between the two authors' points of view?
*9. Read Pico Iyer's "Home Is Every Place." Both authors talk about borders and use geography as a symbol of their own identity. Compare and contrast their views.

Some Subjects for Writing

10. Although not all of us are of mixed or battling heritages, most of us have felt split—"rajetas"—at some point in our lives. For example, we may feel both allegiance to and conflict with the identities prescribed by our family's traditions, our religion, our social class, or our society's ideas about appropriate gender roles. In an essay, describe a way in which you see yourself on the border of any of these identities or others important to you.
11. Do you think society is becoming more or less accepting of people who cross conventional roles of race, ethnicity, or gender? Why or why not? Write an essay giving evidence to support your views.

9

Communicating

How do we communicate? The first answer that is likely to come to most people's minds is through language: we speak, we listen, we read, we write. When we think further, we become increasingly aware that we also communicate in nonverbal ways, through gestures and other visual images. Increasingly, advances in technology—videos, faxes, E-mail, car phones, answering machines, etc.—have relieved us from the necessity of personal, physical contact and, in so doing, have changed the ways in which our messages are relayed. In addition to altering the medium of the message, technology may in fact shape both form and content of the message in subtle ways. For example, in responding to an E-mail message, we may dispense with preliminary common courtesies, necessary in face-to-face interactions. Or, in viewing music videos, we may be presented with fleeting, split-second successions of patriotic images that we are not even aware of, but that leave us feeling proud nonetheless.

When we turn to communication across cultural and social groups, the complexities and subtleties multiply. Language is again the most obvious example. If you speak only English and the person you wish to talk to speaks only Japanese, communication will be limited—although you might be able to understand to some extent by means of gestures. With speakers of the same language, problems may be the result of dialectal or intracultural differences, that is, language distinctions between subgroups. Gloria Naylor, in the first selection, alerts the reader to one such example concerning the use of an incendiary word that takes on different meanings within the African-American community.

Amy Tan, in "Mother Tongue," talks about the effect of growing up in a world of mixed languages: including her mother's ungrammatical but richly expressive Chinese-influenced English. Tan's first attempts as a fiction writer used a stiff and formal style completely unlike the speech she had heard around her.

— **THINKING ABOUT THE THEME** *"Communicating"* —————————

The photo on the opposite page was taken in a middle school science class composed of both hearing and deaf students.

1. Although we usually think of language as speech, American Sign Language is a fully developed language, though it is different from spoken English. Try to learn something about sign language and its place in the deaf community either through a signing friend, or from library or internet research. Share your information with the class.

2. American Sign Language uses facial expression and body posture to accompany the signs and expand their meaning, but we all use gesture and body language to convey meaning. Sometimes our body language expands on the words we say, or even contradicts them. Pair off with someone in your class and focus on describing each person's use of non-verbal communication. One way of highlighting the importance of body language is to start a conversation with your partner back-to-back and then continue the conversation face-to-face.

3. Language is often ambiguous and we frequently miscommunicate our ideas or desires, even if we are talking to someone who speaks the same language. Describe an incident where you misunderstood someone or you were misunderstood. What were the consequences?

4. There are many differences between spoken and written language. List some of these differences and discuss them with your classmates.

5. Turning words into pictures or pictures into words can be a challenging task. You might try one of the following experiments to explore the process: 1) Each person or small group is given six to ten identical blocks or Lego pieces in two or three different colors. Half the class builds a structure out of the blocks and then describes it to someone who cannot see it, but who must try to reproduce it. 2) Working together in pairs or small groups, write a precise description of an animal without naming it. Exchange your description with another group. Each person in that group will attempt to draw a picture of the animal based only on the description. Compare your drawings and descriptions.

Her real career as a novelist begins when she takes advantage of all the Englishes she grew up with and writes with her mother as the imagined audience.

In "Do Ask, Do Tell," Joshua Gamson describes daytime television talk shows, one of the few platforms for the discussion of the lives of gays and lesbians by gays and lesbians themselves. He concludes that, despite the exploitative nature of some of these shows, they do more good than harm in shaping public attitudes towards sexual orientation. Jack G. Shaheen also analyzes the media, in this case the media's one-sided view of Arabs, which he claims are usually viewed stereotypically as oil sheiks or terrorists, and seldom as real people.

In the poem that ends the book, Lisel Mueller shows us how the words we use and the stories we tell shape our lives.

The Meaning of a Word

GLORIA NAYLOR

Gloria Naylor, a native of New York City, was born in 1950 and edu-cated at Brooklyn College and Yale. She has taught at George Wash-ington, New York, and Boston universities. Her first novel, The Women of Brewster Place *(1982), won an American Book Award. Since then she has written* Linden Hills *(1985),* Mama Day *(1988), and* Bailey's Cafe *(1992). She is also the editor of* Children of the Night: The Best Short Stories by Black Writers 1967 to the Present *(1996). The essay included here appeared in* The New York Times *on February 20, 1986.*

The word whose meaning Naylor learned was nigger. *She explains that she had heard it used quite comfortably by friends and relatives, but the way it was uttered to her by a white child in school was so different that she at first did not realize that it was the same word.*

1   Language is the subject. It is the written form with which I've managed to keep the wolf away from the door and, in diaries, to keep my sanity. In spite of this, I consider the written word inferior to the spoken, and much of the frustration experienced by novelists is the awareness that whatever we manage to capture in even the most transcendent passages falls far short of the richness of life. Dia-logue achieves its power in the dynamics of a fleeting moment of sight, sound, smell and touch.

2   I'm not going to enter the debate here about whether it is language that shapes reality or vice versa. That battle is doomed to be waged whenever we seek intermittent reprieve from the chicken and egg dispute. I will simply take the position that the spoken word, like the written word, amounts to a nonsen-sical arrangement of sounds or letters without a consensus that assigns "mean-ing." And building from the meanings of what we hear, we order reality. Words themselves are innocuous; it is the consensus that gives them true power.

3   I remember the first time I heard the word nigger. In my third-grade class, our math tests were being passed down the rows, and as I handed the papers to a little boy in back of me, I remarked that once again he had received a much lower mark than I did. He snatched his test from me and spit out that word. Had he called me a nymphomaniac or a necrophiliac, I couldn't have been more puzzled. I didn't

know what a nigger was, but I knew that whatever it meant, it was something he shouldn't have called me. This was verified when I raised my hand, and in a loud voice repeated what he had said and watched the teacher scold him for using a "bad" word. I was later to go home and ask the inevitable question that every black parent must face—"Mommy, what does 'nigger' mean?"

And what exactly did it mean? Thinking back, I realize that this could not have been the first time the word was used in my presence. I was part of a large extended family that had migrated from the rural South after World War II and formed a close-knit network that gravitated around my maternal grandparents. Their ground-floor apartment in one of the buildings they owned in Harlem was a weekend mecca for my immediate family, along with countless aunts, uncles and cousins who brought along assorted friends. It was a bustling and open house with assorted neighbors and tenants popping in and out to exchange bits of gossip, pick up an old quarrel or referee the ongoing checkers game in which my grandmother cheated shamelessly. They were all there to let down their hair and put up their feet after a week of labor in the factories, laundries and shipyards of New York. 4

Amid the clamor, which could reach deafening proportions—two or three conversations going on simultaneously, punctuated by the sound of a baby's crying somewhere in the back rooms or out on the street—there was still a rigid set of rules about what was said and how. Older children were sent out of the living room when it was time to get into the juicy details about "you-know-who" up on the third floor who had gone and gotten herself "p-r-e-g-n-a-n-t!" But my parents, knowing that I could spell well beyond my years, always demanded that I follow the others out to play. Beyond sexual misconduct and death, everything else was considered harmless for our young ears. And so among the anecdotes of the triumphs and disappointments in the various workings of their lives, the word nigger was used in my presence, but it was set within contexts and inflections that caused it to register in my mind as something else. 5

In the singular, the word was always applied to a man who had distinguished himself in some situation that brought their approval for his strength, intelligence or drive: 6

"Did Johnny *really* do that?" 7

"I'm telling you, that nigger pulled in $6,000 of overtime last year. Said he got enough for a down payment on a house." 8

When used with a possessive adjective by a woman—"my nigger"—it became a term of endearment for husband or boyfriend. But it could be more than just a term applied to a man. In their mouths it became the pure essence of manhood—a disembodied force that channeled their past history of struggle and present survival against the odds into a victorious statement of being: "Yeah, that old foreman found out quick enough—you don't mess with a nigger." 9

In the plural, it became a description of some group within the community that have overstepped the bounds of decency as my family defined it: Parents 10 who neglected their children, a drunken couple who fought in public, people who simply refused to look for work, those with excessively dirty mouths or unkempt households were all "trifling niggers." This particular circle could forgive hard times, unemployment, the occasional bout of depression—they had gone through all of that themselves—but the unforgivable sin was a lack of self-respect.

11   A woman could never be a "nigger" in the singular, with its connotation of confirming worth. The noun girl was its closest equivalent in that sense, but only when used in direct address and regardless of the gender doing the addressing. "Girl" was a token of respect for a woman. The one-syllable word was drawn out to sound like three in recognition of the extra ounce of wit, nerve or daring that the woman had shown in the situation under discussion.

12   "G-i-r-l, stop. You mean you said that to his face?"

13   But if the word was used in a third-person reference or shortened so that it almost snapped out of my mouth, it always involved some element of communal disapproval. And age became an important factor in these exchanges. It was only between individuals of the same generation, or from an older person to a younger (but never the other way around), that "girl" would be considered a compliment.

14   I don't agree with the argument that use of the word nigger at this social stratum of the black community was an internalization of racism. The dynamics were the exact opposite: the people in my grandmother's living room took a word that whites used to signify worthlessness or degradation and rendered it impotent. Gathering there together, they transformed "nigger" to signify the varied and complex human beings they knew themselves to be. If the word was to disappear totally from the mouths of even the most liberal of white society, no one in that room was naïve enough to believe it would disappear from white minds. Meeting the word head-on, they proved it had absolutely nothing to do with the way they were determined to live their lives.

15   So there must have been dozens of times that the word "nigger" was spoken in front of me before I reached the third grade. But I didn't "hear" it until it was said by a small pair of lips that had already learned it could be a way to humiliate me. That was the word I went home and asked my mother about. And since she knew that I had to grow up in America, she took me in her lap and explained.

EXERCISES

Some of the Issues

1. What reasons does Naylor give for considering the spoken word superior to the written? Do you agree or disagree?

2. Reread paragraph 2. What, according to Naylor, gives meaning to words? Do you agree or disagree?

3. In paragraph 3 the author tells a story from her experience as a child. How does it relate to the general statement on language that she made in the first two paragraphs? What is it that made Naylor think that she had been called a "bad" word?

4. At the end of paragraph 5 and in the examples that follow Naylor demonstrates that she had heard the word "nigger" before the boy in her class used it. Why did the previous uses register with her as something different?

The Way We Are Told

5. Naylor starts with a general statement—"Language is the subject"—which she then expands on in paragraphs 1 and 2. What focus does this beginning give her essay? How would the focus differ if she started with the anecdote in paragraph 3?

6. Naylor asserts that "the written word is inferior to the spoken." What devices does she use to help the reader *hear* the dialogue?

7. The essay consists of three parts: paragraphs 1 and 2, 3–13, and 14 and 15. The first is a general statement and the second an anecdote followed by records of conversations. How does the third part relate to the preceding two?

Some Subjects for Writing

8. Many words differ in their meaning depending on the circumstances in which they are used. Write a brief essay on the different words applied to a particular nationality or ethnic group and explain their impact.

*9. "Sticks and stones may break my bones but words can never hurt me." Do you have any experiences that would either confirm or deny the truth of that saying? You may also want to read Countee Cullen's poem "Incident."

10. Do you think teachers should set limits on language permitted in the classroom? Why or why not?

Mother Tongue

AMY TAN

Amy Tan was born in Oakland, California, in 1952, two years after her parents came to the United States from China.

Amy Tan's literary career was not planned—she first began writing fiction as a form of self-therapy. Considered a workaholic by her friends, Tan had been working 90 hours a week as a freelance technical writer; she hoped to eradicate her tendency to overwork by instead immersing herself in fiction writing. Her first efforts were stories, one of which secured her a place in a fiction writers' workshop. Tan's first novel, the semi-autobiographical The Joy Luck Club, *was published in 1989 and made into a very successful film. It tells the story of the lives of four Chinese women and their American daughters in California.*

Amy Tan's writing focuses on the lives of Chinese-American women; her novels introduce characters who are ambivalent, as she once was, about their Chinese background. Tan remarked in an interview that though she once tried to distance herself from her ethnicity, writing The Joy Luck Club *helped her discover "how very Chinese I was. And how much had stayed with me that I had tried to deny."*

Tan has since written two other novels, The Kitchen God's Wife *(1991) and* The Hundred Secret Senses *(1996).*

1   I am not a scholar of English or literature. I cannot give you much more than personal opinions on the English language and its variations in this country or others.

2   I am a writer. And by that definition, I am someone who has always loved language. I am fascinated by language in daily life. I spend a great deal of my time thinking about the power of language—the way it can evoke an emotion, a visual image, a complex idea, or a simple truth. Language is the tool of my trade. And I use them all—all the Englishes I grew up with.

3   Recently, I was made keenly aware of the different Englishes I do use. I was giving a talk to a large group of people, the same talk I had already given to half a dozen other groups. The nature of the talk was about my writing, my life, and my book, *The Joy Luck Club.* The talk was going along well enough, until I remembered one major difference that made the whole talk sound wrong. My mother was in the room. And it was perhaps the first time she had heard me give

a lengthy speech, using the kind of English I have never used with her. I was saying things like, "The intersection of memory upon imagination" and "There is an aspect of my fiction that relates to thus-and-thus"—a speech filled with carefully wrought grammatical phrases, burdened, it suddenly seemed to me, with nominalized forms, past perfect tenses, conditional phrases, all the forms of standard English that I had learned in school and through books, the forms of English I did not use at home with my mother.

Just last week, I was walking down the street with my mother, and I again 4 found myself conscious of the English I was using, the English I do use with her. We were talking about the price of new and used furniture and I heard myself saying this: "Not waste money that way." My husband was with us as well, and he didn't notice any switch in my English. And then I realized why. It's because over the twenty years we've been together I've often used that same kind of English with him, and sometimes he even uses it with me. It has become our language of intimacy, a different sort of English that relates to family talk, the language I grew up with.

So you'll have some idea of what this family talk I heard sounds like, I'll 5 quote what my mother said during a recent conversation which I videotaped and then transcribed. During this conversation, my mother was talking about a political gangster in Shanghai who had the same last name as her family's, Du, and how the gangster in his early years wanted to be adopted by her family, which was rich by comparison. Later, the gangster became more powerful, far richer than my mother's family, and one day showed up at my mother's wedding to pay his respects. Here's what she said in part:

"Du Yusong having business like fruit stand. Like off the street kind. He is 6 Du like Du Zong—but not Tsung-ming Island people. The local people call putong, the river east side, he belong to that side local people. That man want to ask Du Zong father take him in like become own family. Du Zong father wasn't look down on him, but didn't take seriously, until that man big like become a mafia. Now important person, very hard to inviting him. Chinese way, came only to show respect, don't stay for dinner. Respect for making big celebration, he shows up. Mean gives lots of respect. Chinese custom. Chinese social life that way. If too important won't have to stay too long. He come to my wedding. I didn't see, I heard it. I gone to boy's side, they have YMCA dinner. Chinese age I was nineteen."

You should know that my mother's expressive command of English belies 7 how much she actually understands. She reads the *Forbes* report, listens to *Wall Street Week*, converses daily with her stockbroker, reads all of Shirley MacLaine's books with ease—all kinds of things I can't begin to understand. Yet some of my friends tell me they understand 50 percent of what my mother says. Some say they understand 80 to 90 percent. Some say they understand none of it, as if she were speaking pure Chinese. But to me, my mother's English is perfectly clear, perfectly natural. It's my mother tongue. Her language, as I hear it, is vivid, direct, full of observation and imagery. That was the language that helped shape the way I saw things, expressed things, made sense of the world.

8 Lately, I've been giving more thought to the kind of English my mother speaks. Like others, I have described it to people as "broken" or "fractured" English. But I wince when I say that. It has always bothered me that I can think of no way to describe it other than "broken," as if it were damaged and needed to be fixed, as if it lacked a certain wholeness and soundness. I've heard other terms used, "limited English," for example. But they seem just as bad, as if everything is limited, including people's perceptions of the limited English speaker.

9 I know this for a fact, because when I was growing up, my mother's "limited" English limited my perception of her. I was ashamed of her English. I believed that her English reflected the quality of what she had to say. That is, because she expressed them imperfectly her thoughts were imperfect. And I had plenty of empirical evidence to support me: the fact that people in department stores, at banks, and at restaurants did not take her seriously, did not give her good service, pretended not to understand her, or even acted as if they did not hear her.

10 My mother has long realized the limitations of her English as well. When I was fifteen, she used to have me call people on the phone to pretend I was she. In this guise, I was forced to ask for information or even to complain and yell at people who had been rude to her. One time it was a call to her stockbroker in New York. She had cashed out her small portfolio and it just so happened we were going to go to New York the next week, our very first trip outside California. I had to get on the phone and say in an adolescent voice that was not very convincing, "This is Mrs. Tan."

11 And my mother was standing in the back whispering loudly, "Why he don't send me check, already two weeks late. So mad he lie to me, losing me money."

12 And then I said in perfect English, "Yes, I'm getting rather concerned. You had agreed to send the check two weeks ago, but it hasn't arrived."

13 Then she began to talk more loudly. "What he want, I come to New York tell him front of his boss, you cheating me?" And I was trying to calm her down, make her be quiet, while telling the stockbroker, "I can't tolerate any more excuses. If I don't receive the check immediately, I am going to have to speak to your manager when I'm in New York next week." And sure enough, the following week there we were in front of this astonished stockbroker, and I was sitting there red-faced and quiet, and my mother, the real Mrs. Tan, was shouting at his boss in her impeccable broken English.

14 We used a similar routine just five days ago, for a situation that was far less humorous. My mother had gone to the hospital for an appointment, to find out about a benign brain tumor a CAT scan had revealed a month ago. She said she had spoken very good English, her best English, no mistakes. Still, she said, the hospital did not apologize when they said they had lost the CAT scan and she

had come for nothing. She said they did not seem to have any sympathy when she told them she was anxious to know the exact diagnosis, since her husband and son had both died of brain tumors. She said they would not give her any more information until the next time and she would have to make another appointment for that. So she said she would not leave until the doctor called her daughter. She wouldn't budge. And when the doctor finally called her daughter, me, who spoke in perfect English—lo and behold—we had assurances the CAT scan would be found, promises that a conference call on Monday would be held, and apologies for any suffering my mother had gone through for a most regrettable mistake.

I think my mother's English almost had an effect on limiting my possibilities   15
in life as well. Sociologists and linguists probably will tell you that a person's developing language skills are more influenced by peers. But I do think that the language spoken in the family, especially in immigrant families which are more insular, plays a large role in shaping the language of the child. And I believe that it affected my results on achievement tests, IQ tests, and the SAT. While my English skills were never judged as poor, compared to math, English could not be considered my strong suit. In grade school I did moderately well, getting perhaps B's, sometimes B-pluses, in English and scoring perhaps in the sixtieth or seventieth percentile on achievement tests. But those scores were not good enough to override the opinion that my true abilities lay in math and science, because in those areas I achieved A's and scored in the ninetieth percentile or higher.

This was understandable. Math is precise; there is only one correct answer.   16
Whereas, for me at least, the answers on English tests were always a judgment call, a matter of opinion and personal experience. Those tests were constructed around items like fill-in-the-blank sentence completion, such as, "Even though Tom was _____, Mary thought he was _____." And the correct answer always seemed to be the most bland combinations of thoughts, for example, "Even though Tom was shy, Mary thought he was charming," with the grammatical structure "even though" limiting the correct answer to some sort of semantic opposites, so you wouldn't get answers like, "Even though Tom was foolish, Mary thought he was ridiculous." Well, according to my mother, there were very few limitations as to what Tom could have been and what Mary might have thought of him. So I never did well on tests like that.

The same was true with word analogies, pairs of words in which you were   17
supposed to find some sort of logical, semantic relationship—for example, "*Sunset* is to *nightfall* as _____ is to _____." And here you would be presented with a list of four possible pairs, one of which showed the same kind of relationship: *red* is to *stoplight, bus* is to *arrival, chills* is to *fever, yawn* is to *boring*. Well, I could never think that way. I knew what the tests were asking, but I could not block out of my mind the images already created by the first pair, "*sunset* is to *nightfall*"—and I would see a burst of colors against a darkening sky, the moon rising,

the lowering of a curtain of stars. And all the other pairs of words—red, bus, stoplight, boring—just threw up a mass of confusing images, making it impossible for me to sort out something as logical as saying: "A sunset precedes nightfall" is the same as "a chill precedes a fever." The only way I would have gotten that answer right would have been to imagine an associative situation, for example, my being disobedient and staying out past sunset, catching a chill at night, which turns into feverish pneumonia as punishment, which indeed did happen to me.

18 I have been thinking about all this lately, about my mother's English, about achievement tests. Because lately I've been asked, as a writer, why there are not more Asian Americans represented in American literature. Why are there few Asian Americans enrolled in creative writing programs? Why do so many Chinese students go into engineering? Well, these are broad sociological questions I can't begin to answer. But I have noticed in surveys—in fact, just last week—that Asian students, as a whole, always do significantly better on math achievement tests than in English. And this makes me think that there are other Asian-American students whose English spoken in the home might also be described as "broken" or "limited." And perhaps they also have teachers who are steering them away from writing and into math and science, which is what happened to me.

19 Fortunately, I happen to be rebellious in nature and enjoy the challenge of disproving assumptions made about me. I became an English major my first year in college, after being enrolled as pre-med. I started writing nonfiction as a freelancer the week after I was told by my former boss that writing was my worst skill and I should hone my talents toward account management.

20 But it wasn't until 1985 that I finally began to write fiction. And at first I wrote using what I thought to be wittily crafted sentences, sentences that would finally prove I had mastery over the English language. Here's an example from the first draft of a story that later made its way into *The Joy Luck Club*, but without this line: "That was my mental quandary in its nascent state." A terrible line, which I can barely pronounce.

21 Fortunately, for reasons I won't get into today, I later decided I should envision a reader for the stories I would write. And the reader I decided upon was my mother, because these were stories about mothers. So with this reader in mind—and in fact she did read my early drafts—I began to write stories using all the Englishes I grew up with: the English I spoke to my mother, which for lack of a better term might be described as "simple"; the English she used with me, which for lack of a better term might be described as "broken"; my translation of her Chinese, which could certainly be described as "watered down"; and what I imagined to be her translation of her Chinese if she could speak in perfect English, her internal language, and for that I sought to preserve the essence, but neither an English nor a Chinese structure. I wanted to capture

what language ability tests can never reveal: her intent, her passion, her imagery, the rhythms of her speech and the nature of her thoughts.

Apart from what any critic had to say about my writing, I knew I had suc-   22
ceeded where it counted when my mother finished reading my book and gave me her verdict: "So easy to read."

EXERCISES

Some of the Issues

1. What are some possible meanings of the title of Tan's essay?
2. In paragraph 3, how does Tan describe the language used in the speech she made?
3. In paragraph 6, Tan gives us a sample of her mother's speech transcribed from a videotape. Rewrite the paragraph in a more standard from of English. What changes did you need to make? Did you have any difficulty understanding what her mother meant?
4. Why, in paragraphs 8 and 9, does Tan object to the terms "broken" or "fractured" or "limited" English?
5. As a child, how did Tan view her mother's "limited" English (paragraph 9)? What evidence does Tan present that her childhood perception was false?
6. On two occasions, Tan's mother asks her daughter to speak on her behalf— the incident with the stockbroker (paragraphs 10–13) and the more recent incident at the hospital (paragraph 14). Describe each incident. Why are they significant?
7. In paragraphs 15 through 17 Tan talks about how growing up in a family that did not have complete control of English may have affected her ability to do well on standardized English tests. What are the examples she cites of typical questions on those tests? Do you think other imaginative people, even if they did not grow up in an immigrant family, might have trouble with such questions?
8. In paragraph 18, Tan states that she and many other Asian-Americans select, or are guided toward, careers in which mastery of language is less important than skills in math or science. What, according to Tan, are the consequences of this?
9. What were the steps in Tan's own development as a writer (paragraphs 19–22).

The Way We Are Told

10. Tan begins her essay by telling you about herself—her limitations and her interests. What does she gain by doing this?

11. Tan uses quotations at several points in the essay to illustrate both her mother's language and her own. Find several of these quotations and indicate how they help support Tan's ideas about the different Englishes she understands and uses.
12. Why does Amy Tan's mother have the last word in the essay?
13. Writing teachers have probably talked to you about the importance of imagining a reader or an audience when you write. Who does Tan say was the imagined audience for her novel? Who is the audience for this essay?

Some Subjects for Writing

14. Describe an experience in which you felt either very limited or particularly effective when speaking or writing. For example, you could describe a time you took a test and forgot everything you studied because of nervousness or a time in which you managed to explain your ideas or feelings particularly well to a friend.
15. Tan talks about the challenge of disproving early negative assumptions about her abilities as a writer. Write an essay explaining a time in which you, or someone you know, managed to succeed despite others' predictions of failure.
16. Tan tells in paragraphs 2 and 21 of her attempts to use "all the Englishes [she] grew up with." Even if we do not grow up in a bilingual family, as Tan did, we all use several versions of English, depending on audience and situations. For example, we probably use a more relaxed vocabulary and more incomplete sentences when talking with friends about a subject we know well than when we are giving a presentation in class.

    Spend some time listening to your own speech and that of others in various settings. Keep a small notebook with you to jot down what you hear as accurately as possible, or use a tape recorder. Then write up your observations in a short paper.
17. Tan cites evidence that Asian-American students often major in math, science, or engineering, even when they have talents in other areas. Find out if this is the case at your university and, if possible, interview several students about their choices of majors. You could also study sources in the library that would give you information about choice of professions by different ethnic groups. Write the results of what you have found out in a short paper, citing the sources of your information.

Do Ask, Do Tell

JOSHUA GAMSON

In 1995, when this essay was written, the number and popularity of daytime "tell-all" talk shows had increased dramatically, with new additions to the field appearing regularly. In response to keen competition for ratings, talk shows seemed to be stretching in search of ever more provocative and controversial topics. Since this article was written, several of the shows mentioned (including the venerable Phil Donahue show, which is considered to have pioneered the format) have gone off the air, presumably due to increased competition for viewers.

The title "Do Ask, Do Tell" is a play on the Clinton Administration's policy on gays and lesbians in the military, instituted shortly after Bill Clinton's election in 1992. The "don't ask, don't tell" policy allowed gays to serve in the military as long as they stayed silent about their sexual orientation, and prohibited officers from inquiring about the sexual orientation of other service members. This policy, adopted as a compromise between gay rights advocates and those opposed to gays serving openly in the military, was a change from the former policy, which had made homosexuality grounds for immediate discharge.

Several service members have since legally challenged the policy as unconstitutional, arguing that it violates their rights to free speech and equal protection, and that there exists no evidence that shows that being gay is any impediment to serving one's country.

Joshua Gamson teaches sociology at Yale University. He is the author of Claims to Fame: Celebrity in Contemporary America *(1994). This essay was first published in* The American Prospect.

At the end of his 22 years, when Pedro Zamora lost his capacity to speak, all sorts of people stepped into the silence created by the AIDS-related brain disease that shut him up. MTV began running a marathon of *The Real World*, its seven-kids-in-an-apartment-with-the-cameras-running show on which Pedro Zamora starred as Pedro Zamora, a version of himself: openly gay, Miami Cuban, HIV-positive, youth activist. MTV offered the marathon as a tribute to Zamora, which it was, and as a way to raise funds, especially crucial since Zamora, like so many people with HIV, did not have private insurance. Yet, of course, MTV was also paying tribute to itself, capitalizing on Pedro's death without quite seeming as monstrous as all that.

2   President Clinton and Florida governor Lawton Chiles made public statements and publicized phone calls to the hospital room, praising Zamora as a heroic point of light rather than as a routinely outspoken critic of their own HIV and AIDS policies. The Clinton administration, in the midst of its clampdown on Cuban immigration, even granted visas to Zamora's three brothers and a sister in Cuba—a kindly if cynical act, given the realities of people with AIDS awaiting visas and health care in Guantánamo Bay.

3   Thus, according to *People* magazine, did Zamora reach a bittersweet ending. He was unable to see, hear, or speak, yet with his family reunited, "his dream had come true." Behind the scenes, one who was there for Zamora's last weeks told me, the family actually separated Zamora from his boyfriend—quite out of keeping with the "dreams" of Pedro's life. When Pedro had his own voice, he had spoken powerfully of how anti-gay ideology and policy, typically framed as "pro-family," contributed to teen suicides and the spread of HIV; when he died, those who spoke for him emphasized individual heroism and the triumph of the heterosexual family.

4   That others appropriated Zamora on his deathbed hardly tarnishes his accomplishment. As an MTV star, he had probably reduced suffering among lesbian and gay teenagers more, and affected their thinking more deeply, than a zillion social service programs. He spoke publicly to millions in his own words and with the backing of a reputable media institution, and he did not just tell them to wear condoms, or that AIDS is an equal-opportunity destroyer. Nor did he simply fill in the sexual blanks left by prudish government prevention campaigns. He also told them and showed them: Here is me loving my boyfriend; here is what a self-possessed gay man looks like hanging out with his roommates; here is what my Cuban family might have to say about my bringing home a black man; here is me at an AIDS demonstration, getting medical news, exchanging love vows.

5   To speak for and about yourself as a gay man or a lesbian on television, to break silences that are systematically and ubiquitously enforced in public life, is profoundly political. "Don't tell" is more than a U.S. military policy; it remains U.S. public policy, formally and informally, on sex and gender nonconformity. Sex and gender outsiders—gay men, transsexuals, lesbians, bisexuals—are constantly invited to lose their voices, or suffer the consequences (job loss, baseball bats) of using them. Outside of the occasional opening on MTV or sporadic coverage of a demonstration or a parade, if one is not Melissa Etheridge or David Geffen, opportunities to speak as a nonheterosexual, or to listen to one, are few and far between. Even if the cameras soon turn elsewhere, these moments are big breakthroughs, and they are irresistible, giddy moments for the shut up.

Yet, in a media culture, holding the microphone and the spotlight is a com- 6
plicated sort of power, not just because people grab them back from you but
because they are never really yours. If you speak, you must be prepared to be
used. The voice that comes out is not quite yours: It is like listening to yourself
on tape (a bit deeper, or more clipped) or to a version dubbed by your twin. It
is you and it is not you. Zamora's trick, until his voice was taken, was to walk
the line between talking and being dubbed. The troubling question, for the
silenced and the heard alike, is whether the line is indeed walkable. Perhaps the
best place to turn for answers is the main public space in which the edict to shut
up is reversed: daytime television talk shows.

For lesbians, gay men, bisexuals, drag queens, transsexuals—and combinations 7
thereof—watching daytime television has got to be spooky. Suddenly, there are
renditions of you, chattering away in a system that otherwise ignores or steals
your voice at every turn. Sally Jessy Raphael wants to know what it's like to pass
as a different sex, Phil Donahue wants to support you in your battle against gay
bashing, Ricki Lake wants to get you a date, Oprah Winfrey wants you to love
without lying. Most of all, they all want you to talk about it publicly, just at a
time when everyone else wants you not to. They are interested, if not precisely
in "reality," at least not in fictional accounts. For people whose desires and identities go against the norm, this is the only spot in mainstream media culture to
speak on their own terms or to hear others speaking for themselves. The fact
that talk shows are so much maligned, and for so many good reasons, does not
close the case.

The other day, I happened to tune into the *Ricki Lake Show*, the fastest- 8
rising talk show ever. The topic: "I don't want gays around my kids." I caught
the last 20 minutes of what amounted to a pro-gay screamfest. Ricki and her
audience explicitly attacked a large woman who was denying visitation rights to
her gay ex-husband ("I had to explain to a 9-year-old what 'gay' means"; "My
child started having nightmares after he visited his father"). And they went at a
young couple who believed in keeping children away from gay people on the
grounds that the Bible says "homosexuals should die." The gay guests and their
supporters had the last word, brought on to argue, to much audience whooping,
that loving gays are a positive influence and hateful heterosexuals should stay
away from children. The anti-gay guests were denounced on any number of
grounds, by host, other guests, and numerous audience members: They are
denying children loving influences, they are bigots, they are misinformed, they
read the Bible incorrectly, they sound like Mormons, they are resentful that they
have put on more weight than their exes. One suburban-looking audience member angrily addressed each "child protector" in turn, along the way coming up
with a possible new pageant theme: "And as for you, Miss Homophobia…"

The show was a typical mess, with guests yelling and audiences hooting at 9
the best one-liners about bigotry or body weight, but the virulence with which

homophobia was attacked is both typical of these shows and stunning. When Lake cut off a long-sideburned man's argument that "it's a fact that the easiest way to get AIDS is by homosexual sex" ("That is not a fact, sir, that is not correct"), I found myself ready to start the chant of "Go, Ricki! Go, Ricki!" that apparently wraps each taping. Even such elementary corrections, and even such a weird form of visibility and support, stands out sharply. Here, the homophobe is the deviant, the freak.

10   Lake's show is among the new breed of rowdy youth-oriented programs, celebrated as "rock and roll television" by veteran Geraldo Rivera and denigrated as "exploitalk" by cultural critic Neal Gabler. Their sibling shows, the older, tamer "service" programs such as *Oprah* and *Donahue*, support "alternative" sexualities and genders in quieter, but not weaker, ways. Peruse last year's *Donahue*: two teenage lesbian lovers ("Young, courageous people like yourself are blazing the way for other people," says Donahue), a gay construction worker suing his gay boss for harassment ("There's only eight states that protect sexual persuasion," his attorney reports), a bisexual minister, a black lesbian activist, and two members of the African-American theater group Pomo Afro Homos ("We're about trying to build a black gay community," says one), the stars of the gender-crossing *Priscilla, Queen of the Desert* ("I have a lot of friends that are transsexuals," declares an audience member, "and they're the neatest people"), heterosexuals whose best friends are gay, lesbians starting families, gay teens, gay cops, gay men reuniting with their high school sweethearts, a gay talk show. This is a more diverse, self-possessed, and politically outspoken group of non-heterosexuals than I might find, say, at the gay bar around the corner. I can only imagine what this means for people experiencing sexual difference where none is locally visible,

11   Certainly *Donahue* makes moves to counter its "liberal" reputation, inviting right-wing black preachers and the widely discredited "psychologist" Paul Cameron, who argues that cross-dressing preceded the fall of Rome, that people with AIDS should be quarantined, and that sexuality "is going to get us." But more often than not, Donahue himself is making statements about how "homophobia is global" and "respects no nation," how "we're beating up homosexual people, calling them names, throwing them out of apartments, jobs." The "we" being asserted is an "intolerant" population that needs to get over itself. We are, he says at times, "medieval." In fact, Donahue regularly asserts that "for an advanced, so-called industrialized nation, I think we're the worst."

12   Oprah Winfrey, the industry leader, is less concerned with the political treatment of difference; she is overwhelmingly oriented toward "honesty" and "openness," especially in interpersonal relationships. As on Lake's show, lesbians and gays are routinely included without incident in more general themes (meeting people through personal ads, fools for love, sons and daughters you never knew), and bigotry is routinely attacked. But Winfrey's distinctive mark is an attack on lies, and thus the closet comes under attack—especially the gay male

closet—not just for the damage it does to those in it, but for the betrayals of women it engenders.

On a recent program in which a man revealed his "orientation" after 19 years of marriage, for example, both Winfrey and her audience were concerned not that Steve is gay, but that he was not honest with his wife. As Winfrey put it, "For me, always the issue is how you can be more truthful in your life." One of Steve's two supportive sons echoes Winfrey ("I want people to be able to be who they are"), as does his ex-wife, whose anger is widely supported by the audience ("It makes me feel like my life has been a sham"), and the requisite psychologist ("The main thing underneath all of this is the importance of loving ourselves and being honest and authentic and real in our lives"). Being truthful, revealing secrets, learning to love oneself: These are the staples of Winfrey-style talk shows. Gay and bisexual guests find a place to speak as gays and bisexuals, and the pathology becomes not sexual "deviance" but the socially imposed closet.

All of this, however, should not be mistaken for dedicated friendship. Even when ideological commitments to truth and freedom are at work, the primary commitment of talk shows is, of course, to money. What makes these such inviting spots for nonconforming sex and gender identities has mostly to do with the niche talk shows have carved out for ratings. The shows are about talk; the more silence there has been on a subject, the more not-telling, the better a talk topic it is. On talk shows, as media scholar Wayne Munson points out in his book *All Talk* (Temple University Press, 1993), "differences are no longer repressed" but "become the talk show's emphasis," as the shows confront "boredom and channel clutter with constant, intensified novelty and 'reality.'" Indeed, according to Munson, Richard Mincer, *Donahue's* executive producer, encourages prospective guests "to be especially unique or different, to take advantage of rather than repress difference."

While they highlight different sex and gender identities, expressions, and practices, the talk shows can be a dangerous place to speak and a difficult place to get heard. With around 20 syndicated talk shows competing for audiences, shows that trade in confrontation and surprise (*Ricki Lake, Jenny Jones, Jerry Springer*) are edging out the milder, topical programs (*Oprah, Donahue*).

As a former *Jane Whitney Show* producer told *TV Guide,* "When you're booking guests, you're thinking, 'How much confrontation can this person provide me?' The more confrontation, the better. You want people just this side of a fistfight."

For members of groups already subject to violence, the visibility of television can prompt more than just a fistfight, as last year's *Jenny Jones* murder underlined. In March, when Scott Amedure appeared on a "secret admirer" episode of the *Jenny Jones Show*, the admired Jon Schmitz was apparently expecting a female admirer. Schmitz, not warming to Amedure's fantasy of tying him up in a hammock and spraying cream and champagne on his body, declared himself "100 percent heterosexual." Later, back in Michigan, he punctuated this claim by shooting Amedure with a 12-gauge shotgun, telling police that the embarrassment from the program had "eaten away" at him. Or, as he reportedly put it in his 911 call, Amedure "fucked me on national TV."

18   Critics were quick to point out that programming that creates conflict tends to exacerbate it. "The producers made professions of regret," Neal Gabler wrote in the *Los Angeles Times* after the Amedure murder, "but one suspects what they really regretted was the killer's indecency of not having pulled out his rifle and committed the crime before their cameras." In the wake of the murder, talk show producers were likened over and over to drug dealers: Publicist Ken Maley told the *San Francisco Chronicle* that "they've got people strung out on an adrenaline rush," and "they keep raising the dosage"; sociologist Vicki Abt told *People* that "TV allows us to mainline deviance"; Michelangelo Signorile argued in *Out* that some talk show producers "are like crack dealers scouring trailer park America." True enough. Entering the unruly talk show world, one is apt to become, at best, a source of adrenaline rush, and at worst a target of violence.

19   What most reporting tended to ignore, however, was that most anti-gay violence does not require a talk show "ambush" to trigger it. Like the Oakland County, Michigan, prosecutor who argued that "*Jenny Jones*'s producers' cynical pursuit of ratings and total insensitivity to what could occur here left one person dead and Mr. Schmitz now facing life in prison," many critics focused on the "humiliating" surprise attack on Schmitz with the news that he was desired by another man. As in the image of the "straight" soldier being ogled in the shower, in this logic the revelation of same-sex desire is treated as the danger, and the desired as a victim. The talk show critics thus played to the same "don't tell" logic that makes talk shows such a necessary, if uncomfortable, refuge for some of us.

20   Although producers' pursuit of ratings is indeed, unsurprisingly, cynical and insensitive, the talk show environment is one of the very few in which the declaration of same-sex desire (and, to a lesser degree, atypical gender identity) is common, heartily defended, and often even incidental. Although they overlook this in their haste to hate trash, the critics of exploitative talk shows help illuminate the odd sort of opportunity these cacophonous settings provide. Same-sex desires become "normal" on these programs not so much because different sorts of lives become clearly visible, but because they get sucked into the spectacular whirlpool of relationship conflicts. They offer a particular kind of visibility and voice. On a recent *Ricki Lake*, it was the voice of an aggressive, screechy gay man who continually reminded viewers, between laughs at his own nasty comments, that he was a regular guy. On other days, it's the take-your-hands-off-my-woman lesbian, or the I'm-more-of-a-woman-than-you'll-ever-be transsexual. The vicious voice—shouting that we gay people can be as mean, or petty, or just plain loud, as anybody else—is the first voice talk shows promote. It's one price of entry into mainstream public visibility.

The guests on the talk shows seem to march in what psychologist Jeanne   21
Heaton, co-author of *Tuning in Trouble* (Jossey-Bass, 1995), calls a "parade of
pathology." Many talk shows have more than a passing resemblance to freak
shows. Neal Gabler, for example, argues that guests are invited to exhibit "their
deformities for attention" in a "ritual of debasement" aimed primarily at reassuring the audience of its superiority. Indeed, the evidence of dehumanization
is all over the place, especially when it comes to gender crossing, as in the titles
of various recent *Geraldo* programs; the calls of sideshow barkers echo in "Star-
Crossed Cross-Dressers: Bizarre Stories of Transvestites and Their Lovers" and
"Outrageous Impersonators and Flamboyant Drag Queens" and "When Your
Husband Wears the Dress in the Family." As long as talk shows make their bids
by being, in Gabler's words, "a psychological freak show," sex and gender outsiders arguably reinforce perceptions of themselves as freaks by entering a dis-
course in which they may be portrayed as bizarre, outrageous, flamboyant
curiosities. (Often, for example, they must relinquish their right to defend themselves to the ubiquitous talk show "experts.")

Talk shows do indeed trade on voyeurism, and it is no secret that those who   22
break with sex and gender norms and fight with each other on camera help the
shows win higher ratings. But there is more to the picture: the place where
"freaks" talk back. It is a place where Conrad, born and living in a female body,
can assert against Sally Jessy Raphael's claim that he "used and betrayed" women
in order to have sex with them that women fall in love with him as a man because
he considers himself a man; where months later, in a program on "our most outrageous former guests" (all gender crossers), Conrad can reappear, declare himself to have started hormone treatment, and report that the woman he allegedly
"used and betrayed" has stood by him. This is a narrow opening, but an opening
nonetheless, for the second voice promoted by the talk show: the proud voice
of the "freak," even if the freak refuses that term. The fact that talk shows are
exploitative spectacles does not negate the fact that they are also opportunities;
as Munson points out, they are both spectacle and conversation. They give voice
to the systematically silenced, albeit under conditions out of the speaker's control, and in tones that come out tinny, scratched, distant.

These voices, even when they are discounted, sometimes do more than just   23
assert themselves. Whatever their motivations, people sometimes wind up doing
more than just pulling up a chair at a noisy, crowded table. Every so often they
wind up messing with sexual categories in a way that goes beyond a simple
expansion of them. In addition to affirming both homosexuality and heterosex-
uality as normal and natural, talk show producers often make entertainment by
mining the in-between: finding guests who are interesting exactly because they
don't fit existing notions of "gay" and "straight" and "man" and "woman," raising the provocative suggestion that the categories are not quite working.

The last time I visited the *Maury Povich Show*, for instance, I found myself   24
distracted by Jason and Tiffanie. Jason, a large 18-year-old from a small town in

Ohio, was in love with Calvin. Calvin was having an affair with Jamie (Jason's twin sister, also the mother of a three-month-old), who was interested in Scott, who had sex with, as I recall, both Calvin and Tiffanie. Tiffanie, who walked on stage holding Jamie's hand, had pretty much had sex with everyone except Jamie. During group sex, Tiffanie explained, she and Jamie did not touch each other. "We're not lesbians," she loudly asserted, against the noisy protestations of some audience members.

25   The studio audience, in fact, was quick to condemn the kids, who were living together in a one-bedroom apartment with Jamie's baby. Their response was predictably accusatory: You are freaks, some people said; immoral, said others; pathetically bored and in need of a hobby, others asserted. Still other aspects of the "discussion" assumed the validity and normality of homosexuality. Jason, who had recently attempted suicide, was told he needed therapy to help him come to terms with his sexuality, and the other boys were told they too needed to "figure themselves out." Yet much talk also struggled to attach sexual labels to an array of partnerships anarchic enough to throw all labels into disarray. "If you are not lesbians, why were you holding hands?" one woman asked Tiffanie. "If you are not gay," another audience member asked Calvin, "how is it you came to have oral sex with two young men?"

26   This mix was typically contradictory: condemnation of "immoral sex" but not so much of homosexuality per se, openly gay and bisexual teenagers speaking for themselves while their partners in homosexual activities declare heterosexual identities, a situation in which sexual categories are both assumed and up for grabs. I expect the young guests were mainly in it for the free trip to New York, and the studio audience was mainly in it for the brush with television. Yet the discussion they created, the unsettling of categorical assumptions about genders and desires, if only for a few moments in the midst of judgment and laughter, is found almost nowhere else this side of fiction.

27   The importance of these conversations, both for those who for safety must shut up about their sexual and gender identities and for those who never think about them, is certainly underestimated. The level of exploitation is certainly not. Like Pedro Zamora, one can keep one's voice for a little while, one finger on the commercial megaphone, until others inevitably step in to claim it for their own purposes. Or one can talk for show, as freak, or expert, or rowdy—limits set by the production strategies within the talk show genre.

28   Those limits, not the talk shows themselves, are really the point. The story here is not about commercial exploitation, but about just how effective the prohibition on asking and telling is in the United States, how stiff the penalties are, how unsafe this place is for people of atypical sexual and gender identities. You know you're in trouble when Sally Jessy Raphael (strained smile and forced tear behind red glasses) seems like your best bet for being heard, understood, respected, and protected. That for some of us the loopy, hollow light of talk shows seems a safe haven should give us all pause.

EXERCISES

Some of the Issues

1. What is the significance of the title of the essay?
2. What, in Gamson's view, were the benefits and drawbacks of Pedro Zamora's popularity (paragraphs 1 through 3)? How does Gamson point out the irony of Zamora's fame?
3. What does Gamson feel Zamora was able to accomplish as an MTV star (paragraph 4)?
4. What does Gamson mean when he says that the microphone and spotlight are "never really yours" (paragraph 6)?
5. For whom might watching daytime television be "spooky" (paragraph 7) and why?
6. According to Gamson, how do talk shows give more voice to gays and lesbians than other forms of media? Based on your own experience, do you agree?
7. Taking into consideration both Gamson's and your own analysis, why might talk shows be a "safe haven" for gays and lesbians?
8. What is the "primary commitment" of talk shows? What "niche" have they carved out (paragraph 14)?
9. Gamson recounts the murder of Scott Amedure in paragraphs 17–19. How does Gamson analyze the media's response to the murder? Based on Gamson's account and other knowledge you might have about the case, what are your feelings about both the incident and the media's response?
10. How do same-sex desires become "normal" on talk shows (paragraph 20), and what are the consequences of this?
11. Looking at the final paragraph, what, according to Gamson, should "give us pause"?
12. Gamson develops a complicated argument, often presenting two or more sides of the issues and examples he discusses. Working in small groups, pick a short passage that you find particularly difficult and paraphrase Gamson's words.

The Way We Are Told

13. Gamson begins by recounting and analyzing Pedro Zamora's media popularity. How do the events in Zamora's life serve as a good introduction to Gamson's article?
14. Although "Do Ask, Do Tell" is not a personal narrative, Gamson often uses the first person. Why is the author's voice or presence important to the article?

15. Gamson combines both formal and informal language. Find examples of words or passages that you would define as either formal or informal.
16. Who is the audience for this essay? On what basis do you make your conclusion?
17. Conclusions can serve different or multiple purposes: Often, they simply summarize the author's main points, highlighting important ideas. At other times, a conclusion can broaden the issue or even call into question the author's own opinions or ideas. Reread Gamson's conclusion and analyze his strategy. Why might he have chosen to end the article the way he did?

Some Subjects for Writing

18. Pick a television show you watch regularly and analyze it in terms of its treatment of gays and lesbians, or nonwhite racial and ethnic groups. To what extent does the show give voice to diverse characters and how are the characters represented or portrayed? You may choose to compare and contrast two different shows.
19. Consider how you feel about the value and purpose of talk shows. Are they, as Neal Gabler calls them, "exploitalk," or do they serve a more important purpose? In a focused essay, present your views on the subject. Try to create, as Gamson does, an argument that takes into consideration the complexity of the issue.
20. Create a script for a talk show in which you deal with a gay or lesbian theme. Provide a description of each character, and, as you write and revise, give careful consideration to how your characters would act and respond to others on the show. In other words, try to get inside the head of each character and develop each individual voice.

The Media's Image of Arabs

JACK G. SHAHEEN

Jack G. Shaheen, born in 1935, teaches mass communications at Southern Illinois University in Edwardsville. He has also taught at the American University in Beirut and the University of Jordan in Amman. He is the author of The TV Arab *(1984). This essay was written in 1992.*

Lebanon, where Shaheen's family came from, is a small country at the eastern end of the Mediterranean, bordering on Israel to the south and Syria to the east and north. Its capital, Beirut, was once known as the Paris of the Middle East, a lively, sophisticated city that was also the financial center of the region. In recent years Lebanon has been in a state of civil war that has ravaged much of the country and led at times to the occupation of parts of it by its two neighbors.

The media's image of Arabs, Shaheen asserts, is almost invariably hostile and one-sided. It contributes to, perhaps is even responsible for, the negative stereotype Americans have of Arabs.

America's bogeyman is the Arab. Until the nightly news brought us TV pictures of Palestinian youth being punched and beaten, almost all portraits of Arabs seen in America were dangerously threatening. Arabs were either billionaires, bombers, bedouin bandits, belly dancers or bundles in black—rarely victims. They were hardly ever seen as ordinary people practicing law, driving taxis, singing lullabies or healing the sick. Though some TV newscasts may portray them more sympathetically now, the absence of positive media images nurtures suspicion and stereotype.

Historically, the Arab lacks a human face. Media images are almost invariably hostile and one-sided. They articulate to, perhaps are even responsible for, the negative stereotype Americans have of Arabs. As an Arab-American, I have found that ugly caricatures have had an enduring impact on Americans of Arab heritage. For the prejudiced, during the Gulf War, all Arabs, including some of the three million Americans with Arab roots, became to many, "camel jockeys," "ragheads" and "sandsuckers." Whenever there is a crisis in the Middle East Arab-Americans are subjected to vicious stereotyping and incidents of violence and discrimination.

3   I was sheltered from prejudicial portraits at first. My parents came from Lebanon in the 1920s; they met and married in America. Our home in the steel city of Clairton, Pennsylvania was a center for ethnic sharing—black, white, Jew and gentile. There was only one major source of screen images then, at the State movie theater where I was lucky enough to get a part-time job as an usher. But in the late 1940s, Westerns and war movies were popular, not Middle Eastern dramas. Memories of World War II were fresh, and the screen heavies were the Japanese and the Germans. True to the cliché of the times, the only good Indian was a dead Indian. But when I mimicked or mocked the bad guys, my mother cautioned me. She explained that stereotypes hurt; that they blur our vision and corrupt the imagination. "Have compassion for all people, Jackie," she said. Experience the joy of accepting people as they are, and not as they appear in films, she advised.

4   Mother was right. I can remember the Saturday afternoon when my son, Michael, who was seven, and my daughter, Michele, six, suddenly called out: "Daddy, Daddy, they've got some bad Arabs on TV." They were watching that great American morality play, TV wrestling. Akbar the Great, who liked to hear the cracking of bones, and Abdullah the Butcher, a dirty fighter who liked to inflict pain, were pinning their foes with "camel clutches." From that day on, I knew I had to try to neutralize the media caricatures.

5   I believe most researchers begin their investigations because they have strong feelings in their gut about the topic. To me, the stereotyping issue was so important I had to study it. For years I watched hordes of Arabs prowl across TV and movie screens. Yet, a vacuum existed in the literature: research on TV and movie Arabs did not exist. My research began with television because visual impressions from the tube indoctrinate the young. Once a stereotypical image becomes ingrained in a child's mind, it may never wither away.

6   Investigating television's Arabs began as a solo effort. But members of my family, friends, and colleagues assisted by calling attention to dramas I might otherwise have missed. For several years, I examined *TV Guide* and cable and satellite magazines. Daily, I searched for Arab plots and characters, then taped, studied, and categorized them. To go beyond personal observations, I interviewed more than thirty industry leaders, writers, and producers in New York and Los Angeles. In the spirit of fair-mindedness, I invited image makers, those influential purveyors of thought and imagination, to offer sparks of decency that illuminate, rather than distort, our perception of others.

7   It hasn't been easy. Images teach youngsters whom to love, whom to hate. With my children, I have watched animated heroes Heckle and Jeckle pull the rug from under "Ali Boo-Boo, the Desert Rat," and Laverne and Shirley stop "Sheik Ha-Mean-ie" from conquering "the U.S. and the world." I have read more than 250 comic books like the "Fantastic Four" and "G.I. Combat" whose characters have sketched Arabs as "lowlifes" and "human hyenas." Negative stereotypes were everywhere. A dictionary informed my youngsters that an Arab is

a "vagabond, drifter, hobo and vagrant." Whatever happened, my wife wondered, to Aladdin's[1] good genie?

To a child, the world is simple: good versus evil. But my children and others   8
with Arab roots grew up without ever having seen a humane Arab on the silver screen, someone to pattern their lives after. To them, it seems easier for a camel to go through the eye of a needle than for a screen Arab to appear as a genuine human being.

Hollywood producers employ an instant Ali Baba[2] kit that contains scimi-   9
tars, veils, sunglasses and such Arab clothing as chadors[3] and kufiyahs.[4] In the mythical "Ay-rab-land," oil wells, tents, mosques, goats and shepherds prevail. Between the sand dunes, the camera focuses on a mock-up of a palace from "Arabian Nights"—or a military air base. Recent movies suggest that Americans are at war with Arabs, forgetting the fact that out of 21 Arab nations, America is friendly with 19 of them.

Audiences are bombarded with rigid, repetitive and repulsive depictions   10
that demonize and delegitimize the Arab. One reason is because since the early 1900s more than 500 feature films and scores of television programs have shaped Arab portraits.

I recently asked 293 secondary school teachers from five states—Massachu-   11
setts, North Carolina, Arkansas, West Virginia, and Wisconsin—to write down the names of any humane or heroic screen Arab they had seen. Five cited past portraits of Ali Baba and Sinbad; one mentioned Omar Sharif and "those Arabs" in *Lion of the Desert* and *The Wind and the Lion*. The remaining 287 teachers wrote "none."

Nicholas Kadi, an actor with Iraqi roots, makes his living playing terrorists   12
in such films as the 1990 release "Navy Seals." Kadi laments that he does "little talking and a lot of threatening—threatening looks, threatening gestures." On screen, he and others who play Arab villains say "America," then spit. "There are other kinds of Arabs in the world," says Kadi. "I'd like to think that some day there will be an Arab role out there for me that would be an honest portrayal."

The Arab remains American culture's favorite whipping boy. In his mem-   13
oirs, Terrel Bell, Ronald Reagan's first secretary of education, writes about an "apparent bias among mid-level, right-wing staffers at the White House" who dismissed Arabs as "sand niggers."

Sadly, the racial slurs continue. Posters and bumper stickers display an Arab's   14
skull and an atomic explosion. The tag: "Nuke their ass and take their gas."

At a recent teacher's conference, I met a woman from Sioux Falls, South   15
Dakota, who told me about the persistence of discrimination. She was in the

[1]Young boy in *The Arabian Nights* who is given a magic lamp and magic ring to summon genies to fulfill all his wishes.
[2]The poor woodcutter in *The Arabian Nights* who gains entrance into the treasure cave of the forty thieves by saying the words "Open Sesame."
[3]Long black veil worn by Moslem women.
[4]Arab headdress.

process of adopting a baby when an agency staffer warned her that the infant had a problem. When she asked whether the child was mentally ill, or physically handicapped, there was silence. Finally, the worker said: "The baby is Jordanian."

16   To me, the Arab demon of today is much like the Jewish demon of yesterday. We deplore the false portrait of Jews as a swarthy menace. Yet a similar portrait has been accepted and transferred to another group of Semites—the Arabs. Print and broadcast journalists have started to challenge this stereotype. They are now revealing more humane images of Arabs, a people who traditionally suffered from ugly myths. Others could follow that lead and retire the stereotypical Arab to a media Valhalla.[5]

17   The civil rights movement of the 1960s not only helped bring about more realistic depictions of various groups; it curbed negative images of the lazy black, the wealthy Jew, the greasy Hispanic and the corrupt Italian. These images are mercifully rare on today's screens. Conscientious imagemakers and citizens worked together to eliminate the racial mockery that had been a shameful part of the American cultural scene.

18   It would be a step in the right direction if movie and TV producers developed characters modeled after real-life Arab-Americans. We could then see a White House correspondent like Helen Thomas, whose father came from Lebanon, in "The Golden Girls," a lawyer patterned after Ralph Nader on "L.A. Law," or a Syrian-American playing tournament chess like Yasser Seirawan, the Seattle grandmaster.

19   Politicians, too, should speak out against the cardboard caricatures. They should refer to Arabs as friends, not just as moderates. And religious leaders could state that Islam, like Christianity and Judaism, maintains that all mankind is one family in the care of God. When all imagemakers rightfully begin to treat Arabs and all other minorities with respect and dignity, we may begin to unlearn our prejudices. The ultimate result would be an image of the Arab as neither saint nor devil, but as a fellow human being, with all the potentials and frailties that condition implies.

EXERCISES

Some of the Issues

1. What, according to the author, is the standard image of the Arab in the American media? Why is he concerned that Arabs are hardly ever portrayed as ordinary people?

2. When did Shaheen first become aware of stereotypes? Why was he not conscious of them earlier?

---

[5]According to Norse mythology, the hall in which the souls of warriors who had died heroically were ensured immortality.

3. Shaheen is especially concerned about the influence of the media on his children. Why does he believe that children are particularly vulnerable to stereotypes?
4. Shaheen makes specific suggestions for changing the media image of Arabs. What are they? Do you think they would be effective?
5. In April 1995, when the federal building in Oklahoma City was bombed, killing over one hundred people, the first newspapers claimed that the suspected bombers looked "Middle Eastern." In fact, all the suspects were white Americans. What negative stereotypes would account for the false reports? What damage do such reports do?

The Way We Are Told

6. Cite several instances in which Shaheen supports a general assertion with specific examples drawn from his own experience.
7. Shaheen's essay concentrates on the media's treatment of Arabs, yet he mentions unfair treatment of other groups as well. What does his argument gain from this expansion?

Some Subjects for Writing

8. In an essay, describe a character in a film or TV program who belongs to a minority or disadvantaged group. In your opinion is that character presented as a stereotype, either negatively or positively? If so, what changes could be made? One way of testing your opinion is to see if the character appears the same way to a member of the depicted group as it does to someone outside the group.
9. In another article, published in the *Los Angeles Times* in August of 1996, Shaheen criticizes depictions of Middle Easterners in several movies made for children, including Disney's *Aladdin* (1992), *The Return of Jafar* (1994), and *Kazaam* (1996). If you have seen any of these films, or can rent them, analyze the depictions of Arab characters.
10. Fights between "good guys" and "bad guys" have always been a part of drama, fiction, movies, and television. Often the "bad guys" have been members of a group that has been historically discriminated against. Consider the depictions of Native Americans in the classic Western and what influence that might have had on attitudes toward Indian people. Furthermore, could the World War II movies in which Japanese were depicted as subhuman have had any influence on American willingness to drop two atomic bombs on Japan or to intern 100,000 Japanese-Americans (as described in selections by Jeanne Wakatsuki Houston and James D. Houston, and Dwight Okita)? If the media are powerful in shaping opinion, what obligation do they have to present images that will not increase prejudice? Is it enough to present minorities in a realistic way, or is it important to not present them as villains?

Why We Tell Stories

LISEL MUELLER

Lisel Mueller, who came to the United States from Germany at the age of fifteen, is the author of several collections of poetry, as well as a volume of essays. Her latest collection, Alive Together: New and Selected Poems *(1996), won the Pulitzer Prize for poetry.* The Need to Hold Still *(1980), from which this poem is taken, received the National Book Award.*

For Linda Foster

1

Because we used to have leaves
and on damp days
our muscles feel a tug,
painful now, from when roots
5   *pulled us into the ground*

and because our children believe
they can fly, an instinct retained
from when the bones in our arms
were shaped like zithers and broke
10   *neatly under their feathers*

and because before we had lungs
we know how far it was to the bottom
as we floated open-eyed
like painted scarves through the scenery
15   *of dreams, and because we awakened*

and learned to speak

2

We sat by the fire in our caves,
and because we were poor, we made up a tale
about a treasure mountain
20   *that would open only for us*

and because we were always defeated,
we invented impossible riddles
only we could solve,
monsters only we could kill,
women who could love no one else   25

and because we had survived
sisters and brothers, daughters and sons,
we discovered bones that rose
from the dark earth and sang
as white birds in the trees   30

3

Because the story of our life
becomes our life

Because each of us tells
the same story
but tells it differently   35

and none of us tells it
the same way twice

Because grandmothers looking like spiders
want to enchant the children
and grandfathers need to convince us   40
what happened happened because of them

and though we listen only
haphazardly, with one ear,
we will begin our story
with the word and   45

EXERCISES

Some of the Issues

1. Part 1 of Mueller's poem tells us how we are, at least in our imaginations,
   connected to earlier forms of life before "we awakened /and learned to
   speak." Imagine that you were without language. How would that fact
   shape your ability to think, feel, and communicate with others?

2. Part 2 of the poem deals with the time when humans first began to talk and tell stories. Why, according to Mueller, did we invent stories? What function did they serve then? What function do they serve now?

3. Why will we "begin our story with the word *and*"?

4. What is your own answer to the question, "Why do we tell stories?" Do you agree with Mueller that the way we talk about our lives shapes the way we lead our lives? Why or why not?

*5. Read Maxine Hong Kingston's "Girlhood among Ghosts." In that selection, the author remembers a story her mother told her in which the mother cuts a section from under Kingston's tongue. The incident may never have happened, yet it appears to have deep significance in Kingston's life. How does Mueller's idea "that the story of our life becomes our life" apply to Kingston?

Some Subjects for Writing

6. Most of us remember stories our families have told again and again about our childhood. Sometimes these stories are about a funny incident, sometimes they carry a moral. Often, the repetition of the story helps to establish the family's view of that child and may shape the child's own self image. Recount a story told about you and explain its influence then and now.

Credits

Angelou, Maya. "Graduation" from *I Know Why the Caged Bird Sings* by Maya Angelou. Copyright © 1969 by Maya Angelou. Reprinted by permission of Random House Inc.

Anonymous. "Recapture the Flag: 34 Reasons to Love America." *City Pages* (Minneapolis, MN), July 3, 1991. Reprinted by permission of the publisher.

Anzaldúa, Gloria. "To live in the Borderlands means you" From *Borderlands/La Frontera: The New Mestiza* © 1987 by Gloria Anzaldúa. Reprinted be permission of Aunt Lute Books.

Atwood, Margaret. "Canadians: What Do They Want?" by Margaret Atwood. Reprinted with permission from *Mother Jones* magazine. Copyright © 1982, Foundation for National Progress.

Bernstein, Nell. "Goin' Gangsta, Choosin' Cholita" by Nell Bernstein from the *San Jose Mercury News*, Nov. 13, 1994. Reprinted by permission of Pacific News Service.

Bohannon, Laura. "Shakespeare in the Bush" from *Natural History*, August/September, 1966, Vol. 75, No. 7, by Dr. Laura Bohannon. Reprinted by permission of the author.

Brandt, Barbara. "Less is More: A Call for a Shorter Work Week," by Barbara Brandt, from *Utne Reader*, July/Aug. 1991. Reprinted with permission of the author.

Breen, Ruth. "Choosing a Mate." Used by permission of the author.

Brooks, Gwendolyn. "We Real Cool" by Gwendolyn Brooks. Taken from *Blacks*, copyright 1987. Published by the David Co., Chicago. Reprinted by permission of the author.

Brooks, Geraldine. "Unplugged," by Geraldine Brooks, former foreign correspondent for the *Wall Street Journal* and author of *Nine Parts of Desire: The Hidden World of Islamic Women*. Used with permission of the author.

Bruchac, Joseph. "Ellis Island" by Joseph Bruchac from *The Remembered Earth*, Ed. Geary Hobson. Albuquerque: Red Earth Press, 1979. Reprinted by permission of the author.

Cofer, Judith Ortiz. "The Myth of the Latin Woman: I Just Met a Girl Named María," from *The Latin Deli: Prose and Poetry* by Judith Ortiz Cofer, the University of Georgia Press. Reprinted with permission.

Cullen, Countee. "Incident," from the book *Color* by Countee Cullen. Reprinted by permission of GRM Associates, Inc., agents for the Estate of Ida M. Cullen. Copyright © 1925 by Harper & Brothers; copyright renewed 1953 by Ida M. Cullen.

Dorris, Michael. "For the Indians, No Thanksgiving." Copyright © Michael Dorris 1989. From the *Chicago Tribune*, November 24, 1988. Reprinted with permission.

Ehrenreich, Barbara and Annette Fuentes. "Life on the Global Assembly Line." Reprinted from *Ms.* magazine, June, 1981. Barbara Ehrenreich is a freelance writer based in New York.

Eighner, Lars. "On Dumpster Diving, " by Lars Eighner, from *Travels with Lizbeth: Three Years on the Road and on the Streets.* Reprinted by permission of St. Martin's Press Incorporated.

Gamson, Joshua. "Do Ask, Do Tell," by Joshua Gamson. Reprinted with permission from *The American Prospect,* Fall 1995. Copyright New Prospect, Inc.

Gladwell, Malcolm. "Black Like Them," by Malcolm Gladwell in *The New Yorker,* April 29–May 6, 1996. Used with permission of the publisher.

Hoffman, Eva. "Lost in Translation," by Eva Hoffman. From *Lost in Translation.* Copyright © 1989 by Eva Hoffman. Used by permission of the publisher, Dutton, an imprint of New American Library, a division of Penguin Books USA Inc.

Houston, Jeanne Wakatsuki and James D. Houston. "Shikata Ga Nai" from *Farewell to Manzanar* by Jeanne Wakatsuki Houston and James D. Houston. Copyright © 1973 by James D. Houston. Reprinted by permission of Houghton Mifflin Company.

Howard, Jane. "Families," by Jane Howard. Copyright © 1978 by Jane Howard. Reprinted by permission of Simon & Schuster, Inc.

Iyer, Pico. "Home Is Every Place," by Pico Iyer, from *Homeground* (Blue Heron Publishing, Hillsboro, OR), 1996. Used with permission.

Jen, Gish. "An Ethnic Trump," by Gish Jen, from *New York Times Magazine,* July 7, 1996. Reprinted with permission.

Kazin, Alfred. Excerpt from "The Kitchen" in *A Walker in the City,* copyright 1951 and renewed 1979 by Alfred Kazin, reprinted by permission of Harcourt Brace Jovanovich, Inc.

Kincaid, Jamaica. "On Seeing England for the First Time," *Transition* 51 (1991), pp. 32–41. Copyright W.E.B. Dubois Institute. Reprinted by permission of Duke University Press.

Kingston, Maxine Hong. "Girlhood among Ghosts." From *The Woman Warrior: Memoirs of a Girlhood among Ghosts* by Maxine Hong Kingston. Copyright © 1975, 1976 by Maxine Hong Kingston. Reprinted by permission of Alfred A. Knopf, Inc.

Lord, Bette Bao. "Walking in Lucky Shoes." *Newsweek* (July 6, 1992). Reprinted by permission of the author.

Mabry, Marcus. "Living in Two Worlds." From *Newsweek on Campus,* April, 1988. Copyright © 1988, Newsweek, Inc. All rights reserved. Reprinted by permission.

Malcolm X. "Hair." From *The Autobiography of Malcolm X* by Malcolm X, with the assistance of Alex Haley. Copyright © 1964 by Alex Haley and Malcolm X. Copyright © 1965 by Alex Haley and Betty Shabazz. Reprinted by permission of Random House, Inc.

Meier, Daniel. "One Man's Kids," by Daniel Meier, published in *The New York Times Magazine,* Nov. 1, 1987. Reprinted with permission.

Morales, Aurora Levins. "Class Poem," from *Getting Home Alive* by Aurora Levins Morales and Rosario Rosales, Firebrand Books, Ithaca, New York. Reprinted by permission of the publisher.

Morley, John David. "Living in a Japanese Home." From the book, *Pictures from the Water Trade,* copyright © 1985 by John David Morley. Used by permission of the Atlantic Monthly Press.

Morrison, Toni. "A Slow Walk of Trees." From *The New York Times Magazine*, July 4, 1975. Copyright © 1976 by The New York Times Company. Reprinted by permission.

Mueller, Lisel. "Why We Tell Stories," from *The Need to Hold Still*. Reprinted by permission of Louisiana State University Press. Copyright © 1980 by Lisel Mueller.

Muñiz, Maria L. "Back, but Not Home." From *The New York Times*, July 13, 1979. Copyright © 1979/85 by The New York Times Company. Reprinted by permission.

Naylor, Gloria. "The Meaning of a Word," by Gloria Naylor. Reprinted by permission of Sterling Lord Literistic, Inc. Copyright © 1986 by Gloria Naylor.

Novak, Michael. "In Ethnic America." Reprinted with permission of Macmillan Publishing Company from *The Rise of the Unmeltable Ethnics* by Michael Novak. Copyright © 1971 Michael Novak.

Okita, Dwight. "In Response to Executive Order 9066: All Americans of Japanese Descent Must Report to Relocation Centers" by Dwight Okita. From Dwight Okita's new first book of poems, *Crossing with the Light*, published by Tia Chucha Press in Chicago. Copyright © 1992 Dwight Okita.

Orwell, George. "Shooting an Elephant" from *Shooting an Elephant and Other Essays* by George Orwell, copyright 1950 by Sonia Brownell Orwell and renewed 1978 by Sonia Pitt-Rivers. Reprinted by permission of Harcourt Brace Jovanovich, Inc.

Paley, Grace. "The Loudest Voice" from *The Little Disturbances of Man* by Grace Paley. Copyright 1956, 1957, 1958, 1959, renewed © 1984 by Grace Paley. Reprinted by permission of Viking Penguin Inc.

Park, Sun. "Don't Expect Me to Be Perfect" from Special Edition for Teens, 1984, *Newsweek*.

Petrakis, Harry Mark. "Barba Nikos" from *Reflections: A Writer's Life—A Writer's Work*. Lake View Press, Chicago, copyright by Harry Mark Petrakis.

Price, Deb. "Gay Partners Need to Make a Name for Themselves." Reprinted with permission of *The Detroit News*.

Roethke, Theodore. "My Papa's Waltz," copyright 1942 by Hearst Magazines, Inc. From *The Collected Poems of Theodore Roethke* by Theodore Roethke. Used by permission of Doubleday, a division of Bantam, Doubleday, Dell Publishing Group, Inc.

Rose, Mike. "I Just Wanna Be Average." Reprinted with the permission of The Free Press, a Division of Macmillan, Inc., from *Lives on the Boundary: The Struggles and Achievements of America's Underprepared* by Mike Rose. Copyright © 1989 by Mike Rose.

Rose, Wendy. "Three Thousand Dollar Death Song," by Wendy Rose. From *Lost Copper*. Copyright © 1980, Malki Museum, Inc.

Salzman, Mark. "Teacher Mark." From *Iron and Silk*, by Mark Salzman. Copyright © 1986 by Mark Salzman. Reprinted by permission of Random House, Inc.

Shaheen, Jack. "The Media's Image of Arabs," by Jack Shaheen. From *Newsweek*, February 29, 1988. Reprinted by permission of the author.

Shammas, Anton. "Amérka, Amérka," by Anton Shammas. Copyright © 1991 by *Harper's Magazine*. All rights reserved. Reprinted from the February issue by special permission.

Skolnick, Arlene. "The Paradox of Perfection," by Arlene Skolnick. From *Wilson Quarterly*, Summer, 1980. Reprinted by permission of the author.

Soto, Gary. "The Jacket," © 1986 by Gary Soto. Used by permission of the author and BookStop Literary Agency. All rights reserved.

Staples, Brent. "Night Walker," by Brent Staples. From *Ms.* magazine, September 1986. Reprinted by permission of the author.

Tan, Amy. "Mother Tongue." Copyright © 1990 by Amy Tan. First appeared in *The Threepenny Review*. Reprinted by permission of Amy Tan and the Sandra Dijkstra Literary Agency.

Tarkov, John. "Fitting In," by John Tarkov from *The New York Times* (About Men column), July 7, 1985. Reprinted by permission of *The New York Times*.

Thomas, Piri. "Alien Turf." From *Down These Mean Streets* by Piri Thomas. Copyright © 1967 by Piri Thomas. Reprinted by permission of Alfred A. Knopf, Inc.

Touissant, Nicolette. "Hearing the Sweetest Songs," by Nicolette Touissant. From "My Turn" column, *Newsweek* 5/23/94. All rights reserved. Reprinted by permission.

Van Gelder, Lindsy. "The Importance of Being Eleven: Carol Gilligan Takes on Adolescence." Published in *Ms.* magazine, July–August, 1990. Reprinted by permission of the author.

White, Walter. "I Learn What I Am." From *A Man Called White* (Arno Press, 1948). Reprinted by permission of Jane White Viazzi.

Wong, Elizabeth. "The Struggle to Be an All-American Girl," by Elizabeth Wong. Reprinted by permission of the author.

Yezierska, Anzia. "Soap and Water," from *How I Found America: Collected Stories of Anzia Yezierska*, copyright © 1985, 1991 by Louise Levitas Henriksen. Reprinted by permission of Persea Books, Inc.

Photo Credits: © Barbara Rios (p. 2); © Will Hart (p. 60, 98, 366); © Stephen Marks (p. 132); © Robert Harbison (p. 176); © Alain McLaughlin (p. 216); © Michael Geissinger (p. 266); © Mary Beth Camp (p. 302).

Author/Title Index

Alien Turf, 183

Amérka, Amérka: A Palestinian Abroad in the Land of the Free, 85

Angelou, Maya, 13

Anzaldúa, Gloria, 361

Arrival at Manzanar, 205

Atwood, Margaret, 305

Back, but not Home, 139

Barba Nikos, 72

Bernstein, Nell, 165

Black Like Them, 287

Bohannan, Laura, 324

Brandt, Barbara, 246

Breen, Ruth, 113

Brooks, Geraldine, 223

Brooks, Gwendolyn, 172

Bruchac, Joseph, 299

Canadians: What Do They Want?, 305

Choosing a Mate, 113

Class Poem, 261

Cofer, Judith Ortiz, 155

Crèvecoeur, Michel Guillaume St. Jean de, 272

Cullen, Countee, 57

Do Ask, Do Tell, 380

Don't Expect Me to Be Perfect, 100

Dorris, Michael, 201

Ehrenreich, Barbara, 252

Eighner, Lars, 234

Ellis Island, 299

Ethnic Trump, An, 143

Families, 103
Fitting In, 62
For the Indians, No Thanksgiving, 201
Fuentes, Annette, 252

Gamson, Joshua, 380
Gay Partners Need to Make a Name for Themselves, 109
Girlhood among Ghosts, 31
Gladwell, Malcolm, 287
Goin' Gangsta, Choosin' Cholita: Teens Today "Claim" a Racial Identity, 165
Graduation, 13

Hair, 162
Hearing the Sweetest Songs, 146
Hoffman, Eva, 150
Home Is Every Place, 227
Houston, James D., 205
Houston, Jeanne Wakatsuki, 205
Howard, Jane, 103

I Just Wanna Be Average, 43
I Learn What I Am, 195
Importance of Being Eleven: Carol Gilligan Takes on Adolescence, The, 25
In Ethnic America, 78
In Response to Executive Order 9066: All Americans of Japanese Descent Must Report to Relocation Centers, 212
Incident, 57
Iyer, Pico, 227

Jacket, The, 8
Jen, Gish, 143

Kazin, Alfred, 117
Kincaid, Jamaica, 351
Kingston, Maxine Hong, 31
Kitchen, The, 117

Less Is More: A Call for Shorter Work Hours, 246
Life on the Global Assembly Line, 252

Living in a Japanese Home, 318
Living in Two Worlds, 135
Lord, Bette Bao, 268
Lost in Translation, 150
Loudest Voice, The, 36

Mabry, Marcus, 135
Malcolm X, 162
Meaning of a Word, The, 369
Media's Image of Arabs, The, 390
Meier, Daniel, 219
Modest Proposal, A 335
Morales, Aurora Levins, 261
Morley, John David, 318
Morrison, Toni, 67
Mother Tongue, 373
Mueller, Lisel, 395
Muñiz, Maria L., 139
My Papa's Waltz, 129
Myth of the Latin Woman: I Just Met a Girl Named
    María, The, 155

Naylor, Gloria, 369
Night Walker, 178
Novak, Michael, 78

Okita, Dwight, 212
On Dumpster Diving, 234
On Seeing England for the First Time, 351
One Man's Kids, 219
Orwell, George, 343

Paley, Grace, 36
Paradox of Perfection, The, 121
Park, Sun, 100
Petrakis, Harry Mark, 72
Pool Players: Seven at the Golden Shovel, The, 172
Price, Deb, 109

Recapture the Flag: 34 Reasons to Love America, 277
Roethke, Theodore, 129
Rose, Mike, 43
Rose, Wendy, 94

Salzman, Mark, 310
Shaheen, Jack G., 390
Shakespeare in the Bush, 324
Shammas, Anton, 85
Shooting an Elephant, 343
Skolnick, Arlene, 121
Slow Walk of Trees, A, 67
Soap and Water, 280
Soto, Gary, 8
Staples, Brent, 178
Struggle to Be an All-American Girl, The, 4
Swift, Jonathan, 335

Tan, Amy, 373
Tarkov, John, 62
Teacher Mark, 310
Thomas, Piri, 183
Three Thousand Dollar Death Song, 94
To live in the Borderlands means you, 361
Toussaint, Nicolette, 146

Unplugged, 223

Van Gelder, Lindsay, 25

Walking in Lucky Shoes, 268
What Is an American?, 272
White, Walter, 195
Why We Tell Stories, 395
Wong, Elizabeth, 4

Yezierska, Anzia, 280